W9-AXN-375

History in Literature

A READER'S GUIDE TO 20TH-CENTURY HISTORY
AND THE LITERATURE IT INSPIRED

History in Literature

A Reader's Guide to 20th-Century History and the Literature It Inspired

EDWARD QUINN

Facts On File, Inc.

History in Literature: A Reader's Guide to 20th-Century History and the Literature It Inspired

Facts On File, Inc.
132 West 31st Street
New York NY 10001

Library of Congress Cataloging-in-Publication Data

Quinn, Edward.
History in literature ; a reader's guide to 20th-century history and the literature it inspired / Edward Quinn
p. cm.
ISBN 0-8160-4693-X (alk. paper)
1. Literature, Modern—20th century—History and criticism. 2. History, Modern—20th century—Chronology. 3. History in literature. I. Title.
PN50.Q56 2003
809'.9335821—dc21
2003048546

Facts On File books are available at special discounts when purchased in bulk quantities for businesses, associations, institutions, or sales promotions. Please call our Special Sales Department in New York at (212) 967-8800 or (800) 322-8755.

You can find Facts On File on the World Wide Web at http://www.factsonfile.com

Text and cover design by Cathy Rincon

Printed in the United States of America

MP JT 10 9 8 7 6 5 4 3 2 1

This book is printed on acid-free paper.

I wish to thank my four relief pitchers, Bill Herman, Len Kriegel, Karl Malkoff, and Art Waldhorn, who strode to the mound when the starter was tiring and threw nothing but strikes. Also, Barbara Malkoff, who read the manuscript with her customary care and enthusiasm; the staffs of the New York Public, Brooklyn Public, and City University Libraries; Earl Rovit, Leo Hamalian, and Pat Forrestal, who made some key recommendations; David Quinn and Jason Malkoff, who pulled me through more than one computer jam; and Barbara Gleason, for making it possible. I am particularly indebted to Anne Savarese and Jeff Soloway, editors at Facts On File, for their editorial wisdom and personal tact.

CONTENTS

PREFACE

History in Literature is a unique reference book that combines alphabetically arranged summaries of events or biographies of people important to 20th-century history with discussions of works of literature inspired by those subjects. Thus each entry offers a brief account of relevant facts, followed by a description of how and to what purpose novelists, playwrights, or poets used or altered those facts. With this dual goal in mind, we chose our entries both on the basis of their historical importance and the importance of the literature they inspired. Each entry also includes a brief bibliographical note for readers interested in pursuing the topic further.

This history/literature format, we have found, makes for informative, entertaining—often surprising—reading with a wide range of uses. *History in Literature* can serve as a map for the reader with a specific destination: a descendant of immigrants from Greece or Turkey, say, seeking an interesting book on the Greco-Turkish War; an undergraduate or graduate student looking, perhaps, for a term-paper topic relating to existentialism; or a World War I buff on the lookout for a novel that deals with the battle of Gallipoli. On the other hand, it can be a guide for the reader who has no specific place in mind but just wants to ride around the countryside, maybe stopping at a few antique stores to see if there's anything interesting in the area. Or, it can be a kind of Michelin for time travelers, men or women who want to re-experience some aspect of the 20th century, matching their memory of "the way it was" against either the facts or someone's imaginative re-creation of the facts. Doubtless there are other uses (preparation for an appearance on *Jeopardy* comes to mind), but the emphasis on usefulness, perfectly appropriate as it is for a reference book, should not obscure the pleasure the reader will find in the books being referred to. They are not all great, but they are all good reads.

The seed for this book was planted while I was teaching a group of bright, politically active college students in the late 1960s about *Macbeth* and its connections to the Gunpowder Plot. All of these students had read the play; none of them—no surprise here—had ever heard of the plot, a failed attempt by a group of Roman Catholics to blow up a joint session of the

English Parliament on November 5, 1605. Shakespeare had caught the plot when it was today's news, not yet "history," and spun it into gold. With characteristic daring and genius, he seized the term *equivocation* from the trial of the conspirators and made it the central point of Macbeth's relationship with the Weird Sisters.

The Gunpowder Plot played an important role in the subsequent social history of England, in the form of Guy Fawkes' Day (Fawkes was one of the conspirators), a popular celebration in which the straw-stuffed figure of Fawkes is burned in effigy. Guy Fawkes' Day weaves its way through English literature, appearing in the 20th century as the subepigraph ("A penny for the Old Guy") in T. S. Eliot's 1925 poem "The Hollow Men." (The main epigraph to "The Hollow Men"—"Mistah Kurtz—he dead"—is a line from Joseph Conrad's seminal exploration of colonialism, *Heart of Darkness.*)

Thus a single, brief segment of 17th-century history penetrated and enriched later literature, and, at the same time, developed a life of its own. That life took the form of a history of anti-Catholic feeling in Great Britain, which, in turn, generated the kind of terrorist activity (of which the Gunpowder Plot served as a prototype) represented by the Irish Republican Army. This example of an interlocking, recurrent pattern both in history and literature was precisely, it seemed to me, the sort of thing that our rigidly compartmentalized educational system had failed to provide those 1960s students. Not having been taught to look for history and literature in terms of interconnected recurring cycles, they had treated the past as past and, thus, as George Santayana put it, were condemned to repeat it. Since that time, interdisciplinary studies has emerged in American schools and colleges as a far from dominant but nonetheless vigorous movement. This book hopes to serve a modest role in its continued growth.

But the genesis of this book is not the same as its aim. It is designed, not to lecture the young, but to serve them, while it pursues the equally important task of trying to interest and please the no-longer-young, people like those same students, now in their forties and fifties, overcome with nostalgia, who find themselves inclining toward the History Channel, while the youngsters are watching "reality" television. But this book has in mind those—young or old—who have come of age in the most momentous—and, some would say, monstrous—century in history, but who have found solace, satisfaction, escape, wisdom, and, perhaps best of all, joy in its literature, specifically that particular species of literature rooted in historical events.

A word about limits: The literary selections are restricted to fiction, poetry, and drama. Excluded as a result are nonfictional accounts, such as memoirs. To include these would have swelled the book to unmanageable proportions. The same is true of films. An account of the films rooted in historical events of the century would have resulted in an encyclopedia, not a handbook. In those cases where we were unable to track down a suitable literary work, we have not included the entry. As a result, there are some notable absences from a strict historical standpoint, just as from a literary perspective; there are, for instance, no discussions of the works of Marcel Proust or James Joyce, since those two giants of 20th-century literature did not write historical fiction. Another restriction is that only books written in or translated into English are included.

Entries by Contributors

William Herman: Arab-Israeli conflict; cold war; Kennedy, John Fitzgerald; October 3, 1951; Trujillo Molina, Rafael Leónidas.

Leonard Kriegel: War in the Pacific.

Karl Malkoff: Central Intelligence Agency; Einstein, Albert; Greco-Turkish War; Greece, occupation of; Greek civil war; Greek colonels; Knossos, discovery of the palace at; Lambrakis Grigorios, assassination of.

Arthur Waldhorn: colonialism; Great Depression.

HISTORY IN LITERATURE

A

ABRAHAM LINCOLN BRIGADE (SPANISH CIVIL WAR) (1937–1938)

Among the international brigades that fought on the Loyalist (pro-government) side in the SPANISH CIVIL WAR was a group of Americans, most recruited from the ranks of the American Communist Party, but with a substantial minority—about 25 percent—of unaffiliated individuals committed to the fight against fascism. Technically not a brigade, the group consisted of two battalions, forming a part of the XVth International Brigade, which also included British, French, and Spanish battalions.

The group's first engagement, at the battle of Jarama in February 1937, was marked by mishaps and confusion, typical of unprepared troops and compounded by the failure of the Loyalist command to deliver the artillery and air support the brigade had expected. The result was a disastrous defeat in which the "Lincolns" suffered heavy casualties. Subsequent engagements at Belchite, where they experienced their first victory, and at the Ebro River, where after initial success their offensive was halted, added to the casualty list. Of the 2,800 volunteers in the brigade, 900 were killed and virtually all of the others wounded. In December 1938, with a final victory for Franco's forces imminent, the battalion was repatriated to the United States. In their own country, the Lincolns continued to be involved in leftist causes. Although time reduced their numbers to a small band, they remained actively engaged until the end of the century. As one survivor put it, "Struggle is the elixir of life. . . . [I]f you are not struggling, you are dead."

THE LITERATURE

During the war, a significant number of troops in the International Brigades experienced serious morale problems; most were due to the incompetence of its leadership, almost all of whom were Russian officers. The treatment of the brigades offers additional proof that the Soviet Union was less concerned with supporting the fight against Franco than in strengthening its own interests and policies. The Communists tried to subvert the efforts of the socialists, anarchists, and Trotskyites who were their allies in the so-called Popular Front, going so far as to assassinate many of the leaders of these groups. The machinations of the Communist Party are the subject of the novel *Hermanos!* (1969) by William Herrick (1915–). Herrick was a member of the Abraham Lincoln Brigade, wounded at the battle of Jarama. His novel, though written 30 years after the war, seethes with the fresh anger of one who feels betrayed. His protagonist is Jake Starr, a natural leader and a rising star in the Communist Party, whose flaw is a touch of romantic idealism. Jake experiences no internal conflict when fighting alongside his fellow Lincolns, where the air is pure and the group is motivated solely by their antifascist feelings. Once exposed to the battle, they exhibit the usual range of courage and fear, but their commitment to the "good fight," as they called the war, remains untarnished.

But Jake's singular abilities require his attention to duties that take him from the front lines to the fetid air of the "commissars," communist officials overseeing the actions of the military, whose sole function is to carry out direct orders from the Kremlin. Jake's position is further complicated by his passionate love affair with the wife of a Nobel Prize–winning physicist whom the party is wooing for his public relations value. At first, Jake is able to adhere to party discipline and reject his lover, but eventually he rebels, triggered by an incident in which he has to murder a Spanish ally whom the party views as a threat. In the meantime, his Lincoln comrades undergo harrowing battles that decimate their ranks. Eventually, he and they come to see the "good fight" as having been betrayed by its leadership.

Hermanos! is a flawed novel, overstating its case, demonizing its Communist villains, deficient in bringing its protagonist to life. However, the publication in 2001 of secret Soviet state documents relating to the civil war (*Spain Betrayed*, eds. Ronald Radosh, Mary Habeck, and J. Sevostianov) suggests that the novel may have been historically more correct than had previously been imagined. In this respect, *Hermanos!* stands as the fictional equivalent of George Orwell's (1905–50) classic account of the Communist betrayal of the Loyalist cause, *Homage to Catalonia* (1938).

FURTHER READING

Peter Carroll's *The Odyssey of the Abraham Lincoln Brigade* (1994) provides an interesting study of the Lincolns, particularly in its account of their post–civil war history.

AFRICAN-AMERICAN EXPERIENCE (1865–1950)

From the end of the Civil War through the first half of the 20th century, African Americans received the clear message from the larger society that they were, at best, second-class citizens. After moving from slavery, the very existence of which constituted a denial of their humanity, into segregation, the condition of being separate and notoriously unequal, many American blacks found themselves on the bottom rung of the social and economic ladder, often below recent European and Asian immigrants. A matter of law in the South and an unofficial de facto reality in the North, segregation gave birth to discrimination in jobs, housing, and education. The great migration of the early decades, which brought thousands of southern blacks to industrial centers in the North, appeared, at first, to be the critical breakthrough they were seeking. The spirited, creative flowering of the Harlem Renaissance seemed to suggest a new dawn, but the GREAT DEPRESSION soon eclipsed that light, as economic realities overcame cultural aspirations. With WORLD WAR II, northern migration again intensified as war production factories offered opportunities for work; with war's end, the principle of "last hired, first fired" saw blacks once again at the bottom of the ladder, still suffering from the same social indignities and humiliations.

Although the psychological damage inflicted on black people in these years before the CIVIL RIGHTS MOVEMENT took its toll in terms of their own self-image and sense of identity, they nevertheless created a distinctive culture. In black hands, the dour Christianity they had absorbed from their slave masters became a deeply emotional, passionate expression of suffering and joy, captured in soulful spirituals and plaintive gospel music. In the secular world, jazz improvisation gave full rein to the full experience of freedom otherwise denied to them, while the blues rendered the painful conditions of existence into a form of creative play. In the 1920s, jazz entered the American mainstream and transformed the culture, shattering its ties with the Puritan past (see JAZZ AGE). From there, jazz assumed worldwide cultural influence, reflected, for example, in Jean-Paul Sartre's *Nausea* (see EXISTENTIALISM) and Haruki Murakami's *After the Quake* (see KOBE EARTHQUAKE).

The onset of the CIVIL RIGHTS MOVEMENT of the 1950s produced significant changes, notably in the elimination of legal segregation in the South and in fostering racial pride, expressed in the slogan "Black Is Beautiful." But a major reason for the movement's success was no doubt the deep, rich culture out of which it grew.

THE LITERATURE

In his novel *Invisible Man* (1952), Ralph Ellison (1914–94) incorporates the metaphorical invisibility of the black man in the white world with that which many regard as the fundamental theme of 20th-century literature.

Employing elements of jazz, blues, and African-American folklore and fusing them with modernist literary techniques that include realism, surrealism, and overt symbolism, Ellison merges the two traditions to depict the novel's black protagonist as a quintessential existential hero, asking significant questions about identity, choice, and meaning. In a work that combines echoes of Fyodor Dostoyevsky's (1821–81) *Notes from the Underground*, T. S. Eliot's (1888–1965) *The Waste Land*, and Louis Armstrong's recording of "Black and Blue," Ellison, in the words of the critic Albert Murray, "had taken an everyday blues tune . . . and scored it for full orchestra." As a result, the novel won international acclaim, but, at the same time, it drew a certain amount of negative reaction from militant blacks, who saw in the "universalization" of its protagonist a diminution of his particularly black character. Ellison's response to his critics is reflected in his comment that there is no reason why a novel about a black man "could not be effective as literature and, in its effectiveness, transcend its immediate background and speak eloquently for other people." The debate over the novel's racial politics has continued in the years since its publication, although few deny its status as a work of art.

Invisible Man is a picaresque novel, a type of tale in which the protagonist undergoes a series of seemingly unrelated incidents; the plot moves incrementally rather than developmentally. The novel opens with a prologue in which the narrator, an anonymous black man, has taken refuge from a race riot that has broken out in Harlem. He is living in a cellar wired with hundreds of lights. The lighting helps to offset his realization that he is invisible, at least to white people: When they look at him, they see not an individual, but a black man, an object to be used for their own purposes. In the novel's first chapter, the narrator flashes back to his graduation from high school and the puzzling advice he receives from his dying grandfather. The old man instructs the idealistic young man to "yes" the white man to death, to "overcome 'em with yeses, undermine 'em with grins." What follows is a description of a "battle royal" among young black teens, staged for the entertainment of the prominent men in the Southern town, cheering on the boys as they savage each other. At the conclusion of the fight, the bloodied, young narrator, who has been chosen as the speaker of his graduating class, delivers his earnest, pious declaration and is awarded a leather briefcase, containing a scholarship to a southern Negro college (modeled on Tuskegee Institute, which Ellison once attended). But that night he dreams that his grandfather tells him to open the briefcase, where he finds a letter that reads, "Keep This Nigger-Boy Running."

Undaunted, still clinging to his belief in a kind of Horatio Alger–like future, the narrator leaves college without graduating, after a wild, farcical incident with a white benefactor. He comes to New York, where he secures a job in a paint factory, noted for the "purity" of the whiteness of its paint. Here the narrator becomes the hapless victim of another comic catastrophe, losing his job as a result. Now living in Harlem, he becomes acquainted with the Brotherhood (the Communist Party), who enlists him as a black recruiter in the Harlem community. His success there causes some jealousy among the Brotherhood leaders, and he is transferred downtown to speak on women's issues. When trouble appears to be developing in Harlem, partly the result of the activities of a black separatist, Ras the Exhorter, he is called back there, but by now he has become increasingly aware that the party is cynically exploiting him and the entire black population for its own ends. In the meantime a full-blown race riot breaks out in Harlem, which, the narrator realizes, the Brotherhood has provoked. Caught in the middle of the violence, he falls into a manhole and finds refuge in the cellar described in the prologue. In the epilogue that concludes the novel, the narrator prepares to abandon his underground home and to engage the world, chastened and disciplined by his naïve mistakes, but not entirely disillusioned. In spite of everything he has been through, he has not abandoned the possibility, remote as it may be, that the day would come in America, when, as Martin Luther King, Jr., later expressed it, a man would be judged not by the color of his skin but by the content of his character.

FURTHER READING

Albert Murray's *The Omni Americans* (1970) is an affirmative account of African-American culture. *Modern Critical Interpretations: Invisible Man*, edited by Harold Bloom (1999), is a collection of critical studies of the novel.

AIDS (ACQUIRED IMMUNE DEFICIENCY SYNDROME)

In 1980, doctors in Africa and large urban areas of the United States began to confront a new and mysterious disease. In sub-Saharan Africa, the disease appeared to be relatively indiscriminate, while in cities such as San Francisco and New York it attacked a disproportionate number of gay men. In the following year, the disease was identified as Acquired Immune Deficiency Syndrome (AIDS), a lethal infection in the immune system. In 1983, researchers isolated human immunodeficiency virus (HIV), which attacks the immune system, constituting the first phase of AIDS. The virus spreads from the initial site through the lymph nodes. Eventually, usually about 10 years later, it moves into its final phase, AIDS. At that point, diseases such as pneumonia, lymphoma, or sarcoma develop. HIV can be contracted in a variety of ways: through semen or female genital secretions, shared use of a hypodermic needle, blood transfusions, or breast milk. Pregnant women can transmit it to their unborn babies. By the year 2001, the international death toll from AIDS had reached 21.8 million, with another 40 million infected with HIV. Although AIDS is now a worldwide pandemic, the most seriously affected area remains sub-Saharan Africa.

One controversial feature of the response to AIDS in America has been the perceived inadequacy of research efforts to fight the disease. As the AIDS historian Randy Shilts aptly summarized the issue, "the federal government viewed AIDS as a budget problem, local public health officials saw it as a political problem, gay leaders considered it a public relations problem, and the news media regarded it as a homosexual problem that wouldn't interest anybody else." Since those early years, research and treatment have benefited the United States and other Western countries, but the condition in Africa and Asia has become increasingly alarming.

THE LITERATURE

In the relatively brief period since its outbreak in the early 1980s, AIDS has resulted in the production of a large body of literature. Most of this work has formed the central theme of contemporary gay literature. As the disease achieves the dimension of a worldwide epidemic, however, a small but increasing proportion of AIDS literature is being written by heterosexuals.

Much of the early AIDS literature was angry, direct, and combative, striving to overcome the hostility, superstition, and fear that greeted the disease. While more recent literature has retained this angry tone, it has been tempered by infusions of comedy and the themes of love, compassion, and remembrance.

Among the early accounts of the disease was the widely acclaimed "The Way We Live Now," a powerful short story by Susan Sontag (1933–), published in the *New Yorker* in 1986, which depicts the progression of the disease in a young man, as reflected in the conversations of his friends, who continually refer to "it," unable to bring themselves to use the word *AIDS*, and Larry Kramer's (1935–) *The Normal Heart* (1985), the first play to bring AIDS to the attention of the general public. The outstanding chronicler of the disease in literature is Paul Monette (1945–95), who died of AIDS in 1995. Monette's novels *Afterlife* (1990) and *Halfway Home* (1991) affirm the strengths of homosexual love in the face of death. Monette is also the author of a moving collection of poems celebrating the life of his deceased lover, *Love Alone: Eighteen Elegies for Rog* (1988).

In drama, the AIDS crisis forms the center of the most acclaimed American play in many years, Tony Kushner's (1957–) *Angels in America* (1991), a two-part drama that touches on a broad range of themes, with AIDS playing a central role.

Among the nongay literature of AIDS, a notable example is Alice Hoffman's (1952–) *At Risk* (1988), the account of an 11-year-old girl's contracting of AIDS from a blood transfusion. Reynolds Price's (1933–) *The*

Promise of Rest (1995) is a lyrical rendering of a father's reconciliation with his son, who is dying of AIDS.

FURTHER READING

Outstanding among the early histories of the disease is Randy Shilts's *And the Band Played On* (1987). *AIDS: The Literary Response*, edited by Emmanuel Nelson (1992), is a collection of critical essays examining the literature of the crisis from a variety of perspectives. *Confronting AIDS through Literature*, edited by Judith Laurence Pastore (1993), provides a variety of views on using literature as a means of understanding the disease and its ramifications.

ALAMEIN, EL, BATTLE OF (WORLD WAR II) (1942)

In the early stages of the North African campaign, the German Afrika Korps, under the command of the brilliant strategist Field Marshal Erwin Rommel, had driven the British forces from Libya into Egypt before being halted at Alam Halfa, near Alamein, in June of 1942. On October 23, the British Eighth Army, led by its new commander Bernard Montgomery, launched a massive counterattack. Montgomery's strategy involved using artillery and infantry, rather than tanks, as the principal assault instruments, as had been the case previously in the North African desert. In Montgomery's plan, the tanks would be brought into play only after the initial battle. The tactic proved successful. After a week of fierce combat, Rommel, ignoring Adolf HITLER's command to "stand fast," ordered a retreat back to Tripoli, some 1,100 miles east. On the entire route of the withdrawal, the exhausted German army was further pounded by Royal Air Force planes. As had happened four months earlier at Midway and two months later at STALINGRAD, the tide of a major military campaign had turned in the Allies' favor. As Winston Churchill, speaking of Alamein, accurately summarized it, "This not the end, nor even the beginning of the end. It is perhaps the end of the beginning."

THE LITERATURE

The second volume (*The Battle Lost and Won*, 1978) of Olivia Manning's (1911–80) *The Levant Trilogy* contains a highly effective account of the Alamein offensive. Although the bulk of the trilogy deals with wartime English expatriates and the complex marriage of Harriet and Guy Pringle, the battle scenes are seen through the eyes of Simon Boulderstone, an idealistic, 20-year-old lieutenant in the British army. Simon meets Harriet Pringle while on leave in Cairo just after having discovered that his brother has been killed in action. He returns to to the front, assigned the role of liaison officer as the battle is beginning. Sent to deliver an important message to an army group that has lost radio contact, he undergoes the desperate, lost feelings of the soldier in combat. The ensuing scenes capture the confusion, fear, and sense of imminent death that the individual soldier experiences in battle, a scene where everything can seem to go wrong, but out of which sometimes comes sudden, unexpected victory.

Picking his way back from the front lines, stepping over the bodies of dead soldiers, Simon asks himself, "Is this what Hugo [his brother] died for? And am I to die for this?" A week later, the battle still raging, he goes to the front with a land mine map to help an infantry commander advance his troops. He soon discovers that the disparity between headquarters' view of the situation and the front line's reality can be great indeed. As Rommel's troops retreat, the British forces attempt to cut them off, but the Germans evade the trap. Meanwhile, Simon's jeep runs over a mine, and he wakes to find himself paralyzed from the waist down.

In *The Sum of Things* (1980), the third volume of the trilogy, Simon recovers the use of his legs and a new perspective on life, a recognition that he has been living in the shadow of his dead brother. Seasoned by battle and physical pain, he has become his own man. He returns to active service leading troops destined to spend the war in a remote Aegean island, not the return to battle he had hoped for, but he accepts his assignment with a new maturity and a confident anticipation of the future. The battle of El Alamein has been a turning point personally as well as historically.

FURTHER READING

James Lucas's *War in the Desert: The Eighth Army at El Alamein* (1983) offers a detailed account of the battle and its significance.

ALGERIAN WAR OF INDEPENDENCE (1954–1962)

Algeria had been a French colony since 1948, when, in 1954, Algerian nationalists, buoyed by the success of Vietnamese rebels in the INDOCHINA WAR, formed the Front de Libération Nationale (FLN) and launched a series of small attacks on the colonial government. In 1956, the FLN bombed two popular cafés in Algiers, setting off the battle of Algiers, a struggle that lasted for a year, ending with the capture of the FLN chief, Yacef Saadi. But the fight continued elsewhere in Algeria, where the terrorism of the rebels was matched by that of the Organization de l'Armée Secrète (OAS), the most recalcitrant of the French Algerians.

Meanwhile, in a foreshadowing of the American home front during the VIETNAM WAR, the war proved to have a traumatic, divisive effect on the French people. Central figures in this debate were the *pieds noir*, the French Algerians, many of whom had been living in Algeria for generations. Like the Unionists in NORTHERN IRELAND, they identified themselves with the colonizing nation, while refusing to concede compromises with people they regarded as terrorists. Working in conjunction with the military, whose use of torture against the rebels had left many people on the mainland appalled, the French Algerians seemed to be acting independently of the French government. The continuing chaos led to the fall of the Fourth Republic and the call for the return of General Charles de Gaulle to put an end to the war. In 1958, the general was elected president of France. To the surprise of many, the great nationalist and military leader adopted a compromise policy offering "self-determination" to the people of Algeria, a plan that was approved in a national referendum in 1961. In 1962, members of the OAS attempted to assassinate de Gaulle.

Despite continued resistance by the military leadership and the French Algerians, in 1963 the French people approved a referendum on Algeria: Independence was achieved on July 3, 1962. The best estimates indicate that the Algerian rebels lost at least 150,000 fighters and at least that many Muslim civilians. Roughly 25,000 French troops were killed, and more than 100,000 French Algerians were forced into exile. Subsequent years saw an influx of Algerians into France in search of work.

THE LITERATURE

The opposing sides in the war are well represented by two works—Jean Lartéguy's (1920–   ) *The Centurions* (1960; trans., 1961) and Assia Djebar's (1936–   ) *Women of Algiers in Their Apartments* (1980; trans., 1992)—that conflict with each other not only in terms of political ideology but also in their views of men and women. *The Centurions* is a celebration of a group of French paratroopers, who embody a right-wing, masculine ideal: beautifully conditioned fighting machines, equally successful in the bedrooms and the battlefields, courageously courting death and beautiful women, true patriots fighting to save France from the effete decadence that has sapped its strength and sold out French Algeria. Their leader in Colonel Raspéguy, who moulds a disparate group of French soldiers, defeated at the battle of Dienbienphu in the Indochina War, into a special force capable of fighting a guerrilla war. They engage in the "dirty war" of torture and dismemberment because those are the terms the rebels have introduced. American readers, familiar with Robin Moore's 1965 popular novel, *Green Berets* (see VIETNAM WAR), will recognize the similarity of tone and character type in this work.

In dramatic contrast to Lartéguy's paean to French virility stands Assia Djebar's *Women of Algiers in Their Apartments*, a collection of short stories written between 1958 and 1978, a number of which reflect on the critical role that Arab women played in the battle. In the battle of Algiers, for example, the rebels used women to carry bombs into the European quarter of the city, and it was women prisoners who suffered torture and rape at the hands of French troops. But once independence was gained, the traditional Muslim

11

customs in regard to women were reintroduced. In Djebar's words, women were again subject to the "law of invisibility, the law of silence."

Women of Algiers in Their Apartments is the title of a famous painting by Ferdinand Delacroix, who visited Algeria in 1832, shortly after the French invasion and occupation of the country. His painting depicts three women in a local sultan's harem, imprisoned, it seems, in a mysterious, soft light against a dark background. The women evoke a sense of sadness that contributes to the painting's power. Djebar's use of the painting (it is also used as the jacket design of the book) reinforces her attempt at showing that the condition of women in postcolonial Algeria is essentially unchanged. In "There Is No Exile," the narrator, divorced and mourning the death of her two children, is living with her family in exile from war-torn Algiers, all longing to return home. Without any prior notice, she is told that a group of women will be arriving shortly to arrange her marriage. At the same time, a child has died in the apartment next door, so the keening of the women forms a constant background to the daily activities. When the prospective groom's family arrives, she announces, to everyone's astonishment, that she does not wish to marry anyone. She later confides to a friend that she cannot forget the war and the death of her children. She "keeps bumping into the walls of the past." She, as her friend points out, is a "true exile." In an essay, "Forbidden Gaze, Severed Sound," appended to these stories, Djebar comments at length on the significance of the Delacroix painting in its representation of the history of Muslim women.

The war also created personal crises for those French Algerians who recognized the need for compromise. Among the most illustrious products of this community was the renowned writer and thinker Albert Camus (1913–60). Two of his best-known novels, *The Stranger* (1942) and *The Plague* (1947), are set in Algeria, but these were written years before the uprising. During the war itself, Camus, who had been living in Paris for many years, parted company with his peer Jean-Paul Sartre (1905–80) and the great majority of French intellectuals by declaring his opposition to Algerian independence, even though he was acutely aware of the injustices that colonial rule had imposed upon the Arab majority. He found himself caught between justice and, as he put it, his "mother," that is, his deeply rooted identity as a French Algerian.

Camus's dilemma is powerfully captured in his short story "L'Hote" (1957). Daru, a schoolteacher in a remote area of Algeria, is forced to hold an Arab prisoner in his schoolhouse overnight and to bring him to prison the next day. Daru decides not to obey the order. He brings the Arab to a fork in the road, gives him some money, and indicates the road to prison and the road that will take him to a Nomad tribe that will hide him. The prisoner chooses the road to prison. When Daru returns to the schoolhouse, he finds scrawled on the blackboard the message, "You handed over our brother. You will pay for this." The story encapsulates the situation of the liberal French Algerian in general and Camus in particular. Daru's attempt to sidestep the consequences of the decision is doomed in the clash of mighty opposites that the war has unleashed. A key to the dilemma is the title of the story "L'Hote," which translates as either "host" or "guest." In one sense, Daru is the host and his Arab prisoner is the guest. But, in reality, in Algeria, the French are the guests, uninvited and unwelcome. Despite his best efforts, Daru is a guest in the country of his birth, and as the story concludes, he looks north in the direction of Europe, knowing that is where he must go. It would appear that Camus in fiction, if not in fact, was bowing to the inevitable.

FURTHER READING

Martin Windrow's *The Algerian War 1954–62* (1997) looks at the conflict from the perspective of the 1990s. Philip Dine's *Images of the Algerian War* (1994) analyzes French fiction and films dealing with the war. Lartéguy's *Centurions* was reissued in paperback in the United States as *The Lost Command*, the title of a 1966 film based on the novel.

AMIN, IDI (1925–2003)
President of Uganda, 1971–80

Amin joined the army when Uganda was still a British protectorate. After the country gained independence in 1962, Amin rose quickly in the ranks to become commander in chief in 1968. In 1971, he led a successful coup that deposed President Apolo Obote and established himself as president. Soon after, he initiated a number of arbitrary moves, such as the expulsion of the Indian minority from the country, which proved to be disastrous for the Ugandan economy. His regime grew increasingly corrupt and brutal, resulting in the killing of thousands of citizens. In 1978, he attacked neighboring Tanzania, but his forces were defeated; he subsequently fled Uganda and sought sanctuary in Libya and Saudi Arabia, where he died.

THE LITERATURE

In Giles Foden's (1967–) *The Last King of Scotland* (1998), an idealistic young Scottish doctor, Nicholas Garrigan, becomes Amin's personal physician. As a consequence, he finds himself increasingly caught up in the dictator's bizarre world: Among his other fantasies, Amin imagines that he will one day lead a war for the independence of Scotland. Garrigan is alternately appalled, amused, terrified, and mesmerized by the dictator's megalomania.

After a series of near disastrous mishaps, Garrigan escapes from Uganda, only to find on his return to Britain that he is looked upon as having been a willing henchman of Amin. Broken in spirit and profoundly misanthropic, he retreats to a remote island off the coast of Scotland where he receives a call one day from Saudi Arabia. He hears the familiar voice and knows that he will forever be haunted, and tainted, by his association with the dictator. This is a psychologically perceptive study of a mad but shrewd dictator who dominates others by using his knowledge of their knowledge that he is mad. In the character of the young doctor, Foden captures the dilemma of those who are both seduced and repulsed by the appeal of power.

FURTHER READING

Amin is one of the principal subjects in Samuel Decalo's *Psychoses of Power: African Personal Dictatorships* (1998).

AMRITSAR MASSACRE (1919)

In 1919, the British colonial government in India assumed emergency powers in order to ensure calm at a time when Mohandas K. GANDHI was leading his *satya grapha* campaign of passive resistance to British rule. The emergency powers only served to inflame the situation, leading to riots, particularly in the Punjab, the northeastern province of India. Among the trouble spots was Amritsar, a city of 150,000 people, many of whom were protesting the arrest of two of their local leaders. Eventually the protest turned violent, and more than 1,000 troops under the command of Brigadier General Rex Dyer were called in to restore control. On April 13, some 10,000 people gathered in a walled meeting ground within the city, the Jallianwalla Bagh, despite a ban on public meetings that Dyer had proclaimed earlier in the day. British troops arrived at the scene, and without warning Dyer ordered his troops to open fire for a full 10 minutes before giving the cease-fire order. By then 1,600 rounds of ammunition had been fired, leaving 379 people dead and 1,500 wounded. The following day Dyer issued further punitive regulations, including one that required all Indians to crawl on their stomachs when passing a certain spot where a British woman had been attacked by a gang of Indian youth.

On April 18, Gandhi, appalled by the violence, temporarily suspended his campaign. Six months later a parliamentary committee of inquiry found Dyer guilty of an "error of judgment." Forced to resign his post in India, the general returned to England, where he received a hero's welcome from conservative members of Parliament.

THE LITERATURE

The title of Stanley Wolpert's (1927–) novel *An Error of Judgment* (1970) is clearly ironic, reflecting the evasive euphemism of the committee of inquiry's judgment. Wolpert has written extensively on the history of modern India both as a historian and novelist. (His *Nine Hours to Rama* (1962) was a best-selling fictional re-creation of the assassination of Gandhi.) His account of the massacre depicts the Raj as, to a man (and one woman), arrogant, racist, and invincibly ignorant. Not only Dyer but also the rest of the military leadership and the governor of the Punjab, Sir Michael O'Dwyer, sound more like members of the Ku Klux Klan than rulers of the British Empire. (See BRITISH EMPIRE, END OF.) Perhaps Wolpert is historically accurate in his depiction, but from a literary point of view such accuracy renders the novel more melodrama than historical tragedy. One question he might have explored is how and why the experience of being an occupying army brutalizes the occupiers. As it is, the novel offers the brutality and insensitivity of the British as a given. Similarly, the one negative Indian character in the novel is the child of a prostitute and an unknown Englishman—his genes presumably the explanation for his villainy.

The novel's most interesting point occurs near the end when the viceroy, Lord Chelmsford, offers Lord Hunter, head of the commission of inquiry, his theory that the British are masters of India because of a secret weapon, "spirit, our national spirit"; this prompts Hunter, perhaps thinking of Gandhi, to ask what will happen "when the natives [have] caught on to our secret and developed a national spirit of their own?" The viceroy replies, "Then we're finished, Hunter," a remark that proves to be prophetic.

FURTHER READING

Lawrence James's *Raj: The Making and Unmaking of British India* (1998) contains a complete account of the massacre and the Dyer trial.

ANGLO-IRISH WAR (1919–1921)

See IRISH WAR OF INDEPENDENCE.

ANGOLAN WAR OF INDEPENDENCE (1961–1974)

The African nation of Angola had been a colony of Portugal for many years, populated by increasing numbers of European Portuguese following World War II. Resistance to this domination and the exploitation of the country's natural resources took the form of the establishment of native political parties: the Popular Movement for the Liberation of Angola (MPLA) and the National Front for the Liberation of Angola (FNLA). By 1961, these parties, realizing that the Portuguese government had no intention of following other European nations in granting independence to African colonies, engaged in a guerrilla war that was to persist for 13 years. During most of that time, the Portuguese forces had to contend with rebellions in their other African colonies, Mozambique and Guinea, but the fighting was sporadic and contained in limited areas, and the rebels made little headway, despite at one point being secretly supplied with aid from the United States CENTRAL INTELLIGENCE AGENCY (CIA).

With the death of the Portuguese dictator Antonio Salazar in 1970 and the growing disenchantment in Portugal with the conduct of the war, the movement in favor of Angolan independence grew, particularly among leaders in the Portuguese military. The result was a coup in 1974, after which the new military government granted Angola independence. Unfortunately, the new republic was almost immediately plunged into a three-way civil war among the MPLA, FNLA, and the third group, National Union for the Total Independence of Angola (UNITA), a war intensified by the involvement of foreign nations, including the United States and the Soviet Union, 50,000 Cuban troops, and an invasion by South Africa. In addition to the half-million dead and 4 million refugees, the civil war helped to create a famine that raised the mortality rate of newborn children to an unprecedented level.

After many abortive attempts to reconcile the warring groups, a fragile cease-fire was finally concluded in April 2002.

THE LITERATURE

Antonio Lobo Antunes (1942–   ), a Portuguese physician-turned-novelist, served in the early 1970s as a doctor with the Portuguese army in Angola. His novel *South of Nowhere* (1979; trans., 1983) is a graphic, often hallucinatory account of the impact of the war on that desperately poor and oppressed country. The story, whose form borrows heavily from Albert Camus's *The Fall* (1956; trans., 1957), is a first-person narrative set in a bar in Lisbon. The narrator is a guilt-ridden doctor, haunted by his recollections of the horror of the war and his passive acquiescence in the destruction and suffering it brought on both Portuguese soldiers and the starving masses of Angolan natives. The silent listener to the doctor's story is an anonymous woman he has picked up in the bar. The one-night stand that ensues leaves the narrator in the same joyless, unsatisfied, emotional limbo that he exhibits throughout his narration.

But the heart of the story is the Angolan experience: "We died in the asshole of the world one after the other, tripping on wires, being blown up by grenades, zap! . . . [A]ll we had to show were amputated legs, coffins, hepatitis, malaria, corpses." Driven to the brink of madness, the doctor finds a temporary escape in the hut of Tia Theresa, "a fat, black woman, maternal and wise, receiving [him] on her straw mattress with matronly indulgence." But inevitably the war infects every aspect of his life, forcing him to see his family, his city, and all of Portugal as corrupted and debased. The doctor's narrative is a failed attempt to exorcise his guilt and shame, which he shares with Portugal for the rape of Angola.

A powerful indictment of Portuguese colonialism, *South of Nowhere* weakens its case by overstatement, turning righteous anger into a universal indictment of every aspect of Portuguese life and society. The result is that the reader may suspect that here anger has degenerated into self-pity.

FURTHER READING

G. J. Bender's *Angola under the Portuguese* (1978) recounts the history of the colonization of Angola.

ANTARCTIC EXPEDITIONS (1911–1916)

Although the continent of Antarctica was sighted as early as 1820, it was not until the 20th century that explorers were able to penetrate deep into the frozen interior. In 1911, a race to reach the South Pole between a Norwegian group led by Roald Amundsen and a British team under Robert Scott resulted in Amundsen's reaching the Pole on December 15, with Scott arriving a month later on January 18, 1912. Returning to their base, Scott and his crew encountered unusually severe weather and ran out of supplies. Scott and the last two of his men perished within 11 miles of their base camp sometime after March 29, 1912, the date of the last entry in Scott's diary.

A later expedition (1914–16) led by Sir Ernest Shackleton attempted to cross the South Pole; the group endured incredible hardships, and he survived miraculously, although the expedition failed.

At various times in the course of the century, a number of nations claimed the continent as their territory; however, none of these claims has been recognized. Instead, in 1959, 12 nations joined in the Antarctic Treaty, which banned any military presence there and arranged for cooperative international research. This treaty was expanded in 1991, when 40 nations agreed to continue scientific research on the continent for another 50 years.

THE LITERATURE

Beryl Bainbridge's (1933–   ) *The Birthday Boys* (1993) offers a poignant, fictional account of the Scott expedition. The story is alternately narrated by five members of the crew, including Scott himself. Each one carries the story forward chronologically from the ship's leaving port to the death of crew member Edward Oates (dying of gangrene, he crawls out of his tent to expose himself to the elements). Oates's death leaves only two men still alive, Scott and Dr. Edward Wilson, the team medical officer; both men die shortly after.

The tragedy of Scott and his men, as Bainbridge depicts it, lies in their reckless optimism, their faith in the human capacity to overcome unaided any of nature's challenges. Scott, for example, disdained the use of an adequate number of sled dogs, as if they would give his team an unfair advantage in the race. (Amundsen's success was directly attributable to his ready employment of more than 100 dogs.) As Henry Bowers, Scott's strongest supporter among the crew, puts it, "Far better to stride out, nation against nation, man against man." Their idealism and courage is severely tested in the months to come, but the men, none of whom are plastic saints, suffer and die nobly, but unnecessarily, forerunners of millions of men in the trenches of WORLD WAR I.

A relatively short novel, *The Birthday Boys* (1993) tells its story with a cool, spare, precise prose that captures both the beauty of the landscape and the pathos of human failure in an admirable distillation of history, biography, and fiction.

Elizabeth Arthur's (1953–) *Antarctic Navigation* (1994) is the story of Morgan Lamont, a woman with a lifelong dream of retracing Scott's ill-fated journey. The story traces Morgan's obsession from childhood, when she reads about Scott's 1910 expedition; her imaginative quest is realized some 300 pages later, when the adult Morgan arrives on the continent to confront the "white darkness" of a whiteout, an overwhelming totality of whiteness that renders a person, in effect, snow-blind. Once on the continent, Morgan sets about realizing her dream of recreating Scott's expedition. She succeeds in reaching the Pole, but, as with Scott, the difficulties intensify during the return. Morgan breaks her arm in a fall and gangrene sets in. The result is a race to reach the base camp before amputation becomes necessary. This suspenseful race against time is the most engaging section of the novel.

Had it been content to be an exciting adventure story, *Antarctic Navigation* would have been a successful example of that genre. As it stands, however, it is overwritten and frequently pretentious in its reflections on topical events, such as Operation Desert Storm and the nature of imperialism. They are clearly meant to add depth and seriousness to a story that doesn't need it.

FURTHER READING

Susan Solomon's *The Coldest March* (2001) authoritatively updates the history of the Scott expedition.

APARTHEID (1948–1992)

In the aftermath of the BOER WAR, the Union of South Africa, consisting of the British colonies of Natal and Cape Colony, and the Dutch-speaking republics of the Transvaal and the Orange Free State, united as the Union of South Africa in 1910. The country prospered under the impetus of the gold and mining industries. As a result, the native African population started to abandon their traditional tribal life in the country and, in search of employment, moved toward the prosperous industrial centers, where they huddled in shanty towns. The presence of increasing numbers of blacks nearby triggered a reaction in the white community. Segregation of the races had always been a de facto condition, but in 1948 certain elements moved to ensure this condition by setting up a number of specific laws. In that year, the conservative Afrikaner Nationalists were voted back into power and, shortly after, proclaimed their official policy of apartheid (a word meaning "apartness"), arguing that the progress of the races would be enhanced if they were kept separate. Subsequent legislation established specific residential sections for each race, set up laws requiring nonwhites to carry identity cards, developed different educational standards, limited employment opportunities, and forbade social interaction among races. The effect of these laws was to ensure the complete dominance by whites in a land where they represented 20 percent of the population. Protests against the policy in the 1950s culminated in the Sharpeville massacre (1960), in which police fired on black demonstrators, killing 69 people. In 1976, police again opened fire, this time on a group of black school children in the Johannesburg Township of SOWETO protesting inadequate educational facilities. As a consequence, international attention was drawn to the condition of blacks in South Africa, setting off a set of policies involving economic boycotts and sanctions against the government. In 1992, in a national referendum, the white minority voted to abolish apartheid. The following year, the government announced the official end of the practice.

THE LITERATURE

Alan Paton's (1903–88) *Cry, the Beloved Country* was published in the same year, 1948, that apartheid was initiated. Although it does not deal directly with the subject, its moving plea for tolerance and justice among the races established its preeminent claim as an antiapartheid work. The novel consists of three sections, each one viewing its events from a different perspective. In Book I, the point of view is that of Stephen Kuvalo, an African priest in a rural community. Kuvalo travels to Johannesburg to care for his ailing sister and to find his son Absalom, who has moved to the city and dropped out of touch with his family. The city, Kuvalo discovers, is a powder keg of racial tension as a result of the early applications of apartheid. Kuvalo is devastated to learn that Absalom has been arrested for the murder of a white man during an attempted robbery.

In Book II, the story is seen from the point of view of James Jarvis, the father of the murdered man, Arthur Jarvis, who, ironically, had been working for the reform of injustices against blacks. This section ends with the conviction and execution of Absalom. In Book III, Kumalo returns to his village, where his bishop informs him that he can no longer serve in his parish. However, the son of the murdered man, operating with approval of his grandfather, visits Kumalo and establishes a friendship. James Jarvis, the grandfather, hires a farming instructor to help the village improve their agricultural output. The two fathers, united in grief, become friends.

The South African novelist Nadine Gordimer (1923–) has devoted much of her writing life to the struggle against apartheid, an achievement that was recognized in 1990 when she was awarded the Nobel Prize. In the course of a long career that has spanned the rise and fall of apartheid and the government that sponsored it, her recurring theme has been the dilemma of the apolitical or moderate white person opposed to apartheid but inextricably caught up in its social fabric. *The Conservationist* (1974) is a particularly acute portrait of a man who, though trying to avoid racial politics, is drawn into its context and ultimately pays with his life for his willful ignorance. In *Burger's Daughter* (1979), the historical event constructs the identity of her heroine (see SOWETO).

In *July's People* (1981) the revolutionary struggle has erupted into a full-scale civil war. The Smales family—Bam, Maureen, and their two children—escape from a besieged city, thanks to their servant July, who brings them to his remote native village. Bam and Maureen (hers is the central consciousness through which the story is told) pride themselves on being white liberals, opposed to apartheid, and on being generous, open-minded employers of July. Once in the village, however, they begin to experience subtle shifts in the master-servant relationship. These reversals come to a head over the control of two objects: the jeep, in which they made their escape but in which they cannot risk riding openly, and Bam's shotgun, which he uses for hunting. Car and gun are two of the outward signs of white hegemony that Bam and Maureen have been unconscious of until they see them coming under July's control, and their reaction is one of panic. Bam, cut off from the familiar modes of expression and ownership that define a man in white society, grows increasingly weaker and lifeless. Maureen finds herself not accepted by the village women, in contrast to her children, who are easily assimilated. She tries to confront July, and the ensuing argument reveals the gap in understanding that has always been covered over in the past—for example, her recognition that she has never known or tried to find out July's real name, *July* being the name assigned him by whites. What she comes to realize is that she has been benefiting from a psychological apartheid that mirrors the larger social institution. Written with subtle grace and an acute political awareness, *July's People* is a powerful study of people caught at a time when "[t]he old is dying and the new cannot be born."

FURTHER READING

G. M. Gerhart's *Black Power in South Africa* (1978) is a study of the development of the resistance movement growing out of apartheid. Stephen Clingman's *The Novels of Nadine Gordimer* (1986) looks at her work as "history from the inside."

ARAB-ISRAELI CONFLICT (1948–)

The ancient land called Palestine has been settled by both Arabs and Jews since biblical times. A movement called Zionism, designating Palestine as a new nation for the scattered Jewish people, was started in the 1890s by the Austrian journalist Theodor Herzl and quickly began to focus Jewish ambition and Arab discontent. Jews from eastern Europe began to emigrate to Palestine. Before this, Jews and Arabs (mainly Muslims) lived side-by-side, with all the ordinary attendant difficulties associated with two different cultures in close contact. In modern times, Palestine was first in the hands of the Ottoman Empire (until 1918) and then controlled by Great Britain, under an internationally sanctioned mandate (1919–48) following WORLD WAR I . The policy of the Ottomans toward Palestine was benign neglect of both Arabs and Jews. The British looked with favor alternately on one side or the other.

Arabs and Jews clung to legitimate claims to the land by way of two documents: for the Arabs, the McMahon-Husein Correspondence, in which the Arabs were promised the right to a new Arab nation in the lands of the former Ottoman Empire; and for the Jews the Balfour Declaration, issued by the British in 1917, which stated: "His Majesty's Government view with favour the establishment in Palestine of a national home for the Jewish people." Each new wave of Zionist immigration to Palestine in the 1920s and 1930s evoked increasingly violent Arab reactions. The culmination of these responses was the Arab insurrection of 1936 against both the Jews and the British; it lasted three years. WORLD WAR II followed, and its aftermath saw a set of initiatives to reach a peaceful solution. United Nations Resolution 181, mediating Arab and Jewish claims, called for a partition of Palestine into separate states. The Jews agreed. The Arabs did not. At midnight on May 14, 1948, the state of Israel officially came into existence.

Thus began the first of the Arab-Israeli wars. Jewish armies confronted the combined military of Egypt, Transjordan (a state, later Jordan, created by a British division of Palestine in 1922), Syria, and Iraq—as well as loosely organized and lightly armed local Palestinians. Israel won the war, though it sustained heavy casualties. The West Bank region of Palestine came under the control of Transjordan, while Egypt occupied the Gaza Strip. The war also created a large population of Palestinian Arab refugees, who were cared for in camps maintained by the UN in neighboring Arab states. As a result of the war, relations between Israeli Jews and Palestinians deteriorated further. Arabs were angrily disappointed; Jews were warier than ever.

The second of the wars took place in October of 1956, after Egypt, in response to the failure of the Western nations to help finance the Aswân Dam, nationalized the Suez Canal. Britain and France, joint owners of the canal, attacked Egypt a few days later, joined by Israeli forces, which occupied the Sinai Peninsula. Israel eventually withdrew, but, once again, the conflict grew in bitterness.

In 1967, unable to resist calls for war within the Muslim Middle East, Egypt, Syria, and Jordan gathered armies on Israel's frontiers. Israel struck first, however, and, in just six days, defeated these combined forces again. This time, the Israelis took control of the West Bank, Gaza, the Sinai Peninsula, the Golan Heights of Syria, and the whole of Jerusalem. More Arab refugees fled into the camps in Lebanon and Jordan. The loss of Jerusalem was a particularly painful blow to the Arab community, since the enemy now occupied the ancient Islamic holy sites. In late November, the UN Security Council adopted Resolution 242, calling for the exchange of land for peace. Both Israel and the Arabs rejected the proposal.

Then, in 1973, on the Jews' holiest day, Yom Kippur, Egypt and Syria launched a surprise attack that caused enormous destruction and casualties on the Israeli side; the Arab armies' initial success engendered a new sense of confidence in the Arab world. Israel recovered, however, and pushed the armies back from the territory they had recaptured. The Yom Kippur War, also known as the Ramadan War, increased the hatred between the two parties.

In later years, hostilities deepened, exacerbated by the establishment of new Israeli settlements in the occupied territories, Gaza and the West Bank. Continual bloodshed became a hallmark of the region. Extremist Arabs vented their bitterness and made political statements through suicide bombings in the streets of Tel Aviv and Jerusalem; the Israelis answered with savage troop movements into the Arab-controlled towns.

What had begun as a local conflict in the 1920s and 1930s expanded to a regional one in the 1940s and to the whole of the Muslim world and beyond in the 1950s. On a number of critical occasions, the United States as well as the UN has attempted to bring together the two parties for peace conferences, but they have only been partly successful. On both sides, medieval rigidities persist.

The Palestinian Arabs long for a state of their own—an existence free from what they see as Israeli occupation and oppression. They want a homeland, and they mourn the loss of their holy places in Jerusalem. They are also firm in demanding the right of return of the refugees who fled in 1948 and the removal of Israeli settlements in the occupied territories, principally the West Bank. For their part, the Israelis want secure borders and safety from Arab attacks.

THE LITERATURE

Two novelists, one an Israeli, the other a Palestinian, offer differing imaginative conceptions of the conflict. The Israeli writer A. B. Yehoshua (1936–) sets his novel *The Lover* (1977; trans., 1977) in the time of the Yom Kippur

War. The novel is a dense and dreamlike account of Israeli life in the period, describing tensions between Arabs and Israelis, men and women, eastern-European Jews and Jews from Spain and North Africa. The narrators are Adam, a big, strong, impulsive, bearded auto-repair shop owner; his meek and anxious wife, Asya, whose narration consists solely of fantastic dreams; their talented, eloquent, and spirited 15-year-old daughter, Dafi; and an Arab Israeli boy of Dafi's age, Na'im, whom Adam employs in the shop. Later in the novel, this quartet of narrators is joined by Gabriel and Veducha. Gabriel, Asya's lover, is a 30-year-old Israeli orphan, back in Israel after 10 years in Paris. His grandmother, Veducha, is dying, and he wants to secure his inheritance, consisting of her house, formerly owned by an Arab, and her car, a blue 1947 Morris. The lives of these characters are beautifully, painfully, and meaningfully intertwined.

The book begins with Adam's narration: "And in the last war we lost a lover. We used to have a lover, and since the war he is gone. Just disappeared. He and his grandmother's old Morris." Note the use of the pronoun *we*.

Gabriel is introduced to the narrative when he arrives at Adam's shop, breathing heavily, as he pushes the Morris into the garage. The car won't start. Gabriel thinks it needs only a screw, while Adam can see that there are spider webs growing on the engine and that much must be done to repair it. When Gabriel returns to the shop to collect the car, he faints from hunger. He later explains that the car belongs to his grandmother, that she is in a coma, and that he is penniless until she either awakens or dies. Later, in a mysterious spasm of sympathy, Adam takes him home to live for a while. It is there that Asya and Gabriel become lovers.

In the household are Dafi, the daughter, and Na'im, the Arab boy. The boy works in Adam's shop, where all the mechanics are Arabs—one is a cousin who has recruited him for the job. There they listen to Arab music until aware of the presence of Israelis, when their radios go silent. At night they retreat from the city—dominated by Israelis—and return to their villages in the countryside. Na'im is taken up by Adam and in the course of things gets a key to his house. Mesmerized by the opportunity, he enters the house secretly, and encounters Dafi, with whom he falls hopelessly in love. When Gabriel's grandmother miraculously emerges from her coma, Adam arranges that Na'im live with her, as a convenience for him and for Veducha. Na'im is central to Yehoshua's fevered view of Arab-Israeli relations.

At length, Gabriel leaves to meet his obligation to do military service, taking the car with him. When the family does not hear from him, Adam begins a relentless day and night search in the religious areas of Jerusalem. He at last encounters Gabriel, disguised in the traditional clothing and facial hair of the religious sect he has joined to escape from his army unit in the region of the Suez Canal. Three oddly ecstatic, dancing sect members had been in the desert blessing the Jewish forces.

Gabriel then proceeds to narrate his adventures in the Yom Kippur War, scenes of hunger, boredom, fear, chaos, noise, and brutality from his own Israeli officers. The car had at first been appropriated by an officer, who drove them both deep into the Sinai Desert. As his military service dragged on, Gabriel was able, with the help of the three sect members, to steal it back and drive to their compound in Jerusalem.

Now fearful and weak, Gabriel leaves the sect and allows Adam to install him in a hotel room. Asya hurries to join them at the hotel. Adam "liberates" the Morris from the sect. Clearly, the car has a symbolic role: It's a blue 1947 Morris, made in Britain. Blue is the color of the Israeli flag, and 1947 is the year before Israel's independence (from British rule). That the car requires from Adam a mighty effort to bring it to life—as did the Jewish nation—and repeatedly undergoes various problems (described as "exhaustion," for example) is also suggestive.

While Asya, Adam, and Gabriel are at the hotel, Dafi and Na'im consummate their relationship with a fierce sexual encounter at Adam's house. After long sections of the book narrated alternately by Na'im and the old grandmother, Veducha dies, and Na'im summons Adam to her side.

After seeing the dead old lady, Adam has trouble starting the Morris: He says, "It's exhausted after the long journey," and "The car's going to fall apart under me and yet I can't bring myself to leave it. I've spent too much time searching for it up and down the land." Having found Gabriel, now unaccountably with Asya, and dispatched Na'im back to his village, Adam sees himself alone, "standing beside a dead old car from '47," and realizes, "there's nobody to save me."

In the end, the theme of the novel is that Israelis and Arabs are locked in mystery, locked together in unending and unbending relationship. They are like lovers. The pronoun *we* used in the first sentence denotes a collective loss suffered by all. They all, on both sides, have seen their lovers disappear.

In the end, for Adam, the "car battery is absolutely dead." No spark. No movement. He thinks of Na'im, telling himself that Na'im has "become a little lover in the course of a year." The headlights of the "car lose him [Na'im]"—as he moves off to return to his village—and "he disappears around a bend in the road."

The Secret Life of Saeed, the Pessoptimist, (1974; trans., 2001), a novel by Emile Habiby (1919–98) is entirely indebted to Voltaire's *Candide*. The novel makes a detailed and ironic comparison between itself and *Candide* and suggests a likeness between Candide and Saeed.

Saeed, Habiby's comic hero, tells of his life in Israel, in the form of a letter to an unidentified friend. The letter has been sent from outer space, where friendly extraterrestrial beings have taken Saeed after rescuing him. He had been perilously stranded atop a very sharp, pointy pillar, unable to move or dismount. Saeed in this state is a striking image of the Palestinian condition—on the single horn of a perilous dilemma. It has taken supernatural efforts to rescue him. From this perspective, Saeed tells of life between the poles of Zionist colonialism and Palestinian resistance: a life wavering between optimism and pessimism—hence the term *pessoptimist.*

Saeed's character is dense and paradoxical: He is tactless and gullible, shy and fearful, filled with the foolish courage of the innocent and optimistic, yet cowardly and underhanded and convinced that all is lost. Eager to please, personally and politically, he eventually joins and leads the Union of Palestinian Workers and then becomes a spy (unrewarded and unrecognized) in the Zionist secret service. In this role, he befriends his boss, Jacob, and comes under the thumb of Jacob's boss, "the big man," a sinister, cruel, and sometimes stupid overseer.

Self-deprecating and funny, he describes his born-again beginnings: During the fighting in 1948, Zionist forces "waylaid us and opened fire, shooting my father," but a stray donkey came into the line of fire and took a bullet for him. A member of a family sent to the refugee camps outside Israel, Saeed eventually sneaks across the border back into Israel.

Thus begins Habiby's story of a Palestinian catastrophe, propelled by Israeli aggression and reactionary Arab politics. The focus is on institutionalized cruelty, as when Saeed is imprisoned in Shatta jail and beaten to a pulp by guards, each with "thick, strong legs and a mouth wearing a smile worse than a frown. They all seem to have been formed in the same mold." At the same time, ironic criticism is leveled at the "Arabian princes" who make huge profits from the toil and sweat of the people," the same "drunken princes who roar in fury, accusing of treason those who demand implementation of the resolutions of the United Nations Security Council."

Saeed's son, Walaa, has become a rebel against Israeli oppression, a fighter (*a fida'i*). In the contents of the treasure chest Wallaa has found not just money, but arms, which are indeed treasures to a fighter. One of the most touching scenes in the novel is that of Walaa's last stand. He is hiding in a cellar with all his treasured weapons, and he tells his mother, who has come to persuade him to surrender, that he has always lived in a cellar. Then he dies, as Saeed watches from the seashore.

The final chapter finds Saeed back on the stake he sat on at the beginning. There is no one to help him. No friends come to his assistance—a telling comment on the Arab condition. Finally, he sees his "master," the man from outer space, whom he begs to save him; the master, however, replies, "When you can bear the misery of your reality no longer but will not pay the price necessary to change it, only then you come to me." Nevertheless, Saeed is borne aloft, over a jubilant group below expecting a cloud to pass so that the sun will shine.

In an epilogue, the recipient of the letters—that is, the text of the novel—visits a mental institution in search of Saeed. But Saeed is not there. The reader is therefore left to infer from Saeed's not-so-secret life (as the predicament of the Palestinians is also not so secret) the fate of Palestinians: to be deposited on the point of a high stake, an unresolvable dilemma. From there it is a short distance to the madness induced by Israeli oppression, and, finally, there is nowhere else to go but outer space—toward the possibility of a magical intervention and rescue.

FURTHER READING

The reader will find powerful poetic impressions of the Arab-Israeli conflict in *The Selected Poetry of Yehuda Amichai* (trans., 1986). For a sense of how profoundly the two sides are connected, see, for example, Amichai's (1924–2000) "An Arab Shepherd Is Searching for His Goat on Mount Zion." The Palestinian poet Taha Muhammad Ali (1931–   ) has written of an Arab sensibility responding to the loss of the homeland in his *Never Mind: Twenty Poems and a Story* (trans., 2000). Throughout this slender volume, the reader is confronted by Tahas's beautiful evocation of the Arabs' joyous attachment to their land, and their eschewing of violence and embrace of the seasons. A wise commentator has noted that all things said or written about the Arab-Israeli conflict have been open to dispute; nothing can be established as beyond question. Despite this caveat, the reader will find the following books useful. Benny Morris's *Righteous Victims: A History of the Zionist-Arab Conflict, 1881–2001 (2001)* and Rashid Khalidi's *Palestinian Identity: The Construction of Modern National Consciousness* (1998).

—William Herman

ARCTIC EXPLORATION (1905–1909)

Arctic exploration reached fever peak in the first decade of the 20th century, when two American explorers, Frederick Cook and Richard Peary, made separate claims to be the first man to have reached the North Pole. Cook was a New York physician and explorer, who set out in June 1907, ostensibly to lead a hunting party in northern Greenland. Once there, Cook announced his intention to discover the Pole. He traveled to Axel Heiberg Island near the Arctic Circle, and then, accompanied by two Eskimos, he journeyed across the sea ice to the point where on April 21, 1908, he reached what he believed to be the North Pole. Cook's return was so hazardous that it took a full year before he reached Upernavik, Greenland. Peary, who had made several earlier attempts to reach the Pole, traveled in 1908 to Ellesmere Island. From there, accompanied by his assistant Matthew Henson and four Eskimos, he headed for the Pole. On April 6, 1909, he arrived at what his instruments indicated was the North Pole.

Peary proclaimed his discovery four days after Cook had announced his. At first, most authorities supported Cook's claim, but Peary pursued a relentless campaign to discredit Cook, whose cause was further undermined when the two Eskimos who had accompanied him asserted that they had gone only a short distance on the polar ice. Cook's case eroded further when an earlier claim of his to have been the first man to reach the top of Mount McKinley was proven false. In the 1920s, Cook was convicted of stock fraud and spent the rest of his life in prison. Peary's claim came to be generally accepted, although Cook supporters have continued the controversy. A recent argument has suggested that Peary missed the Pole by 50 nautical miles, resolving the controversy not in favor of Cook, but against both explorers.

THE LITERATURE

The dispute between Peary and Cook forms the historical setting of Wayne Johnston's (1958–   ) *The Navigator of New York* (2002). The protagonist is the fictional Devlin Stead, an orphan raised by an uncle in Newfoundland after his physician father disappears on Peary's 1891–92 expedition to Greenland and his mother drowns, an apparent suicide. The father had essentially abandoned his family, caught up in the fever of polar expeditions. At the age of 17, Devlin receives a letter from Frederick Cook, who had been on the expedition from which Devlin's father disappeared. The letter contains a revelation that leaves Devlin astonished, but determined to solve the mystery it opens up. In 1901, he comes to Brooklyn, New York, and moves in with Cook. From there, they participate in a 1905 expedition to rescue Peary, who appears lost on another expedition to Greenland. They succeed in locating Peary and bringing his wife and child back safely, but Peary refuses to return, even after he almost dies; he is eventually rescued by Devlin. Devlin joins the 1907 expedition and, under Cook's direction, becomes, he believes, the first human being to stand on the North Pole. The novel concludes with a complex series of revelations, all of them spinning off the question of Devlin's paternity.

In its plot and tone, *The Navigator of New York* reads like a 19th-century novel, in which Devlin serves as a Pip or David Copperfield, the center of the story, but not its most interesting character. In this respect, the honors go to Peary and Cook. Peary is depicted as a borderline psychotic, fixated on his desire for fame and driven to deceit and murder to achieve it. Cook is a man wracked with guilt and self-hatred for a decision he made as a young man and for which he tries to atone through Devlin. As for the ongoing historical Peary/Cook debate, the author's final word enlists the novelist's prerogative: "This is a work of fiction. At times, it places real people in imaginary space and time. At others, imaginary people in real space and time. While it draws from the historical record, its purpose is not to answer historical questions or settle controversies." Within that frame, the novel succeeds admirably.

FURTHER READING

Robert Bryce's *Cook & Peary* (1997) is an extensively detailed, heavily documented reappraisal of the controversy.

ARDENNES OFFENSIVE (WORLD WAR II) (1944–1945)

The success of the NORMANDY INVASION forced the German army back to the borders of the Rhine. The Allied capture of the port of Antwerp in the Netherlands in 1944 was a critical victory since it considerably shortened the Allied support line. Faced with the prospect of fighting a defensive war against the British and Americans in the west and the Russians in the east, Adolf HITLER chose to gamble on a major offensive effort in the west, with the goal of recapturing Antwerp. He ordered the German commander, Field Marshal Gerd von Rundstedt, to focus the attack in the Ardennes forest on the Belgian, Luxembourg, and French borders, the scene of a major German breakthrough in their victorious campaign against the French in 1940.

On December 16, 1944, the German Fifth and Sixth Armies launched their attack, driving a wedge into the American line that gave the conflict its popular name, battle of the Bulge. The Germans swept over the outmanned and surprised American troops, capturing thousands of prisoners, many of whom were summarily executed by the SS troops, who played a major role in the offensive. But in absorbing the brunt of the initial offensive, the American troops successfully bought time for the Allies' subsequent defense and counterattack. The counterattacks were launched on January 6, 1945; by January 16, the initial bulge created by the German attack was closed up and the line restored to its former position. The final toll of dead and wounded included 19,000 Americans killed and 15,000 taken prisoner. The German toll of killed, wounded, and taken prisoner amounted to more than 100,000 lost in an offensive in which Hitler gained nothing but a little time.

THE LITERATURE

As its title, derived from the opening line of the well-known carol, ironically suggests, William Wharton's (1925–   ) *A Midnight Clear* (1982) is set in the Ardennes Forest during the Christmas season 1944. The action focuses on an I-and-R (intelligence and reconnaissance) infantry squad. Although written in the present tense, the novel periodically flashes back to basic training experiences in Mississippi, where the squad—its members, teenagers fresh out of high school—is formed. The distinctive feature of this squad is that its members are unusually intelligent, originally assigned on the basis of their IQ scores, for specialized army training at American universities. But the army suddenly scuttles this program, and the men are assigned as intelligence-gathering infantry soldiers.

On the Ardennes line, the squad is ordered to occupy an abandoned chateau in a forward position. There they make a series of tentative contacts with a small group of German soldiers, who signify their desire to surrender and be taken out of the war. (One of their peacemaking signs is a Christmas tree, which the German soldiers set up, singing carols in front of it.) The squad's reaction is at first cautious, fearful that the Germans are setting a trap, but eventually they formulate a plan to accept the surrender. The plan tragically misfires, providing its surviving members with an induction into maturity that is both savage and haunting.

The novel's capacity to induce tension, fear, and the anxiety of uncertainty is truly impressive, as is the glimpse it offers of the brightness of youth trapped in the degrading horror of war.

In 1988, Paul Watkins (1964–   ), a 23-year-old American graduate student at Stanford, published his first novel *Night over Day over Night*, remarkable in many respects, not least in its choice of protagonist, a young German who joins the Waffen-SS (Adolf HITLER's elite troops) in 1944 and is sent to fight in the Ardennes. Sebastian Westland is 17 when he enlists as a private in the SS. He could have joined the regular army, but he chooses the SS because it's the natural move for someone who has spent his early years in the Hitler Youth. But behind his choice is an unacknowledged despair over the death of his father earlier in the war and the need to quash the realization that Germany cannot win the war.

In his basic training he is introduced to wanton cruelty by his platoon sergeant Voss, a man whose chief satisfactions derive from sadistic behavior. After the completion of training and a short home leave, the new troops are sent to the Ardennes, opposite the American lines. During the attack, Sebastian's company comes under heavy fire from American artillery, which all but wipes out every man. Sebastian survives in order to avenge the betrayal of his dead comrades' honor by the sadist Voss. The novel concludes with Sebastian racing toward enemy lines to his death.

A Midnight Clear and *Night over Day over Night* pose an interesting contrast to each other. Both focus on soldiers in their teens. Both groups belong to special forces, an American intelligence squad and the SS, who were considered to be Hitler's shock troops. The Americans share a sense of intellectual superiority, reflected, for example, in the fact that one of their diversions is reading the same book and discussing it. The book they are currently reading is Ernest Hemingway's *A Farewell to Arms;* the book before that was Erich Maria Remarque's *All Quiet on the Western Front,* the two most famous novels of WORLD WAR I. (Like *Night over Day, All Quiet* deals with a group of young German soldiers; like *A Midnight Clear,* it is narrated in the present tense. (See WESTERN FRONT.) The Germans' sense of superiority is symbolized by the inscription on the dagger that each SS soldier receives on completing training: "My Honor Is Loyalty." The Americans, despite their youth, are skeptical of heroic rhetoric and deeply distrustful, with good reason, of their immediate officers. The Germans detest their hateful noncommissioned officers, but their respect for their indoctrination as Hitler Youth still persists in the belief that their honor *is* loyalty. Despite these differences, however, once in battle, both groups do their duty, while trying, unsuccessfully for the most part, to stay alive.

FURTHER READING
Hugh Cole's *The Ardennes: Battle of the Bulge* (1994) is a recent authoritative account.

ARMENIAN GENOCIDE (1915)

From the 16th to the 20th centuries, the nation of Armenia was part of the Ottoman Empire under the control of the Turks. Because the Armenians were Christians, they suffered from various forms of ill-treatment by their Muslim rulers. In 1895, the Armenians protested their status within the empire, calling for territorial autonomy. As a result, more than 200,000 Armenians were brutally massacred by Turkish troops. Earlier, part of Armenia had been ceded to Russia in 1878, and, when WORLD WAR I erupted, some Armenians joined the Russian forces to fight against the Turks. In retaliation the Turkish government in 1915 ordered the deportation of the entire Armenian population to Syria and Mesopotamia. The result was a death march of more than 1 million Armenian men, women, and children, during which 600,000 died, many of them from brutality and starvation.

Although the Armenians had little chance of resisting the overwhelming Turkish forces, a group of small villages surrounding the mountain of Musa Dagh on the Syrian coast successfully defied the deportation order. Retreating to the hills above their village, the residents of Musa Dagh constructed a complex series of defensive positions, which they held for close to two months in the face of increasingly large Turkish attacks. In the end, an Allied naval force rescued some 4,000 of the residents of Musa Dagh and brought them to safety.

This small triumph notwithstanding, the massacre of the Armenian population ranks as one of the truly horrifying events of the 20th century, a horror compounded by the refusal of the Turks to this day to acknowledge their guilt. In some ways even more disturbing is the silent complicity of the major world powers in the Turkish denial.

THE LITERATURE
In *The Forty Days of Musa Dagh* (1933; trans., 1934), the Austrian novelist, poet, and playwright Franz Werfel (1890–1945), best known as the author of *The Song of Bernadette* (1941; trans., 1942), provides a fictional reconstruction of the Musa Dagh resistance. With impressive skill, he transforms the historical events into a thoughtful, suspenseful, and moving account of courage and sacrifice. The central figure is Gabriel Bagradian, a westernized Armenian who has been living in Paris, married to a sophisticated French woman. Returning with his wife and son to his native village to settle the estate of his

recently deceased brother, Gabriel finds himself increasingly conscious of his racial identity, becoming caught up in the plight of his fellow Armenians. When his passport is confiscated by the government, he gives himself completely to the struggle. With the help of the village priest Ter Haigasun, the spiritual and political leader of the community, he develops a complex set of plans to defend the summit of the mountain, persuading the villagers to fight rather than submit to deportation and certain death.

Gabriel's plans and tactical command prove to be remarkably effective as the villagers repel a series of Turkish assaults, inflicting serious damage on the invaders. Finally, just as the Turks appear poised for a victorious onslaught, an Allied naval force providentially rescues the Armenian community. Left behind, however, is Gabriel, who is killed while mourning at the grave of his son.

Critics have noted the biblical motif in the novel, in which Gabriel, like Moses, delivers his people to the promised land, which he himself does not enter. (Musa Dagh means "mountain of Moses.") The "forty days" of the title (the historical events actually took place in 53 days) remind the reader of Moses' 40 days on Mount Sinai and of Christ's 40 days in the desert. These allusions reinforce a major theme of the novel: the value and validity of political and military action when founded on a strong spiritual and moral base. A Jew with a strong affinity for Christianity, Werfel introduced into the novel an important subplot concerning Dr. Johannes Lepsius, a German Protestant minister who labored tirelessly to convince the Turks and his own government to intervene on behalf of the Armenians. The year of the novel's publication in Germany, 1933, also saw the election of Adolf HITLER as chancellor of Germany. In that year, Werfel conducted a reading tour of German cities in which he read from chapter 5 of his novel, the account of an interview between Lepsius and the Turkish leader Enver Pasha, in order to underscore the parallel between the Armenians and the impending fate of the Jews in Germany. That Hitler, in his plans for the HOLOCAUST, was entirely conscious of, and made confident by, the Armenian precedent is obvious from his comment, "Who talks nowadays of the extermination of the Armenians?"

FURTHER READING

Michael Arlen's *Passage to Ararat* (1975) is a moving personal account of his discovery of his Armenian heritage and the genocide. The 1990 edition of *The Forty Days of Musa Dagh* contains a useful introduction by Peter Sourian. Cedric Williams's *The Broken Eagle* (1974) examines Werfel's concept of political action as reflected in *The Forty Days of Musa Dagh*.

ATATÜRK, MUSTAFA KEMAL

See GRECO-TURKISH WAR.

ATOMIC BOMB

See HIROSHIMA; MANHATTAN PROJECT.

AUSCHWITZ (1940–1944)

The largest, most notorious of the Nazi concentration and extermination camps, Auschwitz was located in southeastern Poland, about 40 miles from the city of Kraków. Originally, the camp had served as a Polish military base, but under the Nazi occupation in 1940, it became a concentration camp. Auschwitz consisted of three camps: Auschwitz I contained the administrative offices and a forced labor camp of some 30,000 prisoners; it also contained one gas chamber. About a mile away at Birkenau stood Auschwitz II, the largest of the three camps, with a special section for women prisoners, and the terminal point for the railroad bringing in new prisoners. Most of the killing took place at Birkenau, which contained four gas chambers and crematoria. In 1941, the German chemical company I.G. Farben set up a plant nearby to take advantage of the inmates' slave labor. Auschwitz III, called Buna-Monowitz, was built next to the plant to facilitate the use of the slave laborers working there. The word *Buna* referred to the process of producing synthetic rubber at the plant. The Auschwitz administration also supervised 45 sub-camps scattered throughout the region.

The processing of prisoners at Auschwitz began with their arrival in cattle cars at the terminal in Birkenau. There they were divided into the able-bodied and those deemed too weak to work effectively. The selections were made by medical doctors who were also members of the SS. The doctors also set aside a small third group to be the subjects of medical experiments conducted at the camp, notably those associated with Dr. Josef MENGELE. The able-bodied were marched off to receive prisoners' uniforms and to have their heads shaved, then were assigned to barracks at one of the labor camps. The group deemed not able-bodied, mainly the old and very young, were immediately brought to the gas chambers, which they were told were showers, packed into an enclosed space, and gassed with Zyklon B, a poison gas developed at the Farben plant. After the bodies were removed by camp inmates, known as "sondercommandos," they were brought to the crematoria and burned. At times when the traffic was very heavy, the crematoria could not keep pace with the gas chambers, and the bodies had to be buried in mass graves. A similar fate awaited those in the labor camps once they grew too weak to be effective slave laborers or violated one of the many rules that governed life in the camp.

In November 1944, with the Russian army advancing on the area, the camp had to be abandoned. What followed was an infamous death march of

60,000 starving, freezing prisoners, 15,000 of whom died on the way. When the Russian army liberated Auschwitz on January 27, 1945, they found 5,000 emaciated, seriously ill prisoners that had been left behind. According to the best estimates, at least 1.1 million people died at Auschwitz, 90 percent of whom were Jews.

THE LITERATURE

In this book we have restricted the definition of literature to fiction, drama, and poetry, simply for reasons of space, but an exception must be made in this entry in order to acknowledge the central importance of two memoirs, Elie Wiesel's (1928–   ) *Night* (1958; trans., 1960) and Primo Levi's (1919–87) *Survival at Auschwitz* (1947; trans., 1958). In 1944, both writers were prisoners in Auschwitz III (Buna), Wiesel as a 14-year-old boy, Levi as a young man in his 20s. Although there are strong similarities in their accounts, there are also striking differences. Wiesel was an intensely religious boy, for whom the experiences in the camp led to a profound spiritual crisis, a stricken cry of pain and revulsion for a God who would permit the Holocaust. Levi was a trained scientist, with an analytical mind and an artist's gift for language, shocked by the fragility of all civilized values and normal instincts when human life is reduced to the animal instinct to survive. Wiesel's title *Night* captures his dominant theme, the depth of darkness and despair of a world abandoned by God; Levi's original title (changed by his American publishers) *If This Is a Man* explores the inhuman conditions that strip away the layers of habit and culture that we use to define ourselves, leaving us with, in the words of Shakespeare's King Lear, "unaccommodated man . . . a poor, bare, forked animal."

Sustaining young Wiesel in Auschwitz was the presence of his father, but on the death march from Auschwitz to Buchenwald, the boy became the father, driving the totally exhausted older man to keep walking. Once they arrived, the father died, painfully and humiliatingly, of dysentery. The loss of his father cut his connection to life. From that point until his liberation, he describes himself as a living corpse. Levi stayed in the infirmary of the abandoned camp, where he rediscovered the defining human characteristic, a conscience.

Tadeuz Borowski (1922–51) was a non-Jewish survivor of Auschwitz, whose searing collection of short stories *This Way for the Gas, Ladies and Gentlemen* (1948; trans., 1967) is a brutally honest examination of the ways in which the horror and inhumanity that created the atmosphere of Auschwitz filtered into the minds and hearts of its victims, so that they in turn absorbed some of the heartlessness and amorality of the Nazis. At Auschwitz, Borowski was a foreman in "Canada," the prisoners' term for the inmates assigned the task of unloading and transporting to a warehouse all of the belongings brought to the camp by the waves of new prisoners, who arrived on freight trains, having been told that they would be allowed to keep their suitcases, clothing, and other valuables.

In three of the stories in the collection, the narrator is named Tadeuz. As the Polish critic Jan Kott has written, "The identification of the author with the narrator was the moral decision of a prisoner who has lived through Auschwitz—an acceptance of mutual responsibility, mutual participation, and mutual guilt for the concentration camp." Kott is here calling attention to Borowski's refusal to hide behind a fictional persona in recounting his role as both victim and victimizer. As a non-Jewish Pole, he was one step above the Jews (although one step below the German criminals who functioned as "Kapos") in the camp. In the world of Auschwitz, you could only survive by becoming an accomplice, and even then your chances were slim. Moral chaos was the norm, and *This Way for the Gas* captures that chaos without flinching. The title story is a present-tense description of the arrival of a trainload of prisoners, a descent into hell that the "Canada" people gladly enter because they will be allowed to take all the food that the passengers have brought with them. "Auschwitz Our Home" is written as a series of letters by a man being trained as a medical orderly, another privileged position and one that gives a sense of the overall life in the camp, somewhat removed from the horror of the transport's arrival. The author's cynical tone, reflected in the very title of this collection of stories, reflects his point that, although some survived Auschwitz, none survived unscathed.

FURTHER READING

The Holocaust Encyclopedia (2001), edited by Walter Laqueur and Judith Ydor Baumel includes a detailed and authoritative account of the camp. Deborah Dwork and Robert van Pelt's *Auschwitz 1270 to the Present* (1996) sets the development of the camp against a background of the 700-year history of the town.

AZEV, YEVNO (1869–1918)

Between 1893 and 1908, Azev operated as a spy for the Russian State Police (Okhrana), infiltrating the ranks of the Socialist Revolutionary Party. What the Okhrana never suspected was that, for the last five years of that period, their agent Azev had become the head of the "Battle Organization" of the party, its terrorist wing. As chief terrorist, Azev masterminded the assassination of the Russian minister of the interior, V. K. Plehve, Grand Duke Sergei, and many other government officials. As a police spy, he regularly betrayed his colleagues within the revolutionary movement, earning the respect of his superiors in the Okhrana, along with a substantial salary. As for his status in the revolutionary party, he was regarded as something of a genius, an invaluable asset.

In 1908, Victor Burtzev, the editor of a periodical sympathetic to the revolutionary cause hit upon a plan to confirm his suspicion that Azev was a police informer under the name "Raskin." Burtzev boarded a train on which Alexei Lopouhin, the former director of the Petersburgh Police Department, was traveling (the two had known each other already) and began a casual conversation, eventually bringing the topic around to the possibility of a double agent. In response to a question about "Raskin," Lopuhin replied that he knew no one by that name, but that he did know someone of that description, named Azev. Armed with that confirmation, Burtzev exposed Azev to the "Central Committee" of the party. Azev's reputation was so great within the ranks of the party, however, that the leaders decided not to retaliate, allowing him to escape to Germany, where he died in 1918. There he met Burtzev in 1912 and reprimanded him with the assertion, "If you hadn't exposed me, I would have assassinated the Czar." Assuming that this was not an idle boast, the exposure of Azev can be seen as an event that had a profound effect on 20th century history. See RUSSIAN REVOLUTION (1917).

THE LITERATURE

Not surprisingly, Azev has been an attractive figure for a number of novelists. According to his friend and collaborator, Ford Madox Ford, Joseph Conrad (1857–1926) used Azev as the model for Verloc, the sinister *agent provocateur* who convinces his simpleminded brother-in-law to blow up the Greenwich Observatory in *The Secret Agent* (1907). Conrad used Azev as the source of the double agent Nikita (also exposed in a railway carriage conversation) in his *Under Western Eyes* (1911). In Roman Gul's 1931 novel *Provocateur* (retranslated in 1962 as *Azev*), all of the characters are historical figures, allowing the author to explore Azev's motive for his double treachery. On the evidence he supplies, it would appear that Azev engaged in spying partly because of greed (he lived very well on the money he earned from the police and stole from the revolutionaries) and partly because he was a man without a conscience, an important characteristic for a terrorist.

Best known for her nonfiction—especially her analysis of Balkan politics and history *Black Lamb and Grey Falcon* (1941) and her study of traitors in *The Meaning of Treason* (1947), later revised as *The New Meaning of Treason* (1964)—Dame Rebecca West (1892–1983) was also an accomplished novelist. In 1966, she published *The Birds Fall Down*, a novel that reflected her continued interest in the psychology of the traitor. The story, set in the first decade of the 20th century, is told through the eyes of 15-year-old Laura Rowan, the daughter of an Anglo-Irish member of Parliament and a Russian aristocrat. Laura and her maternal grandfather, the exiled former minister of justice in Czarist Russia, are en route by train from Paris to northern France. The grandfather, Nicholas, though no longer in favor at the Russian court, remains devoted to the imperial throne. On the train, Chubinov, a revolutionary with an urgent need to speak to Nicholas, confronts them. What follows is a conversation in which the two men reveal their deepest convictions as they review their roles on opposing sides.

But Chubinov has another purpose in the conversation: He wants Nicholas to confirm his suspicion that Nicholas's trusted private secretary Kamensky is in fact a double agent, a leading member of the terrorist wing of the revolutionary party under the name *Gorin*. In his role as double agent, Kamensky/Gorin betrays both sides, imagining himself as the historical catalyst in a Hegelian synthesis, in which he brings together opposing forces—thesis/antithesis—out of which clash will emerge a new synthesis. The news of Kamensky's betrayal proves too devastating for Nicholas, who is taken from the train after suffering a stroke, from which he later dies. The last section of the novel functions as a thriller, in which Laura narrowly escapes death at Kamensky's hands. As depicted in the novel, the Kamensky figure owes not a small debt to Charles Dickens's Uriah Heep. The novel ends on an ironic note with Laura returning to live in Russia with her mother, who rhapsodizes about how happy they will be there.

In her foreword, West asserts that her novel "is founded on a historical event: perhaps the most momentous conversation ever to take place on a moving railway train." She goes on to claim "that because of this conversation the morale of the powerful terrorist wing of the revolutionary party crumbled, and the cool-headed Lenin found the reins in his hands." West is suggesting, in other words, that the Azev scandal weakened the rival Socialist Revolutionary Party, enabling Lenin's Democratic Socialist Party (later the Bosheviks) to gain more power.

FURTHER READING

Boris Nikolayevsky's *Aseff the Spy: The Russian Judas* (1934) is, as the subtitle suggests, a less than flattering, but probably accurate, portrait of the man.

B

BABI YAR (1941)

During World War II, German SS (Schutzstaffel) troops, who had recently occupied Kiev, the capital of the Ukraine, shot and buried Ukrainian Jews and others, many of whom were buried while still alive, at Babi Yar, a ravine outside the city. The German army captured Kiev on September 19, 1941. (See BARBAROSSA.) A week later, German authorities posted a notice, ordering "all Yids living in the city of Kiev" to report the following day, bringing with them all their documents, money, and warm clothing. Marched to the edge of the ravine, the prisoners were forced to strip naked, whereupon they were lined up and machine gunned as they fell into the mass grave. In this fashion, more than 30,000 Jews were murdered in three days. Later the same fate awaited gypsies, communists, Russian prisoners of war, and many other citizens of Kiev. By the time the Germans retreated from Kiev, the number killed at Babi Yar was more than 100,000.

THE LITERATURE

The massacre is the subject of Anatoli Kuznetsov's (1929–79) *Babi Yar* (1967), which bears the subtitle, "A Document in the Form of a Novel." As a young boy of 12, Kuznetsov witnessed the slaughter at Babi Yar and wrote down "in a thick, home-made notebook everything I saw and heard about Babi Yar as soon as it happened." A heavily censored version was published in the Soviet Union, in which, according to the author, "the whole sense of the book was turned upside down," but Kuznetsov persisted in his determination to call attention to Babi Yar and to protest against the unstated, but strong, opposition of the Soviet authorities, at a time when anti-Semitism pervaded the Communist Party. Kuznetsov prevailed upon the poet Yevgeny Yevtushenko to visit the site. The result was Yevtushenko's poem "Babi Yar," which electrified Soviet audiences when he read it in public in 1961, but the government would not allow the poem to be reprinted in any collections of Yevtushenko's poetry. Nevertheless, the composer Dmitri Shostakovich used the poem as the basis of his Thirteenth Symphony.

Reading Kuznetsov's *Babi Yar* led the British poet and novelist D. M. Thomas (1935–) to integrate the massacre into his very successful and controversial *The White Hotel* (1980). An artfully crafted novel, *The White Hotel* consists of several distinctively different, yet thematically repetitive, sections. The first is a series of letters to and from colleagues of Sigmund Freud, discussing a female patient of Freud's, an opera singer named Lisa Erdman, who is suffering from asthma and mysterious pains in her left breast and left ovary. The next section contains a highly erotic poem written by Lisa, describing an imaginary affair with Freud's son at a "white hotel." Following this section is the patient's journal, recasting the poem in prose. Her journal also refers to a persistent dream vision of a white hotel, which Freud interprets as "the mother's womb"; he analyses her yearning to return as an expression of the death instinct, or what he calls Thanatos.

But even Freud is mystified by her seemingly telepathic gift, one that sees sexuality and death fused in an intense interrelationship. With her therapy complete, Lisa returns to her career as an opera singer. Eventually she unlocks the secret of her hysterical illness: As a child, she came upon her mother engaging in sex with her mother's sister and brother-in-law. She marries Victor Berenstein, a Russian opera director, and becomes the stepmother of his young son, Kolya. The Babi Yar section of the novel opens with Lisa living in poverty in Kiev, her imprisoned husband, a victim of Joseph Stalin's GREAT TERROR. The German authorities have posted a notice that all "Yids" must report for deportation. Lisa, who is half-Jewish, can pass as a gentile, but her son Kolya cannot, and she has no intention of abandoning him. A graphic description of the massacre ensues, culminating in a grotesque scene in which, pretending to be dead, she becomes the prey of two Ukranian workers assigned the task of covering over the mass grave. One worker rapes her by inserting a bayonet into her vagina. Her horrific demise confirms the truth of her earlier premonitions about the fusion of sex and death. In the final section, the author depicts Lisa, whom we know to be dead, as a happy survivor along with her son, her family, even Freud himself, in a settlement camp in Palestine.

When first published in England, the novel received faint praise and was generally overlooked. In America, however, it attracted an enthusiastic critical response that led to its becoming a best-seller. Not a small part of the book's appeal is the convoluted effects of each section: An intense, psychoanalytic experience morphs into a horrifying, realistic depiction of a historical event, which ends, finally, in a quasi-religious portrayal of an afterlife. Asked about his reasons for writing the novel, Thomas has asserted that "the motivation was to write about the real history of the 20th century, which flows through the humanism of Freud into the desolation of the Holocaust." For many critics, this is precisely what the novel achieves. For others, particularly feminist critics, Lisa's violent death is an expression of male sadism indulged in for sensationalist effect, and some question the optimism of the final chapter, which abandons the realism of the rest of the novel to affirm a transhistorical reality.

Added to the controversy attached to *The White Hotel* is the charge that Thomas incorporated, without attribution, material from an eyewitness account of the massacre as it appeared in Kuznetsov's book.

FURTHER READING

The Holocaust and World War II Almanac, Vol. I, edited by Peggy Saari et al. (2001), contains an interesting article on Babi Yar.

BARBAROSSA (1941)

The code name *Barbarossa* stood for perhaps the most significant decision of World War II, the German invasion of the Soviet Union on June 21, 1941. Against the advice of most of his general staff, Adolf HITLER decided to postpone the invasion of England in order to attack the nation with which he had concluded a peace pact two years earlier. He was partly motivated by the poor performance of the Soviet army in its war with Finland in 1940. The Soviet army had been seriously weakened by Joseph Stalin's purge of high-ranking officers during the GREAT TERROR of the 1930s, resulting in the execution of more than half of the army's senior commanders. But despite Stalin's paranoid folly, compounded by his refusal to acknowledge the clear evidence of an imminent German attack, the Soviet army was a formidable force, with more than 5 million combat troops. Hitler, for his part, compounded his mistake by assuming direct command of the invasion. Not to be outdone, Stalin had himself appointed supreme commander. Thus the invasion set the stage for the confrontation of two dictators who were mirror images of megalomania.

German strategy called for an offensive on three fronts, one to the north with the goal of conquering Leningrad, another to the south designed to capture Kiev, and the third a direct central attack on the road to Moscow. Had the Germans concentrated their main force in the central army group, they might have easily captured Moscow before the onset of winter. But Hitler, haunted by the fear of repeating Napoleon's mistake in his Russian campaign, gave priority to the southern and northern fronts. The ironic consequence was that he produced the result that he most feared: Like Napoleon's army, the Germans scored easy early triumphs over the ill-prepared, disorganized Soviet troops, confirming the Hitler's view of himself as a military genius. However, as the months passed, the Russians invoked the aid of two of their greatest allies—autumn, whose relentless rain turned roads into seas of mud, and winter, whose subzero temperatures ground the ill-clad, disease-ridden German army to a halt. The offensive stopped within 18 miles of Moscow, at which point a Russian counterattack succeeded in forcing the Germans back to a position where they then waited for the renewal of hostilities in the spring. That offensive was to result in the decisive battle of STALINGRAD.

THE LITERATURE

Theodor Plievier's (1892–1955) *Moscow* (1952; trans., 1953) opens on the eve of the invasion in German-occupied Poland, where the preparations for the central army group's attack have been completed, and the initial forays are made against little or no opposition. The scene then shifts to the Soviet encampment around Bialystok, where the unprepared Russians engage in a disordered retreat. Gradually the Russian tanks begin to hold the enemy in check. One of the main figures in the book is Lieutenant Colonel Vilshofen, a resourceful German tank commander, who appears in Plievier's two other war novels, *Stalingrad* and *Berlin*. Vilshofen soon realizes that the Soviet tanks are superior and orders a retreat, an unheard of move. Forced to attack again, Vilshofen's tanks are again beaten back. But the Russians, lacking ammunition and supplies, are unable to capitalize on the victory. The German forces push on, creating chaos among the civilian population. Among these are Nina, the wife of a missing Russian captain, and Anna Pavlovna, a young, genteel woman horrified by the savage destruction she witnesses. Their stories, along with a half dozen others, create a panoramic view of wanton cruelty, inflexible bureaucracy, and individual heroism that culminates in the onset of the Russian winter. The novel concludes with a quiet anecdote illustrating the tenacity of the human spirit. *Moscow*, though not as powerful as the author's *Stalingrad*, is a worthy prequel to that work.

FURTHER READING

John Keegan's *The Second World War* (1989) contains a vivid, insightful account of the Barbarossa campaign.

BELLEAU WOOD, BATTLE OF (WORLD WAR I) (1918)

As part of a large-scale Allied counterattack near the Marne in June 1918, the U.S. Marines and Army invaded Belleau Wood, a small forest that had been a hunting preserve on a private estate. The American troops, particularly the marines, suffered heavy casualties but eventually captured the area.

Although the battle was of little strategic importance, it sent an important message to the Allies and their enemy. Despite their inexperience and relative lack of training, U.S. troops represented a vast new army whose sheer numbers made Allied victory inevitable. And, in addition to their numerical contribution, they brought new energy to the conduct of the war. As one German intelligence officer reported of the Americans, "The spirit of the troops is high and they possess an innocent self confidence."

THE LITERATURE

William March's (1893–1954) *Company K* (1933) deals with the experiences of an American army company from their basic training days to the action in Belleau Wood and beyond into postwar civilian life. However, the novel is not structured in the simple chronological fashion this description would imply. Instead, it offers 116 separate mini-narratives, each one told by a different member of the company, and headed by the name and rank of the narrator recording his reminiscence. The stories run from comedy to cruelty, from the sentimental to the savage. The general effect of the whole is a searing indictment of the war, a theme epitomized in a selection in which a soldier charged with sending letters of condolence home to bereaved families decides to write the truth for a change:

Dear Madam:

Your son died needlessly in Belleau Wood. At the time of his death, he was crawling with vermin and weak with diarrhea. His feet were swollen and rotten and they stank. . . . Then on June 6th, a piece of shrapnel hit him and he died in agony, slowly. . . . He lived three full hours screaming and cursing by turns. He had nothing to hold on to, you see: He had learned long ago that what he had been taught to believe by you, his mother who loved him, under the meaningless names of honor, courage and patriotism, were all lies. . . .

Reading the letter to an impassive fellow soldier, he realizes that the truth doesn't matter either, and he tears the letter up.

March is best known as the author of *The Bad Seed* (1954), a novel about an inherently evil little girl, adapted into a highly successful play and, later, a film. March earned his credentials to write about World War I: In 1917, he enlisted in the marines, saw action in Belleau Wood and Chateau Thierry, was wounded, and received the Distinguished Service Cross. The ring of authenticity sounds throughout this work.

FURTHER READING

Byron Farwell's *Over There* (1994) is a lively, intelligent account of the American army in World War I.

BERLIN, FALL OF (WORLD WAR II) (1945)

Following Operation BARBAROSSA and the battle of STALINGRAD, the siege and fall of Berlin in the spring of 1945 marked the third and final phase of the war on the eastern front. Encircled by British and American forces in the west, the German army faced a more feared enemy in the east in the form of two Russian armies led by Marshals Georgi Zhukov and Ivan Konev. These two commanders waged a heated competition to see which army would reach Berlin first. (An earlier international agreement had stipulated that Berlin would fall to a Soviet army in recognition of Russia's heavy casualties and its critical role in the defeat of Germany.) By April 20, Adolf HITLER's 56th birthday, it was clear that Berlin's fall was imminent. The following day Russian troops from Zhukov's army entered the northern suburbs of the city. Five days later, Berlin proper was ringed with 500,000 Soviet troops, subjecting it to unceasing air and artillery bombardment. By April 29, despite fierce resistance by the hopelessly outmanned remnants of the German army, the Russians advanced to within a quarter mile of the remains of the Reich Chancellory building. Fifty-five feet beneath its ruins, in his lavishly constructed bunker, Hitler, following a ceremony in which he married his long-time mistress, Eva Braun, made his farewells to those who had remained with him. Shortly after, he administered cyanide to his bride and himself and, for added measure, shot himself in the head.

The Russians continued to bombard the small portion of the city not yet in their hands, demanding unconditional surrender. On May 2, the fall of Berlin was complete. Six days later, May 8, 1945, V-E Day, the war in Europe that had begun on September 1, 1939, had come to an end.

THE LITERATURE

Theodor Plievier's (1892–1955) *Berlin* (1954; trans., 1956) is the third volume of his World War II trilogy. Here, as in the other two books, Plievier chooses the panoramic view of events, the collapse of the city as viewed from the perspectives of Hitler's bunker, the officers and soldiers ordered to fight to the death, and German civilians, enduring pitiless shelling and bombing, desperate at the prospect of the Russian army's pillage and rape of the city. It is the latter view that dominates the novel, although some of the most compelling scenes take place within the bunker. Pliever employs the technique of a range of perspectives interspersed with one another to build a sense of the whole from the concrete depiction of individual stories. One story concerns a doctor picking his way through the relentless bombardment looking for his wife, who has been raped and carried off in a Russian tank. The wife, Dolores Linth, confined in the bottom of the tank, becomes the exclusive property of the tank's commander until he is killed. At that point she is brutally raped by another one of the crew. She escapes but suffers serious physical and psychological damage; eventually her husband recovers her dead body. Thus the total terror with which the German civilians anticipate the Russian army proves to be not unreasonable. The whirligig of time brings in its revenge as the Russians, remembering German atrocities during the 1941 invasion, retaliate brutally, spurred on by a government exhorting them to loot, rampage, and, particularly, "to destroy the pride of Teutonic women."

Standing out from the many memorable scenes in the bunker is the portrait of the exhausted "restless corpse, Uncle Adolph, . . . with nothing left to murder," hosting a tea party for Joseph Goebbels's five beautiful blond children. Within a week, these children will be poisoned by their parents, who will then commit suicide.

From this world in ruin, Plievier carries his story into the postwar era. Here it loses much of its force and focus. But the heart of the book is memorable for its devastating account of the fall of the city.

FURTHER READING

H. R. Trevor-Roper's *The Last Days of Hitler* (1947) is a celebrated historian's description of the fall of Berlin.

BERLIN WALL (1961–1988)

At the end of WORLD WAR II, the Allies divided Germany into four zones, each one administered by one of the four Allied powers—France, Great Britain, the United States, and the Soviet Union. Berlin was also divided into four zones, even though geographically it was situated in the eastern zone, administered by the Soviets. In 1948, the Soviets tried to control all of Berlin by blockading all roads and railroad traffic into the city. The western Allies responded with the Berlin Airlift, flying in huge amounts of food and supplies to the Allied zones. The airlift proved to be a success, as did the economy of western Germany, which in the 1950s underwent a remarkable recovery, West Berlin along with it. The economic success produced mass migrations from the Soviet controlled zone. In 1960 alone, 200,000 Germans emigrated to West Berlin.

In August of the following year, the East German government erected a wall, sealing off the eastern zone of the city—in effect, imprisoning its citizenry. Reinforced by barbed wire, manned by armed guards with orders to shoot anyone attempting to scale it, the wall stood as a grim symbol of totalitarian socialism and of a divided Germany until 1989. In that year, a series of widespread demonstrations throughout Eastern Europe led to the overthrow of Communist governments (see COMMUNISM, FALL OF). Thousands of East Germans escaped to West Germany by crossing the newly opened border between Hungary and Austria. Mass demonstrations in Leipzig and other East German cities provoked the ouster of Ernest Honecker, the East German leader. On November 7, the East German cabinet resigned. On November 9, while the rest of the world watched on television, hundreds of thousands of Berliners took to the streets, breaching the wall in a frenzied celebration. To the astonishment of most observers, the overthrow of the East German government and the fall of the wall were accomplished without violence.

On November 28, West Germany outlined a proposal calling for the reunification of the nation.

THE LITERATURE

In Ian McEwan's (1948–) *Black Dogs* (1992), Bernard, a prominent English politician, present at the fall of the wall, suffers a severe beating at the hands of a group of neo-Nazi skinheads. He is rescued by the efforts of his son-in-law, Jeremy, and by a woman who bears a strong resemblance to Bernard's late wife, June. June and Bernard were married in 1946, right after the end of World War II. While on their honeymoon hiking in a remote area of the Midi section of France, June is separated from Bernard and finds herself confronting two huge, ravenously hungry black dogs. One of the dogs attacks her, and in defense she repeatedly stabs the animal with a pocket knife until he finally retreats. Shortly after, she and Bernard learn from a local resident that the dogs had belonged to a Gestapo unit stationed in the area. The animals had been left behind when the Gestapo troops were ordered to frontline duty.

June is profoundly affected by this incident. Prior to it, she and Bernard had been ardent young communists, committed to social justice as the highest good. Now she becomes increasingly spiritual in her concerns, withdrawing from the world of politics and ideology. She and Bernard, although still very much in love, separate since neither can accept the other's point of view. Even after her death, Bernard is embittered by what he views as her destruction of their marriage. For June, the black dog incident had been a revelation, an expression of the afterlife of evil—in the case of the dogs, the legacy of Nazism, but this persistent wickedness is not limited to Nazism:

> The evil I'm talking about lives in us all. It takes hold in an individual, in private lives. . . . And, when conditions are right, in different countries, at different times, a terrible cruelty, a viciousness against life erupts, and everyone is surprised by the depth of hatred within himself. . . . It is something in our hearts.

As the attack on Bernard demonstrates, the evil that the wall embodied did not entirely disappear on November 9. Its residue taints the hearts of the people of the city. But Bernard's rescue, by someone who looked like June, also suggests the final triumph of love over hate.

John Marks's (1943–) *The Wall* (1998) focuses on the dilemma that followed the collapse of the wall, which in effect ended the COLD WAR. The decades-old confrontation of superpowers had created a relatively simple and straightforward standoff, both sides handcuffed by the knowledge that because each side had nuclear weapons, neither side could use them. The Berlin Wall stood as a symbol of that reassuring assumption. Its sudden collapse upset all the rules by which the superpowers played and opened the field up to individual entrepreneurs and hard-line fanatics on both sides. This is the situation explored in *The Wall*, a novel that combines elements of the spy thriller with a probing examination of a serious historical dilemma.

The novel opens at an Allied listening post in Berlin on November 9, 1989. A few hours before the celebration at the wall, Captain Nester Cates, an American intelligence officer, hears two members of an enemy intelligence unit discussing him, when the computer next to him suddenly catches fire and a programmer working on the machine is killed. Cates's friend Stuart Glemnik is a suspect, and Cates is ordered to find him. The search, weaving its way through a diverse group of people, including Douglas, Stuart's brother, leads to Czechoslovakia, Hungary, and Romania, as those nations are in the throes of revolt against the local communist regimes. Douglas eventually finds Stuart, dying in a Romanian prison cell, who tells him the complex, involved story of a planned terrorist act in Berlin that misfired because it had been scheduled on November 9, the day that the wall came down. *The Wall* is a superior thriller, adroitly fusing its action to the collapse of communist world.

FURTHER READING

Misha Glenny's *The Rebirth of History: Eastern Europe in the Age of Democracy* (1990) is an eyewitness description of the events of 1989.

BLITZ, THE (WORLD WAR II) (1940–1941)

A shortened form of the German word *Blitzkrieg* ("lightning battle"), the term is used to describe the bombing of London and other English cities in 1940–41. The blitz was a test of the nerves and courage of the English civilian population. English unflappability reached its quintessential expression in the behavior of the civilian population faced with nightly raids that took the lives of thousands and destroyed numberless buildings and homes—all of it occurring with the threat of imminent German invasion looming on the horizon. As the alarm sounded evening after evening, the citizens of London would calmly gather up some bedding and proceed to the Underground stations or other shelters until the "all clear" signal was given. At that point some would return home to find a crater or the shell of the building that had been their house. Their calm, often wryly humorous acceptance of perilous circumstances made a powerful impression on foreign observers, particularly American correspondents like Edward R. Murrow, whose nightly broadcasts from London on CBS radio helped create an image of the indomitable English spirit that won many Americans to the Allied side. The figure who embodied that spirit most emphatically was the English prime minister, Winston Churchill, who memorably characterized both the blitz and the air war (see BRITAIN, BATTLE OF) as Britain's "finest hour."

A later version of the blitz occurred near the end of the war when the Germans, in a desperate attempt to win the war with vaunted "secret weapons," unleashed first the V1 (the "buzz bomb") and later V2 rockets on English cities. After some serious initial damage, the V1s proved to be less effective than manned bombers. The V2s, on the other hand, were highly effective and deadly, but not any more destructive than the conventional Allied bombers that were conducting at this time massive, relentless, daily raids on German cities.

THE LITERATURE

Two novels that capture the blitz experience in vivid and precise detail are Henry Green's (1905–73) *Caught* (1943) and Elizabeth Bowen's (1899–1973) *The Heat of the Day* (1949). Green's novel describes a group of men and women in the London Auxiliary Fire Service, charged with the task of fighting the fires that resulted from the bombings. Much of the novel deals with events leading up to the blitz, the so-called phony war period, spanning the declaration of war in 1939 and the actual military engagement in the spring of 1940, when people were cut adrift from their traditional lives but not yet involved in the war itself. The protagonist is Richard Roe, whose only son has been evacuated to the country. A loner by nature, Roe joins the Auxiliary Fire Service, where he finds himself caught, that is, trapped, by the lives of other fire fighters to whom he feels distant and alien. Part of this alienation is the inevitable product of the gap between his English, middle-class background and the working-class men and women in the service. Roe and his working-class supervisor, Pye, are at odds but coincidentally bonded by the relationship of Pye's sister to Roe's son. Pye's tragic suicide is one of the events that breaks down the distance between Roe and the other members of the service. The other is the onset of the actual bombing, which extricates Roe and his fellow workers from the limbo of waiting and gives them the freedom to perform meaningful action.

In *The Heat of the Day*, the protagonist Stella Rodney meets her lover, Robert, in "that first heady autumn of the London air raids." This fact immediately encloses their relationship: "Their time sat in the third place at their table. They were creatures of history whose coming together was of a nature possible in no other day—the day was inherent in the nature." The novel's greatest strength lies in its evocation of that time, in which the fellowship engendered by the blitz counterpoints the novel's additional theme of treason: "Strangers saying 'Goodnight, good luck,' to each other at street corners as the sky first blanched, then faded with evening, each hoped not to die that night, still more not to die unknown."

At the critical moment of Graham Greene's *The End of the Affair* (1951), a buzz bomb scores a direct hit on the house that the protagonist Maurice and his married lover, Sarah, use for their trysts. When Maurice goes to investigate, another bomb goes off, and he is cast down the staircase, apparently dead. Sarah, a nonbeliever all her life, falls to her knees and prays, "I'll give him up forever, only let him be alive." A moment later Maurice appears, and Sarah thinks "now the agony of being without him starts." She remains true to her vow, turning Maurice, who is convinced she left him for another man, into an embittered cynic. Only after her death does Maurice discover the true cause of her rejection along with the evidence that she may have died a saint. As a result, he declares his defiant hatred for God, his victorious rival for the love of Sarah, not realizing that his hatred nullifies the atheism that had been a central feature of his life.

In radical departure from these straightforward treatments of the blitz stands Thomas Pynchon's (1937–) *Gravity's Rainbow* (1973), a novel that, befitting its status as one of the founding texts of postmodernism, deconstructs the traditional conception of the aerial attacks. In its place, it offers as a plot premise the correspondence between the location of V2 strikes in various parts of London and the sexual conquests of Tyrone Slothrop, an American lieutenant assigned to work with British intelligence. He is assigned the task of determining the connection between the V2's machinery and his own. In the process, he comes to see himself and all humanity as forms of matter not all that different from the rockets. Both have been launched into space for a brief period, wired to self-destruct on impact.

The opening chapter of David Lodge's (1935–) *Out of the Shelter* (1970) casts the blitz experience through the eyes of a young boy. (See WORLD WAR II: AFTERMATH.)

FURTHER READING

Philip Ziegler's *London at War, 1939–1945* (1995) offers a portrait of the city and its citizens coping with six years of aerial attacks.

BLUNT, ANTHONY (1907–1983)

The most respected British art historian of his time, Blunt was exposed as a longtime Soviet spy in 1979. Blunt began his career in espionage while a student and fellow at Cambridge, where he was recruited by fellow spy Guy Burgess. During WORLD WAR II he worked for MI5, British domestic intelligence, a job that enabled him to pass on much valuable information to the Soviets, which they apparently never put to good use. After the war, as an art historian specializing in the work of the Renaissance artist Nicolas Poussin, he became the director of the Courtauld Institute of Art and surveyor of the Queen's Pictures. In 1951, he assisted Burgess and Donald MacLean in their escape to the Soviet Union after they were exposed as spies. By this time he did very little spying, but the authorities became aware of his treason in 1964 in the wake of Kim Philby's defection to Moscow. The government chose not to reveal the truth until forced to do so in 1979. At that time he was stripped of a knighthood he had earlier received and had to resign his membership in the British Academy. In the popular press, Blunt became the notorious "Fourth Man" of the Cambridge spies. He died in 1983, disgraced but presumably unrepentant.

In his personal life Blunt was, like Burgess, a homosexual, at a time when homosexuality was grounds for imprisonment in England. Some have argued that the necessity for deception in this area fostered the sense of alienation that led to lack of loyalty to the English government. Others point to the historical circumstances. The Cambridge spies were recruited during the SPANISH CIVIL WAR, when many young intellectuals saw communism as the only viable alternative to fascism. In any case, the revelation that old-school English gentlemen with impeccable credentials could be communist spies left a permanent suspicion in the public mind about the so-called ruling class.

THE LITERATURE

In John Banville's (1945–) *The Untouchable* (1997), the character closely modeled on Blunt is Victor Maskell, a celebrated art historian who, as the novel opens, has just been unmasked as a Soviet spy. He has chosen to write his apologia for a young woman who is planning to write a book about him. What emerges from his narrative is a man who has had one real passion in his life: art, embodied for him in a small picture he owns, Nicolas Poussin's *The Death of Seneca*. Everything else—his friends, his wife and children, his long-time male lover, his country, he views with ironic detachment. This is particularly true of his supposed commitment to communism. He is an aesthete at heart, contemptuous of the working classes, with a sentimental attachment to the monarchy, two of whom, King George VI and his daughter Elizabeth II, he comes to know familiarly, if not intimately. As Banville describes Maskell, the reason he betrayed his country remains a mystery to himself as well as to others. He has been a spy, presumably, for the pleasure of deception and because being a spy made life more interesting. Also, it offered him a kind of family, the fellowship of the other Cambridge spies, particularly the irrepressible Boy Bannister (the Guy Burgess figure in the novel), all of them additionally motivated by what they perceive as America's threat to European culture. He sums up his mixed motives with the image of a Frankenstein monster, made of scattered bits and pieces, which may remind the reader of

Samuel Taylor Coleridge's words about Shakespeare's Iago: "the motive hunting of a motiveless malignity."

The novel ends with Victor, alone as he has been all his life, preparing to commit suicide, an echo of the suicide of Seneca, acting on the orders of the state. Among the novel's surprising turns are the important role played by Querell, a novelist who bears a strong resemblance to Graham Greene, and the suggestion that Maskell's brother-in-law, now a high-ranking Tory minister, was also a communist mole. These and other deviations from the strict facts of Blunt's life give the novel an added depth, as does the brilliant, ice-cold style that captures both the voice and the heart of the narrator.

FURTHER READING

Miranda Carter's *Anthony Blunt: His Lives* (2002) is an objective and authoritative account of Blunt's career as scholar and spy.

BOBBY THOMPSON HOME RUN

See OCTOBER 3, 1951.

BOER WAR (1899–1902)

In the late 19th century, present-day South Africa consisted of two British colonies, Cape Colony and Natal, and two independent republics, the Orange Free State and the Transvaal. Governing the latter two were the Boers, descendants of early Dutch settlers in the region. The abundant natural resources of these two Boer republics constituted an attractive lure to their British neighbors, especially entrepreneurs like Cecil Rhodes, onetime prime minister of Cape Colony. In particular, the discovery in 1886 of rich veins of gold in the Transvaal provided a powerful incentive for the British to extend their control into the two republics.

Alarmed by the obvious intentions of their powerful neighbors, the Boers attacked Natal in October 1899, submitting the British towns of Mafeking and Ladysmith to sieges that lasted for many punishing months. In Ladysmith, besieged for four months, the population dwindled, succumbing to hunger, unclean water, and a variety of infectious diseases. Only after the intervention of vastly superior numbers were the British able to lift the sieges and eventually capture Pretoria, the capital of the Transvaal, in June 1900. Even then the Boers carried on a successful guerrilla campaign. In response, the British commander, Lord Kitchener, created the first 20th-century example of one of the horrors of modern life, the concentration camp for civilians, mostly women and children.

The Boer leader Louis Botha, recognizing that defeat was inevitable, accepted a truce on reasonably favorable terms in the Treaty of Vereeniging on May 31, 1902, which paved the way seven years later for the establishment of the Union of South Africa. Technically, the British had won, but considering their vast superiority in numbers and weapons, it was a dubious victory. It had been a dirty war, leaving a stain on the national honor, signaling the beginning of the end of the glory days of the BRITISH EMPIRE.

THE LITERATURE

A compellingly detailed account of the siege of Ladysmith forms the core of the American novelist Johnny Kenny Crane's (1942–   ) *The Legacy of Ladysmith* (1986). The siege is described in the form of a diary kept by Dr. Robert Menzies, a Scottish physician attending a large number of patients in the besieged town. Faced with a serious shortage of medical supplies and with outbreaks of typhus and enteric fever, Menzies agrees to trade the secret codebooks of the British forces in exchange for medicine. He is both a totally dedicated, compassionate physician and a traitor, implicated in the deaths of many British soldiers. The duality of his character is also evident in his extramarital affair with a young Boer woman while his pregnant wife works selflessly at his side as a nurse. Framing this story is a historically and aesthetically irrelevant overplot (with a preposterous conclusion) involving a contemporary American commissioned to write a biography of Menzies. However, the account of the siege and the psychology of the fictional Dr. Menzies are compelling.

Giles Foden's (1967–   ) *Ladysmith* (1999) also deals with the four-month siege. While rummaging in his family attic, Foden came across copies of letters written by his great-grandfather, a British soldier at Ladysmith, which provided the inspiration for his novel. The story is refracted through a collage of points of view. Mixed in with the fictional characters are some historical figures, notably Mohandas K. GANDHI, who did humanitarian work during the war, and Winston Churchill, who was captured by the Boers and later escaped while serving as a war correspondent. The fictional characters include Bella and Jane Kiernan, the daughters of an Irish hotel keeper in Ladysmith, who provide the novel's love interest, in which Bella sacrifices her chance of winning her lover in order to right an injustice within the besieged community.

FURTHER READING

James Barbary's *The Boer War* (1968) describes the events and discusses the issues of the war.

BOLSHEVIK REVOLUTION

See RUSSIAN REVOLUTION.

BONHOEFFER, DIETRICH (1906–1945)

A German Lutheran theologian and pastor who became an early opponent of the Nazi regime, Bonhoeffer was one of eight children in a wealthy, highly educated, Lutheran family. Early on, he chose a career as a pastor and theologian, establishing contacts with other prominent theologians in Europe and America. In 1934, the year Adolf HITLER assumed the title of *Führer* of Germany, Bonhoeffer joined the Confessing Church, which seceded from the government-controlled Reich Church, immediately marking its members as potential enemies of the state. In 1940, friends and relatives helped him narrowly escape arrest by the Gestapo by securing him a post with German military intelligence. Military Intelligence was headed by Admiral William Canaris, a secret opponent of Hitler who peopled his command with a group of dedicated anti-Nazis. In this position, Bonhoeffer established contact with Allied clergy and was privy to the various abortive attempts to overthrow or assassinate the führer.

He was arrested in 1943. His brother, uncle, and two brothers-in-law were executed for their roles in the JULY 20 PLOT to assassinate Hitler. Even though he was in prison at the time, he was, along with thousands of others, peripherally related to the conspiracy. On April 9, 1945, one month before the end of the war, he was hanged at the Flossenburg concentration camp. But he achieved a posthumous fame when letters and poems he had written in prison were collected and published. The thinking exhibited in his theological work, a complex and subtle position, had a powerful influence on the development of theology as that discipline evolved in postwar Europe. In addition to his formal theological works, he is best known for *Prisoner for God: Letters and Papers from Prison* (1955; trans., 1951), the spiritually passionate, inspiring collection of his letters from prison.

THE LITERATURE

Mary Glazener's (1921–1992) *The Cup of Wrath* (1993) is a novel based on Bonhoeffer's role in the German resistance to Hitler. She tells a straightforward, meticulously researched story, devoid of stylistic flourishes, allowing the story to tell itself. Although at times somewhat plodding, the author's plain style serves the reader well, bringing us directly into the lives of its characters. Bonhoeffer was clearly a man of great moral courage and compassion. His struggles to overcome his scruples regarding what most of his fellow citizens would see as high treason and his religious compunctions about the use of assassination as a weapon are quietly and effectively portrayed. To a fellow conspirator's question, "You think we can kill this man [Hitler] and not be guilty of breaking the commandment?," he replies, "It is worse to be evil than to do evil. . . . Should we set our own personal innocence above our responsibility to the Jews and all others who are suffering and dying at this man's hand? Are we not in fact killing when we fail to stop his murders in the only way left to us?" Very near the end, when offered the opportunity to try to escape, he refuses, knowing that if he succeeds, his family will be arrested: "Sometimes, the only way to keep one's freedom is to give it up. . . . But we won't give up hope, even so. God is still in charge of this world, no matter how dark it looks." The Third Reich, and all the evil it harnessed, was no match for the strength of this man.

FURTHER READING

Theodore Gill's *Memo for a Movie: A Short Life of Dietrich Bonhoeffer* (1971) tells Bonhoeffer's story in the form of a memo, written as an outline for a projected film.

BOSNIAN WAR (1992–1995)

Bosnia, long a part of the OTTOMAN EMPIRE, was annexed by Austria-Hungary in 1908. (Bosnian opposition to this annexation led to the assassination in 1914 of Archduke FRANZ FERDINAND in Sarajevo, the Bosnian capital, and the start of WORLD WAR I.) In 1918, the province became a part of Yugoslavia. After the collapse of communism and the breakup of Yugoslavia in 1990, Bosnia-Herzegovina became an independent republic, with a coalition government representative of its three leading ethnic communities, Muslim, Serb, and Croat. However, supported and armed by the Serbian-Yugoslav president Slobodan Milošević, the Bosnian Serbs declared an independent Serbian Bosnia, under the leadership of Radovan Karadzic. In April 1992, the European Community and the United States officially recognized Bosnia-Herzegovina as an independent state, but they refused to intervene when, in the same month, Serbs overran the rural areas of the new republic. Initiating a program of "ethnic cleansing," the Serbs interned thousands of Muslims and Croats, murdering civilians and engaging in mass rapes. Much like the Jews in Nazi-occupied Europe, the victims were taken from their homes, confined to concentration camps, and forced to watch the executions of their community leaders. But the Serb campaign stalled when it attacked the urban areas, particularly Sarajevo. The Serbs then resorted to long-range artillery bombardment.

Media exposure of Serb atrocities eventually forced the Western powers to intervene. Ongoing European mediation efforts proved ineffective until the aggressive intervention of the Clinton administration forced the Serbs to the bargaining table. These negotiations resulted in the Dayton Accords in 1995, an agreement calling for two semiautonomous states united in the conduct of foreign affairs and defense. The realignment created a mass migration in which the ethnic groups moved to their respective sections within the country.

THE LITERATURE

Slavenka Drakulić (1949–) is a Croatian journalist, whose novel *S.* (1999; trans., 2000) grew out of her interviews with women who had been raped by Serbian soldiers during the war. During the interviews, it became clear that many of these women were too traumatized to put into words the horror they had experienced. After one such interview, Drakulić writes, "[I]t then occurred to me for the first time, that her story was precisely in what she could not say. And I must find a way to say it for her." The result is a narrative of one composite character, whose experience represents that of thousands.

S., a 29-year-old substitute teacher in a small Bosnian village, is a native of Sarajevo, where she lives with her parents, a Muslim father and a Serbian mother. This mixed ethnic identity, an "impurity" that must be cleansed in the eyes of her captors, results in her being transported to a concentration camp, specifically to the "women's room," a building within the camp housing young, attractive women, forced each night to service the local Serb soldiers. Any resistance on the women's part means death. Her indoctrination consists of being brutally raped by three soldiers. In time she becomes the mistress of the camp commander. Although this privileged position markedly improves her life, inwardly she is torn by self-doubt. She sees herself as despicable since, unlike the other women, she has to strive to please and be agreeable with her captor. The commander has chosen her because she is educated and refined, and he treats her respectfully: "But she cannot conceal from herself that she is sleeping with a murderer."

Eventually she becomes part of a prisoner exchange that permits her to emigrate to Sweden, but her joy is shattered by the realization that she is five months pregnant. She sees her unborn child as "a disease . . . a tumor," the crowning humiliation by her captors that she should bring another of them into the world. She notifies the hospital that she will be giving the child up for adoption. But when the baby is born, she recognizes that she must not try to escape her past but must accept it. With that she turns to nurse her baby.

Asked about the apparent optimism of this ending, the author has replied, "The consequences of accepting a child conceived by rape are grave. The child will have, in a way, a completely false identity. . . . Really, what do you tell such a child? The truth? Imagine the child's horror. I would say that the ending of the novel can be interpreted in several different ways, it is certainly not simply optimistic." From a strictly literary standpoint, *S.* is not a flawless novel. The writing is somewhat prolix, exhibiting a tendency to tell rather than show, but as a text translating a historical event into a fully human experience, it is a powerful and important work.

FURTHER READING

Christopher Bennett's *Yugoslavia's Bloody Collapse* (1995) argues that the ethnic conflict in the Balkans is less the product of ancient enmity than of the political manipulation of Slobodan Milošević. The Penguin edition of *S.* includes an interview with the author.

BOXER REBELLION

In 1899, a northern Chinese military group, known as the Society of Righteous and Harmonious Fists (hence the name *Boxers*), rose in protest against the growing influence of foreigners in Chinese life. More specifically, they were objecting to the colonizing designs of the Western powers and to the spread of Christianity. With the tacit support of the imperial court under the dowager empress Tsu Hsi, the Boxers conducted raids against Christian missions, slaughtering Chinese Christians and some foreign missionaries. By 1900, the uprising had spread to the capital, Peking, where the group lay siege to the embassies of the Western powers.

A combined force of British, American, German, Austrian, French, Italian, and Japanese troops lifted the siege and crushed the rebellion. The empress, who had fled the Forbidden City, seat of the imperial court, was restored to her throne, but only after accepting humiliating peace terms from the victorious forces. The rebellion was instrumental in precipitating the downfall of the Ching dynasty in 1912.

THE LITERATURE

C. Y. Lee (Ching Yang) (b. 1917), best known for his novel *The Flower Drum Song* (1957), approaches the rebellion from an interesting angle in his *Madame Goldenflower* (1960). Based on the life of Sai-chin-hua (1874–1936), a beautiful "singsong girl" who as a teenager became the concubine of the Chinese ambassador to Germany and subsequently had a passionate affair with a German army officer, the novel opens in 1900, 18 years after these events. Sai-chin, now the middle-aged courtesan Madame Goldenflower, confronts the growing menace of the Boxer uprising. The novel also depicts the dowager empress, an isolated, imperious, and whimsical ruler, and Li Shan, Goldenflower's lover and a highly principled government official, who risks his life to prevent the uprising. Once the allied forces overcome the Boxers, they emerge as a new threat. Looting and pillaging by European soldiers is so widespread, it endangers the existence of the city.

The critical moment in the novel arrives, after the defeat of the Boxers, with the discovery that the man Goldenflower had an affair with in Germany is now commander in chief of the allied forces, Field Marshal Count Waldersee. When she receives an invitation from Waldersee, she refuses to see him out of loyalty to Li Shan, but the suffering caused by the war forces her to relent. She ends up sleeping with Waldersee and convincing him to end the looting and killing by allied soldiers, thereby saving the city of Peking from complete destruction. For her efforts she is despised and attacked by the local population until rescued by Li Shan. The reunited couple decide to shun the newly restored court and seek a quiet, peaceful life in the country.

FURTHER READING

Paul Cohen's *History in Three Keys: The Boxers as Event, Experience, and Myth* (1997) offers a comprehensive analysis of the rebellion and its aftermath. A biography of Madame Goldenflower by the pseudonymous "Drunken Whiskers" is available in English under the title *That Chinese Woman* (1959).

BRAUN, EVA

See HITLER, ADOLF.

BRITAIN, BATTLE OF (WORLD WAR II) (1940)

After the FALL OF FRANCE in June 1940, the German general staff began its preparations for the invasion of England. The invasion was to be preceded by massive air attacks, designed, in the words of the Luftwaffe (German Air Force) chief, Field Marshal Göring, "to have the enemy . . . down on its knees in the nearest future so that an occupation of the island by our troops can proceed without any risk." Göring's overconfidence suffered serious setbacks from the beginning of the battle. Although the Luftwaffe had a greater number of trained pilots, the Royal Air Force (RAF) had more planes, and the British fighter planes—spitfires and hurricanes—were equal, if not superior, to the German Messerschmidts. The British enjoyed the additional advantage of being close to their own bases, whereas the German pilots were constantly threatened by a lack of fuel. Also invaluable to the English cause were the 50 warning stations throughout Britain, equipped with the new British invention, radar. The unacknowledged hero of the battle, British air chief marshal Sir Hugh Dowding, who, in the prewar years championed the development of radar, devised the brilliant RAF defensive strategy.

In early August, the Germans began air attacks on airfields in southern England, suffering severe losses both from ground fire and the RAF. After a month of aerial battle, German losses had risen to an unacceptable level, and Adolf HITLER shifted his strategy to air attacks on London and other major cities in the hopes of completely demoralizing the British civilian population. Here again the Germans seriously underestimated the will of the people and its indomitable prime minister Winston Churchill. If anyone was demoralized, it was the Luftwaffe when, on September 15, the RAF shot down 60 German bombers in one day. By October, a seaborne invasion was no longer feasible, and Germany decided to postpone the invasion while maintaining air attacks on English cities (see the BLITZ). The English nation had scored its first, and most important, victory of the war. Churchill's famous tribute to the RAF eloquently summarized the triumph: "Never in the field of human conflict was so much owed by so many to so few."

THE LITERATURE

Although the battle was a great British victory, other nationalities played a critical role, particularly the Polish and Czech fliers, who after the defeats of their own countries had flown to England to continue the fight against Hitler. Homage to these fighters, and to the Women's Auxiliary Air Force (WAAF) who operated the radar equipment, forms a central feature of Andrew Greig's (1951–   ) novel *The Clouds Above* (2001). In fact, the entire novel is a paean, as its dedication puts it, to "the vanishing generation." Opening with a poetic evocation of the period, the paradoxically beautiful summer of 1940, the novel then takes the form of alternating diarylike entries by its two protagonists, Stella Gardam, a WAAF radar operator, and Len Westbourne, an RAF pilot. Their romance is paralleled by that of their best friends Maddy, a nurse, and Tad, a Polish pilot, both of whom are life-loving, rule-breaking free spirits, teaching the more cautious Stella and Len to wrench life from the jaws of death. Tad, the most skilled and daring fighter in Len's squadron, is the epitome of what Len terms "regardless," the defining characteristic of the true fighter pilot. But Tad's seemingly carefree approach sits atop a barely suppressed rage against the Nazis who murdered his father.

The aerial dogfights have a powerful immediacy, often as brief as lightning in the night, creating a more vivid effect with language than the many dogfight scenes in films of the period. Nor is Stella exempt from danger as the German planes increasingly target radar stations. Staring at the blips on her radar screen, she suddenly hears "a curious howling wail. Then the screen went blank, the floor rose and the walls leaned in. [She] saw the major lift and fly across the room. Then the air imploded and [she] was deaf and saw the room soundlessly turn gray with smoke and dust." Similarly powerful is Stella's description of the bombing of a London nightclub, in which Maddy is killed.

The presence of death confers on the lovers a depth and maturity that deepens their relationship. Forged in the crucible of war, in a period of two months, their passion achieves the solidity and permanence of a long marriage. Love and death are the basic elements of romantic tragedy, but Greig writes not in a tragic mode but in a celebratory one. He makes this clear in an authorial "Last Word," in which we learn that Stella is modeled on the author's mother, "now finally gone into the silence to join the rest of her vanishing generation, whose code was sacrifice and whose quest was a decent normality, though it was one that never quite existed. Who were so baffled by our turning away from what they made." Greig's achievement was admirably summarized in the London *Times* review of the novel: "The Battle of Britain may be rightly regarded as the most famous air conflict in history, but Greig has made it something much more important for a generation now almost unimaginably removed: he has made it real."

FURTHER READING

John Keegan's *The Second World War* (1989) offers an insightful account of the battle. Norman Franks's *The Battle of Britain* (1981) includes interviews with both German and British pilots and contains 100 photographs.

BRITISH EMPIRE, END OF THE

At the beginning of the 20th century the British Empire, which had established itself on every continent but Antarctica, was so vast that it validated the boast that on it "the sun never set." It appeared as permanent as the long reign of the queen in whose name it was ruled. However, by 1902, Victoria was dead, and the empire had suffered its first major setback in the BOER WAR. Five years later, in 1907, finding imperial administrative burdens overwhelming, England agreed to confer "dominion" status—de facto self-government—on Australia, New Zealand, Canada, and South Africa. Although the empire seemed to rebound after the victory in WORLD WAR I, when it acquired added power in the Middle East, it was forced, after a face-losing war, to grant free-state status to its oldest, geographically closest, and most intransigent colony, Ireland (see IRISH WAR OF INDEPENDENCE). At the same time, trouble loomed in the "jewel in the imperial crown," India, where the frail figure of Mohandas K. GANDHI developed a policy of passive resistance to British rule that proved to be an extraordinarily effective weapon in India's fight for independence.

Nevertheless, the British clung to control of India and its African colonies, although increasingly relying on a policy of "indirect rule," which meant using existing native rulers to administer the colonies while the British pursued their own economic and political interests. Discontent with imperial rule grew with the economic turmoil of the GREAT DEPRESSION, but WORLD WAR II proved how vulnerable the empire really was. In Southeast Asia, the Japanese easily overcame British colonies, most notably in the ignominious fall of Singapore and the first phase of the BURMA CAMPAIGN in 1942.

In the aftermath of World War II, even indirect rule was unable to assuage the tide of nationalism and cries for independence that emerged from the colonized peoples. Britain, exhausted and impoverished by the war, acceded to these demands, granting independence to India and Pakistan in 1947, Palestine and Burma in 1948, Uganda in 1962, Kenya in 1963,

Northern Rhodesia (now Zambia) in 1964, and Southern Rhodesia (now Zimbabwe) in 1980. For many, the empire's coup de grâce was delivered in its bungling of the SUEZ CRISIS in 1956. The sun over the empire had finally set in the blazing heat of the Egyptian desert. (See also COLONIALISM.)

THE LITERATURE

The writer most associated with the British Empire is Rudyard Kipling (1865–1936), whose poems, stories, and novels celebrate what he and his public regarded as essentially "English" virtues: military valor, moral responsibility, administrative skill, and the principle of "fair play" that had been instilled in the ruling classes by English public schools. In the Darwinian atmosphere of the late 19th and early 20th centuries, these virtues seemed to be nature's and God's way of indicating their manifest destiny to rule. From this perspective, Kipling's focus fell inevitably on the English hero, with little or no attempt to perceive the empire from the vantage point of the colonized. The one partial exception is Kipling's novel *Kim* (1901), in which an orphan of a British soldier stationed in India grows up thinking of himself as an Indian. Kim travels through northern India guided by a Tibetan lama, who introduces him to Indian religious beliefs. But once Kim's English paternity is discovered, he is adopted by a British regiment and soon recruited as a young secret agent for the British. Kim struggles with the conflicting claims of colonizer/colonized even as he plunges into the "great game" of spying. The novel does provide a rich and largely sympathetic description of Indian life, but Kim's ultimate "whiteness" triumphs in his quest for identity.

Kipling's view of the empire did not survive the post–World War I period. A much more complex view of the relations between the governors and the governed in India emerges in E. M. Forster's (1897–1970) *A Passage to India* and Paul Scott's (1920–78) *Raj Quartet*. An early example of an attempt by an English writer to depict directly the native's dilemma is Joyce Cary's (1888–1957) *Mister Johnson* (1939). Mister Johnson, a government clerk in a remote village in Nigeria, has a rich, natural sense of the joy of life, but he also aspires to be an English gentleman. Alienated from his own culture, unable to enter the English world of his imagination, he is nevertheless not discouraged. His energy, enthusiasm, and unrelenting optimism result in the production of a road that changes the life of the village, with mixed results. Ultimately Johnson is fired for stealing, while in his mind he is merely imitating his superiors. In the novel's climactic conclusion, he meets his death at the hands of Rudbeck, the white man he most admires. In executing Johnson, who had been sentenced to death, Rudbeck attempts to acknowledge his own responsibility for Johnson's tragic situation. For the author, Johnson is a symbol of colonized Africa, torn from its roots by imperial rule, educated to be an efficient cog in the imperial machine, tossed aside and later destroyed when he proves troublesome. In the character of Rudbeck, we see the Englishman's recognition of responsibility for the violation of others that is endemic to imperial rule.

According to the critic Jeffrey Meyers, "The phoenix of the African novel has arisen from the ashes of the colonial novel." With the arrival of independence, African novelists have set out to revise the European view of African history and culture. Foremost of these novelists has been the Nigerian novelist Chinua Achebe (1930–   ), who has argued that even anticolonialist works, such as Joseph Conrad's (1857–1926) *Heart of Darkness*, and sympathetic portraits of natives such as *Mister Johnson*, exhibit the limitations and prejudices of an outsider. In his novels, he has set himself the task of charting the effects of imperialism from the perspective of one who knows the experience of the natives and the price they have paid for the British presence in Nigeria.

Starting with *Things Fall Apart* (1958), his celebrated account of the intrusion of colonial government into the tribal life of the Ibo community in the late 19th century, Achebe then moved into the 20th century in *Arrow of God* (1964). *Arrow of God* is set primarily in 1921 in the Nigerian Ibo village Umuaro, where the chief priest Ezeulu presides over a series of rituals and festivals that have created a cohesive community, strengthened by tradition. A short distance away is a British administrative post at Okperi, where a group of Englishmen, led by Captain Winterbottom, live their isolated, alienated lives. When Ezeulu is invited by Winterbottom to come to Okperi to receive an honor, he refuses at first because his priestly duties forbid leaving his village. But the Ibo tribesmen, fearful of offending the British, insist that he go to Okperi. When he arrives, the British, insulted by his earlier refusal, detain him for some months in the local guard room. Because of this detention, he fails to calculate the correct number of new moons for the harvest, a critical responsibility of the chief priest. When he returns to Umuaro, his miscalculation results in the threat of famine. As a result, the tribe shifts its allegiance to the British god, "the son." The people of the village realize that "these are not the times we used to know and we must meet them as they come or be rolled in the dust." Feeling betrayed, Ezeulu adopts the inflexible, rigid posture of a tragic hero with inevitably disastrous results for him.

Achebe recognizes the Ibo's need for adaptation, but he sees the greater loss in the destruction of the beautiful traditions and rituals, without which, "things fall apart." In his postindependence novels, he traces the continuing dissolution of the Ibo tradition, culminating in the disastrous Nigerian civil war.

A similarly negative view of the imperialist presence is evident in the works of the Kenyan novelist Ngugi wa Thiong'o (1938–   ). (See MAU MAU REBELLION.)

FURTHER READING

Colin Cross's *The Fall of the British Empire, 1918–1968* (1968) traces the last 50 years of the empire up to Prime Minister Harold Wilson's 1968 announcement of the return of the last of British military units from former colonies. Jeffrey Meyers's *Fiction and the Colonial Experience* (1973) and M. M. Mahood's *The Colonial Encounter* (1977) offer perceptive analyses of selected novels of the empire.

BULGE, BATTLE OF THE (WORLD WAR II)

See ARDENNES OFFENSIVE.

BURMA CAMPAIGN (WORLD WAR II) (1942–1945)

Burma (now Myanmar) became a part of the British Empire in 1885, as a province of India. Once the British entered the Pacific war against the Japanese, Burma assumed critical importance, since the Burma Road, a one-lane highway that stretched from Burma to Chungking, China, was the only land route by which Chinese forces could be supplied in their battle against the Japanese.

In January 1942, the Japanese invaded Burma, easily overwhelming the undermanned British forces, and two months later were able to seal off the Burma Road. By February, they had captured the capital, Rangoon (now Yangon). Chinese reinforcements, one group led by an American general, Vinegar Joe Stilwell, were unable to stem the Japanese tide. By May 1942, the remaining British troops had retreated across the Indian border and Stilwell's Chinese force returned to China. Plans for a reinvasion of Burma became tangled by the questions of priority (the Allied command always operated on the principle of "Germany First") and strategy differences between the British and Americans. The Americans tended to set greater store in the importance of Chiang Kai-shek and his army than the British did.

In February 1944, the Japanese launched an offensive on the Indian border, which succeeded in surrounding Anglo-Indian forces at Kohima and Imphal, but the Anglo-Indians stood fast, reinforced by American planes airlifting necessary supplies. After a long siege, the Japanese army, starving and riddled with disease, retreated back to Burma. In October 1944, the Allies launched attacks into Burma, resulting in the reopening of the Burma Road in January 1945 and the recapture of Rangoon on May 2. Upon entering the capital, the Allied troops discovered that the Japanese had already abandoned it.

THE LITERATURE

In Burma and neighboring Thailand, the Japanese put 60,000 Allied prisoners to work building a railroad from Rangoon to Bangkok. This incident provided the French novelist Pierre Boulle (1912–94) with the background for *The Bridge over the River Kwai* (1954), his best-selling, fictional account of the building of a railroad bridge on the Burmese-Thai border by a group of British prisoners. The story focuses on the commander of the British troops, Colonel Nicholson, a man whose "sense of duty, observance of ritual, obsession with discipline, and love of a job well done" cause him to lose sight of the reality of his situation—the fact that he is building a bridge for the enemy. Nicholson's implacable will is strong enough not only to control the 500 men he commands but to transform the sadistic camp commandant, Colonel Saito, into his bemused and intimidated accomplice. Nicholson begins modestly with the intention of requiring that the commandant adhere to the Geneva convention in the treatment of prisoners, but he ends as a fanatic, who sees the bridge as a personal testament, his life's greatest accomplishment.

His delusory state persists even as he comes upon the presence of an English commando about to blow the bridge up. The conclusion is melodramatic, but gripping, as the colonel's mind struggles to get around an inconceivable idea: "Blow up the bridge?" The novel offers a darker ending than that of David Lean's famous 1957 film *The Bridge on the River Kwai*, in which Alec Guinness's performance as Nicholson lends the character a tragic grandeur.

One of the features of the novel that contemporary readers will find ironically amusing is its errant racism, not simply in the language of the characters, which would be historically justified, but in the authorial narration. Time and again we are reminded of the inherent superiority of the Europeans to the Japanese, particularly in technical matters. The completed bridge, we are told, is yet another example of "the craftmanship of the European and the Anglo-Saxon sense of perfection."

FURTHER READING

Raymond Callahan's *Burma 1942–1945* (1979) explores the political as well as military aspects of the campaign.

C

CAMBODIAN GENOCIDE

Cambodia had been a colony of France until 1953, when it gained independence under the rule of Prince Sihanouk. Sihanouk pursued a policy of neutrality in the COLD WAR, alternately wooing the Soviet Union and the United States. During the VIETNAM WAR, North Vietnamese forces used Cambodia as a supply base along the border. As a result, American planes steadily bombed areas of the country, and in 1970, while Sihanouk was out of the country, American troops supported a coup that brought General Lon Nol to power. Communist guerrillas in Cambodia, known as the Khmer Rouge and led by Pol Pot, began to step up their campaign against the government. In 1975, the capital city of Pnomh Penh fell to the Khmer Rouge. The American strategy that helped overthrow Sihanouk and support Lon Nol had backfired, leading to a communist coup and the installation of a murderous, insane regime for the next four years.

Pol Pot, influenced by the example of Mao Zedong's CULTURAL REVOLUTION, set about transforming the country in an extraordinarily radical and barbarous manner. Determined to start from "year zero," Pol Pot abolished money in favor of a barter system; emptied out urban areas, forcing the population to live in agricultural communes; suppressed all forms of religion, laying waste to the Buddhist monasteries; and eliminated traditional education. Children were removed from their families and sent to live in barracks, where they learned that the state was their true, and only reliable, parent. All of this was accompanied by one of the most brutal and savage genocides of the 20th century. Among those singled out for extermination was the middle class, particularly its intellectual and educated segments. Pol Pot also declared war on the ethnic minorities, particularly the Chinese and Vietnamese living in Kampuchea, the new name for Cambodia. The preferred mode of execution, in an effort to save ammunition, was to smash a pickaxe or spade into the skull of the kneeling victim. The estimated number of people killed is 1.7 million, approximately 20 percent of the total population.

Pol Pot also caused strained relations with the neighboring Vietnamese government, newly powerful after its triumph in the Vietnam War. After a series of border disputes, Vietnam invaded Cambodia, driving Pol Pot into retreat to the countryside, where the Khmer Rouge continued to wage guerrilla war well into the 1990s. Under the new Vietnamese-supported communist government, urban residents returned to the cities, Buddhist temples reopened, and foreign aid was sought to mitigate the severe suffering and hunger of the population, but the new government was unable to restore order in the war-torn land. In 1989, the Vietnamese army withdrew, and in 1991 a United Nations–mediated peace led to the proclamation, in 1993, of Sihanouk as king, with limited powers. Pol Pot died in 1998, after having been rejected by his Khmer Rouge.

THE LITERATURE

In a complexly plotted novel that ranges from strife-ridden Cambodia to contemporary London, Margaret Drabble's (1939–   ) *The Gates of Ivory* (1991) explores the possibility of establishing a moral norm in an age of atrocity. How do people who think of themselves as living more or less decent lives absorb and integrate such unimaginable horrors as that which occurred in Cambodia? This question, similar to the one that arose for the previous generation in confronting the HOLOCAUST, now emerges in the 1980s, as the truth about the "killing fields" of Cambodia becomes known. In an echo of the beginning of Charles Dickens's *A Tale of Two Cities* ("It was the best of times; it was the worst of times"), *The Gates of Ivory* opens with a reference to the "Good Time and Bad Time," asking you, the reader, to imagine yourself by a river on the border of Thailand and Cambodia. Behind you is "the Good Time of the West. Before you, the Bad Time of Cambodia." On one level, the novel explores the irony underscoring the antithesis of good and bad, focusing on the degree of the good's culpability for the existence of the bad.

In London, Liz Headeland receives a package containing a manuscript, a diary, a booklet of "Atrocity Stories," and "the two middle joints of a human finger bone." The source of this material is Stephen Cox, a writer and old friend of Liz, who has gone to Cambodia with the intent of writing a play about Pol Pot, "to find out what went wrong" with Pol Pot's attempt to "take Cambodia out of history." The rest of the novel is narrated from a number of viewpoints, principally those of Stephen and Liz, who, in attempting to determine what has happened to Stephen, travels to Thailand. Liz discovers that Stephen has died in a remote clinic in Cambodia. A doctor at the clinic, who had become friendly with Stephen, mailed the package containing his effects because her name was listed as next of kin on his passport. After becoming ill herself in Bangkok, apparently a victim of toxic shock syndrome, she returns to London. In Stephen's account, we learn that his death is precipitated by an ill-advised attempt to enter Cambodia, where he and his companion, a young English photographer, Konstantin Vassiliou, are captured by Khmer Rouge guerrillas and force-marched to a remote village, which ultimately results in Stephen's death. Back in London, Liz arranges Stephen's memorial ceremony, where the guests' behavior epitomizes lines from the poet W. H. Auden: "[Suffering always] takes place / While someone is eating or opening a window or just walking dully along."

The emblematic figure in the novel is Madame Savet Akrun, an educated Pnomh Penh resident, who loses her husband, brother, mother, and sisters in the genocide. She is thrust out into the jungle with her three children, the oldest of whom is 18-year-old Mitra, a medical student, who has luckily survived—the novel explains, "Out of 6,000 doctors, 57 remained alive in 1979"—by pretending to be a street vendor of cigarettes. Mme. Akrun's family forms part of a group forced to trek through the jungle to a designated area where they will do agricultural work. They are stopped by Khmer Rouge soldiers, "boys of sixteen and seventeen . . . ignorant children . . . mad with power," who, after killing most of the men in the group, force the rest, Mitra included, aboard a truck. Now living in one of the Thailand camps bordering Cambodia, Mme. Akrun is photographed by Konstantin, and the photograph—with the caption, "Where is my son?"—becomes the official poster for the refugees' international relief fund. At the conclusion of the novel, we learn that Mitra has survived and become a Khmer Rouge guerrilla: "He does not care whether his mother lives or dies. He marches on. He is multitudes."

References to the novels of Joseph Conrad (1857–1926) appear often, particularly in the suggestion that Stephen is entering "the heart of darkness," and in the finger bone among his effects, which alludes to the skulls adorning Kurtz's hut in Conrad's story (see COLONIALISM). Mitra assumes the Kurtz role, the young medical student so transformed by the "horror" that he becomes the enemy, while Liz, who had thought of marrying Stephen at one point, might function as the "Intended" of Conrad's tale, enmeshed in "Good Time" without recognizing its imperceptible slide into "Bad Time." Stephen, on the other hand, dying, awakens in the middle of a storm to see the woman who has been tending him swaying in a strange dance: "Stephen feels an intense happiness. It is a vision. It is the heart of darkness, it is the heart of light," a suggestion, perhaps, that from the absolute perspective of imminent death, the distinction between the two times vanishes.

FURTHER READING

Sydney Schanberg's *The Death and Life of Dith Pran* (1985) is the account by a *New York Times* correspondent of the Khmer Rouge atrocities in the immediate aftermath of their victory in 1975 and the fate of his heroic young assistant, Dith Pran, which formed the basis of the 1984 film *The Killing Fields.*

CAPORETTO, THE RETREAT FROM (WORLD WAR I) (1917)

In a WORLD WAR I battle in October 1917, the Italian army suffered a disastrous rout by a combined Austro-German force. The fighting occurred along the Isonzo River on the Italian-Austrian border. Anticipating an attack on the northern end of the front, the Italians heavily fortified that area. But the Austro-German forces focused their attack on the southern end, penetrating deep into Italian territory, capturing the town of Caporetto. As a result of the poor strategy of its commander, General Luigi Cadorna, the Italian army found itself cut off by the enemy, resulting in a chaotic attempt to retreat, exacerbated by Cadorna's order that all stragglers be executed on the spot as deserters. Through death, captivity, and desertion, the Italians lost more than 600,000 men. (The Austro-German breakthrough of the Italian lines was spearheaded by a small company commanded by Lieutenant Erwin Rommel, who in WORLD WAR II rose to the rank of field marshal in charge of the German army in Africa.)

THE LITERATURE

The Caporetto retreat forms a memorable episode in Ernest Hemingway's (1899–1961) *A Farewell to Arms* (1929). Its narrator, Frederic Henry, an American volunteer serving with an ambulance unit in the Italian army, is wounded and sent to a hospital in Milan, where he is visited by an English nurse he has met earlier, Catherine Barkley. The two fall in love and spend an idyllic time together before he returns to the front. When they part, Catherine tells him that she is pregnant, and they agree to join each other as soon as possible.

Henry arrives back at his unit just as the battle of Caporetto is underway. Driving an ambulance that gets caught in the long line of retreating vehicles, Henry provides a powerful, vivid account of the retreat. Beginning in an orderly fashion, the retreat soon degenerates into chaos. The novel's descriptions of the ravaged, demoralized army trudging in the rain and the summary executions of Italian officers for desertion, serve, in the words of the historian John Keegan, as "one of the greatest literary evocations of military disaster." Threatened with execution himself, Henry escapes by leaping into a river. Eventually he makes his way back to Catherine, but, fearful of Henry's being captured and shot as a deserter, the two escape to Switzerland. There they turn their backs on the war and forge "a separate peace." Their idyll comes to a tragic conclusion when Catherine dies in childbirth. Catherine's death underscores the idea that just as life is penetrated by the senseless folly of war (at least of the kind of war that the Caporetto retreat exemplifies), so is love defeated by the "dirty trick" that is death.

A memorable statement in the novel is its protest not only against war but against the rhetoric of war: "[A]bstract words such as glory, honor, courage or hallow were obscene." The sentiment has a double significance, representing both the rejection of abstract ideas and language and, inferentially, the endorsement of the celebrated Hemingway style—the simple, clean, concrete language of understatement.

FURTHER READING

John Keegan's *The First World War* (1999) provides an incisive account of Caporetto. Robert Penn Warren's *Selected Essays* (1958) contains a perceptive treatment of *A Farewell to Arms*.

CENTRAL INTELLIGENCE AGENCY (CIA)

Odd as it may seem today, the United States of America was one of the last major nations in the world to field an international intelligence agency. The Office of Strategic Services (OSS) was formed in 1941, in anticipation of WORLD WAR II, and disbanded in September 1945. In spite of strong protests on the part of J. Edgar Hoover, to the effect that the Federal Bureau of Investigation (FBI) was more than adequate to handle all of the nation's security needs, the onset of the COLD WAR impelled President Harry Truman to create the successor to the OSS, the Central Intelligence Agency, in December 1947, with Admiral Roscoe Hillenkoetter as its first director. Under his aegis, and with the particular help of former OSS agent James Jesus Angleton, the CIA helped prevent a Communist electoral victory in postwar Italy.

Under Allen Dulles, whom President Dwight Eisenhower appointed director in 1953, the agency grew in scope and sophistication. In 1954, it abetted the overthrow of Jacobo Arbenz's leftist regime in Guatemala. E. Howard Hunt, later involved in WATERGATE, was a key figure in this operation. In 1955, the CIA oversaw the digging of the Berlin Tunnel, which for a time gave American intelligence access to the cable carrying messages to and from Soviet military and diplomatic offices in East Berlin.

Dulles's tenure as CIA director was largely contemporary with that of Nikita Khrushchev as first secretary of the Soviet Communist Party. (Khrushchev lasted longer: He was deposed by Brezhnev in 1964, while Dulles was forced to resign in the wake of the Bay of Pigs fiasco in 1961.) In

1956, the agency obtained a copy of a speech given by Khrushchev to the Twentieth Party Congress denouncing the crimes of Joseph STALIN. The CIA ran U2 spy planes in the Soviet Union from 1956 until pilot Gary Powers was shot down in 1960, tried, and later exchanged for the Komitet gosudarstvennoĭ bezopasnosti (KGB) agent Rudolf Abel. But it was the Bay of Pigs episode, in which a group of Cuban exiles with CIA support attempted to undo the revolution led by Fidel Castro, that revealed how an ideologically unified group, operating in secret, insulated from opposing points of view, can lose touch with reality. The agency imagined that Castro was so reviled a figure that the island would rise up against him en masse at the first opportunity. That being largely untrue, the invasion soon became a debacle, with most of the invaders killed or captured. From that time, in spite of certain successes, the CIA was revealed as a fallible—even an extremely fallible—instrument. In turn, many CIA operatives hated the Kennedy administration, whose lukewarm, stumbling support for the invasion had, in their view, been the real cause of failure.

Nonetheless, under the direction of John McCone, the CIA had one of its major triumphs, when in 1962 its spy planes revealed Cuban installations being prepared for Soviet missiles. This led to the Cuban Missile Crisis, which brought the world to the brink of nuclear war; ultimately it ended with Russian ships turning back in the face of an American blockade of the island. But the assassination of John F. Kennedy in 1963 produced further criticism of the CIA for not having kept track of his assassin, Lee Harvey Oswald, of whom the agency had already been made aware. Some critics went so far as to accuse the CIA of being complicit in the crime, although no evidence has ever emerged to prove such a claim.

Under Richard Helms, who ran the agency from 1966 to 1973, Vietnam was the chief focus. As in the case of the Bay of Pigs, an overly optimistic assessment of prospects contributed to one of the great military and foreign policy failures in American history. Also, under Helms's aegis, the CIA began the illegal surveillance of political figures in the United States. (Frequent violations to the contrary, the agency was in fact limited by charter to gathering intelligence outside the Western Hemisphere.) The Watergate scandal, in which the CIA may not have been directly involved, led to the disclosure of its illegal activities.

President Richard Nixon fired Helms in 1973 and appointed William Colby to withstand the pressures now brought to bear on the intelligence community by Congress. It was during Colby's tenure that James Jesus Angleton, whom Norman Mailer (1923–   ), in his author's note to *Harlot's Ghost*, acknowledges to be the prototype of his eponymous protagonist, was forced to resign. Angleton, the former OSS agent who had helped prevent a Communist victory in postwar Italy, had been a powerful, and somewhat extreme, figure in the agency until 1974, embodying and exaggerating the paranoia on which it fed. Certain that any possible rift in what he took to be the monolithic Communist world was no more than a trick designed to take in the innocent West, he finally became convinced that there was a KGB mole in the CIA and grew obsessed with discovering him. He found no mole, but he ruined the careers of more than a dozen agents, subsequently exonerated, while trying to do so.

The CIA regained much of its power and secrecy under President Ronald Reagan's appointee, William Casey, director from 1981 to 1987. These were the years of the IRAN-CONTRA SCANDAL, in which the CIA was deeply involved, as well as of the agency's support of Afghan rebels against the Soviet Union.

In 1994, the mole that Angleton never found—and who did not begin his betrayal until 1985, when Angleton was long gone—was finally discovered. Aldrich Ames, son of a CIA agent, and himself an employee since 1959, had been selling information, including the identities of American agents in Russia, to the Soviets. Ironically, in 1983, he had been put in charge of counterintelligence, as the search for a mole discredited by Angleton's obsessiveness had reemerged as an important concern. His acts of treason stand among the most damaging ever performed against the United States.

In the aftermath of September 11, 2001, the CIA again was criticized, this time for its failure to anticipate the attack on the World Trade Center. On the other hand, the dangers of terrorism also ensured widespread support for the agency's activities, albeit with reservations from many who believed that the search for terrorists provided an excuse to extend government control beyond constitutional limits.

THE LITERATURE

Nearly 1,300 pages long, *Harlot's Ghost* (1991), Norman Mailer's novel about the CIA, ends with the seemingly ironic tag: "To Be Continued." But, in fact, the novel, long as it is, has little sense of narrative finality. It does, however, stand on its own as Mailer's reading of the history of the CIA from 1955 to 1965, and as a quasi-serious presentation of a dualist view of human nature. Mailer's spokesman in this endeavor, promulgating the theory of Alpha and Omega, is Kittredge Gardiner, wife first of Hugh Montague (aka Harlot), then the narrator, Herrick (Harry) Hubbard.

As Kittredge puts it, Omega is "about the mysteries—conception, birth, death, night, the moon, eternity, karma, ghosts, divinities, myths, magic, our primitive past, so on. The other, Alpha, creature of the forward-swimming energies of sperm, ambitious, blind to all but its own purpose, tends, of course, to be more oriented toward enterprise, technology, grinding the corn, repairing the mill, building bridges between money and power." Alpha and Omega exist within each of us. Mailer's universe consists of dichotomies in conflict. The Americans are at odds with the Russians, the CIA with the FBI,

Hugh Montague's faction in the CIA with William Harvey's, and all individuals, it seems, are at war with themselves. As a type, the CIA agent catches up all of these conflicts, and so it becomes the concrete embodiment of the novel's metaphysical thrust.

The narrative begins at a point in time shortly before its conclusion. CIA agent Harry Hubbard, son of CIA agent Cal Hubbard and godson of CIA legend Hugh Montague, returns through a deadly storm and an almost mythic landscape to his home in Maine, where he lives with Kittredge. Having survived the hero's perilous journey home, Harry then encounters catastrophe. Before the night is over, he has word that Montague is dead and that his wife is leaving him for his opposite and adversary in the agency, Dix Butler. A few days later, he learns that the house has been burnt to the ground, and that his ally Arnie Rosen is dead; Harry himself is soon in flight.

The novel then moves back in time to the beginning of Harry's career in the CIA. After completing his training in 1955, he is sent to work for Bill Harvey in Berlin, at the time the Berlin Tunnel is in operation. He is in a sense Hugh Montague's agent, leading to an adversarial relationship between himself and Harvey and, finally, to Harry's reposting to Uruguay, where he works for E. Howard Hunt, fresh from his triumph in Guatemala. Here Harry runs his first agent, the Uruguayan Communist Chevi Fuertes. He also has an ongoing affair with the wife of a fellow agent and a sexual encounter with Libertad La Lengua, a courtesan who may be able to get close to Fidel Castro and who turns out to be transsexual. For Mailer, spies, lovers, homosexuals, bisexuals, and transsexuals are all double agents. All the while, Harry keeps up his correspondence with Montague's wife, Kittredge, as well as a surreptitious stream of communication with Harlot himself.

Harry follows E. Howard Hunt to Miami, where attempts to assassinate Castro are already underway. From this post, Harry monitors the entire Bay of Pigs catastrophe, even briefly setting foot on Cuban soil. After the fiasco, efforts to assassinate Castro intensify. Harry begins an affair with the airline stewardess Modene Murphy, a character based to some extent on Judith Exner. Like Exner, she has affairs with Frank Sinatra, John F. Kennedy, and mobster Sam Giancana. The last years of the narrative cover the Cuban missile crisis and the assassination of Kennedy.

The novel's conclusion finds Harry Hubbard in Moscow in March 1984, shortly after the events with which it began. Harry is defecting not because of any change of heart regarding his work for the CIA, but rather because he first hopes, then begins to believe, that Hugh Montague is not really dead, that he has defected to Moscow, and that he, Harry, will be able to join him. At this point, we can either take Mailer's word that the story will be continued or look back on what we have read and conclude that the author has had his say about the universe of conflict and betrayal in which the CIA and its agents become appropriate symbols for the whole.

FURTHER READING

Philip Agee's *Inside the Company: CIA Diary* (1975) and Victor Marchetti and John Marks's *The CIA and the Cult of Intelligence* (1974) are accounts by former CIA agents. *The Central Intelligence Agency: History and Documents* (1984), edited by William M. Leary, and the much praised *The U.S. Intelligence Community* (1999) by Jeffrey T. Richelson provide factual and historical analysis.

—Karl Malkoff

CHERNOBYL DISASTER (1986)

On April 26, 1986, reactor no. 4 exploded in a Soviet nuclear plant at Chernobyl, a village in Ukraine. The explosion tore the cap off the reactor, releasing large amounts of radioactive material into the atmosphere. At first, the Soviet authorities attempted to cover up the disaster, but as the evidence of radioactive elements in the atmosphere spread throughout northern Europe, the Soviets were forced to acknowledge the catastrophe. Chernobyl proved to be the most serious nuclear accident in history, resulting in the evacuation of more than 100,000 people in the Chernobyl vicinity. An estimated 500,000 people in the Soviet Union were exposed to the radiation. Traces of radiation were also found in other nations of eastern Europe.

THE LITERATURE

The journalist Vladimir Gubaryev, at the time the science editor of *Pravda*, was the first journalist on the scene of the disaster. What he witnessed so moved him that he set about writing a play, *Sarcophagus: A Tragedy* (1986; trans., 1987), which he completed within three months. Set in the fictional Institute of Radiation Surgery, which is receiving early victims of the disaster, the play deals with the efforts of the medical staff and their patients to come to terms with what has happened. Ten isolated cubicles are on stage, nine of them occupied by recent victims, the 10th by the self-styled Bessmertny (the immortal), a patient who has previously been exposed to radiation and survived. Bessmertny functions as the chorus to this tragedy, interacting with the victims and doctors and interpreting both the immediate and larger significance of Chernobyl. In the course of the play, the victims begin to die, one by one.

The play's title is a pun. *Sarcophagus* is the term used at Chernobyl for the concrete structure that encloses the core of the reactor. Bessmertny compares this use of the term to its traditional meaning: "You're building the pyramids, the tombs of the pharaohs. You're our nuclear pharaohs. . . . The pyramid of the pharaohs have been there for a mere five thousand years. But to contain the nuclear radiation your nuclear pyramid must remain for a hundred thousand years. That's some monument to leave our descendants, isn't it?"

Gubaryev has pointed out that he hopes the play's warning will be noticed by the generations born after 1960, who have come to take nuclear energy for granted: "They must understand that the level of their knowledge and culture must be far higher than their parents." The nuclear age demands "a new level of thought and knowledge and, most importantly a new attitude toward it." An English translation of the play has been performed in Great Britain, and, in 1987, at the Los Angeles Theatre Center.

Christa Wolf (1929–) is a distinguished and controversial novelist/essayist who grew up in Nazi Germany and, during the postwar years, chose to live and work in East Germany. Despite the fact that she suffered for her outspoken criticism of the East German regime, until the time of its collapse in 1989, she remained loyal to the basic principles of socialism, a committed Marxist.

Her novel *Accident* (1987; trans., 1989) takes place in one day, shortly after the Chernobyl disaster, a day in which the brother of the female narrator is undergoing surgery for a brain tumor. The two events—the public and the personal crises—completely occupy the mind of the narrator, a professional writer strongly resembling Wolf herself, as she goes about her usual daily activities. These mundane routines—tending the garden, listening to the radio, talking on the telephone—are fraught with new meaning as she reflects on the frailty and beauty of nature and human life. The novel opens with a description of "one of the most beautiful days of the year." The new spring blossoms on the cherry trees have "exploded," but the narrator can no longer use that metaphorical verb to express the fecundity of nature, now contaminated by nuclear activity. Later she will learn that the fruit of these trees are unsafe to eat. The environment has become, like the skull of her brother, so sensitive that the slightest mishap can be fatal. The comparison also brings to the fore the two faces of science, that which is being applied (successfully, as it turns out) in the operating room and that which goes on in a place like the Livermore Laboratory in California, peopled with modern Fausts, who have sold their souls for scientific knowledge. To a reader in the West, this Faustian allusion seems to leap out from the text: We become aware of the fact that the narrator has never mentioned the word *Chernobyl*, never referred to the blatant attempts of the Soviet government to cover up the disaster, thereby escalating the risk of spread. Instead the villains are sitting in California "shackled to their computers." At one point, the narrator discusses with her daughter "our blind spot." It would appear that her blind spot here revolves around her propensity to look for a scapegoat rather than acknowledge the Soviet government's responsibility.

This short novel concludes with the narrator in bed reading Joseph Conrad's (1857–1926) *Heart of Darkness* (see COLONIALISM), which leads to the realization that, in the darkness surrounding life, there is an occasional flicker of light, "'like the flash of lightning in the clouds.' We live in the flicker—may it last as long as the old earth keeps rolling." Though Chernobyl is never mentioned, it is unquestionably the subject of the work. In one sense, Chernobyl doesn't need to be named, but the fact that Wolf avoids the word allows her to shift blame away from the Soviet authorities. Nonetheless, in its ability to capture the interior consciousness coming to grips with an insidious threat, *Accident* constitutes a memorable, if flawed, work of literature.

FURTHER READING

Iurii Shcherbak's *Chernobyl* (1989) is a record of interviews with eyewitnesses to the disaster, government officials, and local media representatives, including the comments of Vladimir Gubaryev. Margit Resch's *Understanding Christa Wolf* (1997) explores her achievements and controversial status in modern European literature.

CHILEAN MILITARY COUP (1973)

In 1970, after a campaign in which he promised sweeping reforms, Salvador Allende, backed by a fusion of Socialist and Communist Parties, was elected president of Chile. He immediately nationalized the copper mines, many of which had been foreign-owned, thereby antagonizing foreign governments and investors. In addition, he broke up large estates in a poorly organized attempt at land reform, thereby alienating even further wealthy and middle-class citizens. Soon economic chaos pervaded the nation. Supported by the United States CENTRAL INTELLIGENCE AGENCY (CIA), a military junta led by Augusto Pinochet staged a coup in September 1973, during which Allende was killed and Pinochet declared the new president. Pinochet presided over a brutally repressive military regime, imprisoning and torturing thousands of Chileans, but his economic policies, which encouraged foreign investors, proved to be on the whole successful. As a result, Pinochet remained in power for 15 years, during which time civil rights violations and other repressive measures steadily increased. In 1988, he was voted out as president, but he retained the powerful position of commander in chief of the army. Ten years later, he was arrested in England, charged with crimes against Spanish citizens in Chile during his reign.

THE LITERATURE

The novelist Isabel Allende (1942–), the niece of Salvador Allende, was working as a journalist at the time of the coup and was forced to leave the country. While in exile, she drew on her family's background to write *The House of the Spirits* (1985), a family chronicle focusing on three generations of women in an aristocratic Chilean family: the grandmother Clara, the daughter Blanca, the granddaughter Alba, and their frequently contentious relationship with the family patriarch, Esteban Truez, Clara's husband. Esteban is a large landowner and strongly conservative member of the Chilean senate. Although well advanced in years, he is still a fiery, combative politician, and he plays a significant role in undermining the Allende government and colluding with the military forces.

Once the coup is successful, however, the Pinochet regime has little use for any form of parliamentary power. In the meantime Esteban's granddaughter Alba is arrested as the lover of a leader of the anti-Pinochet faction. While in detention she is tortured and raped, but Alba is sustained by the deep identity she shares with her mother and grandmother, enabling her to overcome the horrors of torture and imprisonment. Finally released, she rejoins her grandfather in their house, where the two effect a quiet reconciliation.

The early sections of the novel, set before the brutal reality of the coup period, are interspersed with fantastic elements, reminiscent of Gabriel García Márquez's (1928–) *One Hundred Years of Solitude* (1967; trans., 1970). These touches of magic realism help to suggest a theme of female strength offsetting the traditional paternalism and machismo embodied in the figure of Esteban. But magic realism is absent from the latter parts of the novel, which deal with the depiction of the coup. For some readers, this incongruity fatally weakens the novel; for others, it suggests that the magic has been deliberately deleted, testifying to the triumph of brutal reality represented by the Pinochet regime.

FURTHER READING

Stefan de Vylder's *Allende's Chile* (1976) is an analysis of the weaknesses of the Allende regime that led to the overthrow.

CHINA, EMERGENCE OF (1911–)

By the beginning of the 20th century, the weaknesses of the Manchu dynasty reign of the dowager empress Cixi led to the increasing encroachment of Western commercial powers on Chinese soil. Chinese discontent erupted in the BOXER REBELLION (1900), in which foreigners and Christian missionaries were massacred and the Western consulates in the capital city of Peking (Beijing) were placed under siege. As a result, an international Western military force descended on China. This army soon quelled the uprising, wreaking damage and extracting demands that further weakened the imperial government.

For the rest of the decade, the alienation of the imperial Qing dynasty from the mass of Chinese people created increasing discontent. Foremost of the opponents of the government was the exiled Dr. Sun Yat-sen (Sun Yixian or Sun I-hsien), who promoted the principles of a democratic republic as opposed to the tradition of imperial rule. In October 1911, revolutionary forces in the city of Wuchang began a spontaneous uprising that ended in their controlling the city. The movement soon spread to other cities. Sun Yat-sen returned to China and proclaimed the establishment of the Republic of China. However, European and American international business interests feared the new republic and silently funded the remnants of the imperial army commanded by Yuan Shikai. As a result, Sun was forced to compromise. In order to save the republic, he agreed to step down as president in favor of Yuan. Yuan became president, and the new capital of China was established at Beijing. From the very beginning, Yuan proved to be a military autocrat. He overrode all of the newly established democratic policies, forced Sun into exile once again, dissolved Sun's political party, the Kuomindang, and attempted to have himself proclaimed emperor. With Yuan's death in 1916, Sun returned to serve as president. His tenure was marked by continual struggles with the WARLORDS, who had come to power during the Yuan regime.

In the 1920s, Sun's successor, his son-in-law Chiang Kai-shek, had some success in subduing the warlords, but he made a serious miscalculation in turning on his allies, the Chinese Communists (see SHANGHAI INSURREC-TION). Outmatched by Chiang's superior strength, the Communists were forced to retreat to a remote corner of China (see LONG MARCH), but they made the best of a bad situation by enlisting the support of the peasant popu-lation in many of the rural areas. Led by Mao Zedong, the Communists car-ried on guerrilla warfare until 1937. In that year the Japanese invaded China, and the warring Chinese forces formed a coalition against the invaders. The first two years of the war saw the Japanese score a number of victories, includ-ing the capture of Chiang's capital (see NANKING [NANJING], RAPE OF). From 1939 to 1941, the positions of the rival forces saw little change—the Japanese controlling the large urban centers, Chiang's forces occupying the southwest, and Mao's Communist troops engaging in effective guerrilla warfare in the northwest. With the entry of the United States and Great Britain into the war with Japan, the invaders found themselves fighting an increasingly defensive battle.

The defeat of the Japanese in 1945 brought renewed hostilities between the Nationalists and the Communists, which by 1946 had blossomed into a full-scale civil war. Despite economic aid from the United States, Chiang's government proved inefficient and unable to control runaway inflation. Added to this was the alienation of the peasant population, who enlisted in the Communist cause in large numbers. Eventually Chiang conceded main-land China to the Communists, retreating to the island of Taiwan, 100 miles off the Chinese coast. Chiang proclaimed the island the Republic of China while the mainland became the People's Republic of China.

Under Mao's rule, the government undertook radical reforms, including the distribution of land to the vast peasant population. Less popular and less feasible was the government's attempt to eliminate the four "olds": old ideas, habits, customs, and culture. This change penetrated the private lives of every citizen, creating a totalitarian state, which made a mockery of the "liberation of the people" idea that had been Mao's proclaimed goal. The new government also embarked on an aggressive foreign policy that sent more than 1 million troops to North Korea in the KOREAN WAR and to the invasion of Tibet.

In the 1960s, Mao inaugurated the CULTURAL REVOLUTION, his attempt to purge the Communist Party of "bourgeois influences." The result, mirroring Joseph STALIN's GREAT TERROR of the 1930s, was a massive assault on human rights, in which citizens were encouraged to denounce friends and family. The Cultural Revolution dominated Chinese society until Mao's death in 1976. Mao's successor Deng Xiaoping adopted a policy of liberalization that called for individual initiative and, to a limited extent, private ownership. His pragmatic, less ideological approach was evident in foreign affairs as well when he established diplomatic relations with the United States.

The late 1980s saw the emergence of a democratic movement among university students calling for the elimination of corruption in government and economic reform. The movement culminated in a rally held in Tiananmen Square on April 21, 1989. Many of the 100,000 student protesters camped out in the square, erecting a 30-foot Styrofoam statue of the Goddess of democracy. Government troops moved into the area and proceeded to kill and wound thousands of unarmed students. When the massacre was over and order restored, the Chinese government had suffered a severe loss of credibility both at home and abroad. In the 1990s, Jiang Zemin succeeded Deng as leader of the party and president of the republic.

THE LITERATURE

One literary work that sets out to encompass most of the major events of 20th-century Chinese history—and succeeds in doing so to an impressive extent—is John Hersey's *The Call* (1985). Hersey himself was born in China in 1914, the son of Protestant missionaries. The protagonist of *The Call*, David Treadup, is modeled to a significant degree on Hersey's father. Treadup is a young American, who as a college student undergoes a religious experience in which he hears God calling him to become a missionary. He answers the call through the YMCA's Student Volunteer Movement. After courting and marrying a woman (at least in part because he has been told that a missionary must be married), he arrives in China in 1905, determined to spread not just the word of God but also the splendors of Western scientific progress. He achieves great success with the latter message. When the Revolution of 1911 succeeds, his hopes soar with the ascendance of the Western-trained, progressive Christian Sun Yat Sen coming to power. With Sun's death, anti-Christian, anti-Western fervor begins to reemerge, this time encouraged by the new Communist government in the

Soviet Union. In the fighting that erupts after the SHANGHAI INSURRECTION between Chiang Kai-shek's Nationalist forces and the Communists, Treadup narrowly escapes death.

But for him political events are subsumed under his mission to bring his brand of enlightenment to China; he becomes totally absorbed in his work, developing a successful literacy campaign among the peasants in his area. In addition, his lectures extolling science achieve great popularity. However, these successes reflect an increasingly secular tone, and he is accused by other missionaries of having abandoned his religious role, a charge in which he recognizes more than a grain of truth.

During WORLD WAR II, Treadup is interned by the Japanese, where he undergoes his dark night of the soul: "I am out of touch with God. . . . It may be that now I think that there is no God." But his participation with the community of prisoners breathes new energy into his life. He begins to keep a new journal, which he titles "The Search," a quest "for the inner frame on which the house of me stands." In the middle of the war he is the beneficiary of a prisoner exchange program, and he sails back to the United States, where he is reunited with his wife and son. He returns to China in 1945 as a United Nations employee in time for the Chinese civil war. Treadup resigns his post with the UN and returns to the villages he worked in before his internment. With the Communist victory, he is arrested, subjected to a show trial, and expelled back to the United States. After his death, his son Philip attempts to honor his wish to be buried in China. In the 1980s, Philip returns to China with his father's ashes, but the Christian cemetery his father had designated has been replaced by a "large, boxlike, concrete apartment house, as bleak as a prison." His attempt to travel to the villages where his father worked is rejected by the Communist bureaucracy. Philip's reaction pinpoints his anger: "What burns me is that no one has ever heard of him. He might just as well never have existed."

When John Hersey visited China in 1983, he had undergone a similar disillusionment, leaving him to ask whether his parents' life in China "had been worth living." This novel is his attempt to answer that question. At one level, the answer seems to be that even a heroic individual's attempt to make a difference will be overwhelmed by the relentless, impersonal, and random march of history. As Treadup himself records in his diary, "I began to realize that I was caught up in vast forces—world currents . . . —which were to overwhelm the puny efforts of one small person." On the other hand, the very existence of literature such as *The Call* suggests that the effort itself yields an alternative answer. When historical literature is done well, history and the individual spirit are evenly matched and mutually enhanced.

FURTHER READING

Edwin Hoyt's *The Rise of the Chinese Republic* (1988) covers the history of the republic up to the eve of the Tiananmen Square demonstrations in 1989. In *John Hersey*

Revisited (1990), David Sanders pays particular attention to *The Call*, extolling it as Hersey's finest novel.

CHOSIN RESERVOIR RETREAT (KOREAN WAR) (1950)

The United Nations intervention in the KOREAN WAR in July 1950 halted the advance of the invading North Korean troops, forcing them into a rapid retreat across the thirty-eighth parallel, the dividing line between North and South Korea. Buoyed by the success of his strategy, notably his surprise landing of United States Marines at Inchon Harbor, the UN supreme commander Douglas MacArthur divided his forces on either side of the impassable Tabaek mountain range, which runs north-south. Supporting this disastrous decision was the inept military intelligence that seriously underestimated the strength and intention of the Chinese troops massed on the border. On the western side of the range, MacArthur placed his largest force, the Eighth Army, and on the eastern side, the X Corps, made up chiefly of the First Marine Division. After reaching the Chosin reservoir, close to the Manchurian border, the marines found themselves confronting more than 100,000 Chinese troops.

The subsequent marine retreat has become one of the most famous episodes of the war. From the end of November to December, a time when the fierce North Korean winter was settling in, the marines fought their way back along a narrow road, stretching 80 miles to the port city of Hungnam. Suffering from severe frostbite, exposed to relentless winds blowing down from Siberia, the heavily outnumbered marines maintained the discipline and fighting spirit for which they are noted, inflicting far more casualties than they suffered.

THE LITERATURE

The novelist and columnist James Brady (1928–) served as a marine in Korea during this period, an experience he recorded in his memoir *The Coldest War* (1990). In *The Marines of Autumn* (2000), he casts the retreat in fictional form, focusing on the figure of Captain Thomas Verity, a WORLD WAR II veteran called back into the service because of his knowledge of the Chinese language. His job is to intercept Chinese radio transmissions and interrogate prisoners to determine the extent of Chinese strength. To do so, he must operate close to the front line. No sooner does he arrive than the Chinese attack occurs, forcing him and his two noncommissioned aides to join in the retreat. The first leg of the retreat brings them to the town of Hagaru, from which he expects to be evacuated, but Verity is ordered to remain with the retreat to Hungnam. The march continues with the enemy attacking every night: "The Chinese were killing them. So was the cold." Interspersed with the main action are flashbacks in which Verity recalls his late wife and his daughter and experiences the dread of knowing that if he doesn't make it, his 3-year-old daughter will be an orphan. The flashbacks appear to be designed to provide a romantic counterpoint to the war scenes, but their saccharine sentimentality adds little to the story. However, the description of the march, which grows increasingly brutal as it progresses, powerfully captures both its horror and the enduring spirit of the men who undergo it.

In an afterword, Brady acknowledges that the character of Captain Verity was inspired by his company commander in Korea, John Chafee. Chafee later became secretary of the navy and United States senator from Rhode Island.

FURTHER READING

Martin Russ's *Breakout* (1999) provides a detailed account of the Chosin reservoir retreat.

CIVIL RIGHTS MOVEMENT (UNITED STATES) (1954–1964)

On May 17, 1954, U.S. Supreme Court chief justice Earl Warren announced the court's decision in the case of *Brown v. Board of Education:* "We conclude that in the field of public education, the doctrine of separate but equal has no place. Separate educational facilities are inherently unequal." On December 1, 1955, in Montgomery, Alabama, a woman named Rosa Parks was arrested and fined for refusing to give up her seat on the bus to a white man who was standing. These two events sparked the American Civil Rights movement, the African-American campaign to obtain equal rights. The Supreme Court decision calling for the desegregation of public schools "with all deliberate speed," effectively overruled the laws requiring school segregation in 17 southern states. The arrest of Rosa Parks triggered a black boycott of Montgomery's buses. These events also defined the areas where the struggle would take place: in the courtroom and on the streets.

The key figure in the boycott was Martin Luther King, Jr., a clergyman with a Ph.D. from Boston University, who would emerge as the single most important figure in the movement. King preached and practiced the doctrine, derived from Mohandas K. GANDHI, of nonviolent resistance even when violently attacked. This behavior was on display and sorely tested in 1957, when the Arkansas governor, Orval Faubus, tried to prevent the integration of nine black students into Central High School in Little Rock. President Dwight D. Eisenhower finally had to call in federal troops to guarantee the safety of the students.

The beginning of the 1960s saw the movement expressed in sit-ins, in which blacks occupied privately owned facilities, such as the Woolworth's lunch counter in Greensboro, North Carolina; freedom rides, in which northern whites joined blacks in attempting to desegregate bus and train stations; the integration of public colleges, such as the state universities of Mississippi and Alabama; and nonviolent demonstrations, conducted with extraordinary dignity in the face of tear gas, fire hoses, and attack dogs used by the local police in Birmingham, Alabama.

The high point of the movement occurred in August 1963, when 200,000 people (about one-quarter of them white) massed in front of the Lincoln Memorial to listen to King's "I have a dream" speech. It was an event that many people had feared would erupt in violence. Instead it produced what the columnist Murray Kempton characterized as "the largest religious pilgrimage of Americans that any of us is ever likely to see." The Civil Rights Act of 1964, begun by the Kennedy administration and enacted, thanks to the legislative skill of President Lyndon Johnson, in the Johnson administration, capped this early stage of the campaign.

The success of the movement led to an expansion of its goals. The murder of civil rights workers Medgar Evers, Mickey Schwerner, Andrew Goodman, and James Chaney; the brutality of the local police in reacting to a peaceful demonstration in Selma, Alabama; and the outbreak of race riots in northern cities, notably Detroit and the Watts section of Los Angeles, led to increasing militancy among younger blacks, impatient with King's nonviolent approach. Some adopted the principle of "black power," stressing the need for independence from well-meaning white allies as part of an altered self-consciousness, expressed in the slogan "Black Is Beautiful." Two extreme forms of this development were the Black Panthers movement in California, which called for armed retaliation against white society, and the Black Muslim movement, which sought total separation from whites. The charismatic spokesman of the latter position was Malcolm X, who later split from the Black Muslims and was assassinated by them in 1965.

Three years later came the event that shocked the nation and the world, the murder of Martin Luther King, Jr., by James Earl Ray, a southern white who offered no motive for his crime, leading to the suspicion that he had been part of a plot. The assassination triggered a series of riots in many American cities, as black Americans exploded in rage and frustration. The assassination a few months later of Robert Kennedy, the presidential candidate thought to be the most sympathetic to the African-American people, only intensified those feelings.

The legacies of Martin and Malcolm, the former representing the principle of nonviolence and the latter seeking justice "by any means necessary," represent the two currents of the movement, which now appear to have flowed into the mainstream. (See also AFRICAN-AMERICAN EXPERIENCE.)

THE LITERATURE

Alice Walker's (1944–   ) *Meridian* (1976) boldly abandons chronology in its account of the impact on the lives of three young people called to the service of the movement. The novel opens in the 1970s, some years after the movement's high point, then flashes back to a series of episodes that relate the experiences of three civil rights workers: Truman Held, a southern black artist; Lynne Rabinowitz, a northern, white, Jewish college student; and, principally, Meridian Hill, a southern black woman, who, at 17, is abandoned by her husband after the birth of her baby. Accepting a scholarship to attend a black college in Atlanta, a decision which involves leaving her child to be raised by others, Meridian meets Truman and, later, Lynne, and the three become involved in the Voter Education Project. Truman has a brief affair with Meridian but leaves her for Lynne. He and Lynne get married, and continue the movement's work in Mississippi, while Meridian, committed to the original cause exemplified by Martin Luther King, Jr., finds herself alienated by the rising tide of militancy in the movement. The emergence of this new militancy, excluding white participation, ostracizes Lynne, who becomes abused and self-destructive, guilty of the sin of whiteness. Despite the birth of their child and their move to New York City, Truman and Lynne separate. Lynne, who has been disowned by her parents, is left to struggle in poverty to raise her child. When the child is attacked and murdered, Lynne falls apart, and Truman abandons the struggle. Meridian discovers that she can accept the need for violence, but only from the traditional, simple, churchgoing people, "the righteous guardians of the people's memories," not the calculating, aggressive, educated young militants. In the conclusion, Truman is reunited with Meridian, but as a follower, not a leader. Meridian's patient, difficult struggle for self-identity serves as Truman's model of selfless service to the cause.

As a meditation on the Civil Rights movement, *Meridian* is notable for the honesty with which it explores the questions of violence, sexual roles, and the complexity of interracial relations. But the movement's major misstep, from the novel's point of view, is illustrated early on in the emblematic story of the "Sojourner," a beautiful, enormous magnolia tree that stands in the center of the college Meridian attends. Student demonstrators, furious at the college administration's refusal to permit a funeral ceremony for an expelled student, destroy the tree, the rich repository of folklore dating back through slave days. The destruction of the past in the name of future justice is a fatal error that Meridian comes to recognize and, in the course of the rest of her life, tries to rectify. The fact that the protagonists in this novel pay a severe price for their commitment does not, finally, negate the value of their struggle. In her 1967 essay "The Civil Rights Movement: What Good Was It?," writer Alice Walker summarized that value: "It brought us to Life."

FURTHER READING

Andrew Young's *An Easy Burden: The Civil Rights Movement and the Transformation of America* (1996) is a history by an important participant in the movement. Melissa Walker's *Down from the Mountaintop* (1991) offers perceptive analyses of black women's novels dealing with the Civil Rights movement.

COLD WAR (1946–1991)

The term *cold war* denotes the period of unarmed struggle between the United States and its allies and the Soviet Union and its allies in the aftermath of WORLD WAR II. In the course of 45 years, the two superpowers engaged in struggles and confrontations that fell short of actual hostilities, each side motivated by the fear of the other's achieving world domination. Although the period witnessed a number of "hot" wars that were rooted in the superpower struggle, notably in Korea and Vietnam, none of them directly pitted American and Soviet military forces against each other (always excluding the "military advisers," who seemed to be hovering in the background of all the hot spots).

This ideological struggle was geopolitical in nature. Each side was wary—even paranoid—about the spread of the other's influence, and each worked both overtly and covertly to undermine and counter the other. United States foreign policy—chiefly directed at the height of the cold war by John Foster Dulles, secretary of state during the Eisenhower administration, and first spelled out in an article by George Kennan, a noted Russian scholar and later American ambassador to the Soviet Union—was that of containment. To counter Soviet expansionism, the United States was willing to concede a huge sphere of influence to the Soviet Union but not to let it grow. American cold warriors feared the "domino effect," the toppling of one after another nonaligned, neutral, or democratic states when and if its neighbor was "subverted to communism."

The closest the two sides came to direct armed conflict was the Cuban Missile Crisis, in which the United States confronted the Soviets over the missiles the Soviets had installed in Fidel Castro's Cuba. The crisis proved to be a turning point in the cold war, suggesting to both sides the perilous possibility that the scenario of mutually assured destruction (MAD) could easily become a reality. Thus, in one of history's ironies, the brinksmanship of the missile crisis led to the beginning of disarmament talks.

Although the nuclear possibility receded, the conflict continued in the 1970s amid developments that favored the Soviets, as increasing numbers of developing nations chose the socialist road at a time when the Western nations, wounded economically by the Arab oil crisis and politically by the debacle of the VIETNAM WAR, appeared to be backing the wrong side, such as, in the CHILEAN MILITARY COUP.

Meanwhile, there was an ongoing hot version of the cold war, conducted by the secret services of both sides. Since neither side trusted the other to be truthful about its economic and military strength, especially concerning missile capabilities and atomic weapons, military intelligence assumed a significant role. The CENTRAL INTELLIGENCE AGENCY (CIA) for the United States, the British Secret Intelligence Service (SIS, sometimes also abbreviated as MI-6, its wartime name) for Britain, and the Komitet gosudarstvennoy bezopasnostĭ (KGB) in the Soviet Union all expended enormous sums on spying, contriving with surprising success to penetrate each other's intelligence agencies with double agents ("moles"). In the late 1950s, the CIA flew U2 spy planes 60,000 feet over the Soviet Union and deployed the Corona, the first space spy satellite. In addition, disseminating information or disinformation—elaborately structured fabulations about secret weapons and codes—was central in engaging each side's paranoiac tendencies. Paranoia intensified in the Western nations with the gradually released, increasingly sensational revelations that three high-ranking British diplomats (Guy Burgess, Donald MacLean, and Kim Philby), men with impeccable, establishment credentials, were spies, followed years later by the revelations concerning ANTHONY BLUNT.

THE LITERATURE

No imaginative writer successfully wrote one book on the cold war as a whole, although Norman Mailer's (1923–) *Harlot's Ghost* represents a heroic effort in that direction. But the cold war period and the atmosphere of anxiety that characterized it proved to be a boon for one genre, the spy novel. The cold war ushered in a golden age of espionage fiction, none more successful than Ian Fleming's (1908–64) romantic fantasies, the James Bond novels, counting among its fans President John F. Kennedy.

But the author who, working in the tradition of Joseph Conrad (1857–1924) and Graham Greene (1904–91), moved the spy novel into the realm of serious fiction, was John Le Carré (1931–), who used the spy novel, in the words of the critic Julian Symons, "as a means of conveying an attitude towards life and society."

In his *Tinker, Tailor, Soldier, Spy* (1974), Le Carré takes the reader into the labyrinthine depths of a continuing, sinister struggle between Moscow Centre, headquarters of the worldwide Soviet spy apparatus, and its counterpart Cambridge Circus, named for its London location, shortened to the "Circus." The Circus has recently undergone sweeping changes, caused by the death by heart attack of its head, known as "Control." A new management team has come in and proceeded to push into retirement Control's trusted colleague, George Smiley, a man whose unimpressive appearance, "small, podgy, and at best middle-aged," belies his cool intelligence and flawless intuition.

Olive Lacon, senior adviser to the "Cabinet Office" and watchdog of intelligence affairs, asks Smiley to conduct a private investigation to uncover a dangerous and destructive mole in the top echelon of the Circus. Smiley discovers that before his death Control had dispatched an agent, Jim Prideaux, to Czechoslovakia to bring back a Czech general, who could identify the traitor. Prideaux's mission was a complete failure: He had walked into an ambush and been shot, captured, and interrogated by the KGB, who seemed to know everything he had been sent to do. Prideaux was later repatriated and forced to retire. He is now teaching, under another name, at a preparatory school.

Control and Prideaux had narrowed the suspects to five people, one of whom was Smiley himself. The remaining four suspects are all part of the new team now running the Circus. Issues of trust and loyalty arise on virtually every page of the novel. Only Smiley, because of his disinterested stance, seems solidly outside the ray of mistrust. Yet as Lacon—who trusts him—puts it to Smiley: "It's a little difficult to know when to trust you people and when not. You do live by rather different standards, don't you? I mean you have to, I accept that. Our aims are the same even if our methods are different. . . . Difficult to know what one's aims *are*, that's the trouble, specially if you're British." Ricki Tarr, a marginal British spy, whose knowledge is crucial to Smiley's investigation, declares as he makes his revelations: "You must tell no one in the Circus, for no one can be trusted until the riddle is solved."

Domestic betrayal is a another prominent motif: Smiley's wife, Ann, a wealthy aristocrat, has had a public affair with her cousin, Bill Haydon, a respectable artist before he joined the secret service, and now one of the leading figures at London Station, headquarters of British intelligence. She is, in fact, "living quite wildly, taking anyone who would have her." And Peter Guillam, Smiley's trusted associate—the only Circus agent he does trust—is cuckolded by his Camilla, a beautiful 20-year-old flute player with whom he is living.

Smiley sets a trap for the mole at a safe house, from which it becomes clear that Bill Haydon is indeed the mole. He learns from Haydon that the betrayal was an "aesthetic decision" tied to the collapse of the BRITISH EMPIRE, which Haydon and his generation had been trained to administer. In his eyes, Britain is now reduced to being an American lap dog. (Haydon declares that the SUEZ CRISIS was the final indignity.)

Smiley also learns that Haydon's affair with Ann had been dictated by Karla, head of Moscow Centre, on the grounds that Smiley, knowing of the affair, would be blinded by it and thus unable to see Haydon clearly, underscoring the theme of the interrelationship of political and personal betrayal. At the end, Jim Prideaux, who was the former lover of the bisexual Haydon, exacts his revenge by penetrating the safe house where Haydon is being kept and murdering him, although, in keeping with the moral ambiguity that pervades the novel, no one accuses Jim of the deed.

Le Carré's novel seems to assert that governments are locked into an unending dance, of which the cold war is a model. As Le Carré put it in a letter to the periodical *Encounter* in 1966, "[T]here is no victory and no virtue in the Cold War, only a condition of human illness and a political misery." (As an added historical irony, it was later revealed that *Encounter* itself had been secretly supported by funds from the CIA, as part of the "cultural cold war.")

FURTHER READING

For overviews of the cold war, see Deborah Welch Larson's *The Anatomy of Mistrust: U.S.-Soviet Relations during the Cold War* (1997) and Scott Lucas's *Freedom's War: The American Crusade against the Soviet Union* (1999). Peter Lewis's *John Le Carré* (1985) is a perceptive study of the author's work.

—William Herman

COLONIALISM

Modern colonialism, which exploded during the 19th century, may be defined as the social, economic, political, and administrative measures powerful nations use to exercise control over less powerful people or less developed regions. By the time of WORLD WAR I, many European nations—France, Germany, Portugal, Belgium, the Netherlands, and, supremely, Great Britain (see BRITISH EMPIRE)—had relentlessly expanded. The United States played its colonial hand shrewdly too, acquiring Hawaii, Alaska, Puerto Rico, the Philippines, Samoa, Guam, Wake Island, and portions of Cuba.

World War I had a decisive impact on the international colonial scene. Germany and the Ottoman Empire lost the few colonial possessions they had left to Britain and France. But at the same time, certain colonies of the British Empire, notably Ireland and India, were exhibiting various forms of defiance, leading in the case of the former to the quasi-independent Irish Free State (see IRISH WAR OF INDEPENDENCE) and, in India, to the astonishing success of the civil disobedience movement, led by Mohandas K. GANDHI. WORLD WAR II left the European imperial powers too exhausted to maintain order in their troublesome empires. In 1945, Syria and Lebanon, and, in 1947, India and Pakistan, gained independence. The French attempted to hold on to Indochina, but they were defeated in the INDOCHINA WAR, which led to the independent states of Vietnam, Cambodia, and Laos. The 1950s witnessed the decolonization of Africa, a process that, with the exception of South Africa, was completed by 1962.

Neocolonialism (a term credited to Kwame Nkrumah, Ghana's first postindependence president) describes the condition of economic and technological control exercised by former colonial powers, particularly the United States and Soviet Union, in the postwar world. With the breakup of the

Soviet Union, the United States emerged as the major source of economic and cultural neocolonialism, aptly summarized in the term *McWorld*.

THE LITERATURE

Among the many novels dealing with the colonial experience, two rank among the fictional masterpieces of the 20th century, Joseph Conrad's *Heart of Darkness* (1902) and E. M. Forster's *A Passage to India* (1924). Each of these works incorporates a powerful theme, emerging out of the history of colonialism. Conrad's story examines the moral disintegration that the colonizer undergoes, while Forster explores the tragic gap, the failure "to connect," that inevitably emerges in the relationship between the colonizer and the colonized. The two works also describe two different forms of colonialism: in Conrad's, the rapacious exploitation of the resources of the colony for the benefit of the colonizer; in Forster's, "settler colonialism," in which Europeans occupy the colony, constituting a separate and privileged class within it.

Conrad's short but unforgettable novel, one that has much affected the course of modern fiction, is set in the Belgian Congo and narrated by a ship's captain in the Congo, Charles Marlow. At the core of Marlow's tale is the company's chief agent, Mr. Kurtz, whom Marlow has been sent to rescue from the interior. As he travels down the river, Marlow gathers fragmentary impressions of Kurtz. He hears company functionaries speak at once admiringly and bitterly of Kurtz's genius at collecting ivory and complain that everything belongs to him: It is *his* station, *his* river, *his* "Intended" (the woman left behind in London). Marlow's purpose, however, is to discover not what belongs to Kurtz but what he belongs to, "how many powers of darkness claimed him for their own."

Marlow discovers a partial answer in an essay Kurtz wrote to teach Europeans facing savage customs how to "exert a power for good practically unbounded" and to which he later added the postscript, "Exterminate all the brutes!" Increasingly, Marlow thinks of Kurtz as mad, more so when, looking through his glass from aboard the ship, he sees knobs atop the fence posts outside Kurtz's house—knobs he soon recognizes as human heads. Appalled, Marlow concludes that Kurtz has become dehumanized, "hollow at the core," but he fails to consider that, despite everything, the natives adore Kurtz and want him to remain. What Marlow will ultimately recognize is that Kurtz, however mad, "had kicked himself loose of the earth" and had become for the natives a kind of existential force they both dread and worship.

Terminally ill, Kurtz is carried to Marlow's ship, where he registers his eloquent protestations about his plans, his ivory, and his Intended. At last, he breathes his final words: "The horror! The horror!" Later, a native attendant enters, saying, "in a tone of scathing contempt: 'Mistah Kurtz—he dead.' " (In 1925, T. S. Eliot was to use the phrase as the epigraph to his poem "The

Hollow Men," one example among many of the novel's influence on later literature.) A year after his return to England, Marlow visits Kurtz's Intended, finding her in mourning. She begs to hear Kurtz's last words; Marlow replies that Kurtz spoke her name.

For most of the 20th century, *Heart of Darkness* has been read as a powerful attack on the rapacious greed and hypocrisy that characterized the type of colonialism exhibited in the Belgian Congo.

However, the Nigerian novelist Chinua Achebe's (b. 1930) stinging critique of the novel as racist marks a significant chapter in the ongoing debate over the historical limitations of certain works of art. Although literature lays claim to a kind of universal truth in its depiction of human nature, it is true that literary artists, for the most part, share the limited vision of their own culture. Achebe acknowledges that *Heart of Darkness* attacks European colonialism, but he argues that it betrays a view of Africa and Africans as primitive and barbaric that is not only typical of 19th- (and 20th-) century Europe, but also a distinctive feature of Conrad's personal psychology. Defenders of the novel hold that the prejudices it displays do not displace the essential truth of the human condition that it explores. Others maintain that readers, like authors, are also limited by their historical/personal frameworks and that their reactions should be seen within those frameworks.

"Only connect! . . . Only connect the prose and the passion, and both will be exalted, and human love will be seen at its height." Those hopeful but unspoken thoughts in E. M. Forster's (1897–1976) *Howards End* (1910) form a mantra that echoes silently through the tragicomic pages of *A Passage to India*. The novel is divided into three sections: Mosque, Caves, and Temple, and it is in the Caves of Marabar that the risks, frustrations, and possibilities of connection are exposed for the reader to contemplate. The novel's central characters are Dr. Aziz, a young Muslim doctor, cautiously pro-English, offended by, but willing to accommodate, the arrogance and rudeness of the Raj, the English settlers; Cyril Fielding, a middle-aged teacher and former head of the Government College who is Aziz's close friend among the British; Mrs. Moore, an elderly woman, newly arrived in India to attend the wedding of her racist son, the City Magistrate; and her son's fiancée, Adela Quested, also newly arrived, a plain, well-intentioned, but priggish, young Englishwoman. Another significant character is Professor Narayan Godbole, a wizened, elegantly clad, gracious, and articulate Brahman priest. Except for Professor Godbole, all agree to Aziz's suggestion that they visit the Marabar Caves.

Overwhelmed by the heat and the smells of the crowd also visiting the caves, Mrs. Moore tries to get out, but she is swept back, grows faint, hits her head, and is, above all, terrified by a dull echo, a "boum" that resonates in her consciousness. When the group emerges from the cave, Adela is missing. Aziz had accompanied her until, at one point, he loses his balance and lets go of her hand. Adela then wandered off to another cave. Aziz cheerfully reassures all that

Adela has surely joined her friends down the road, and he is appalled the next morning when he is arrested on charges of having assaulted Adela in the caves.

The arrest creates a severe strain between the English and Indian communities. Fielding defends Aziz, in defiance of the "club set," and writes to Adela arguing his friend's innocence. Adela begins to doubt the validity of her own charges, finally realizing that she had scratched the wall, producing an echo that frightened her, and had struck out at Aziz and fled untouched. Before an outraged court she withdraws all her charges. Aziz faints. Free from the law but not from his rage, Aziz seeks revenge, demanding damages or public apology from Adela. Fielding tries to deter him, but unfounded rumors of an affair between Fielding and Adela stir Aziz's fury once more, and Fielding, in disgust, breaks their friendship and leaves India. Adela returns to England—alone but having grown through suffering.

The brief final section of *A Passage to India*, Temple, counterpoints the reality of the cave with a transcendent time of rebirth, the rainy season. Professor Godbole, Aziz, and Fielding are reunited as Godbole presides at a Hindu birth ceremony; Fielding marries Mrs. Moore's daughter; and Fielding and Aziz almost become reconciled, but will not truly become friends again, Aziz says, until "we shall drive every blasted Englishman into the sea."

Forster's efforts to explore in the novel the political, philosophical, theological, and human implications of colonialism command respect. Beyond any of these, however, are the superb characterizations that dramatize his unforgettable but perhaps unattainable mantra—"only connect."

An assault also triggers the events in the *Raj Quartet*, Paul Scott's (1920–78) tetralogy about India between 1942–45: *The Jewel in the Crown* (1966), *The Day of the Scorpion* (1968), *The Towers of Silence* (1971), and *A Division of the Spoils* (1975). This time, however, the rape is real, its impact a terrible force throughout the tetralogy. The victim is Daphne Manners, a young Englishwoman profoundly aware of the strains separating the English, the natives, and the Anglo-Indians. The rape occurs at night on the mosaic floor of an isolated garden pavilion where Daphne and her Anglo-Indian lover, Hari Kumar, are sharing the passion of their first sexual encounter. Suddenly, a group of men is upon them, tearing Kumar away, binding his mouth and limbs, and then raping Daphne. Within a few days, several youths are arrested for the crime—Kumar among them.

Hari Kumar is a handsome, dark-skinned Anglo-Indian, well educated in England, incapable of speaking Urdu or Hindi, the basic Indian dialects in his canton, and hopelessly misplaced in the turmoil of caste and class—too English for the Indians, too Indian for the English. His particular nemesis is the superintendent of police, Ronald Merrick, a red-armed, blue-eyed, malevolent force omnipresent in the tetralogy and Scott's symbolic representation of the cruelest manifestations of colonialism. An English grammar-school boy of lower middle class origins, he has—an ironic touch Scott cannot resist—

absolute mastery of the dialects Kumar cannot speak, but also an English accent far less precise than Kumar's. He has long known about and resented the open affection shared by Daphne and Kumar (indeed, Merrick has proposed to her and been rejected).

Before the first novel had ended, Daphne dies in childbirth without ever implicating Kumar. A child of color survives to be raised by Daphne's aunt, Lady Manners, in blatant defiance of the outraged British community. Kumar refuses to testify at a preliminary hearing, is jailed, and, only two years later (in *The Day of the Scorpion*) does he learn of Daphne's death. Kumar wins his release, then disappears from the tetralogy. He is mentioned only once more at the close of the final volume when, in 1947, Guy Perron, a former classmate in England, calls on him, only to be told by a native boy that Kumar was out visiting a pupil. Perron leaves his card, but no message, convinced that Kumar was at last among people who wished him well. Scott's narrative ranges far beyond Daphne and Kumar, but Merrick remains a diabolical and destructive force throughout. He rises in status, leaving the police force to become an army captain, then a lieutenant-colonel.

In 1947, as England faces its inevitable loss of India and the *Raj Quartet* draws to a close (in *A Division of the Spoils*), Merrick does at last fall, his obituary indicating him as a staunch defender of the jewel in the British crown. The facts of his death are never released, but Guy Perron learns from native sources that Merrick was found on his bedroom floor "hacked about with his own ornamental axe and strangled with his own sash." There were cabalistic signs on the floor and "Bibighar" (the name of the garden where Daphne had been raped) scrawled in lipstick across a dressing-table mirror. The cause? One possibility is that Merrick, assigned the task of keeping peace between Hindu and Muslim on the eve of Indian independence, may have been felled by either side. It matters little which, for what is happening beyond the Merrick bedroom is the grisly train massacre of Muslims by Hindus. Guy Perron and Sarah Layton work side by side to help the victims. The jewel, much tarnished, will at last be loosed from the crown.

Whatever its flaws, the *Raj Quartet*, 25 years after its completion, remains a formidable achievement, deserving to be read as well as to be seen in the 14 episodes of its more famed Masterpiece Theater television version, *The Jewel in the Crown* (1983). The Indian-born novelist Salman Rushdie (1947–), who objected to what he regarded as stereotypical characterizations of English and Indians in the novel, thought the television adaptation "a marked improvement on the original."

FURTHER READING

Edward Said's *Culture and Imperialism* (1994) offers a reasoned but highly controversial point of view. Chinua Achebe's critique of *Heart of Darkness*, "An Image of Africa," is included in his *Hopes and Impediments* (1988). Michael Gorra's *After Empire: Scott,*

Naipaul, Rushdie (1997) is a useful study of how these authors reflect England's adjustments to its loss of empire. Salman Rushdie's comments appear in *Step across This Line* (2002), a collection of his essays.

—*Arthur Waldhorn*

COMMUNISM, FALL OF (1989–1991)

By the mid-1980s, the governments of the Soviet block in Eastern Europe—Poland, East Germany, Czechoslovakia, Hungary, Bulgaria, Romania, and the Soviet Union itself—began to reveal political and economic weaknesses of critical proportions. By 1989, the people's simmering rage over the suppression of freedom and, in Timothy Garton Ash's phrase, "the structures of organized lying," that defined Communist governments, erupted in public, nonviolent demonstrations. Another underlying cause of the demonstrations was discontent with the standard of living, the product of outmoded and rigid economic policies, summed up by a striking shipyard worker in Gdansk (see DANZIG), Poland: "Forty years of socialism and there's still no toilet paper."

The first of the nonviolent revolutions to topple a Communist government took place in Poland. Lech Walesa's Solidarity movement had agitated for free elections, hoping that the movement would be able to achieve a substantial minority. To its surprise, in June 1989, Solidarity won a landslide victory, establishing the country's first non-Communist government since 1945.

On October 23, 1989, the anniversary of the HUNGARIAN REVOLT of 1956, Matyas Szuros proclaimed a new Hungarian republic. On November 11, 1989, thousands of East Germans passed through the gates of the BERLIN WALL, an event that symbolized the reunification of Germany. Six days later in Prague, a peaceful, candlelit demonstration was broken up by police using truncheons to beat the men, women, and children demonstrators. The reaction set off two weeks of nationwide demonstrations, resulting in the fall of the Communist government and the establishment of the playwright and political leader Václav Havel as president. In Romania in December 1989, the corrupt Communist regime of Nicolae Ceauşescu collapsed. All of these events occurred within six months and all, with the exception of the overthrow of Ceauşescu, were nonviolent.

THE LITERATURE

In *Proofs and Three Parables* (1992), a novella by the distinguished scholar and critic George Steiner (1929–), the collapse of communism is seen through the fading eyes and broken heart of an aging, Italian proofreader, known to his comrades as "Professore." As a proofreader, Professore is a master craftsman, bringing to his job an attention to detail that reflects the high standards by which he lives. But he faces a personal crisis, the realization that he is losing his sight.

Professore had been a lifelong Communist Party regular until 1968, when his objection to the ruthless Soviet suppression of the Prague revolution led to his being drummed out of the party. He has joined a group, the Circle for Marxist Revolutionary Theory and Praxis, largely made up of expelled dissidents like himself carrying on the principles of Karl Marx, despite their impotent status as party outcasts. Together with his comrades, he watches the television scenes of Communist governments being overthrown in Warsaw, Berlin, Prague, and Budapest, appalled at the triumph of consumer capitalism and the illusion of freedom it offers. In a rich, rhetorical exchange with another member of the group, a Marxist Catholic priest, he sees communism's fatal flaw in having "overestimated man," having held too high an opinion of human beings, unlike the church, which offers the illusion of an afterlife, and capitalism, which distracts the people with toys and gadgets. The priest replies that communism's mistake lay in trying to ram its truth, if truth it is, down the world's throat. He praises America for its take-it-or-leave-it attitude—that is, its freedom.

Eventually the group, fearful of a neofascist takeover of the Italian government, agrees to dissolve. Professore, his eyesight seriously deteriorating, travels to Rome to visit a now-defaced memorial to a group of partisans, tortured and killed by the Nazis in WORLD WAR II. While there, he has a sexual encounter with a woman whose mother was a partisan, an experience that leads to a kind of reawakening. When he returns to his city, he applies for readmission to the old party, confirmed in his conviction that he had never really left it. He descends the dark stairway of the party building, realizing that "he had not held on to the banister. Not even once. But then one doesn't need one, does one, when coming home." Steiner seems to be suggesting that, like the Professore, communism had become blinded, having lost its way in the pursuit of power. Any possibility of its resurgence would depend upon its ability to regain the original ideas and ideals with which it began. This is the task of a proofreader: the correction of error, the restoration of the original intention. There is nothing to suggest that the author considers such a renewal possible or desirable; what he does seem to imply is the nobility of the effort.

FURTHER READING

Timothy Garton Ash's *The Magic Lantern* (1990) is an engrossing eyewitness account of the events that took place in Warsaw, Budapest, Berlin, and Prague in 1989.

CRETE, BATTLE OF (WORLD WAR II) (1941)

In April 1941, the German army invaded Greece in an attempt to save face for an Italian army whose 1940 invasion of Greece had been routed. Despite valiant Greek opposition, aided by British troops, on April 27, Greeks had to endure the sight of the swastika waving over the Acropolis in Athens. The final step in the German campaign in the Balkans was the island of Crete. To cap off the triumph on the mainland, the German general staff decided on an airborne invasion of the island. Although the British and Greek forces on Crete were hopelessly ill equipped to withstand a German invasion, they had one distinct advantage: prior notice of the German plans, thanks to the code-breaking activity of British intelligence (see ULTRA). As a result, when German paratroopers descended on Crete on May 20, 1941, they were met by troops who knew exactly when and where they would be dropped. As they floated to earth, the Germans were ducks in a shooting gallery. Of the 600 men in one battalion, 400 were killed on the first day of battle. But the lack of sufficient equipment and arms, along with the infusion of German reinforcements, overwhelmed the Allied forces. In a chaotic retreat, the British troops reached the southern port of Sphakia, from which some 18,000 soldiers were evacuated to Egypt.

Looking at the German casualties for an island whose strategic importance proved to be minimal, Adolf HITLER became skeptical about further use of paratroopers. The invasion of Crete proved to be their first and last attempt at a massive airborne invasion. From that point on, airborne German troops were used only for relatively small tactical advantages. Adding to the sense that Crete proved to be a Pyrrhic victory was the fierce Cretan resistance during the German occupation of the island, prompting extremely brutal German reprisals.

THE LITERATURE

The English novelist Evelyn Waugh (1903–66) was a member of a commando force that arrived in Crete just as the retreat was under way. Waugh's group was under orders to hold the line at Sphakia until the last possible moment, but his superior officer, acting not out of cowardice but on the feeling that the order would involve the waste of an elite corps of fighters, chose to have his men "jump" the line of troops waiting to be evacuated. The experience left Waugh feeling guilty and disillusioned. He recorded this experience in *Officers and Gentlemen* (1955), the second volume of his World War II trilogy *Sword of Honor*. The action is seen through the eyes of Guy Crouchback, the author's surrogate, who has enlisted at the advanced age of 36, relishing, in the wake of the Hitler-Joseph STALIN pact, a war against the twin evils of fascism and communism. But his ideals suffer considerably when faced with the inanities and injustices of army life. Here Waugh's genius for satire is given full expression.

Assigned to a commando unit, Guy is sent to Crete, where the retreat is a shambles, the kind of disorder that brings out the best and worst of human behavior. Representative of the latter is Major Fido Hound, a replacement officer who promptly deserts his troops and disappears, having been apparently murdered by a sinister noncommissioned officer. Guy's fellow officer and friend, Ivor Clair, also deserts. Under orders to surrender after the evacuation is complete, Guy instead escapes in an open boat. He narrowly avoids death on the boat and is recuperating in an Egyptian hospital when he learns of the German invasion of the Soviet Union (see BARBAROSSA). For Guy, a conservative Catholic, the acceptance of the Soviet Union as an ally has fatally wounded the cause for which he enlisted. In the third volume of the trilogy, *Unconditional Surrender* (1961), his anticommunist sentiments are confirmed when he acts as liaison officer for Communist partisans in Yugoslavia.

Waugh's trilogy bears a strong resemblance to Ford Madox Ford's (1873–1939) *Parades End* (see WORLD WAR I), in that both spotlight flawed men of good intentions who operate from what the world regards as an outmoded code of honor. Waugh's trilogy is laced with richly comic, farcical figures, but the comedy does not trivialize the historical events—it humanizes them.

FURTHER READING

Antony Beevor's *Crete: The Battle and the Resistance* (1991) discusses the fall of the island and the bloody aftermath. The second volume of Martin Stannard's biography, *Evelyn Waugh: The Later Years 1939–1966* (1992), offers a highly critical view of the conduct of Waugh's commando group in Crete.

CUBAN REVOLUTION (1956–1959)

In 1895, Cuba was still a colony of Spain when Jose Martí's Cuban Revolutionary Party launched a war of independence. Three years later, the United States joined the battle against Spain, and, in 1902, Cuba was proclaimed an independent republic. From the beginning Cuba's "independence" was seriously compromised by the Platt Amendment to the Cuban constitution, permitting the United States the right to intervene in Cuban affairs under special circumstances. In 1934, President Franklin Delano Roosevelt revoked the Platt Amendment, but by that time the island's economic dependence on the American market for its principal export, sugar, was an accepted fact. In 1952, a military coup overthrew the republican government, installing General Fulgencio Batista as president. Batista's corrupt regime maintained close ties with U.S. businesses, including the business of organized crime, which ran many hotels and casinos in Havana.

In 1956, Fidel Castro formed a group of exiles in Mexico, trained to fight a guerrilla war. With 80 men, he landed on the Cuban coast, where he suffered a serious defeat in his first encounter with government troops and was forced to retreat to the Sierra Maestra. For the next two years, the rebels, led by Castro, his brother Raul, and the legendary Argentine rebel Ernesto "Che" Guevara, gained the support of increasingly large numbers of rural peasants, as they engaged in guerrilla warfare. Accompanying the peasant support, a significant group of middle-class and business people, disgusted with the Batista regime, helped to finance Castro's cause. In late 1958, the rebels captured the provincial capital of Santa Clara. On New Year's Day, 1959, Batista abandoned Cuba, seeking refuge in the Dominican Republic. On the same day, Castro led a victory march along Cuba's main highway.

For Castro, the military action was only the first phase of what he proclaimed to be a "permanent revolution," which began with the nationalization of American industries, characterizing the United States as a "vulture . . . feeding on humanity." American overreaction to this rhetoric resulted in the 1961 Bay of Pigs fiasco, the CENTRAL INTELLIGENCE AGENCY (CIA)–inspired attempt to overthrow Castro using Cuban exiles. The following year, the United States initiated an economic blockade, followed later in the year by the Cuban missile crisis. By this time, Castro had moved into the Soviet sphere of influence, assuming more and more the role of a European communist nation, with Castro as dictator. Despite success in developing literacy and health care programs, the economy continued to suffer, leading to more repressive moves on the government's part. With the collapse of the Soviet Union in 1991, Cuba lost its most important trading partner. As a result, Castro, departing from his rigid communist principles, began to encourage foreign investments and to revivify the tourist industry.

THE LITERATURE

An interesting account of the military aspect of the revolution is contained in Jay Cantor's (1948–) *The Death of Che Guevara* (1983). Guevara was an Argentine physician and Marxist intellectual who joined Castro in Mexico, participated in the rebels' landing in Cuba, played a critical role in the final victory at Santa Clara, and became Castro's director of the national bank and later minister of industry. Cantor's novel is cast in the form of a first-person narrative, interspersed with excerpts from Guevara's fictionalized diary. In the section devoted to the revolution, Guevara describes Castro's "mad" plan to spark a revolution with a mere 80 men, but listening to Castro, he feels "limitless possibility. . . . Fidel was amplitude, Fidel was sweep, Fidel was permission." They set sail for Cuba on the "Granma," a hopelessly inadequate vessel that soon spouts a leak, forcing them to jettison some of their heavier weapons. Storms batter the ship, which runs aground in a swamp. There the rebels are almost wiped out by government troops lying in wait. A remnant escapes to the Sierra Maestra and, against all probability, becomes the core of the successful revolution. The novel goes on to explore his break with Castro over the economy and his attempt to spread the principles of the revolution to Bolivia, where, in 1957, Guevara is captured and killed. Implicit in this account is the assumption that the reader is aware of the mythical stature Che Guevara had acquired among young people in the 1960s and 1970s, as the embodiment of the revolutionary hero.

A less romantic view of the revolution emerges from two novels published in the 1990s, Cristina Garcia's (1958–) *Dreaming in Cuban* (1992) and Pico Iyer's (1957–) *Cuba and the Night* (1995). *Dreaming in Cuban* examines the divisive impact of the revolution on a family, some of whom became exiles in the United States and some of whom remained behind. The story looks at three generations of Cuban women, Celia del Pino and her daughter Felicia, who continue to live in Cuba, and Celia's older daughter Lourdes, who flees in 1959 after the birth of her daughter Pilar. The novel opens in 1972, as Celia, empowered by the revolution, is serving as a domestic court judge in her native village, Santa Teresa del Mar. Further evidence of her commitment to the revolution is her willingness to stand watch daily from her beachfront home on the lookout for a repeat of the Bay of Pigs invasion. Her daughter Felicia, once jailed for setting the face of her unfaithful husband on fire, lives in Havana, where she has become increasingly involved in Santería, the Cuban mix of Catholicism and an African tribal religion. Lourdes Puente, Celia's other daughter, lives in Brooklyn, operating a bakery that she runs with an iron hand. Her rebellious daughter Pilar is an aspiring artist, completely Americanized except for the deep connection she feels to her grandmother, whom she has never met. While pregnant with Pilar, Lourdes had been raped by rebel soldiers and, as a result, is vehemently anti-Castro. The story is told from the vantage point of these four women, particularly Celia and Pilar, whose bond, leaping across generations and cultural differences, forms the heart of the story. Eventually Lourdes and Pilar visit Cuba, where Pilar comes to recognize that she cannot live there, but where she achieves a deeper connection to her identity, particularly with Celia, who bequeaths to her a collection of letters to the man she loved, written from 1935 to 1958 but never mailed. These letters constitute a history of Cuba, seen within the confines of one family. Celia's last letter to her lover, dated January 11, 1959, summarizes the theme: "The revolution is eleven days old. My granddaughter, Pilar Puente del Pino, was born today. . . . I will no longer write to you, *mi amor*. She will remember everything."

Iyer's *Cuba and the Night* is set in 1987, when the stagnant Cuban economy and the increasingly totalitarian character of Castro's regime have created an atmosphere of decay and desperation. In this context, Richard, an American news photographer, engages in a passionate love affair with Lourdes, a beautiful young Cuban woman. But Richard cannot overcome the skepticism and emotional frigidity that controls his life. As a result, he loses her to a mild-mannered, unprepossessing English schoolteacher, willing to make the effort to rescue her from a Havana pervaded by secret police, privation, and despair, an atmosphere that intensifies erotic pleasure, but it also renders love impossible. Lourdes's critique of Castro invokes the other famous Cuban rebel: Jose Marti, "Martí was bigger than Castro. He had room for revolution and for Love."

FURTHER READING

Che Guevara's memoir, *Reminiscences of the Cuban Revolutionary War* (1968), remains an interesting, but necessarily biased, account. Kathleen Brogan's *Cultural Haunting* (1999) includes a detailed analysis of *Dreaming in Cuban*.

CULTURAL REVOLUTION (GREAT PROLETARIAN CULTURAL REVOLUTION) (CHINA) (1966–1976)

In 1966, Mao Zedong, chairman of the Chinese Communist Party, disturbed by what he claimed were increasingly bureaucratic and bourgeois tendencies within the party, launched the Great Proletarian Cultural Revolution. Mao's real motive was his fear of losing power to the party establishment and of the rivalry represented by Liu Shaoqi, who had assumed the title of president after Mao's "Great Leap Forward" program, an attempt to revolutionize Chinese agriculture, had proved to be a disaster. Mao promoted the Cultural Revolution as a power-to-the-people program that would bypass party leadership. After ensuring the continued support of the military, he enlisted in his crusade students in the universities and senior classes of secondary schools. The suddenly empowered students rose up against their elders, scorning traditional scholarship and humiliating their former teachers. Children were encouraged to denounce their families, and adults were ordered to report neighbors and friends for lacking the true Communist spirit. The students organized themselves as Red Guards, militant groups with the goal of enforcing the new policy, designed to eliminate any traces of Chinese traditional life as anticommunist and bourgeois. The Red Guards soon were out of control, creating terror and chaos, particularly in the cities. Eventually the army had to be called in to control the young militants.

Never openly committing himself to the revolution, though his tacit support was evident, Mao left its implementation to two close allies, his minister of defense, Lin Biao, who oversaw the spread of the new spirit among the military, and Jiang Qing, Mao's third wife, who was in charge of cultural activities, particularly opera and films. After the death of Lin Biao in 1971, the conduct of the revolution was left in the hands of Jiang Qing, Wang Hongwen, Zhang Chunqiao, and Yao Wenyuan; the group became known as "the Gang of Four." The death of Mao on September 9, 1976, led to the arrest, less than a month later, of the Gang of Four and 20 of their top associates and the formal end of the revolution.

During the 10 years of the revolution, more than 3 million Chinese, most of them party members, were denounced and purged. Under the guise of ideological purity, the Cultural Revolution created chaos and despair, from which China is still recovering.

THE LITERATURE

Anchee Min's (1957–) *Becoming Madame Mao* (1999) is a fictional biography of Jiang Qing, narrated by Jiang from her prison cell just before she commits suicide. Raised by her grandparents, Jiang (her childhood name was Yunhe) becomes entranced when her grandfather takes her to a Chinese opera. Determined to be an opera star, she runs away from home and joins an acting company. She marries a Communist Party official, joins the party herself, and is imprisoned, released only after she signs a paper denouncing the party. She changes her name (to Lan Ping) and wins the part of Nora in a Shanghai production of Henrik Ibsen's (1828–1906) *A Doll's House*. When the Japanese capture Shanghai, she travels to Yenan, the headquarters of Mao's Communist forces. She and Mao meet and fall in love, and after Mao disposes of his third wife, they marry.

The Cultural Revolution occupies a significant portion of the novel, it being the highpoint of Madame Mao's public life. Newly empowered by her husband, she uses her position not only to advance the revolution but to settle old scores with enemies and friends that she is jealous of or threatened by. She operates from her old Shanghai base to produce operas and films strictly adhering to the party line. At the same time she plays an influential role in the actions of the Red Guard. As the revolution proceeds, she manages to antagonize just about everyone but a few associates, relying on Mao to bail her out. Although he supports her in general, he manipulates her, alternatively fueling and frustrating her ambition.

Sections of the novel employ a first-person narrative, in which Jiang generally represents herself as the servant, if not the slave, of her husband, committed to carrying out his wishes even at the expense of neglecting her children and her life: "I live to please Mao. . . . I can't live without Mao's affection." But contradictions to this self-effacing claim occur throughout the novel. The other ingredients that go into the making of Madame Mao are the narcissism of the actress and the power drive of the politician. She overplays her role, expecting Mao to name her his successor. But it is clear that the fox has used her as a lightning rod, drawing negative criticism away from himself. On his death, she is imprisoned, ready to play the final act of her role as tragic heroine. What she fails to see is that the role she has been playing is not of a diva but of a Lady Macbeth. The novel is not a sympathetic portrait of Madame Mao, but, to its credit, she emerges, not as a monster, but as a badly flawed human being.

One might find a moral of sorts in Madame Mao's life, contrasting her to another actress who became the wife of a dictator, EVA PERÓN. Equally devoted to her husband's regime, Evita nevertheless maintained a genuine commitment to the cause of the poor and the women of Argentina. Her loyalty to them inspired a devotion that has continued into the 21st century, while Madame Mao is reviled in her native country.

FURTHER READING

Jiaqi Yan's *Turbulent Decade: A History of the Cultural Revolution* (1996) traces its rise and fall.

CURLEY, JAMES MICHAEL (1874–1958)

The mayor of Boston, intermittently from 1914 to 1950, and the governor of Massachusetts from 1935 to 1937, Curley was a product of the Boston slums who talked, charmed, and schemed his way up the political ladder. He came of age at a time when Boston was changing from a city controlled by the old Yankee aristocracy to one dominated politically by the immigrant Irish. Curley early on mastered the secrets of ethnic politics, which, combined with his personal charisma, helped him rise from alderman to congressman to mayor, despite having served time in jail for taking a civil service examination for a friend—just the kind of lawbreaking that endeared him to his constituents.

He was also a man who never quit. In 1918, after losing a reelection bid for mayor, he ran for Congress and was defeated. In 1920, he was reelected mayor, an office he was in and out of for the next 30 years. In the interims he served as governor of Massachusetts (1935–37) and congressman (1943–47). In 1947, at the age of 73, convicted of mail fraud and sentenced to federal prison, he was pardoned by President Harry S. Truman in response to a petition signed by more than 100,000 citizens of Boston and 100 members of the U.S. House of Representatives. At his death in 1973, he received the largest funeral in the history of the city, beloved by people who revered him as a saint, although they knew him as a sinner.

Curley serves as a prototype of a uniquely American phenomenon, the big-city "boss" politician who combined a populist appeal to his constituency with a casual approach to ethics.

THE LITERATURE

Edwin O'Connor's (1918–68) *The Last Hurrah* (1956) was a best-selling novel and successful film, whose main character, Francis Skeffington, was closely modeled on Curley. The novel focuses on Skeffington's final campaign for mayor, his "last hurrah," in which his nephew Adam serves as an observer. Like Curley, Skeffington lives in a large beautiful house, built under suspect auspices, quotes Shakespeare regularly, and delivers witty lines at press conferences, all the while enjoying the sport of politics and, in his fashion, overseeing an efficient, if not strictly speaking honest, government.

Some critics have pointed out that Skeffington is a romanticized portrait of Curley, faulting O'Connor for choosing to downplay the moral compromises and outright ruthlessness that any big-city boss would inevitably be guilty of. But the idealized portrait of Curley resulted in an enormously popular novel, to which was added the John Ford film adaptation in 1958, starring Spencer Tracy.

O'Connor said he wanted "to do a novel on the whole Irish-American business. What the Irish got in America, they got through politics; so, of course, I had to use a political framework." In doing so, he created a comic hero, who proved the truth of the adage attributed to another Irish-American politician from Massachusetts, Tip O'Neill: "All politics is personal."

FURTHER READING

Jack Beatty's *The Rascal King* (1992) is an intelligent, well-written biography of Curley's life and times.

D

DANZIG (GDANSK)

The city of Danzig (now Gdansk), long the site of conflict between Germany and Poland, has played a critical role in the 20th-century European history. In the 1919 Treaty of Versailles, the city, a seaport on the Baltic with a 96 percent German population, was declared a "Free City" under the protection of the League of Nations. The decision to cut Danzig off from Germany opened old wounds and became a symbol of the wrongs done to Germans by the treaty. In 1933, the newly elected German chancellor Adolf HITLER called for a revision of the treaty. Danzig welcomed the prospect of becoming part of a new, powerful German state and elected a Nazi local government. In 1939, the conflict between the Polish government and that of the city provided Hitler the excuse to intervene, leading to the invasion of Poland on September 1 and the outbreak of WORLD WAR II. Danzig was also the scene of heavy fighting near the end of the war when the Soviet army besieged the city. By the time it surrendered, most of the city's historic buildings were destroyed. After the war, Danzig became a part of Poland, was renamed *Gdansk*, and its German population was expelled. In 1980, Gdansk was the scene of a shipyard workers' strike that gave rise to a national organization known as Solidarity. By 1990, the leader of the Solidarity movement, Lech Walesa, was elected president of Poland.

THE LITERATURE

The German novelist Günter Grass (1927–) was born and came of age in the Free City of Danzig. Three of his best-known novels, *The Tin Drum*

(1959; trans., 1962), *Cat and Mouse* (1961; trans., 1963), and *Dog Years* (1963; trans., 1965), are for the most part set in Danzig in the period from the 1920s to the end of the World War II. The three novels have been published in one volume under the title *The Danzig Trilogy* (1980; trans., 1987). The city occupies a central role in these works, its checkered history constituting a microcosm of 20th-century Germany.

The Tin Drum opens with its narrator, Oskar Matzeroth, who is a 30-year-old inmate in a mental institution. He was born in Danzig in the 1920s to a woman whose husband may or, more likely, may not be his father. Oskar, even at birth, is painfully, often hilariously, conscious of the debased world he is entering. He chooses to stop growing at the age of three and, by incessantly beating a drum, communicates his rejection of the growth of Nazism in Danzig. Among the things the Nazis destroyed in Danzig was childhood, turning every little boy into a miniature soldier and every girl into a submissive daughter of the Reich, a potential breeder of the new super race. Oskar's refusal to grow also suggests his protest over the denial of his childhood.

But Oskar is no innocent victim. He is guilty, in the complex paradoxical scheme of the novel, of trying to evade guilt. In this respect Oskar represents his readership—primarily postwar Germany, attempting to blot out its past and, by extension, denying the connection between individual acts and collective history. He also represents the artist who cannot evade his responsibility to disrupt the accepted norms of an evil system. One example of Oscar's playing this role is his effective disruption of a Nazi demonstration. Because of his small size, Oskar is able to slip beneath the speakers' grandstand and sabotage the event by playing "The Blue Danube" and jazz tunes that leave the audience dancing rather than listening to Nazi rhetoric. But there are other times when Oscar goes along with the system, suggesting that Grass's satire is sometimes directed at himself.

Cat and Mouse, the shortest of the three works, focuses on the war years in Danzig. Its narrator, Pilenz, tells the story of his classmate Joachim Mahlke, whose distinguishing characteristic is an unusually large and unstable Adam's apple. At one point in their childhood, Pilenz sicks a cat on Mahlke, because the shifting Adam's apple gives the impression of being a mouse. Mahlke embarks on a career of strenuous heroism, ultimately winning the Iron Cross for bravery in battle, but the Danzig "cat," in the form of a Nazi schoolmaster, refuses to acknowledge his achievement, a rejection that precipitates Mahlke's death. This emblematic story underscores the cruelty and victimization visited upon those whose individualism poses a threat to totalitarian society.

Like *The Tin Drum*, *Dog Years* covers the period from the 1920s to the 1950s, the decade of the *wirtschaftwunder* ("economic miracle") of postwar Germany. The novel's complex, exuberant shifts in language and the various transformations of its characters make it difficult to follow, but its unifying tone, irony barely suppressing rage, compels the reader's attention. The chief characters are Walter Matern and Eddi Amsel, who meet as children in Danzig in the 1920s. Matern defends Amsel, a half-Jewish boy, from schoolyard bullies, from which emerges their complex, mutually dependent relationship of German and Jew, one of the novel's key themes. Amsel early on has developed a distinctive skill, the ability to create lifelike scarecrows that can move somewhat like toy soldiers. Nazi groups like the SA (Sturmabteilung) in the early 1930s prove to be ideal models for his art until a group of masked SA youth attack him, knocking out all of his teeth. Among the group is Matern himself, who has joined the SA as part of his restless search for an ideology to which he can commit himself. At the end of the war, Matern, a prisoner of war, is released and heads home, accompanied by a stray German dog he adopts. The dog happens to be Prinz, one of Hitler's dogs, a gift to him from the city of Danzig. Prinz has escaped from his master's doomed bunker in the last days of the war. Matern and dog team up to form a formidable antifascist duo, hunting down ex-Nazis, particularly the members of the group who attacked Matern's friend Amsel. In the course of these events Matern is himself exposed as an ex-Nazi and plans to flee to East Germany. The novel ends with a reunited Matern and Amsel returning to the abandoned potash mine in Danzig where the story began. In the mine—"hell itself"—they come upon 32 stalls in which scarecrows represent the full range of human folly and iniquity. Despite these revelations Matern clings stubbornly to the illusion that he can ignore the past and start over with a clean slate.

Still another Grass work that focuses on Danzig is *From the Diary of a Snail* (1972; trans., 1973). A mix of fact and fiction, the book is cast as a diary kept by Grass in 1969, while he was assisting the presidential campaign of Willy Brandt. Interwoven into his journal of the campaign is a historical account of the fate of the Jews of Danzig in the Nazi years and a fictional rendering of Hermann Ott, nicknamed "Doubt" (after the allegorical figure Melancholy in the famous engraving of Albrecht Durer). Doubt is a Jewish schoolteacher, hiding out in the cellar of Anton Stomma, an illiterate peasant, whose condition for helping is that he be allowed to beat Doubt regularly. The point both in Doubt's relations with Stomma and in Grass's political campaign is that progress moves at a snail's pace and that patience and persistence are critical virtues in the painfully slow journey to a just society.

FURTHER READING

Michael Hollington's *Gunter Grass: The Writer in a Pluralist Society* (1980) offers a cogent analysis of the role Danzig plays in Grass's work.

D DAY (WORLD WAR II)

See NORMANDY, INVASION OF.

DEPRESSION

See GREAT DEPRESSION.

DRESDEN, BOMBING OF (WORLD WAR II) (1945)

During the war, Dresden, Germany, was considered an unofficial "open city," in effect, a demilitarized zone, a designation that acknowledged its rich historical and cultural heritage, as well as its strategic unimportance. As a result of its open-city status, Dresden was filled to overflowing with refugees, orphans, and wounded soldiers. Nevertheless, on February 13 and 14, 1945, first British, and later American, bombers attacked Dresden, killing an estimated 80,000 civilians in the overcrowded city. Many died in the firestorm created by the bombing, which reduced the beautiful town to rubble. The one military target in Dresden was the rail yards, through which German troops could move from the western front to the east. The attack on the rest of the city was part of a policy designed to demoralize the German population and thus hasten the conclusion of the war. It has also been suggested that the patent heartlessness of the attack was an indirect message to Joseph STALIN from Winston Churchill, a reminder, as the war was drawing to an end, that the western Allies could be just as brutal as the Soviets.

THE LITERATURE

The Dresden bombing is a recurrent theme in the writings of the American novelist Kurt Vonnegut (1922–). Vonnegut served in the army during WORLD WAR II. Captured during the ARDENNES OFFENSIVE, he was a prisoner of war in Dresden before and during the bombing. He alludes to it in several of his novels, most significantly in *Mother Night* (1961) and *Slaughterhouse-Five* (1969). *Mother Night* focuses on Howard Campbell, a German American living in prewar Germany who is recruited as an American spy. He spends the war years pretending to be a loyal Nazi, but in the process the pretense becomes a reality. In the introduction to *Mother Night*, Vonnegut offers this description of the bombing: "There were no particular targets for the bombs. The hope was that they would create a lot of kindling. . . . And then hundreds of thousands of incendiaries were scattered like seeds on freshly turned loam."

Vonnegut's most sustained treatment of the bombing is in *Slaughterhouse Five*, a satiric but serious view of humankind's addiction to war. The subtitle of the novel, *The Children's Crusade*, alludes to the 13th-century religious movement in which children were enlisted in an attempt to recover the Holy Land from the Muslims. The implication is that all wars are children's crusades—manifestations of the immaturity of the human species.

The novel opens with a description of Vonnegut's return to Dresden as a middle-aged man, still trying to come to terms with his earlier experience there. This serves as an introduction to the story of Billy Pilgrim, an optometrist living in upstate New York, who is suddenly kidnapped by aliens, the Tralfamidorians. They bring Billy back to their planet and place him in a zoo, where he mates with another kidnapped human, a sexy movie star named Montana Wildcat. Eventually Billy returns to Earth to spread the gospel according to the Tralfamidorians, one of whose principles is that after death we go on living in some other form. In a flashback we see Billy, like his creator, a prisoner of war in Dresden. During the bombing, he and the other prisoners are locked in a cellar under a slaughterhouse and survive unharmed. In the aftermath they are assigned the task of carrying out dead bodies from the ruins. The descriptions of the removal of the bodies are particularly gruesome reminders of the insanity that war engenders, underscored here by the fate of one prisoner who is tried and executed for stealing a teapot from the ruins. The novel ends with the war's end: "And then one morning [the prisoners] got up to discover that the door was unlocked. World War Two in Europe was over." The quiet tone of the conclusion suggests that Vonnegut's long internal struggle to tell the story of Dresden has finally ended here, with it a personal peace, an acceptance of that "over which we have no control."

FURTHER READING

Alexander McKee's *Dresden 1945: The Devil's Tinderbox* (1982) provides a complete account of the bombing. Jerome Klinkowitz's *Kurt Vonnegut* (1982) is a concise critical study.

DUNKIRK, THE EVACUATION OF (WORLD WAR II) (1940)

The German blitzkrieg offensive in the spring of 1940 was so successful that the German high command feared they had advanced too far too quickly, just as they had in the opening months of WORLD WAR I (see MARNE). As a result, after encircling the British army and 100,000 French troops in the port of Dunkirk in Belgium, Adolf HITLER issued a stop-order, halting the German advance on May 24, 1940. The order was revoked two days later, but the halt had given the British just enough time to initiate Operation Dynamo, the code name for the evacuation from Dunkirk across the North Sea to England. The evacuation involved, in addition to a large British fleet, hundreds of small boats, carrying troops from the shore to the large ships. Many English civilian volunteers, sailing their own boats into waters in which German submarines and bombers were a constant threat, participated in the operation.

Exposed to enemy air attacks, the British troops seethed with anger over the relative paucity of protective cover by the Royal Air Force (RAF). The RAF had decided—wisely, as it turned out—not to commit its full strength in anticipation of the next, and even more vital, phase of the war, the BATTLE OF BRITAIN.

Despite the heavy German air bombardment, Operation Dynamo succeeded in rescuing more than 338,000 British and French troops. Were it not for the two-day halt, the greater part of these men would have been trapped in the Dunkirk pocket. Thus the culmination of a crushing defeat became, in the popular press and the minds of the English public, a miraculous deliverance. The disaster proved to be a propaganda victory that would help to sustain morale in the ensuing battle of Britain and the blitz.

THE LITERATURE

The Snow Goose (1941), a story by the American writer and journalist Paul Gallico, captures the view of Dunkirk as a miracle quite literally. The protagonist is Rhayader, a hump-backed hermit-artist living in a lighthouse on the English coast, where he has established a bird sanctuary. A young girl, Frith, brings him an injured goose. The artist and the girl nurse the goose back to health. Seven years pass and Frith, now a young woman, continues to visit the goose, who returns every year to the sanctuary. On one visit she discovers Rhayader outfitting his boat for the journey to Dunkirk. As she bids him farewell, she realizes that she is in love with the man.

The rest of the story is narrated by British soldiers recounting the extraordinary appearance of a goose hovering protectively over a small boat as it rescues soldiers through the night and by a British naval officer who spots a small boat with a dead pilot and with a goose perched on the deck of the boat drifting on the sea. The story concludes with the return of the goose to the sanctuary and Frith's recognition that the goose's flight embodies that of Rhayader's soul.

This story enjoyed great popularity in England and America, providing both consolation and uplift in the early years of the war. In that respect it is a representative example of the popular literature of the period, combining sentimentality with a vaguely spiritual theme. Similarly, in William Wyler's film adaptation of Jan Struther's (1901–53) *Mrs. Miniver* (1940), the husband of the heroine leaves in the middle of the night to sail his boat to Dunkirk. The film was an enormous success in England and America, winning the Academy Award for best picture in 1942.

Elleston Trevor's (1920–95) *The Big Pick-Up* (1955), written 15 years after the event, takes a more realistic view of the evacuation. *The Big Pick-Up* tells of the attempt of three soldiers in the chaos of a hurried retreat to find their company. When one of the three is killed, they connect with four other troops who are also cut off from their company. The leader of the group, the resourceful, steady Corporal Bains, displays the cool command and common sense that enables them to reach the beach. As they are being taken out to a ship, their boat is hit by a torpedo. Picked up by a barge, they eventually reach, in the words of one of the men, "'ome bleedin' 'ome."

The Big Pick-Up is a fast-moving, worthy war story. Its characters—the stoical leader, the quivering, fragile young man always on the verge of a crack-up, the salty working-class types who use wit and mechanical ingenuity to survive—are recognizable stock figures but well drawn in a story filled with exciting incidents. Added to these virtues is its efforts to de-romanticize the events it describes.

From both a literary and historical perspective, the outstanding depiction of the evacuation and its immediate aftermath occurs in Ian McEwan's (1948–) *Atonement* (2001), a beautifully written, riveting tale of guilt, penance, and forgiveness. The overall story deals with the consequences of a young girl's overactive imagination, which result in the humiliation and imprisonment of an innocent man who becomes the lover of the young girl's sister. Four years after the incident, in 1939, the man, Robbie Turner, is released from prison to serve in the army, where he participates in the retreat from Dunkirk. In the meantime the young girl, Briony Tallis, stung with guilt and shame for the suffering she has caused, becomes a nurse in an army hospital treating the Dunkirk evacuees.

The descriptions of the evacuation are breathtakingly vivid, as in this account of a dive-bombing attack on the road to Dunkirk, following Robbie's unavailing attempt to help a Flemish woman and her child:

> The blast lifted him forward several feet and drove him face-first into the soil. When he came to, his mouth and nose were filled with dirt. He was trying to clear his mouth, but he had no saliva. He used a finger, but that was worse. He was gagging on the dirt, then he was gagging on his filthy finger. His snot was mud and it covered his mouth. . . . [H]e turned to look back. Where the woman and her son had been was a crater. Even as he saw it, he thought he had always known. That was why he had had to leave them. His business was to survive, though he had forgotten why. He kept on towards the woods.

One incident on the evacuation beach illustrates McEwan's skill in integrating history into his fictional framework. An angry mob of British soldiers, furious over the apparent lack of support from the RAF, gather around a lone British airman and come very close to killing him. In its picture of an innocent victim condemned by appearances (in this case, his RAF uniform), the incident echoes the earlier injustice, Briony's false accusation against Robbie.

Similarly, in the hospital scenes, which we see through Briony's eyes, the accumulated pain and suffering, often described in excrutiatingly precise prose, suggests that she, as well as her patients, undergoing a penitential purgatory, although the book is not weighed down with thematic symbolism. On the contrary, the author never loses sight of the advice Briony receives at the beginning of what will later prove to be a successful career as a writer, "Your most sophisticated readers may be well up on the latest Bergsonian theories of consciousness, but I'm sure they retain a childlike desire to be told a story, to be held in suspense, to know what happens.' *Atonement* combines psychological depth, eloquent prose, and a powerful narrative line. In addition, as a fictional recounting of Dunkirk and its aftermath, it belongs in the front ranks of modern historical fiction.

FURTHER READING
Robert Carse's *Dunkirk, 1940* (1970) is a colorful account of the evacuation that includes excerpts from diaries and the personal recollections of participants. John Keegan's *The Second World War* (1990) contains a perceptive analysis of the evacuation.

DUST BOWL (1930–1936)

In 1930, at the beginning of the GREAT DEPRESSION, overproduction and overgrazing had stripped the Great Plains of the United States of its topsoil. Later, when a severe drought reduced the soil to a fine powder, violent winds then lifted the soil to create dust storms that left devastation in their wake. Crops were destroyed, and large numbers of livestock, lacking any grazing soil, died of starvation. Particularly hard hit were the Oklahoma and Texas panhandles and parts of Kansas and Colorado.

In desperation more than 300,000 farmers and their families abandoned their exhausted land and headed west, primarily to California, in the hope of finding work. Many of these refugees were from Oklahoma, but all of them came to be called "Okies." Long caravans of their cars and trucks snaked their way across the highways of the Southwest. When they finally arrived in California, they found that the only available work was as migrant farmworkers. Federal assistance programs enabled them to survive and, with the coming of WORLD WAR II, thrive, securing work in defense plants on the West Coast.

THE LITERATURE
The first 11 chapters of John Steinbeck's (1902–68) *The Grapes of Wrath* (1939) take place in the dust bowl, where a family of tenant farmers, the Joads, prepares to join the thousands like them and seek a new life in California. In Oklahoma, tenant farmers like the Joads have been evicted from their farms by banks and land companies. The land is arid, left parched by the drought, the relentless sun, and the winds that have sprinkled the shriveled crops with dust. To this scene Tom Joad returns from four years in prison and

joins his family in preparation for the trip west. Tom's mother, Ma Joad, is a stoic, courageous matriarch, who serves as the moral center of the family and the novel. The trip itself is a painfully slow and dogged test of endurance and patience, but the family eventually arrives in California.

Once there, they discover that the promised land is not what they had hoped. Efforts to exploit the migrant workers lead to violence that is only alleviated when the family moves to a government camp. At the camp, the family learns the value of collective social action, but the lack of work in the area forces them to continue their trip, bringing Tom into contact with striking workers. When the strikers are attacked by thugs, hired by the landowners, Tom kills a man and is forced to separate from the family, vowing to continue the fight for working people. His indomitable mother also promises to continue the struggle, asserting, "They ain't gonna wipe us out. Why, we're the people—we go on."

Published in 1939, *The Grapes of Wrath* became an international bestseller, translated into many languages and adapted, in the following year, into a prize-winning film directed by John Ford. Its success propelled John Steinbeck into the front rank of American novelists. In the ensuing years, the novel has been attacked as being mawkishly sentimental and thinly disguised propaganda. Nevertheless, *The Grapes of Wrath* continues to enjoy a wide popular audience, a fact that suggests that it has captured an American, if not universal, spirit. More than 60 years later, the simple dignity of the Okies justifies Ma Joad's optimism.

FURTHER READING

James Gregory's *American Exodus: The Dust Bowl Migration and Okie Culture in California* (1989) is a scholarly study of the Okies' experience and their later history. *The Steinbeck Question: New Essays in Criticism*, edited by Donald Noble (1993), reexamines Steinbeck's work in general and *The Grapes of Wrath* in particular.

E

EASTERN FRONT (WORLD WAR I) (1914–1918)

The war in the east began in August 1914 with a rapid Russian advance into East Prussia that came to a decisive halt in the battle of TANNENBERG. This demoralizing Russian defeat was at first offset by Russian victories in Poland against the Austrians at the battles of Lemberg and Warsaw. But, as they were to do throughout the war, the Germans came to Austria's rescue and eventually pushed the Russians back inside their own borders. Czar Nicholas II took command of the army, but the Russians continued to suffer serious setbacks. In the meantime the Russian home front had gone from bad to worse as the administration came under the influence of the czarina, Alexandra, and the mad monk Rasputin. By 1917, discontent within Russia had erupted into the full-scale RUSSIAN REVOLUTION (1917), toppling the czar's regime and eventually installing the Bolshevik government under Vladimir Ilich LENIN. In March of 1918, the beleaguered Communist government, fighting a civil war (see RUSSIAN CIVIL WAR) within its borders, negotiated a peace with Germany and Austria-Hungary.

When Italy entered the war on the Allies' side in 1915, Germany once again had to bail out the Austrian forces, fighting on the Italian border. German intervention led to the disastrous Italian defeat at CAPORETTO, from which the Italians were not to recover until near the end of the war, when they delivered a crushing defeat to the Austrians at the battle of Vittorio Veneto.

Elsewhere on the eastern front, the undermanned Serbian army, former subjects of Austria, proved to be more formidable opponents of the Hapsburg forces than had been anticipated. As a result they constituted a persistent and effective threat to the Austrians, already employed on the Italian and Russian fronts. Eventually, however, the Serbs were forced to abandon their positions before the Allies, slow to recognize the importance of the area, could provide reinforcements.

Further east lay the Dardanelles, controlled by troops of the Ottoman Empire. In 1915, the British attempted a joint naval and land offensive. The aim was to break through this "back door" to Europe and link up with Russian allies in eastern Europe. The offensive culminated in the disastrous British defeat at GALLIPOLI, which ended any effort to open up a new front.

THE LITERATURE

A famous novel set in the eastern front is Jaroslav Hasek's (1883–1923) *The Good Soldier Schweik* (1920–23; trans., 1930), a merciless satire of the military mind in general and the Austrian army in particular. In the deceptively simpleminded Schweik, Hasek created one of the great anarchic and disruptive figures in literature. The novel opens with the news of the assassination of Archduke FRANZ FERDINAND, an event that Schweik confidently predicts will have no serious consequences. Although he has been earlier discharged from the army for "feeble-mindedness," Schweik, like many Czechs, is called upon to defend an empire to which he unwillingly belongs. He is assigned the job of orderly to a chaplain until the chaplain, an inveterate gambler, loses Schweik in a poker game to Lieutenant Lukash. Soon the "Good Soldier" proves to be the bane of Lukash's existence, eventually getting the lieutenant and Schweik himself transferred to the Russian front. Schweik gets thrown off the train heading for the front and undergoes a number of Schweikian adventures before reuniting with the lieutenant. On the front lines he proceeds to wreak havoc with the Austrian effort. The final episode of this incomplete novel finds our hero being mistaken for a Russian soldier (he is wearing a Russian uniform at the time) and being placed in a prisoner-of-war work battalion. There Schweik's story ends, his tale left incomplete by the death of his creator.

Generally regarded as the satirical masterpiece of WORLD WAR I, *The Good Soldier Schweik*, like its WORLD WAR II descendant *Catch-22*, takes as its target the rigidity and arbitrary nature of military life. Schweik is the direct descendant of the "wise Fool" figure in literature, whose simplicity and literalness shine a revealing light on the hypocrisy and pomposity that surround him. He is the embodiment of folk wisdom and its awareness that mockery of the great and powerful is a weapon that the weak and powerless can always bring to the battle.

FURTHER READING

Winston Churchill's *The Unknown War: The Eastern Front* (1931) is a highly readable history of the war in the east. The 1963 New American Library edition of *The Good Soldier Schweik* contains a perceptive foreword by the critic Leslie Fiedler.

EASTER RISING, THE (1916)

On Easter Monday, April 24, 1916, armed members of the Irish Volunteer Army took control of the General Post Office and several other buildings in Dublin, proclaiming an Irish republic. The Dublin action was originally conceived as the first step in a national insurrection, but the national uprising had been cancelled when a ship bearing 20,000 rifles was captured by the British authorities off the coast of Ireland. Nevertheless, the Dublin contingent, led by James Connolly and Padraig Pearse, chose to implement the plan despite their certain knowledge that the insurrection would fail. Pearse, in particular, was convinced that nothing less than a blood sacrifice, drawing the analogy to Christ, would bring about the liberation of Ireland.

On Easter Monday morning, some 1,800 rebels took over several government buildings, using the post office as their headquarters. Outside the post office on that day, the rebels read their famous Proclamation: "[W]e hereby declare the Irish Republic as a Sovereign Independent State; and we pledge our lives . . . to the cause of its freedom, its welfare, and its exaltation among nations." The following day, British troops counterattacked, sealing off the post office. On April 27, the British began shelling the building. Within a week, the insurgents surrendered; by May 12, 15 of the leaders, including Pearse and Connolly, were executed for treason. The effect of the executions was to create martyrs of men who had initially been seen by many of their compatriots as merely foolish romantics. As a consequence the rising seized the popular imagination, galvanized the rebel forces, and led to the IRISH WAR OF INDEPENDENCE three years later. The Irish Republican Army (IRA), which assumed its name in 1919, has always maintained that its fighters are the direct ideological descendants of the leaders of the rising.

THE LITERATURE

Three of the leaders of the rising (Pearse, Thomas MacDonagh, and Joseph Plunkett) were practicing poets, but the insurrection achieved literary immortality at the hands of another poet, William Butler Yeats (1865–1939). In "Easter, 1916," Yeats, who was personally acquainted with a number of the leaders, describes the "casual comedy" of their lives suddenly transformed by the "terrible beauty" born of their tragic deaths. The description of this movement from comedy to tragedy perfectly mirrored the reaction of the Irish people to the event:

> All changed, changed utterly:
> A terrible beauty is born.

Yeats returned to the subject in "Sixteen Dead Men," in which he enlists the executed leaders among those figures from the past who died fighting for Irish independence.

In 1926, Sean O'Casey's (1880–1964) *The Plough and the Stars* (the plough and stars were the insignia on the rebels' flag) opened at the Abbey Theatre in Dublin. With bitter, tragicomic irony, O'Casey depicts the lives of Dublin slum dwellers against the background of the rising. For the poor, the military action is not an occasion of liberation but simply an opportunity for looting for some and, for others, a tragic waste of human life. In the latter category is Nora Clitheroe, who loses her husband, miscarries her unborn child, and finally goes out of her mind with grief. In O'Casey's rendering, the true heroes of the rising are some of the poor, comic people in the slums, like Fluther Good, who leads Nora back though the bullet-riddled streets, and Bessie Burgess, who feeds a child dying of tuberculosis.

The play sets up an ironic contrast between the high-toned rhetoric of military heroism and the bawdy, comic lyricism of the streets. For O'Casey, the former is the language of oppression and death, the latter the affirmation of freedom and life. Historical statistics would seem to support O'Casey's position: Of the 450 people killed during the rising, 200 were combatants on both sides and 250 were civilians, many of them residents of the slums.

The production was greeted with protests and riots by outraged Irish nationalists, appalled at its irreverent treatment of the event that, by 1926, had come to be regarded as the founding moment of the new nation. On opening night, Yeats, the artistic director of the Abbey Theatre, strode on to the stage to rebuke the angry crowd. Alluding to similar riots that had occurred at the Abbey in 1907 at the performances of J. M. Synge's (1871–1909) *The Playboy of the Western World*, he denounced the mob: "You have disgraced yourselves again. Is this to be an ever recurring celebration of the arrival of Irish genius. . . . From such a scene in this theatre went forth the fame of Synge. Equally the fame of O'Casey is born here tonight. This is his apotheosis." O'Casey, always true to his working-class roots, recalled that walking home after the performance, he wondered, "What in God's name does apotheosis mean?"

FURTHER READING

Joseph Coohill's *Ireland: A Short History* (2000) summarizes conflicting historical interpretations of the rising. Carmel Jordan's *A Terrible Beauty* (1987) argues that both the rising and Yeats's poem can only be fully understood seen against the Gaelic tradition, specifically the fate of the mythical Gaelic hero Cuchulain.

EINSTEIN, ALBERT (1879–1955)

Albert Einstein was born in Ulm, Germany, the son of a featherbed salesman. His family moved to Munich in 1880 and then to Pavia, Italy, when Albert was 15. He remained in Munich to finish his schooling but left within a year. Famously mediocre in his early studies, he gained admittance to the prestigious Eidgenossische Technische Hochschule (ETH) in Zurich on a second try and graduated in 1900, a good but not exceptional student. He became a Swiss citizen and fell in love with a Serbian woman, Mileva Malic. They had a daughter, who was given up for adoption, but they married in 1903 and would later have two sons. Because his grades had not been high enough to earn him a teaching position at ETH, Einstein worked first as a high-school teacher and, in 1902, took a job at the Swiss Patent Office in Bern. A most unlikely stage was set for a major revolution in modern science, which would permanently alter our conception of time.

Time, in the view of Isaac Newton (1642–1727), and according to our common sense, existed independent of any observer and flowed at a constant rate everywhere in the universe. But experiments performed in the late 19th century involving the propagation of light called these self-evident principles into question.

According to Newton, motion in space must be measured in relation to the speed of the observer. Light, for example, would move away at the same speed in every direction from a body at rest in absolute space, but it would seem to move slower relative to a body moving in the same direction (you would subtract the speed of the body from that of light) and faster relative to a body moving in the opposite direction (you would add the speed in this case). However, in an experiment measuring the speed of light performed in 1881 by Albert Michelson and Edward Morley, Newton and common sense were contradicted. Earth is a body moving in absolute space, and therefore light moving in the same direction as Earth should appear to be moving more slowly than light moving in the opposite direction. But Michelson and Morley found that light appeared to travel at the same speed in all directions, despite the Earth's movement. The electromagnetic laws of James Clerk Maxwell also showed troubling deviations in calculations when the observer was in motion. These results could be explained only by questioning the experimental methods and execution or by acknowledging that since the speed of light remained constant in all directions regardless of the speed of the observer with relation to any arbitrarily fixed frame of reference, there must be distortions in space and time to accommodate the data.

As early as 1899, Einstein, as he indicated in a letter to Mileva, had suspected that the classical Newtonian model of the universe was at fault. Working in the same patent office in Bern was Michele Besso, of whom Einstein said he "could not have found a better sounding board in the whole of Europe." In May 1905, Besso helped Einstein get past the difficult-to-abandon claims of classical physics. Einstein realized that neither time nor space was absolute, since the speed of light was. Time and space are relative: Time moves slower and space contracts for a person or object the greater the speed relative to an observer. Newtonian calculations and Einsteinian calculations are difficult to distinguish in everyday life, that is, while traveling at comprehensible speeds. But as bodies approach the speed of light, the differences are highly significant. And the consequences even for our commonsense reality are momentous as well. Relativity, when applied to mass and energy, yields the famous equation $E=mc^2$ (energy equals the mass multiplied by the speed of light squared), the underlying principle of the atomic bomb.

As the 19th century ended, many scientists were proclaiming the "end of physics," insisting that all major theories were in place and that there was nothing left for physicists to do but to fill in the details. On June 30, 1905, with Einstein's submission of his paper "On the Electrodynamics of Moving Bodies," a decisive challenge had been offered to the Newtonian universe, and new worlds of inquiry would soon open.

In 1911, Einstein became a professor at the German University in Prague. By 1912, he was professor of theoretical physics at ETH. In 1915, with his marriage to Mileva falling apart, Einstein completed his general theory of relativity. (The special theory of 1905 had dealt with bodies in isolation from other forces; the general theory took gravity into account.) In the following years, he became seriously ill, near death, in fact, and was nursed back to health by his cousin Elsa, whom he married in 1919. In 1921, Einstein won the Nobel Prize for physics, but steering away from controversy, the committee honored him for neither the special nor the general theory of relativity, but for his work on the photoelectric effect, also completed in 1905.

Einstein had never been a practicing Jew, but with the rise of Nazism his position in Germany became untenable. In 1933, he and Elsa sailed for the United States, where Einstein accepted a position at the Institute for Advanced Study in Princeton. In 1936, Elsa died.

The menace of Nazi Germany continued to grow. In August 1939, nuclear physicist Leo Szilard drafted a letter, which was signed by Einstein and sent to President Franklin Roosevelt, warning that a nuclear weapon could be developed in the near future and that Germany might already be working on it. There were three follow-up letters, which contributed significantly to the launching of the MANHATTAN PROJECT and the development of America's first atomic weapons. Einstein himself never took part in the project. He became an American citizen in 1940 and remained at Princeton until his death from heart failure in 1955.

THE LITERATURE

Alan Lightman's (1948–) *Einstein's Dreams* (1993) is a remarkable novel that focuses on the days leading up to Einstein's great breakthrough in 1905. A prologue, three interludes, and an epilogue show us Einstein in his perplexity and give us a glimpse of his friendship with Michele Besso. But the meat of the novel is the series of dreams Einstein is imagined to have had from April 14 until June 28, all set in a meticulously described Bern. The dreams explore different conceptions of time. In one dream, for example, time is a circle, and everything that happens will happen again and again. Most are unaware of this, but some townspeople know and are tormented by their knowledge. In another dream, cause and effect are related erratically, so that causes sometimes precede and sometimes follow effects, with the consequence that people learn to live in the present. In another, time is a "rigid, bonelike structure, extending infinitely ahead and behind, fossilizing the future as well as the past." Here there is no free will, no sense of responsibility for one's actions.

We do not directly gain insight into the particular theory of time developed by Einstein, but we understand the immense anxiety of overturning the Newtonian, commonsense conception of time and get a taste of what possibilities are unleashed by such iconoclasm. In addition, the connection between conceptions of time and moral outlook is made explicit, making us aware that a conception of time is an essential part of any moral vision, whether acknowledged or not.

FURTHER READING

For a biography of Einstein, see *Albert Einstein: A Biography* by Albrecht Folsing (1998). A more technically oriented account can be found in Abraham Pias's *Subtle Is the Lord: The Science and the Life of Albert Einstein* (1982). For an intelligible account of the implications of Einstein's theories, see Paul Davies's *About Time: Einstein's Unfinished Revolution* (1995) or, for those with elementary mathematics, Wesley C. Salmon's *Space, Time & Motion: A Philosophical Introduction* (1975).

—Karl Malkoff

EXISTENTIALISM

Although rooted in 19th-century ideas, particularly those of the Danish philosopher Søren Kierkegaard and the German philosopher Friederich Nietzsche, existentialism assumed a prominent role in philosophical and literary life in the West after WORLD WAR II, mirroring as it did the spiritual crisis that many were undergoing at that time. Alienation, the loss of sustaining religious belief, the sense of anxiety and guilt, the growing conviction that life was, at bottom, meaningless—all were given powerful and explicit voice in existentialist thought. Central to existentialism is a critique of the traditional idea that within each human being there is a distinctive essence, a soul, in religious terms, that is the source of the true self. In place of this conception, existentialism holds that we create our selves by our individual choices, that one's "essence" is nothing more the sum total of one's existence. The existentialist formula expressing this conception is "Existence precedes essence." Equally important is the focus on the individual responsibility for the choices he or she makes and the actions that express these choices. Choice implies freedom. But freedom exists within the twin boundaries that frame our choices, birth and death, the two absolutes that admit no choice and illustrate life's absurdity. It is absurd that we are born and absurd that we die.

THE LITERATURE

The most important 20th-century philosopher associated with existentialism was Martin Heidegger (1889–1976), whose *Being and Time* (1927; trans., 1962) offered an alternative to the traditional separation of subject and object, observed and observer, by describing human existence as a "being there," a "situated" time-bound consciousness aware of the past and the future and filled with anxiety by the knowledge of its own death. To evade that awareness, we use language to shield ourselves, thus living an "inauthentic" life, a life of denial, characterized by depersonalizing generalizations. An example of the latter, drawn from Leo Tolstoy's (1828–1910) *The Death of Ivan Ilych* (1886), is the statement "all men are mortal," a truth rendered abstract and unreal by its universality; in saying "all men," we arm ourselves against the reality of "I am mortal." But the authentic life is there for us to choose, and in that choice lies our freedom. Heidegger's difficult language and arcane ideas were adapted and made more accessible by Jean-Paul Sartre (1905–80), whose work bridged the gap between philosophy and literature. In literature, the term *existentialist* necessarily takes on a looser, less systematic meaning than it does in philosophy, but even existential philosophers, notably Kierkegaard, Nietzsche, and Sartre, have had a tendency to rely on literary devices in communicating their ideas.

As in philosophy, there were 19th-century forerunners of existential literature, notably Leo Tolstoy, as we have seen, and his great Russian contemporary Fyodor Dostoyevsky (1821–81), whose *Notes from Underground* (1864) is a passionate monologue by an embittered, angry, self-destructive figure, defiantly asserting his freedom to say "no" to technological progress and the "good life." His transatlantic equivalent is the eponymous hero of Herman Melville's (1819–91) *Bartleby the Scrivener* (1853), whose simple but resolute "I prefer not to" exhibits the individual's ontological freedom.

In the 20th century, existentialist ideas take a more nihilistic turn in the novels and stories of Franz Kafka (1883–1924), which are peopled with characters engaged in a quest to determine the meaning of existence, but who are frustrated and condemned by an inexplicable system. His Spanish contemporary Miguel de Unamuno represents in his fiction and nonfiction the need to create meaning in one's life regardless of the final truth. In France, André Gide (1869–1951) explored the theme of the "gratuitous act," the unmotivated deed, a demonstration of the essential freedom that underlies the human condition.

The three figures most intimately associated with literary existentialism are Jean-Paul Sartre, Simone de Beauvoir (1908–86), and Albert Camus (1913–60). Although the relationship of Sartre and Camus was a stormy one and the personal life of De Beauvoir and Sartre raises eyebrows among feminists, all three benefited creatively and intellectually from their interactions.

For many, the quintessential existentialist fiction is Sartre's *Nausea* (1938; trans., 1949), a novel cast in the form of the diary of Antoine Roquentin, a historian/biographer. The diary details Roquentin's daily routine, his library research on the 18th-century subject of his projected biography, his casual encounters, sexually and socially, with others, but it primarily deals with his overwhelming sense of nausea. The nausea becomes the precondition for a revelation that comes to him upon encountering the root of an old chestnut tree: "And then, all of a sudden, there it was, clear as day; existence had suddenly unveiled itself." And the unveiling brings with it the realization that it exists for no reason. It is absurd. Existence is not necessary; it is contingent, something that has happened by chance. Existence is naked and formless and therefore beyond rational categories. Worse still, it is nothingness. And yet, Roquentin discovers something of value, represented in the song "Some of These Days," written by a New York Jew and sung by a black American woman. Listening to the tune, Roquentin declares, "I feel something brush against me and I dare not move because I am afraid it will go away . . . a sort of joy." He resolves to write a novel. Perhaps, as the song does for the composer and the singer, it will justify his existence.

During his lifetime, Albert Camus always rejected the term *existentialist.* But his fiction, such as his 1942 novel *The Stranger,* and his plays, such as his 1945 *Caligula,* as well as his powerful 1942 metaphysical essay "The Myth of Sisyphus," invoke certain existentialist themes, particularly the notion of the absurd. In the novel commonly regarded as his finest, *The Fall* (1956; trans., 1957), Camus engages the basic existentialist question of the inauthentic life. The first-person narrator, who calls himself Jean-Baptiste Clamence, is a Parisian, now living in Amsterdam, telling his story, his confession, to a silent listener in a local bar. In his former life in Paris, Clamence had been a successful lawyer or, rather, had played that role, since role-playing and judging people are the chief occupations of a Parisian. Clamence had enjoyed great success in this world, both professionally and socially. He is on top of the world. His fall begins when, one evening, returning home over a bridge, he hears the sound of laughter but looking around, can find no one. Some time later, while passing over the same bridge in Paris, he walks by a woman leaning against the rail. A moment later he hears a splash and a voice crying for help. He moves on without helping. Years later, when he is on board a ship, he sees something floating in the ocean, thinks for a moment that it might be a person drowning, but a second later recognizes that it is simply flotsam. He realizes that the laughter and the cry for help that he ignored will haunt him for the rest of his life. As a result, he begins to examine his life and to see himself as split in two, the outer self, acting, and the inner self, alienated by the process of self-reflection. In response, he develops the split role of judge/penitent. It is his role to bring others to acknowledge their guilt (for everyone is guilty), while continuing to acknowledge his own. In the novel's conclusion his listener visits him as he lies suffering from a fever in his room. As he tries to draw his listener into the elaborate web of guilt and penance he has woven, the listener responds with a laugh. The laugh, plus the revelation that the listener is himself a Paris lawyer, leaves open the question of whether or not Clamence is talking to himself in some delusional state. The final interpretation, as well as the application of Clamence's confession to life, becomes the responsibility of the individual reader.

The critic Brian Fitch raises an interesting point about the novel's relation to existentialism: In 1952, Camus had a falling out with Sartre, more serious and long-lasting than the rift depicted in de Beauvoir's *The Mandarins*. Echoes of the language of the quarrel appear in *The Fall* in a manner that might suggest Camus's acknowledging the validity of Sartre's criticism of him. But Fitch argues that Clamence's comments—"Once upon a time, I was always talking of freedom. At breakfast I used to spread it on my toast"—constitute "a kind of parody of Sartrean existentialism."

Simone de Beauvoir's *The Mandarins* (1954; trans., 1956) is less an existentialist novel than a novel about existentialists. Drawing on her long relationship with Jean-Paul Sartre and their friendship with Albert Camus, she creates an autobiographical story that fictionalizes the events surrounding the lives of these three people. The story opens in 1944 at a Christmas party in recently liberated Paris, when Anne (the de Beauvoir character) and Robert (Sartre) join Henri (Camus), his lover, Paula, and their friends, who had assisted Henri in publishing the Resistance newspaper *L'Espoir*. Anne and Robert are the married parents of a teenage daughter, Nadine.

The story is told in a first-person narration by Anne and, alternately, from the third-person perspective of Henri. Anne's account primarily centers on her passionate love affair with an American writer Lewis (based upon de Beauvoir's love affair with the Chicago-based novelist Nelson Algren, best known as the author of *The Man with the Golden Arm*). Although deeply in love, Anne finds herself more profoundly connected to Robert and her life in France. Eventually frustrated by her ambivalence, Lewis breaks off the relationship. The central event in Henri's story is the breakup of his friendship with Robert. He and Robert had been the leaders of a postwar effort to establish a left-wing alternative to communism, but sympathetic to the goals of the Soviet Union. The split, which mirrors closely an actual quarrel between Sartre and Camus, erupts over Henri's revelation in 1949 of the existence of slave-labor camps (see GULAG) in the Soviet Union. To Robert, such exposure undermines the efforts to spread socialism throughout the world and strengthens the hand of the United States in the newly emerging COLD WAR. For Henri, any attempt to cover up the truth is a basic betrayal of his ideals. The rift is healed when Henri finds himself in a similar dilemma, where he has to compromise his integrity in order to save the life of his mistress. Both come to recognize that other demands, personal or political, inevitably complicate and taint one's idealism, leaving one, at best, with a choice between the lesser of two evils.

Among American novels influenced by existentialism, the most notable are Ralph Ellison's (1914–94) *The Invisible Man* (1952), Saul Bellow's (1915–) *Herzog* (1964) and Norman Mailer's (1923–) *An American Dream* (1965). The protagonists of these novels are searching in an alien world, undergoing the crisis of identity and loss of faith that are the existentialist preconditions for the discovery of the self. Among those works that reflect the religious influence of Kierkegaard are Flannery O'Connor's (1925–64) powerful short stories and her novel *The Violent Bear It Away* (1960) and Walker Percy's (1916–90) *The Moviegoer* (1961).

FURTHER READING

An excellent introduction to existentialist ideas is William Barrett's *Irrational Man* (1958). Catharine Brosnan's *Existential Fiction* (2000) provides a useful overview of the subject, and Brian Fitch's *The Fall: A Matter of Guilt* (1995) offers a number of interesting approaches to Camus's novel.

F

FASCISM

A political ideology that glorifies the state, fascism also emphasizes the superiority of the race associated with the state and stresses the danger to the national health of the "contaminating" presence of minority populations, such as Jews or foreigners. A fascist government is headed by an all-powerful leader, "a strong man," who claims that he will lead the nation to recapture its idealized past glory.

Fascism developed in Europe in the aftermath of WORLD WAR I in response to economic turmoil and the growing threat represented by various forms of socialism. Like socialism, fascism made its appeal to the masses. Its torch-lit parades, featuring massive columns of men in uniform, stirred the blood and emotions of many of those disaffected in the aftermath of the great war. But in addition to the circus, fascism offered bread, promoting economic recovery and governmental efficiency ("making the trains run on time") for its followers, as well as terror and death for its opponents.

In 1922, Benito Mussolini adopted the term *fascism* to describe his newly established government in Italy. In this early manifestation, following his successful coup in 1922, Mussolini acted within the framework of a democratic system. In 1925, after murdering a prominent political opponent, Italian Fascists moved toward a totalitarian regime in which all other parties were outlawed. Adolf HITLER's rise to power in Germany followed a similar pattern. When he became chancellor in 1933, he was in effect the head of a coalition government. In the following year, after the death of the German president Hindenburg, he became the *Führer*, the absolute dictator. In the case of the third prominent fascist dictator of the century, Francisco Franco, fascism took a more conciliatory turn, after his victory in the SPANISH CIVIL WAR. His military dictatorship was mitigated by his attempts to balance the claims of important groups within Spain. Finally, after WORLD WAR II, during which Spain had wisely remained neutral, he abandoned fascist ideology itself. Examples of modified fascist regimes include those of Antonio Salazar in Portugal and Juan PERÓN in Argentina.

THE LITERATURE

The writer most conspicuously associated with fascism is Louis-Ferdinand Céline (1894–1961), the pen name of Louis-Ferdinand Destouches, a practicing physician, who used his writing as an outlet for the extraordinary hatred and contempt he felt for human life in all its forms. The publication in 1932 of his most famous work, *Journey to the End of the Night* (1932; trans., 1934), created a literary sensation, both for its tone and its content. The tone derives from the language and attitude of its first-person narrator, Bardamu, who raises vituperation and hatred to the level of art. (This is at least the opinion of some readers; others are so repelled by the novel's nihilism as to deny it the label *art*.) Its story begins with the narrator's impulsive enlistment in the army prior to the outbreak of World War I. His description of the generals, politicians, profiteers, and passive, ignorant citizenry amounts not just to a denunciation of war but of the entire civilization. After the war, Bardamu goes to West Africa (Cameroon), where the evils of COLONIALISM are matched, in the narrator's view, by the inferiority of the African race. From here he travels to America, affording him the opportunity to denounce the greed and materialism of American society. (His one exception is American women, whom he celebrates.) Unable to find any satisfaction in these places, he returns to Paris to work as a doctor in Clichy, a working-class section of Paris. There he ministers to prostitutes, pimps, and criminals. But by this time it's clear that it's not the sordid society that is the subject of the novel but the impact of that sordidness on the disordered mind of the narrator. His reaction to the disease of modern life is so extreme that he looks for an apocalyptic resolution, the blood and fire of a cleansing war that brings his vision into line with that in Hitler's *Mein Kampf.* And just as Hitler did, Céline sees the source of the decay of modern civilization in the Jews.

In and of itself, *Journey* is more nihilist than fascist, but as the 1930s moved on, Céline's nihilism steadily metamorphosed into fascism. His next novel, *Death on the Installment Plan* (1936; trans., 1938), focuses on the childhood and adolescence of its main character, Ferdinand. As in *Journey*, the outline of the events closely corresponds to Céline's own life history. These incidents are not really autobiographical; they are distortions of his actual life designed to make them appear infinitely worse than they appear to have been. Between 1936 and 1941, he wrote several virulently anti-Semitic pamphlets;

in one he called for a Franco-German alliance that would get rid of Jews and their influence on the culture. His collaboration with the Nazi occupation of France forced him to escape to Germany before the liberation of Paris. After the war, he was imprisoned for a brief period, but eventually he was allowed to return to France and to practice medicine until his death in 1961.

The debate as to whether Céline was truly a fascist or merely a half-mad misanthrope is important only to those who see *Journey to the End of the Night* and *Death on the Installment Plan* as works of genius. In any case, his two novels exist as reminders that even true works of art can be malevolent when they appear to justify brutality and mass murder.

An early and notable example of antifascist literature is Thomas Mann's (1875–1955) novella *Mario and the Magician* (1930). In 1926, Mann and his family vacationed at a resort in Italy, four years after the newly Fascist regime of Benito Mussolini had come to power. During their stay, the family attended a performance by a magician and hypnotist that both impressed and disturbed Mann. A few years later, confronted with the rising tide of fascism within his native Germany, Mann recast the Italian experience into the story of a German family on vacation who notices the changes in attitude of the Italian guests at a resort, as they demonstrate an increasingly obvious hostility to foreigners. The climax of the story is a show put on at the resort by Cipolla, a renowned hypnotist. During the performance, Cipolla hypnotizes a young waiter into imagining that he is standing with the young woman he loves and incites him to kiss his "beloved," Cipolla himself. Humiliated by the audience, the awakened young man rushes out and returns to kill the hypnotist. Clearly the allegorical implications are strong: The rhetorically powerful performer, relying on illusionist tricks, hypnotizes his people into loving him. But eventually he goes too far and triggers a retributive reaction.

Another renowned 20th-century novelist, the Austrian Hermann Broch (1886–1951), relied on an allegorical form to examine the appeal of fascism. In *The Spell*, which Broch wrote in 1935, later revised and published in German in 1953 (English translation, 1987), the residents of a beautiful mountain village become enthralled by the itinerant stranger Marius Ratti, a mesmerizing public speaker. Rejected at first as a crackpot, Ratti steadily wins over the villagers, aided by some rich farmers in the region, who stand to gain by his success. Ratti preaches the necessity of returning to a mythic past of purity and love of nature, but his doctrine also includes hatred of the enemy, embodied here in the figure of an insurance salesman who becomes the local scapegoat. The story is told by the village doctor, a man who prides himself on his scientific rationalism, but who also succumbs to Ratti's mysterious power. The climax occurs at the village fair where mass hysteria grips the crowd, resulting in a tragic death. Eventually the village resumes its normal pattern of life, but it has paid a price, "a portion of humaneness has been lost forever."

Although the Hitler analogy is clear throughout, Broch sees the appeal of fascism as a specific instance of a broader phenomenon—the human longing for some type of absolute, one intimately associated with nature, that seems destined to lead to the diminishing of human values. The complexity of his ideas matches the complexity of his style: long, cadenced sentences that make for difficult reading but that often achieve an austere beauty.

FURTHER READING

Patrick McCarthy's *Céline* (1976) is a balanced and discerning critical and biographical study. Ilsedore Jonas's *Thomas Mann and Italy* (1969) contains a careful account of the genesis of *Mario and the Magician.*

FEMINIST MOVEMENT (1963–)

Inspired by the CIVIL RIGHTS MOVEMENT of the 1960s, an increasing number of American women began a campaign "to raise the consciousness" both of other women and the male population to the inbred, unrecognized sexism that pervaded American society. Although the success of the suffragist movement in the 1920s and the employment of women in traditional male jobs during WORLD WAR II seemed to be evidence of equality, the underlying reality revealed a different picture of economic, political, social, linguistic, and personal male domination.

The impetus for this newer phase of the women's movement, frequently referred to as the "new feminism" or "second-wave feminism," emerged from the publication of two books, Simone de Beauvoir's *The Second Sex* (1949) and Betty Friedan's *The Feminine Mystique* (1963). De Beauvoir, one of the most prominent French exponents of EXISTENTIALISM, argued that women, trapped by the biological drive of maternity, inevitably succumb to the undertow of marriage, a condition that perpetuates their economic, social, and psychological dependence. Friedan translated that general proposition into its specifically 1950s, American application, the idealized suburban housewife, supposedly immersed and fulfilled in the roles of wife and mother. This figure, her smiling image projected in ads in glossy magazines and on popular television sitcoms, was, Friedan maintained, a prisoner, the neat lawns and split-level houses of her community a "comfortable concentration camp."

Friedan's book struck a responsive chord among American women, leading to the formation in 1966 of the National Organization of Women (NOW), of which Friedan served as first president. NOW embraced a wide range of issues, including the longstanding abuse of paying women less than men for the same job. Other work-related issues were sexual harassment and the implicit assumption that women were unfit for certain types of jobs, for example, those requiring mathematical skills or tough "leadership" qualities.

A measure of the success of the movement was the inclusion, in 1971, of women within the federal guidelines for affirmative action.

The movement soon spread to Western Europe, where *The Second Sex* had already laid out the fundamental issues. These were amplified and radicalized in Germaine Greer's *The Female Eunuch* (1970), whose title refers to Greer's argument that modern society "castrates" women, imbuing them with self-hatred and men with contempt. Among her other targets was "the Middle-Class Myth of Love and Marriage," which, echoing de Beauvoir, she saw as a powerful vehicle in the enslavement of women and the perpetuation of consumer capitalism. Greer's polemic was translated into 12 languages and created a firestorm reaction, both pro and con. Her highly idiosyncratic views branded her a maverick even within the movement, but her book was a powerful consciousness raiser.

Lagging behind political and public developments was a change in the personal relations between men and women. This was particularly true among working-class people. From the beginning, the feminist movement had appealed to a white, middle-class audience, while working-class and poor women at first took a dim view of "women's lib," as it was derisively called. Black women, influenced by a similar, separatist development in the Civil Rights movement, chose to go their own way, convinced that their issues, rooted for many in poverty and racism, would be lost in the mainstream. Another setback was the defeat of the Equal Rights Amendment, although its defeat was mitigated by the sense among many women that it was no longer necessary.

The continuing controversy over the legalization of abortion remains the most controversial issue of the movement. The 1973 Supreme Court decision in *Roe v. Wade*, which invalidated all state laws prohibiting abortion in a woman's first trimester, was hailed by feminists as a major triumph. But the subsequent success of the antiabortion right-to-life movement in bringing about a ban on all funding for abortion through medicaid has proven to be a major obstacle.

The overall success of the international feminist movement, however, is indisputable. The end of the 20th century saw extraordinary expansion of equal rights in the developed countries, East and West, and, allowing for some notable exceptions, the beginnings of an even profounder change throughout the rest of the world.

THE LITERATURE

The towering literary figure in 20th-century feminism is the novelist and essayist Virginia Woolf (1882–1941). Among her novels, *Mrs Dalloway* (1925) and *To the Lighthouse* (1927) are notable for their renderings of women's subjectivity through the use of the stream of consciousness mode, and in *Orlando* (1928) Woolf explores the nature of androgyny and its relation to creativity.

But it is Woolf's nonfictional *A Room of One's Own* (1929), a collection of lectures given at a women's college, that established her centrality to the development of the new feminism. There she makes her case against the patriarchal structure of English society, which has resulted in the suppression of the female voice. She cites as a central example of her thesis the hypothetical figure of "Shakespeare's sister," who might have matched her brother in creativity, but who would never have been permitted to express it. Woolf concludes with an expression of hope to her student audience: "For my belief is that . . . if we have rooms of our own; if we have the habit of freedom and the courage to write exactly what we think . . . then the dead poet who was Shakespeare's sister will put on the body which she has so often laid down."

For many women, the fictional equivalent of *The Second Sex* and *The Feminine Mystique* is Doris Lessing's (1919–   ) novel *The Golden Notebook* (1962). Published at the beginning of the 1960s, the novel reflected the personal, political, and historical upheaval set in motion during that decade. The protagonist is Anna Wulf (her name a possible homage to Virginia Woolf), a novelist suffering from writer's block, whose writing is confined to her notebooks: "I keep four notebooks, a black notebook, which is to do with Anna Wulf, the writer; a red notebook, concerned with politics; a yellow notebook, in which I make stories out of my experience; and a blue notebook, which tries to be a diary." The different notebooks represent Anna's attempt to impose order on the impending chaos, the mental breakdown she fears she is headed for. She is attempting to complete a novel entitled *Free Women*.

The novel consists of five sections, each one designated "Free Women 1, 2, 3" and so on, followed by entries in the black, red, yellow, and blue notebooks. "Free Women 5" is preceded by a section called "The Golden Notebook," in which Anna and her lover, Saul Green, an American writer, break through their inner chaos with each other's help. The sign of their mutuality is that each one writes the first line of the other's novel. For Anna, Saul writes, "The two women were alone in their London flat," the opening line of *The Golden Notebook*.

The elaborate and unusual structure of the novel sets up a basic distinction between the "facts," as recorded in the notebooks, and the transformation of those facts in the fictional narrative recorded in the "Free Women" sections. The existence of the "Free Women" sections testifies to the fact that Anna has overcome her block, so that the novel offers us both the process, in the notebooks, and the product, in the "Free Women" parts.

Why did *The Golden Notebook* become the critical fictional text in the early years of postwar feminism? One answer is that it offered an encyclopedic view of a modern woman writer's attempt to fuse politics, psychoanalysis, history, and the relations between the sexes into a language and a form that could restore sanity and order to the fragmented chaos of modern lives. But the novel seems to suggest that sanity—wholeness—can come about not by the rigid compartmentalizing of experience, as Anna tries to do in the note-books, but by submitting to the chaos and reconstructing a kind of synthesis, as she does in the "golden notebook." Whatever the answer to the question, the irony is that Lessing was not consciously writing a feminist novel, but one which she hoped would explore universal questions of general relevance. Set-ting out to be a broadly philosophical novel based on her own experience, she produced a profoundly feminist one.

The steady, ironic, often satiric vision of the novelist Alison Lurie (1926–) focuses in on feminism in *The Truth about Lorin Jones* (1988). Polly Alter, an art curator whose recent divorce has soured her on men, sets out to write a biography of Lorin Jones, an artist who is achieving posthumous recognition after having been neglected in her lifetime. Polly is convinced that Lorin had been mistreated by the men in her life: Paolo Carducci, the gallery owner who refused at one point to exhibit any more of her work; Lorin's half brother, Leonard Zimmern, who rejected her while she was alive, but quickly claimed ownership of her paintings after her death; Lorin's ex-husband, Garrett Jones, a celebrated art critic who may have wrecked her career out of revenge; and Hugh Cameron, "an unsuccessful, ex-hippie poet, who took Lorin to Key West and then left her when she was ill and dying."

All of these simple scenarios prove to be misconceptions that lead Polly to revise some basic ideas not only about her biographical subject but, more important, about herself. In the process, Polly comes to terms with life issues related to the nature and extent of her feminism. She experiments with les-bianism but finds herself "addicted" to heterosexuality. She begins to understand that her ex-husband was not the ogre she had conjured him up to be and that the persons she loves most in the world, her father and her 12-year-old son, happen to be males, although the son "was not like most males; he had been raised on non-sexist principles from birth." What she dis-covers about Lorin Jones (with the help of a male lover, whose identity is a surprise) is that there is no single truth about Lorin Jones, only a series of contradictory partial truths.

The scarred history of slavery and its impact on the relations of black men and women and consequently on the black family has given a distinctive weight and tone to African-American feminism. Two writers who have attacked this subject with extraordinary intensity and power are Alice Walker (1944–) and Toni Morrison (1931–). Essentially the story of Celie, a poor black woman living in the South who is sexually abused and manipulated first by her stepfather and later by her husband, Walker's *The Color Purple* (1982) focuses on the power of black women's solidarity with each other. Celie, for example, achieves a measure of self-respect and control over her life as a result of a lesbian relationship with her husband's mistress. Contrasted to the degradation to which Celie is subjected is the experience of her sister Nettie, who is a missionary in Africa, which suggests that the oppression of black women by black men, a depiction that created a good deal of controversy when the novel was filmed by Steven Spielberg in 1985, is a specifically American phenomenon, a by-product of the racism which has warped the lives of blacks in America.

The preeminent recorder of the lives of African-American women is Toni Morrison, whose novels draw on the rich resources of black oral culture, creating fictions that are permeated with magical and mythic episodes and are written in a haunting poetic prose. In *The Bluest Eye* (1969), she tells of Pecola, a black girl growing up in the 1930s, victimized by the blue-eyed, blonde-haired model of beauty, represented by Shirley Temple, that dominates her life and those of the people surrounding her. Raped by her father, she loses her mind. In *Sula* (1973), Morrison depicts a rebellious woman who violates her community's sense of morality, but who infuses life and a sense of freedom into that community. Morrison's masterpiece, *Beloved* (1987), set in the 19th century, vividly explores the profound depths of black motherhood and the extent to which the ghost of slavery haunts African-American life, a theme she explores further in *Jazz* (1992) (see JAZZ AGE).

FURTHER READING

Elaine Showalter's *A Literature of Their Own* (1977) is a pioneering effort to establish a separate tradition of women's writing. Alice Walker's *In Search of Our Mother's Gardens* (1983) is a collection of essays that lays out a specific feminist (she employs the term *womanist*) agenda for minority women.

FITZGERALD, F. SCOTT

See JAZZ AGE.

FRANCE, FALL OF (WORLD WAR II) (1940)

On May 10, 1940, a full eight months after the formal declaration of war in September 1939, German troops launched a long-expected attack in western Europe, but, in a surprise maneuver, the main German assault came through Luxembourg and the Ardennes Forest. With astonishing speed, German Panzer (motorized) divisions slashed through Allied lines, cutting off British and French troops in the north, leading to the evacuation at DUNKIRK. Meanwhile French forces in the south were forced to retreat from the numerically superior German army, which had simply bypassed the "impregnable" Maginot Line, the core of French defensive strategy. On June 10, Mussolini's Italian government, delighted to get in on a sure thing, declared war on France, moving its troops into areas along the French-Italian border. On

June 13, the Germans entered Paris and, two days later, occupied VERDUN, the city that in WORLD WAR I had stood as the symbol of an indomitable France.

On June 16, 1940, the French prime minister, Paul Reynaud, resigned. His successor, Marshal Henri Pétain, hero of the battle of Verdun in the First World War, sued for peace on June 22. By the terms of the treaty, the southern area of the nation was to be nominally autonomous, governed by Pétain from its capital in Vichy, a well-known health spa. The remaining French territory (about two-thirds of the total) would be under direct German command. The German army had defeated their great traditional enemy in six weeks of fighting, a humiliating debacle for the nation of Joan of Arc and Napoleon. When he heard the news, Adolf HITLER danced a celebratory jig. Vehemently protesting this collapse, French general Charles de Gaulle broadcast from London, calling for the continuation of the war from the French colonies by "Free French" troops. Fearful that the French naval fleet would fall into German hands, British ships and planes attacked the fleet while it was anchored in harbor off Algeria, destroying almost the entire fleet and killing nearly 1,300 French sailors. As a result, the Vichy government broke off diplomatic relations with the British, who continued to support the Free French troops under de Gaulle.

THE LITERATURE

The French philosopher, novelist, and playwright Jean-Paul Sartre (1905–80) served in the French army during this period and was interned as a prisoner of war in 1940. These experiences became the basis of *Troubled Sleep* (1949; trans., 1951), the third volume of his trilogy, *The Roads to Freedom*. The second volume of the trilogy, *The Reprieve*, set in 1938, deals with the impact of the MUNICH PACT on a group of French citizens. Carrying over some of the main characters from the first two novels, *Troubled Sleep* depicts the French army, confused and demoralized, anticipating surrender with a mixture of shame and relief. Immediately following their surrender, while in a temporary camp, they are comparatively well treated by the Germans, raising hopes that they will soon be allowed to return to their homes. This illusion is cruelly shattered at the end of the novel when the troops discover that the cattle cars they are traveling on are taking them to labor camps inside Germany. For many of the prisoners, this marks a shocking revelation: "For the first time since September '39, this was war."

Troubled Sleep marks a significant advance for Sartre in his development as a novelist. In an earlier novel, *Nausea* (1938; trans., 1949), he explored some of the central themes of EXISTENTIALISM, intensely focusing on the individual's subjective consciousness. In *Troubled Sleep*, he turns to the engagement of the individual with the forces of history in the context of ideological conflict. Writing in the aftermath of WORLD WAR II, Sartre sees the subjective crisis explored in *Nausea*, transformed by the twin catastrophes of war and ignominious defeat. Private life fades in the face of the large collective spectacles of mass destruction and death, of refugees and defeated armies roaming aimlessly through the countryside. The protagonist of the first half of the novel, Mathieu, an intensely private soldier, a former philosophy teacher, chooses to go on waging a last-ditch battle immediately after the defeat as a way of affirming his freedom of choice: "Mathieu went on firing. . . . [H]e was cleansed, he was all-powerful, he was free."

The novel also dramatizes a political conflict between two political factions, the communist and the noncommunist left, as they come to terms with the defeat. Brunet, a committed communist, looks on the internment of French prisoners as an opportunity to capitalize on their discontent, creating more converts to communism. His fellow prisoners are merely the means to his goal—the ultimate triumph of communism. Schneider, a fellow prisoner, sympathetic to the party in certain respects, perceives Brunet's flaw. "What worries me is that you don't seem particularly fond of us." In the final scene Brunet discovers the total estrangement from ordinary human feeling that his commitment to the party has created. He has lost a sense of his individual identity in pursuit of a collective dream.

FURTHER READING

In *Encounters with Darkness* (1983), Frederick Harris studies the portrayal of World War II in French and German literature. S. B. John analyzes the political theme in *Troubled Sleep* in an essay reprinted in *John-Paul Sartre*, edited by Harold Bloom (2001).

FRANZ FERDINAND, ASSASSINATION OF (1914)

In 1878, the Austro-Hungarian imperial army occupied the Baltic province of Bosnia-Herzegovina, even though the province was nominally a part of the Ottoman Empire. In 1908, Austria announced its formal annexation, despite a storm of protests from Turkey and the major nations of Europe, who saw the move as a further destabilization of a region already on the brink of war. Opposition was even stronger within Bosnia itself, whose strong Serbian majority desired independence, like that of their fellow Serbs in neighboring Serbia. In the years that followed, increasingly militant opponents of Austrian rule emerged both in Bosnia and Serbia. Among the latter was "the Black Hand," a group of Serbian army officers determined to win independence for Bosnia.

Archduke Franz Ferdinand was the nephew and presumptive heir of the aging Emperor Franz Joseph of Austria-Hungary (see HAPSBURG EMPIRE). Ignoring warnings of possible danger, Franz Ferdinand visited Bosnia to inspect the maneuvers of the imperial troops stationed in the region. The following day, he and his wife traveled to Sarajevo, Bosnia's principal city, for a formal ceremony. While they passed in procession, someone threw a hand grenade at their car, but they emerged unscathed. Continuing their journey, their car made a wrong turn, at the very place where another conspirator, Gavrilo Princip, an 18-year-old Sarajevo student, coincidentally happened to be standing. As the car moved into reverse to return to its proper route, Princip drew a pistol, then shot and killed both the archduke and his wife. Princip and his fellow conspirators were apprehended. He was spared the death penalty because of his age, but he was confined to a military prison in Theresienstadt (the site of a future Nazi ghetto/concentration camp), where he died of tuberculosis in 1918.

Subsequent investigation revealed that the conspirators had been trained and armed by the Black Hand. The head of this group, known by the code name *Avis*, was the chief of intelligence for the Serbian army; thus the Serbian government appeared to be implicated in the assassination. The connection was enough for Austria, once assured of Germany's cooperation, to declare war on Serbia, the first step in a chain reaction leading to WORLD WAR I, whose consequences shaped the 20th century more than any other single event. In the words of the Bosnian historian Vladimir Dedijer, "No other political murder in modern history has had such momentous consequences."

THE LITERATURE

Hans Koning's (1924–   ) *Death of a Schoolboy* (1974) is a first-person novel, narrated by the assassin Gavrilo Princip. In an introductory note, the Dutch-born American novelist explains, "[I]t may depress some people, and cheer up others, but there were indeed freedom marches of schoolboys as far back as 1913, and they were called just that. . . . I did not want to create an aura of foreignness. . . . My story is not taking place in a far country." Writing in the early 1970s, Koning appears to be referring to the student activism of the late 1960s, relating to the CIVIL RIGHTS MOVEMENT and the VIETNAM WAR. Koning never loses sight of this parallel as he explores Princip's mind and revolutionary spirit.

The story begins with Princip's dismissal from school for having organized a freedom march from his high school in Sarajevo to the Town Hall. Expelled for this activity, he decides to continue his education in Belgrade, Serbia. Here he meets two other students, who share his intense Slavic nationalism and his eclectic reading knowledge of revolutionary theory. The announcement of the impending visit of the archduke on June 28, the anniversary of the defeat of the Serbs at Kosovo in 1389, adds salt to the Bosnian wounds. Princip decides that "the only proper response to his visit, the only action that would be commensurate, would be to kill him." After being armed and assisted in crossing the border into Bosnia by the Black

Hand, the three conspirators feel a sense of exaltation and purpose that creates an unbreakable bond uniting them. During the assassination itself, Princip, momentarily stunned by the sudden appearance of the archduke's car, fails to act in time. But the sudden, seemingly miraculous reversal of the car's direction gives him a second chance, and this time he fires two shots, killing both the archduke and his wife. The assassination itself seems to be blessed by Providence, or, as the revolutionary Princip sees it, history.

At this point, consistent with his plan to commit suicide after the deed, he swallows cyanide pills, purchased in Belgrade. But the chemist has tricked him; the pills are harmless. The rest of the novel deals with his thoughts and experiences during his imprisonment, as he tries to come to terms with his guilt for the death of the archduchess and for the punishments inflicted on dozens of people convicted of aiding the conspiracy. In his last year, dying of tuberculosis of the bone, he undergoes an amputation of an arm and hears of the collapse of empires and of the revolution in Russia, but these events do not eradicate the doubt he now experiences: "I no longer have the strength to understand my fellow man. I think I've lived just at the dawn of my species."

The Death of a Schoolboy is an impressive novel. In exploring the psychology of a famous terrorist, it subtly moves that story to a universal level, using a muted style that gathers strength as it reveals the depths of its main character.

FURTHER READING

Vladimir Dedijer's *The Road to Sarajevo* (1966) is an impressively detailed account of the assassination.

FRENCH-INDOCHINA WAR

See INDOCHINA WAR.

G

GALLIPOLI, BATTLE OF (WORLD WAR I) (1915–1916)

In 1915, the stalemate on the WESTERN FRONT compelled the Allies to look elsewhere for a breakthrough that would bring the war to a swift conclusion. In the British war cabinet, Winston Churchill, then first lord of the admiralty, argued eloquently for a combined land-sea offensive in the Dardenelles, the 40-mile strait separating southeast Europe from Asia. The plan called for an expedition that would establish naval control of the strait, followed by the capture of Constantinople (now Istanbul), thereby establishing a direct connection with Russian forces fighting the Turks in the Caucusus.

In March 1915, the naval plan was put into action. It failed—due to the effective mining of the strait by the Turks. As a consequence, in April, English and Australian forces landed on various parts of the Gallipoli Peninsula, a long stretch of land on the European side of the strait. Despite a fiercely heroic effort, particularly on the part of the Australian troops, the outnumbered Turks held their fortified positions from heights that made the British easy targets for machine guns and snipers. The offensive, repeated a number of times at different points, was a fiasco. The British lost more than 100,000 dead or wounded, with nothing strategic to show for it. In January 1916, they withdrew from the area. Had they succeeded, the offensive might have knocked the Turks out of the war and turned the tide of the war in Russia. As it was, the defeat further demoralized the Russian army and its people, setting the stage for the 1917 RUSSIAN REVOLUTION.

THE LITERATURE

A. P. Herbert's (1890–1971) *The Secret Battle* (1919) contains a memorable account of Gallipoli and its impact on one particular soldier. Harry Penrose is an idealistic young Oxford graduate who approaches the campaign with an enthusiasm intensified by the association of the area with the Trojan War in Homer's *Iliad*. His story, narrated by an anonymous fellow officer, describes the hideous conditions under which Penrose and the soldiers under his command struggle. Fighting on an exposed plain under blazing sun, afflicted by ceaseless sniper attacks and flies that converge by the thousands whenever they try to eat or sleep, the men contract dysentery that renders them too weak to wage an effective attack. Despite these conditions Penrose, severely weakened with dysentery, carries on in a quietly heroic manner, engaging nightly in dangerous scouting missions under heavy fire. Eventually he collapses and is evacuated to England. After recuperating, he requests a return to his old outfit, now on the front line in France. Here he is brutalized by a new commanding officer, until he is wounded again and returned to England. By this time his nerves are obviously gone:

> "Harry had black moods. . . . He lost his keenness, his cheerfulness, and his health. Once a man starts on that path his past history finds him out like an old wound. In Harry's case it was Gallipoli. No man who had a bad time in that place, ever got 'over it' in body or soul."

When he returns to the front again, he gives way under fire. As a result, he is brought up on charges of cowardice and found guilty with a recommendation of mercy, which is rejected by his commanding officer. In the end he is executed by a firing squad of men from his own battalion. The narrator's final comment summarizes the story: "my friend Harry was shot for cowardice—and he was the bravest man I ever knew."

The Secret Battle is one of the most poignant and memorable novels of the Great War. The critic Samuel Hynes sees Harry Penrose as the prototype of "the victim-as-hero," a figure that was to develop into the antihero, a staple of modern literature: "Herbert . . . found a structure, a language, and a subject for a new kind of narrative of human destiny."

In his introduction to later editions of the novel, Winston Churchill, the architect of the Gallipoli campaign, also calls attention to the novel's capacity to universalize its hero, calling it "a monument not of one but of millions, standing impassive in marble to give its message to all wayfarers who pass it."

FURTHER READING

Alan Moorehead's *Gallipoli* (1956) gives a detailed account of the campaign. Samuel Hynes's *A War Imagined* (1990) contains an insightful discussion of *A Secret Battle*.

GANDHI, MOHANDAS K. (1869–1948)

Born in India and trained as a lawyer, Gandhi worked in South Africa, where he became involved in protesting discriminatory acts against Indians in the British crown colony of Natal. In the ensuing years, he became a leader of the Indian community throughout South Africa, developing his doctrines of nonviolent resistance and of maintaining of and respect for the roots of one's culture.

In 1915, he returned to India, continuing his campaign against the British authorities. As the unofficial leader of the Indian National Congress, he led thousands of followers in nonviolent demonstrations throughout the 1920s and 1930s; as a consequence he was jailed numerous times. In the meantime his policy of civil disobedience and passive resistance resulted in significant reforms in the British administration of India, but it fell short of Gandhi's demands for Indian independence. When independence was achieved in 1947, it came at a great price for Gandhi, since it included the partition that created the Hindu state of India and the Muslim state of Pakistan, a development about which he had severe misgivings. He believed that Hindus and Muslims could live together in peace. In January 1948, Gandhi, while on his way to deliver his daily prayer message, was assassinated by a Hindu fanatic. Gandhi's influence extended far beyond India. He inspired, among others, Martin Luther King, Jr., and the American CIVIL RIGHTS MOVEMENT of the 1960s. A significant source of Gandhi's strength lay in the fact that he was not merely a political leader, but a spiritual leader as well. ("Mahatma," a title conferred on Gandhi by the famous Indian poet Rabindranath Tagore, means "holy man.")

THE LITERATURE

R. K. Narayan (1906–2001), one of the most important Indian writers of the 20th century, set almost all of his novels in the fictitious South Indian city of Malgudi. Among these is *Waiting for the Mahatma* (1955), the story of Srinam, a feckless young man who lives with his grandmother. Srinam seems to be living his life in a trance when suddenly he falls in love with a beautiful young woman who is a follower of Gandhi. To be near her, Srinam joins the movement without really understanding the Mahatma's message. He violates the principle of nonviolence by indulging in certain acts of sabotage for which he is jailed. While in prison, he begins to sympathize with the plight of his fellow prisoners, the first step in his transformation from self-centered individualism to a genuine commitment to others. After his release he rejoins his beloved, and the two appeal to Gandhi for permission to marry. After some subtle questioning of Srinam, Gandhi approves the marriage and promises to perform the ceremony. A moment later Gandhi experiences a strong intuition that he will not be present at the wedding, but he blesses the couple and advises them to marry even if he is unable to be there. Moments later, he goes out to address a prayer meeting and is shot dead. In his valedictory, his disciple Jawaharlal Nehru summarizes his death: "A light has gone out of our lives."

Stanley Wolpert's (1927–   ) *Nine Hours to Rama* (1962) focuses on the assassination of Gandhi on January 30, 1948. The central figure is the assassin, Naturam Godse, a journalist and member of an extreme Hindu sect that sees Gandhi's tolerance of Muslims as a threat to India. In a series of flashbacks interpolated into the events of the day, the author reveals the shaping of Godse's character—his rejection by the British when, as a young man, he attempts to join the army, and his passionate relationship with a beautiful married woman. Despite his deep attraction to this woman, he cannot overcome his traditional view of the proper place of women in society. He is both attracted and repelled by her free spirit. In the last seconds of his suicide mission, he becomes fully conscious of the loss of this love, but the realization arrives too late. He kills Gandhi while hallucinating that his victim is his father. Among the other characters is a police inspector, aware of the threat and anguished over the refusal of the Mahatma to cancel the prayer meeting where the assassination will take place. Of the interior life of Gandhi himself, Wolpert, perhaps wisely, limits himself to a description of the saint revered by all.

The success of the novel stands and falls on its ability to render Godse as a believable human being. In this effort, Wolpert is not entirely successful. Godse's conversion to extremism is not convincing because never shown, and the picture we have of him does not add up to that of a fanatic. Nevertheless, *Nine Hours to Rama* is an exciting, suspenseful adventure story.

FURTHER READING

Glyn Richards's *The Philosophy of Gandhi* (1982) provides a clear exposition of Gandhi's ideas.

GREAT DEPRESSION (1929–1939)

In the 1920s, America underwent a period of seemingly unmatched prosperity, signaled by high levels of consumption and production. Much of that prosperity was founded on debit spending by businesses and consumers. Innovative technology had created sharp increases in industrial production and installment buying. The STOCK MARKET CRASH of 1929 exposed the fragility of that economy, with consequences that stretched far beyond the borders of the United States. The American economy sneezed and the rest of the world caught a cold. Western European nations, struggling to recover from a disastrous war and relying heavily on American loans, had serious problems, now exacerbated by raised tariffs in the American market. Unemployment and social unrest followed, leaving countries like Italy and Germany susceptible to the appeal of FASCISM in the form of "strong men," demagogues who offered easy answers to complex economic problems.

In the United States, the shock of failure seemed to intensify in the early years. By 1932, 5,000 banks had failed; farmers' incomes, never that high even in the go-go 1920s, declined by 65 percent, while in the cities unemployment rates tripled. Ecological disasters—droughts in some sections of the country, which led to the DUST BOWL, and floods in others—contrived to produce a combined sense of paralysis and fear. By 1933, about 15 million Americans were unemployed. For the first time in its history, more people were emigrating from America than immigrating to it.

In the 1932 presidential election, the Democratic nominee, Franklin Delano ROOSEVELT, campaigned on his pledge of "a new deal for the American people." Roosevelt won the election with a plurality of more than 7 million votes. His New Deal represented an aggressive attack on the depression, reanimating a nearly lifeless society. Swift legislation regulated the stock market and the banking system, improved the agricultural economy, and introduced a social security program. Throughout the 1930s, public works programs changed the face of the nation: Dams, roads, and schools were built; forests were protected and replenished; and electric power was extended to impoverished areas (especially in the Southeast).

Enemies on the right denounced this ambitious range of policies as socialistic. Ironically, New Deal policies helped save capitalism in the United States by overcoming a climate of despair. But the Great Depression did not really end until WORLD WAR II put the American economy on a wartime basis.

THE LITERATURE

Many novelists during the 1930s committed themselves to documenting both the causes of the Great Depression and the quest for substantial improvement in the lives of that "one-third of the nation" who most suffered its grim effects. John Steinbeck's (1902–68) *In Dubious Battle* (1936) lacks the dramatic sweep of his *The Grapes of Wrath* (1939) but avoids that novel's misplaced epic pretensions. Instead, Steinbeck focuses here on three men: Mac, a communist; Jim, his younger protegé; and Doc Burton, an apolitical figure who nevertheless sympathizes with the apple pickers Mac and Jim are trying to organize against "the capitalist sonsobitches." Although Mac's rigid, doctrinaire politics ultimately prove ineffective, he does manage to stiffen Jim's gentle, rather passive humanity. As Jim prepares to make his first speech to the workers, he is murdered by a shotgun blast to his face. Burton has, by the time Jim dies, already left the scene of this "dubious battle" (a reference to the struggle in Milton's *Paradise Lost* between Satan and the heavenly forces), a hint—which is all Steinbeck provides—that the struggle will continue, but without a predictable outcome.

Josephine Herbst's (1897–1969) *Rope of Gold* (1939) is the final novel in a trilogy about the Trexler family of Iowa (where Herbst was born) and its descendants. The first novel, *Pity Is Not Enough* (1933), explores their involvement in social, economic, and political events from 1868–96, including late 19th-century railroad frauds, grain monopolies, and Klondike fever. *The Executioner Waits* (1934) covers 1902–29: profiteering during WORLD WAR I and the social and economic excesses of the 1920s. *Rope of Gold* ranges through the 1930s to 1937 and a climactic sit-down strike inside an auto factory in Detroit. Like the first two novels, it exposes and assails the weaknesses of capitalism. In *Rope of Gold*, one of the Trexler descendants, Victoria Chance (whose life in many ways parallels Herbst's), becomes the center of the novel. She and her husband, Jonathan, drift slowly but inevitably apart, their once deep love shriveling beneath family pressures, poverty, miscarriage, affairs, and failed reconciliations. A handsome, articulate writer, Jonathan identifies with social protest earlier than his wife and even gains prominence in the Communist Party. But the party exploits him as a "front," useful merely as a fund-raiser. While Jonathan wallows in self-pity, Victoria compensates with action and commitment. She develops her skills as a reporter and thrusts herself into situations where those skills are tested (especially when she investigates corruption in corporate sugar dealings in dictator Fulgencio Batista's Cuba). The society in which the couple dwell certainly contributes to the destruction of their love, but Herbst makes clear that it is Victoria, the woman, who commands the ability to discover and fulfill her emotional and intellectual potential.

Herbst's portraiture extends beyond these two. Jonathan's father is a tight-fisted reactionary, unwilling to offer financial help so long as Jonathan continues writing instead of going into business. One of Victoria's sisters, Nancy, is wed to Clifford Radford, a decent, simple fellow helpless in the web of economic depression, reduced at last to earning a substandard wage as an orderly in an asylum—where he must live, apart from his family. Another sister, Margaret, despises her gross, bigoted, union-busting husband, Ed Thompson, the most stereotypic of Herbst's characters. Newly returned from Europe, Lester Tolman, a writer and friend of Victoria and Jonathan, has seen the terrors of Nazism and is intellectually attracted to radicalism, but he finds it difficult to give up the pleasures offered by his mistress, a beautiful but faithless actress. When at last he does and joins Victoria in Cuba to develop their story of international corruption in the sugar industry, he becomes so convinced that Cuban and American business interests will prevail over justice that he abandons their assignment and gets drunk.

Few of Herbst's characters are willing to make Victoria's radical political commitment. One who does is a character she never meets and about whom she knows nothing. Steve Carson grows up as the surviving child of Walt Carson, a socialist Nebraskan homesteader whose wife and four other children die when a cyclone destroys their new home. Walt marries Steve's schoolteacher and moves his new family to a farm in South Dakota, where the family prospers until World War I, when land becomes more valuable than produce. Banks and real estate interests force farmers off land they own but can no longer afford to work. The farmers picket, a strike breaker is killed, and Steve is arrested as a scapegoat, though he goes free for lack of evidence.

Ten years later, fired with memories of betrayal by the "bloated Capitalists," frustrated by years of drought, hail, frost, and grasshoppers, and enraged by the corruption and cruelty of banks and insurance companies, Steve Carson enlists in the workers' movement. He despises the technology at his factory because it takes production out of the hands of labor; he despises his father-in-law for keeping him on a farm and paying him too little to live on. When his best friend is murdered by a gang of "town guys" and "Legion fellows," Steve begs his wife to let him go, determined to stand beside the worker rather than lie beside his wife. He reappears in the final chapter of the novel, writing a love letter to his wife as he squats inside a Detroit auto plant where he and his fellow workers are staging a sit-down strike to protest the company's demands of increased speed on the assembly line. The last man to swing over the fence and join the workers inside shouts to the crowd—National Guardsmen and workers' wives—"Brothers and sisters, we're only fighting for our human rights, better to die like men than live like dogs on the speedup."

Steve Carson is a lovable character but also a stereotypic one—the idealized proletarian whose vision presages ultimate victory. Compared with Victoria, Steve lacks complexity. But whatever the weaknesses in his characterization, Herbst offers in *Rope of Gold* an intricate portrait of life during the Great Depression and in the trilogy as a whole a valuable portrait of the events that led to that catastrophe.

FURTHER READING

Studs Terkel's *Hard Times: An Oral History of the Great Depression* (1970) records the thoughts of people from every level of American society. T. H. Watkins's *The Great Depression: America in the 1930s* (1993) is a useful account. Walter Rideout's *The Radical Novel in the United States: 1900–1954* (1956) is another excellent resource. Daniel Aaron's *Writers on the Left* (1961) is the best study of the effect of communism on American writers during the first half of the 20th century.

—*Arthur Waldhorn*

GREAT TERROR, THE (1934–1938)

The assassination in 1934 of Sergey Kirov, the head of the Communist Party in Leningrad and a loyal supporter of Joseph STALIN, provided the Soviet dictator, faced with growing criticism of his regime, with an excuse to begin a ruthless hunt for the murderer. Most historians believe that Stalin, fearful of Kirov's growing popularity, had ordered the murder. In any case, the investigation of the murder became the starting point for the Great Terror—purges conducted by Stalin's henchmen that laid waste the leadership of the Communist Party and the general staff of the Soviet army. Among its distinctive barbarities were three public "show trials" of leading Communist figures, men who had distinguished themselves in the 1917 RUSSIAN REVOLUTION, forced under torture to confess to nonexistent crimes, whereupon they were immediately executed. In the backdrop of these trials were widespread campaigns of terror against leading officials of the Communist Party, most of them accused of conspiring with Leon TROTSKY, Stalin's exiled Communist rival, to overthrow the Soviet government. By 1938, the purges had succeeded to such an extent that there were only 41 survivors of the 139 members of the Central Committee elected at the party congress in 1934. The purges also extended beyond party members to include intellectuals, writers, and whatever remained of traditional class enemies, the bourgeoisie and the landed aristocracy. Technically the terror came to an end in 1938, although, after WORLD WAR II, Stalin initiated another series of purges against Jews and former Russian prisoners of war that continued up to his death in 1953. In 1956, in a secret speech to the 20th Congress of the Communist Party, Nikita Khrushchev detailed and denounced the purges of the Stalin era.

THE LITERATURE

Among the best known of the show-trial defendants was Nikolai Bukharin (1888–1938), former editor of *Pravda*, the official newspaper of the Soviet Union and a member of the Politburo, the highest policy-making body of the Soviet government. Bukharin is widely considered to be the model for the protagonist of Arthur Koestler's novel *Darkness at Noon* (1940). Arthur Koestler (1905–83), a prototype of the 20th-century author, activist, and thinker, was a Hungarian Jew who emigrated to Palestine at the age of 18, later joined the German Communist Party, was imprisoned by Francisco Franco's forces in the SPANISH CIVIL WAR, and barely escaped the Nazis after the FALL OF FRANCE in 1940. Koestler recounted his disillusion with, and defection from, the Communist Party in a celebrated collection of essays by former communists, *The God That Failed* (1950).

Darkness at Noon uses the purges as a case study of a tragically flawed ideal. Acknowledging that the Russian Revolution was betrayed by the arrogance of power and implacable will of Joseph Stalin, Koestler nevertheless argues, through his main character Rubashov, that Stalin's thought processes were consistent with one principle that emerged from the revolution—the justification of the means by the end. Once that idea gained acceptance among the ruling Communist elite, a cancer cell was introduced into the

Soviet system. Stalin was a uniquely effective carcinogen, but the disease would have emerged in any case.

Rubashov is one of the founding fathers of the revolution, totally dedicated to the cause. He has learned early on to subordinate any humane and compassionate instincts to the demands of the party. Arrested as a spy by the Nazis in 1933, the year of Adolf HITLER's assumption of power, he was tortured and imprisoned before being returned to the Soviet Union. But he discovers that the country he has returned to is not the one he left. Although his criticism of the regime is muted and indirect, he is arrested and charged with plotting to assassinate "Number One," as Stalin is referred to in the novel. Most of the story focuses on Rubashov's imprisonment and interrogations. Finally benumbed by a ruthless interrogator, one of the "new men" of the Soviet system, he confesses to deeds he did not commit and is executed.

One feature of the purge underscored by the novel with bitter irony is the description of the old revolutionaries, drained of physical and moral energy, unable to mount any sort of challenge to the new order: "Worn by the years of illegal struggle, eaten by the damp of prison walls, between which they had spent half their youth, spiritually sucked dry by the permanent nervous strain of holding down the physical fear, of which one never spoke . . . Worn by the years of exile, the acid sharpness of factions within the Party, the unscrupulousness with which they were fought out; worn out by the endless defeats and the demoralization of the final victory."

But the heart of the novel is the transformation of Rubashov from the cool, rationalist, Marxist machine into a recognizable human being. Although the cause to which he devoted his life now appears to have been fatally flawed, he does not succumb to despair or to self-defense. Instead he dies with the dignity of a man who committed himself to a corrupted ideal of human betterment, a classic example of a tragic hero.

The Yugoslavian novelist Danilo Kís's (1935–89) *A Tomb for Boris Davidovich* (1976; trans., 1978) is a collection of seven interconnected stories, most of which relate to the terror. The title story deals with a figure strongly resembling Koestler's Bukharin-inspired Rubashov. Boris Davidovich (his party name is Novsky) is a brilliant, ruthless, true believer in communism. All of his interrogator's efforts to induce him to confess are futile. Finally, he is told that for every day he holds out, some other prisoner will be executed in his presence. To save the lives of others, he confesses to his alleged crimes, but, to his dismay, instead of being executed, he is sent to a GULAG. He escapes, is tracked down by dogs, and commits suicide rather than let himself be taken, but his image, a man who represents the dignity of the individual, survives.

FURTHER READING

Robert Conquest's *The Great Terror: A Reassessment* (1990) makes a convincing argument that both the casualties and the consequences of the terror were much greater than had previously been thought. Sidney Pearson's *Arthur Koestler* (1978) is a critical discussion of the man and his work.

GRECO-TURKISH WAR (1921–1922)

One of the defining events of modern Greek history is what the Greeks themselves refer to as the Asia Minor catastrophe, the failed invasion of Turkey that in 1922 resulted in the massacre of many Greeks whose families had lived in Turkey for centuries and in the next year forced an exchange of Christian and Muslim populations that created considerable logistic, economic, and social burdens for the Greek government.

The Greek War of Independence from Turkey (1821–28) had established a core state, but it had also left much to be desired by those who thought that much more of the Greek-speaking world should have been included within its borders. Gradually the "Great Idea," the conviction that modern Greece should consist of the entire Greek world, including large portions of Turkey, grew and became a formidable political force. In the wake of the war between Russia and Turkey, and under British pressure, Turkey ceded Thessaly and Arta to Greece (1881). But as late as 1908, Greece was far short of its current size. Crete had been freed from Turkey in 1898 by the so-called Great Powers (Britain, France, Russia, and Italy) but was not yet united with Greece. What is now northern Greece, including Thessalonika, was still under Ottoman rule, as were islands of the eastern Aegean, such as Lesbos, Chios, and Samos, and the Dodecanese, including Rhodes. Eleftherios Venezelou (1864–1936), a proponent of the Great Idea who had made his political reputation in Crete during uprisings against Turkish rule, became prime minister in 1912 and led his country into the first and second Balkan Wars (1912–13), at the end of which Crete, the islands of the eastern Aegean, and Thessalonika were incorporated into Greece.

When WORLD WAR I broke out, a bitter struggle between the Greek king, Constantine, who sympathized with Germany, and Venezelos, who saw an opportunity to advance the Great Idea, delayed Greece's entry into the war until 1917. By that time, Constantine had resigned, and his dismissed prime minister, Venezelos, had returned to Athens. After the armistice on November 11, 1918, the Allies occupied Constantinople (now Istanbul), and the Greeks, in 1919, Smyrna (now Izmir). In 1921, Greece, with presumed Allied support, launched an offensive whose goal was the capture of Ankara. This expedition, however, was frustrated for a variety of reasons: supply lines stretched thin, the withdrawal of support by the Great Powers, especially Britain, and the genius of Turkey's Mustafa Kemal Atatürk (1881–1938), who, like Russian generals facing Napoléon Bonaparte and Adolf HITLER, counterattacked and defeated an overextended invading enemy. In September

1921, the Greeks were stopped at the Sakarya River, just short of Ankara. A year later, the Turks sacked Smyrna, which had a large Greek quarter. The Greeks had not been gentle in their march into the heartland of Turkey, and the Turkish response was even more brutal, resulting in wholesale slaughter of Greeks unable to buy or beg their way onto boats. The Great Powers, which remained shockingly neutral, had ships in the harbor that stood by and watched as Greeks were literally driven into the sea in their efforts to escape the advancing army and the burning city. The city's archbishop, Chrysostomos, was hacked to death by a Turkish mob.

In a power vacuum created by the catastrophe—Constantine had abdicated, Venezelos had as yet refused to return—a cadre of army officers put to death five senior ex-ministers and the former commander in chief, a universally condemned act of misdirected vengeance. Venezelos did help negotiate the Treaty of Lausanne (1923), which at least preserved most of the gains of the previous decade, but there was no longer any question of Greek claims to Constantinople or Smyrna, and the resulting exchange of Turks from Greece and Greeks from Turkey forced Greece to deal with a million refugees and all the social and economic problems they brought with them. Exempt from this exchange were the Greeks of Constantinople, the Turks of Thrace, and both the Greeks and Turks of Cyprus.

THE LITERATURE

In *Beyond the Aegean* (1994), Elia Kazan (1909–   ) completes his trilogy focused on the life of Stavros Topouzoglou, an Anatolian Greek whose dream it has always been to escape Turkish oppression by starting a new life in America. This he succeeds in doing in the first two novels (*America, America,* 1962; *The Anatolian*, 1982), but *Beyond the Aegean* finds him back in Turkey in 1921, drawn by the excitement of the Greek offensive directed toward Ankara and the opportunity to profit by buying up Turkish rugs at bargain prices. The novel's plot involves Stavros's various relationships with his business partners, his former lover Althea, his siblings and mother, and Thomna, an Anatolian woman who sees in Stavros the fulfillment of her own dream of life in America. Although he is not sexually attracted to her at the start, his feelings evolve quickly, due to his appreciation of her shrewdness and feisty spirit. He finally grows to love her, and perversely, from her point of view, intends to make a home with her in Greek Anatolia.

Beyond the Aegean is as much the story of the Asia Minor catastrophe as it is of its hero. Stavros, in his pompous certainty that the Greek army will easily achieve its goal, embodies the enthusiasm with which so many contemporary Greeks embraced the Great Idea. Greek victories against Serbs and Bulgars in World War I had boosted confidence. Success seemed a matter of destiny. But before too long, it is clear that the war is not going well. First, the Greeks are stopped short of their crucial objective, Ankara. Then there is a pause, the Greek retreat, in which Stavros is involved, and, finally, the overwhelming Turkish offensive. Kazan puts Stavros in key places to make events more realistic. In particular, he uses his hero's acquaintance with Archbishop Chrysostomos to give him access to the councils of generals and even King Constantine.

The book's climax is the burning of Smyrna, depicted in cinematographic detail. Stavros escapes aboard an American boat. He, like Greece, must adapt to a new reality. In Athens, he manages to combine business acumen with a sense of altruism by helping some of the refugees from this disaster. Though still connected with Greece, he lives out his life in New York, where he has success in business and finds a certain peace. But he has lost Thomna, who, swept away by the chaos of Smyrna's last days while Stavros was saving his rugs, ultimately reclaims her life in the New World with his brother.

Coincidentally, the masterpiece of Anatolian Greek writer Elias Venezis (1904–73) was also published in the United States under the title *Beyond the Aegean* (1943; trans., 1950 in England as *Aeolia*, 1957 in the United States). Set in Anatolia in the years before World War I, this autobiographical novel complements Kazan's trilogy by depicting in detail the way of life destroyed by the catastrophe and by keeping to a rural setting, as opposed to Kazan's focus on cities. The brilliance of this narrative derives from its conflation of the innocence of childhood and its growing awareness of the darker adult world with the Eden of Anatolia and its premonitions of the coming fall into war and disaster.

The first section of Jeffrey Eugenides' (1960–) Pulitzer Prize–winning novel *Middlesex* (2002) describes the escape of the grandparents of the novel's hermaphrodite protagonist from Asia Minor. Desdemona and Eleutherios (Lefty) are orphaned siblings living in Bursa when the Greek offensive starts to unravel in 1921. The confusion that accompanies the rout of the Greek army sweeps them up just as the problem of dealing with the young man's sexuality emerges and throws them together in a desperate attempt to escape through Smyrna, which, with the protecting war boats of the Great Powers in the harbor, seems to them a safe choice. The Turkish army loots and rapes and murders, and the carnage drives the Greeks, spurned by the warships, into the harbor. Lefty manages to secure passage to Greece for himself and his sister by pretending to be a French citizen. In the passions of the moment, they are drawn toward an incestuous union, consummated on the voyage to America. The fifth chromosome with a single recessive gene is thus unleashed. Skipping a generation, it produces the hermaphrodite, Calliope Helen (Cal) Stephanides, born in Detroit in 1960, the narrator and focus of attention of the rest of the novel, which then turns to the immigrant experience of the family and to the complicated life of its protagonist.

Ernest Hemingway's (1899–1961) "On the Quai at Smyrna," a brief but powerful view of the slaughter in the harbor of Smyrna, was published in *In*

Our Time, a set of sketches (1924). Hemingway then used the vignette to begin, and to set the tone for, his first collection of short stories, *In Our Time* (1925).

FURTHER READING

For detailed accounts of the Greco-Turkish War, see Michael Llewellyn-Smith, *Ionian Vision: Greece in Asia Minor, 1919–22* (1973) and Marjorie Housespian, *Smyrna 1922: The Destruction of a City* (1972). C. M. Woodhouse in *Modern Greece* (1991) and Richard Clogg in *A Concise History of Greece* (1992) provide briefer treatments in the context of modern Greek history.

—*Karl Malkoff*

GREECE, OCCUPATION OF (1941–1944)

On October 28, 1940, Benito Mussolini issued an ultimatum to Greek dictator General John Metaxas, demanding passage through Greek territory. Although Greece was in many respects itself a country ruled by FASCISM, acquiescence to the ultimatum would have been a major humiliation. Metaxas's reply, a simple and resounding "no," is still celebrated as a national holiday in Greece. The Italians attacked. They expected an easy time of it but were soon pushed back into Albania, where winter weather led to a stalemate. Unwilling to let that result stand, Germany invaded Greece on April 6 of the following year and entered Athens on April 27. King George II and the government of Emmanuel Tsouderos (Metaxas had died in January) fled to Crete. When the Germans invaded Crete by air on May 20 and captured the island (see CRETE, BATTLE OF), the Greek government took refuge in Egypt. Keeping for themselves the larger centers of population like Athens and Thessalonika and various other key locations like Crete, the Germans turned the occupation of much of the country over to the Italians, until the fall of Mussolini later in the war.

The occupation was severely punishing to Greek citizens in a variety of ways. While in rural Greece it was usually possible to find something to eat, in the cities, particularly Athens, famine was devastating. A black market was necessary, but the greed and self-interest of those who profited from it brought another dimension of pain to the situation. Inflation was rampant; modest quantities of basic foodstuff could cost millions of drachmas.

Although Greece had its collaborators and Nazi sympathizers, resistance was widespread. A month after the German victory, two Greek teenagers snuck past guards and lowered the swastika that had been raised over the acropolis. In addition to many anonymous acts of resistance, there were guerrilla movements. In 1941, the KKE (Communist Party of Greece) created EAM (National Liberation Front) and its military arm, ELAS (National

Popular Liberation Army). The EDES (National Republican Greek Army), monarchist, or at least anticommunist, in its leanings, was a smaller resistance force. In spite of the inherent hostility between ELAS and EDES (see GREEK CIVIL WAR), in 1942 they cooperated with the British Special Operations Executive (SOE), Britain's behind-the-lines presence in occupied Europe, and Colonel C. W. Myers to accomplish one of the single most noteworthy acts of sabotage of the war. Under the leadership of EDES general Napoleon Zervas, they blew up the viaduct at Gorgopotamos, disrupting the flow of German supplies to North Africa.

The Germans responded to resistance with reprisals that involved executions, razing of villages, and horrific massacres at such places as Kalavryta, Komeno, Klisura, Distomon, Khalkis, and Hortiati (see Kurt WALDHEIM). Large-scale killing took place chiefly in the villages, where guerrillas operated, but in some urban areas as well: In Athens as many as 200 hostages were shot in a single day. As for the 80,000 Greek Jews, in spite of a generally sympathetic attitude on the part of Eastern Orthodox Greeks, who in many individual instances hid and saved Jews, and even of the Athenian police, who issued fake identity papers to protect others, all but about 5,000 were deported to concentration camps and killed (see the HOLOCAUST). The gendarmerie in general, however, along with "Security Battalions," substantially composed of fascistically inclined thugs, were responsible for bloody incidents near the end of the occupation.

One of the crueler ironies of the occupation is that when the Germans were finally chased from Greece, rather than having the opportunity to recover and rebuild in peace as was the case elsewhere in Europe, Greece found itself already involved in the Greek Civil War, which would plague the country until 1949.

THE LITERATURE

Apartment in Athens (1945), by Glenway Wescott (1901–87), is set in Greece early in the German occupation, in the apartment of the Helianos family, a Greek household that has felt the impact of the war. Their oldest son, Cimon, has been killed in the battle of Mount Olympus. Mr. Helianos, Nikolas, is a small publisher who has gone out of business since the advent of the Germans. The family now lives on his wife's modest inheritance. Their children are troubled. But things are made considerably worse when Captain Kalter, a German quartermaster, is housed in their apartment.

The captain's presence and his manner—ranging from aloof to sadistic—accentuate the family's problems. But when Kalter, now a major, returns after a two-week absence, it is clear that something cataclysmic has happened to him. He seems less impatient and demanding, more human. He begins to invite Mr. Helianos into his study for evening chats, and when the major tells Helianos of the recent loss of his entire family in the war, the Greek, drawn to him by human grief, forgets himself long enough to offer criticism of Adolf HITLER and Benito Mussolini, as the men who have brought this suffering into the world. Kalter becomes furious, beats Helianos, and denounces him to the Gestapo. Helianos is arrested, leaving his family on its own. Kalter commits suicide. When her husband is executed, the heretofore passive Mrs. Helianos finds resources of which she was totally unaware and, as the novel ends, resolves to do what she can to use the trap the Germans have set for her—to get information about the Resistance—against them.

The novel is extraordinary for its psychological insight, its refusal to simplify complex states of mind, and its ability to avoid sentimentalizing even the most pathetic situations. If, in the broadest sense, it falls within the category of propagandistic literature that celebrates the resiliency of the spirit of the ordinary human being, it earns its insights far more than most.

Corelli's Mandolin (1994; first published in England, 1994, as *Captain Corelli's Mandolin*) by Louis de Bernières (1954–) deals chiefly with the German occupation, but it slides inevitably into the civil war. Set on the island of Cephallonia just before the Italian invasion of Greece, the novel first focuses on Pelagia, the daughter of the skilled, humane, and somewhat ironical Dr. Iannis. She falls in love with Mandras the fisherman and is soon engaged to him, but the war intrudes, and Mandras goes off to join ELAS. We also see events through the eyes of the Italian soldier, Carlo Guercio, homosexual, immensely strong, gentle, and the most heroic figure in the novel. Through him, the hypocrisy, ineptness, and brutal cynicism of the Italian invasion, which soon becomes a fiasco, are revealed.

After the German intervention, Italians and their German overseers occupy the island. Carlo becomes the aide of Captain Antonio Corelli, who is quartered in the house of Dr. Iannis and his daughter. Corelli is a disillusioned patriot, a lover of music, and, above all, a decent human being. In spite of her persistent refusal to give aid and comfort to the enemy, Pelagia falls in love with him as she falls out of love with Mandras. The fisherman himself has come under the sway of ELAS leader Hector, who takes orders directly from Aris Veloukhiotis. The guerrilla leader, responsible for numerous atrocities, is treacherous, petty, and far more interested in personal gain and in jockeying for position in postwar Greece than in fighting the Nazis. His encounter with the historical figure Colonel Myers makes the case against the leftist guerrillas in its strongest form.

When Italy surrenders to the Allies in 1943, the Italians, who vastly outnumber the Germans on the island, are betrayed by the indifference of the British and the incompetence of their own officers. When Germans arrive in force, most of the Italians are executed. Carlo dies protecting Corelli with his body. Severely wounded, but alive, Corelli is tended to by Iannis and his daughter and is finally smuggled off the island by the British.

With the liberation, Mandras returns to claim his betrothed, but her contempt and that of his mother lead him to suicide. The novel now moves at a quicker pace toward its conclusion. Pelagia adopts an abandoned baby whom she names Antonia. Corelli, returning, sees her with the baby and assumes Pelagia has a new love. Only at the novel's conclusion are they reunited.

Bernières's lively prose and the witty edge that hovers between satire and tragedy won the novel critical acclaim, but the author's anger at the Greek Left produces a politically distorted version of events, not so much by exaggerating the excesses of the Communists, but by ignoring the abuses of the Greek right and the heavy-handed intervention of the Allies in Greek politics.

FURTHER READING

Mark Mazower gives a lucid and well-documented account of the occupation in *Inside Hitler's Greece* (1993). See also C. M. Woodhouse's *The Struggle for Greece, 1941–1949* (1976), as well as appropriate sections in Woodhouse's *Modern Greece* (1991) and Richard Clogg's *A Concise History of Greece* (1992) for further historical analyses.

—*Karl Malkoff*

GREEK CIVIL WAR (1945–1949)

During Germany's WORLD WAR II occupation of GREECE, marked by devastating famine in the cities and retaliatory massacres in the villages, the civilian population as a whole may have suffered more intensely than any in Western Europe. But during the attempt to organize an effective resistance and to make common cause with the British, then the only enemy of Germany able to assist, Greece slipped inexorably and almost seamlessly into an even crueler civil war.

King George II's questionable decisions during the electoral crises of 1936, in which long-standing tensions between right and left resulted in an impasse, created the fault lines along which the murderous midcentury schism developed. Two indecisive elections within several months had given the balance of power to the Communists, a situation unacceptable to the king, who began to rely more and more on the right-wing leader General Ioannis Metaxas. Ultimately George declared a state of emergency that gave dictatorial powers to the general. As a result, the legitimacy of the Greek government in exile during the Axis occupation would be in doubt and beyond resolution as long as the war continued. Disagreements that might have otherwise ended in shouting matches in Parliament and demonstrations in the street became lethal in the context of war.

Greece entered World War II in October 1940, when it repelled an Italian invasion, but the German offensive of April 1941 quickly brought the country under Axis control. As in other instances during this war, the Communists offered the most effective, most organized resistance to the occupation. In 1941, they created EAM (National Liberation Front) and soon after its military counterpart, ELAS (National Popular Liberation Army), led by guerrilla leaders such as Aris Veloukhiotis. Although communist-inspired, EAM nonetheless attracted many others who opposed both constitutional monarchy and dictatorship and who favored the creation of a more egalitarian society. The EDES (National Republican Greek Army), which owed its allegiance to the right, formed a much smaller center of resistance. In 1942, Winston Churchill ordered British support for all groups actively resisting the Nazis, but he directed most assistance to monarchist groups, and in 1943 he and Franklin Delano ROOSEVELT urged the king to maintain his government in exile.

Strengthened by the acquisition of equipment after the surrender of Italy in 1943, ELAS dominated the rural areas of Greece, while EAM set up an alternative to the government in exile. The formation in Cairo of a new cabinet by Emmanouil Tsouderos, who had succeeded Metaxas as prime minister in 1941, was followed by a mutiny of Greek armed forces operating in Egypt. Two brigades of Greek soldiers who had been evacuated from Greece and elements of the Greek navy revolted and purged themselves of anticommunist officers. The infantry surrendered when confronted with overwhelming British force, and the Greek navy loyal to the government supported by the British Royal Navy similarly put down the mutiny at sea. Nonetheless, ELAS seemed in an advantageous position from which to seize power as the Germans withdrew from Greece. In the end, British pressure, and behind the scenes negotiations with Joseph STALIN, undermined the Communists and resulted in their surrender of power to George Papandreou's National Unity government in 1944.

When British troops landed at Patras in October 1944, their operations seemed at least as concerned with neutralizing still-active ELAS units as with pursuing the Germans. With Churchill's support and American neutrality, General Nicholas Plastiras formed a government that promised, in an agreement reached at Varkiza in February 1945, amnesty, democratic elections, and a plebiscite on the monarchy. But before elections were held, there was a ferocious onslaught against the left, during which right-wing thugs were turned loose in the countryside. The election of a Labor government in Britain brought no relief, but rather a continuation of Churchill's policies.

In October 1946, Markos Vafiadis formed the Democratic Army out of the remnants of ELAS and soon had a guerrilla force of 100,000. In March 1947, Britain informed the United States that it could no longer fulfill its responsibilities in Greece, leading to further involvement of the United States in Greece's affairs through the Truman Doctrine—America's vow to combat communism wherever it might appear in the world. On the other side, Communist forces loyal to Moscow were taking control of the Democratic Army, creating a wave of leftist terror, including the kidnapping of children sent to be raised in Eastern European countries. Stalinist Nikos

Zachariadis succeeded in influencing and finally controlling the mode of combat. He supported terrorist activities that alienated liberals in the population and ultimately made the unwise decision in 1948 to fight the government as a regular army rather than a guerrilla force. Even more decisive a blow to the leftist cause was struck by the split between Stalin and Marshal Tito, leader of Yugoslavia, which resulted in the sealing of the Yugoslavian border in 1949. In October of that year, the Communists proclaimed a temporary halt to hostilities that was soon understood to be permanent.

THE LITERATURE

The Greek civil war provides the subject for *The Fratricides* (1963; trans., 1964) by Nikos Kazantzakis (1883–1957), well known outside of Greece for novels such as *Zorba the Greek* (1946; trans., 1952) and *The Last Temptation of Christ* (1955; trans., 1960), and for his epic poem, *The Odyssey: A Modern Sequel* (1938; trans., 1958). The fratricidal fury of the civil war provides a gruesome laboratory in which the claims of a beneficent, all-powerful divinity are tested. Set during Holy Week, the novel begins with the civil war well under way. Three times the Reds (members of ELAS) have captured the village Castello; three times the Blacks (supporters of EDES and the government) have recaptured it. Father Yánaros, the village priest, is appalled by the spectacle of brother against brother, both literally and figuratively. He is momentarily attracted by the notion that Lenin is the new Christ, come to right the many wrongs of the contemporary world, to redeem the poor and the oppressed, and that "this unjust world would crumble by the hand of God." But he inevitably concludes, "earthly paradise is the work of the devil." The contending forces are crucifying Greece. In protest against the incessant slaughter, he decides he will not resurrect Christ this Easter season. (In Kazantzakis's work, and perhaps in the villages of Greece as well, Easter Mass is not so much a celebration of the Resurrection as a yearly reenactment of it.)

Father Yánaros has decided there is no right side. Simply refusing to resurrect Christ is not enough; he must save his village. Knowing the guerrillas plan to attack Castello again soon, he goes into the mountains to meet with their leader, his own son, Captain Drakos. With some difficulty, he persuades Drakos to promise not to kill anyone if the village is handed over to him. Drakos is a fighter for freedom rather than a Communist, but looking over his shoulder at all times is his doctrinaire Communist second-in-command, Loukas. In Castello, Father Yánaros has difficulty persuading the villagers to surrender the city in exchange for promises of no reprisals, but with the aid of a villager's vision of the Virgin, which Father Yánaros does not see, but (with serious reservations) capitalizes upon, he persuades them.

Captain Drakos and his men descend on Castello and meet no resistance. But Drakos has already betrayed his father and threatens to execute all fighters who will not switch sides. With his enemies against the wall, Drakos hesitates, but Loukas eggs him on. The villagers are executed, and Father Yánaros, their blood on his hands, goes off, promising to preach against the Communists wherever he goes. Drakos is on the verge of letting him go, but Loukas again pushes him over the edge, and the priest is shot dead.

As is often the case in Kazantzakis's work, the novel focuses on a man's attempt to engage God, to struggle with Him, even to give Him meaning. But *The Fratricides* encounters the heart of the historical moment as well. There is a real sense of the need for revolution, for social justice, and therefore sympathy for the guerrillas, but the character of Loukas dramatizes the pernicious effect of dogmatic communism controlled by Stalin. The only character in the novel for whom Kazantzakis shows no sympathy whatsoever, Loukas embodies the excesses that deprived the left of the broader popular support it needed to prevail.

Stratis Tsirkas's (1911–80) trilogy, *Drifting Cities* (*The Club*, 1960; *Ariadne*, 1962; *The Bat*, 1965; trans., 1974), presents another aspect of the civil war, from a decidedly different political perspective. This intricately designed novel, marked by a variety of points of view and narrative modes, has at its center the fight for the soul of the Greek army that, along with the government, has regrouped in Egypt after the German victory. The "Drifting Cities," where the books are respectively set, are Jerusalem, Cairo, and Alexandria. The hero, Manos Simonidis (also known as Kaloyannis), an intellectual in the Communist Party and a Greek army officer, is caught in the labyrinthine cities and in an equally convoluted series of events. Each book of the trilogy is presided over by its own Ariadne (the daughter of Minos and the woman who helped Theseus find his way out of the labyrinth): Emmy, the promiscuous aristocrat whose desire for Minos is never consummated; Ariagne (whose name represents the way the name *Ariadne* is pronounced on Naxos), the maternal figure protecting her real and figurative children from the Minotaurs of war and intrigue; and Nancy, the upperclass Englishwoman with socialist leanings.

After deserting from army units controlled by right-wing political forces, Manos labors to rejoin the First Greek Brigade fighting with the Allies at EL ALAMEIN in October 1942. Ironically, he succeeds in reaching the Greek army in Egypt only when their adversaries are the British, who in the spring of 1943 treat the mutinous Greek anti-Royalists more harshly than they do their Nazi prisoners.

All the while, he struggles with the Communist Party hierarchy, whose orders, which rarely fit the circumstances, seem to be generated by motives, personal or political, not open to scrutiny. But with all of Manos's frustration with Communists, they have their redeeming points, and all—or almost all—believe they are working toward a better world. The true villains are the Greek right, the British and Americans attempting to ensure the continuance of the monarchy after the war, and those who allow themselves to be manipulated by these reactionary forces. In the trilogy's climax, after the leftists have purged right-wing officers, British forces surround the Greek brigades and disperse some and send others on a death march across the desert, and the ships that have mutinied are surrounded by the British and loyalist Greek navy and disarmed.

Tsirkas, a Marxist literary critic whose biases are quite clear, nonetheless offers an accurate representation of the extent to which fears of the left undercut the war against FASCISM.

FURTHER READING

See appropriate sections in C. M. Woodhouse's *Modern Greece* (1991) and Richard Clogg's *A Concise History of Greece* (1992) for more insight. Woodhouse, who replaced Myers as colonel in command of the Allied military mission to the Greek guerrillas, strives with fair success for objectivity in *The Struggle for Greece, 1941–1949* (1976). See also Edgar O'Ballance's *The Greek Civil War, 1944–1949* (1966) for further analysis.

—Karl Malkoff

GREEK COLONELS

In the wake of the assassination of Grigorios LAMBRAKIS in 1963, the center-right government of Constantine Karamanlis could not hold. Elections in November brought George Papandreou's Center Union party to power. Papandreou relied heavily on his American-educated economist son, Andreas, who was suspected of being affiliated with ASPIDA (Shield), a left-wing cabal within the army. King Constantine, who ascended to the throne in 1964, maneuvered the elderly Papandreou into resigning in July of 1965. The subsequent government had little legitimacy, and when new elections were finally called in 1967, a cadre of junior officers, anticipating a left-wing landslide, initiated a coup d'état, which led to the seven-year dictatorship of the colonels. United by their fear of the left, the colonels pursued contradictory goals, rejecting Western values as inimical to Greek Orthodox traditions, but at the same time depending militarily and politically on American and North Atlantic Treaty Organization (NATO) support and economically on tourism from and trade with the Western nations. Colonel George Papadopoulos served as prime minister until 1973. Political enemies were treated brutally, sent to detention islands, or exiled. Protest was stifled, although sporadic demonstrations were held, and in 1968 Center Union activist Alexander Panagoulis famously, and unsuccessfully, attempted to assassinate Papadopoulos. A student uprising at the Polytechnic Institute in Athens in 1973, in which dozens of students were killed, weakened the unpopular regime severely, causing the removal of Papadopoulos and the ascension of

General Phaedon Gizikis as president, with General Dimitrios Ioannides in real control. The junta's initiation of a failed coup aimed at President Makarios of Cyprus led finally to its downfall. The return of Karamanlis to power and a referendum that rejected the monarchy soon followed. When the Communist Party was once again made legal, it seemed that while the fault lines in Greek society remained, democracy had been irrevocably established. The episode, however, left many wounds. The Greek left, for example, has never forgiven the United States for its putative involvement in the colonel's coup or its overt support of the regime.

THE LITERATURE

In *A Man* (1979; trans., 1980), Oriana Fallaci (1930–) gives a fictionalized account of the life of Alexander Panagoulis, from the day of his unsuccessful attempt to assassinate George Papadopoulos in August 1968 until his death in a highly suspicious traffic accident in 1976. Fallaci, who was Panagoulis's lover from his release in 1973 until his death, gives a disturbingly detailed account of the brutal torture to which Panagoulis was subjected. He is sentenced to death, and when the sentence is commuted because of international pressure, he is repeatedly led to believe that it has only been postponed for another 24 hours. He then endures years of solitary confinement in a prison only several paces square. Panagoulis not only survives, but in his total abandon—especially when he realizes that Papadopoulos needs to keep him alive for propagandistic reasons—he succeeds in mentally tormenting his keepers and in persuading some of his guards to aid him in ultimately unsuccessful attempts to escape.

Panagoulis is a loner, committed to freedom rather than to any ideology. When he is free, even after the dictatorship is toppled, his life is immensely difficult, since he is unable to align himself with any political party. He has contempt for Karamanlis, whom all but the far right hail as a savior, and he seems to hate Andreas Papandreou more than Papadopoulos or the even more ruthless Ioannides. And Evangelos Averoff, to many an enemy of the colonels, one who attempted to depose them, but to Panagoulis the archetype of the hypocritical survivor, becomes his new dragon.

Panagoulis never does what anyone expects him to do; he always chooses the harder path and becomes such a gadfly to so many interests that his unrelenting paranoia becomes justified, as he hurtles toward the death he feels fated for, the victim of an attack on the road that is thinly disguised as a traffic accident. (C. M. Woodhouse, however, in his *The Rise and Fall of the Greek Colonels*, seems to dismiss this account as a symptom of the Greek need to account for every misfortune as being the fault of some malevolent outside force.)

Fallaci's love for Panagoulis, although fully sexual, is driven by her abstract view of him as a hero committed to sacrificing himself for his people.

Their preconceived, and to a large extent justified, ideas of each other are crucial to their affair, which is underway almost before they meet, he the slayer of dragons, she the justice-loving journalist who chronicles the exploits of such men and women. Told in the second person, her account, a paean to her dead lover, cannot be free of bias, but it is searingly persuasive.

FURTHER READING

The Panagoulis case is described by C. M. Woodhouse in *The Rise and Fall of the Greek Colonels* (1985), and in *Greece under Military Rule*, edited by Richard Clogg and George Yannopoulos.

—*Karl Malkoff*

GULAG

Gulag is a Russian acronym for "Chief Administration of Corrective Labor Camps," the bureau of the secret police that administered the hundreds of prisons and camps, stretched throughout the Soviet Union during the reign of Joseph STALIN, from the 1920s to his death in 1953. In the course of that period, an estimated 15 million perished in these camps, many of them the victims of Stalin's 1920s attempts to impose collectivism in agriculture, or his 1930s policy of the GREAT TERROR, or his post–WORLD WAR II purges of returning Russian prisoners of war, Jews, and professionals. The government's early justification for the system invoked the idea of "corrective labor," the use of work to rehabilitate all those who had committed crimes against the state. As the number of inmates grew, it became clear that a vast slave labor population added significantly to the national economy. Thus the policy served a dual purpose: smashing internal opposition while boosting the economy. Three years after Stalin's death, Nikita Khruschev exposed his crimes at a closed meeting of the 20th Congress.

THE LITERATURE

The full extent of the horror and murderous brutality of the gulag system was brought to world attention in 1973 with the publication in Paris of the first volume of Aleksandr Solzhenitsyn's (1918–) *The Gulag Archipelago* (1973–75; trans., 1974–79), a massively documented three-volume combined history/memoir. Solzhenitsyn (1918–), a great writer as well as one of the most heroic Soviet dissidents, was imprisoned for eight years in a gulag camp. His experience forms the nucleus of his voluminously detailed, exhaustive history of the horrors of the gulag, adding up to a massive indictment of the Soviet system.

Seven years before writing his enormous nonfictional history, Solzhenitsyn published a novel that set the stage for his later work. *One Day in the Life of Ivan Denisovich* (1962; trans., 1963) chronicles life in the gulag on a typical day, as experienced by one prisoner, Ivan Denisovich Shukhov. Ivan's first chore on arising is to dispose of the heavy toilet bucket. Then he must mop the floor at headquarters. After breakfast, he marches to his work site, with the other members of his squad, who represent a cross section of gulag prisoners: a man whose only crime is that his father was a *kulak* (a land-owning peasant); a former soldier who had survived internment at Buchenwald only to be imprisoned on returning home; a former communist official accused of spying; and a young man imprisoned for being a devout Baptist, who happily embraces this opportunity to "die for the sake of the Lord Jesus." Ivan is serving a 10-year sentence for high treason. It seems that during the war he was captured by the Germans. In Stalin's vocabulary, "surrender" is synonymous with "betrayal."

Ivan's task on this day is to be a mason, building a wall. This proves to be the highpoint of his day, as he constructs a good, solid, straight wall, feeling the pride and satisfaction of a job well done. The satisfaction is enough to sustain him, and he goes to sleep that night "fully content" for "a day without a dark cloud. Almost a happy day."

The irony of the last line is typical of the tone of the whole book, written in a racy, colloquial style that is infused with empathy for the suffering prisoners. According to the Russian literature scholar Edward Brown, *One Day* "burst upon the Soviet reader in 1962 like a shot in the night. As a revelation of the daily misery experienced by the inmates of Stalin's concentration camps, the novel had an immediate and sensational success." Permission to publish the novel came directly from Nikita Khruschev, who saw it as a splendid vehicle in his campaign to de-Stalinize (by exposing the Stalin myth) the Soviet Union. What the Soviet governments later learned to their regret was that *One Day* was merely the first salvo in Solzhenitsyn's war, not simply on Stalin, but on every aspect of communism.

Supplementing and expanding *One Day* is Vasily Grossman's *Forever Flowing* (1970; trans., 1972), which examines not just life in the camps, but the "free" society in the Soviet Union. Grossman's protagonist, Ivan Gregoryevich, is a political prisoner who has been freed after 30 years in the camps. He returns to a world that has moved on without him; relatives, friends, some of whom had survived by informing, are all nursing unexpressed guilt and resentment at his presence, and the woman he loved long ago is now married to someone else. He moves to a small city in South Russia, where he falls in love with and marries his landlady, a gentle widow.

Interlaced within the story are Ivan's passionate memories and meditations on Soviet Russia, the accounts of the disasters of forced collectivization, the widespread use of informers, and the personal outrages that poisoned everyday life. Stalin's betrayal of the revolution was completed with the GREAT TERROR. After the 1930s came a new generation: "They were not the children of the Revolution. They were the children of the state the Revolution had created." This and later generations exist in a world permeated by the absence of freedom, a void antithetical to the "Russian soul." In a surprising turn, Ivan does not lay all of the blame on Stalin. For Ivan, before Stalin there was Vladimir Ilich LENIN. It was Lenin who established the secret police, setting in motion the murderous machinery that Stalin put to work. In the novel's melancholy conclusion, Ivan, his wife having died, takes a trip to his childhood home, only to find it in ruins, a symbol of the fate of freedom in the Soviet Union.

In *The Mandarins* (1954), a novel by Simone de Beauvoir (1908–86), French leftist intellectuals, particularly the characters based upon EXISTEN-TIALISTS Albert Camus and Jean-Paul Sartre, undergo a crisis of conscience about revealing their knowledge of the gulag system.

FURTHER READING

Michael Jakobson's *Origins of the GULAG* (1992) is a carefully detailed account of the ongoing conduct of the system. Edward Brown's *Russian Literature since the Revolution* (1963), an eloquent and authoritative study of its subject, includes an excellent chapter on the literature of the gulag.

H

HAPSBURG [HABSBURG] EMPIRE, FALL OF (1918)

From the 15th to the 20th centuries, the House of Hapsburg was the most enduring and powerful dynasty in Europe. For a good part of that time, Hapsburg rulers also held the title of Holy Roman emperor. Although the empire varied in size throughout the centuries, its core consisted of Austria, Hungary, northern Italy, Bohemia (Czech Republic), Slovakia, Croatia, and Slovenia. Attempts to retain control over this wide range of peoples and lands became increasingly difficult in the wake of the strong movements for independence that sprang up in the late 19th century. Added to the administrative problems were the continual power struggles with foreign governments that further weakened the empire.

At the turn of the 20th century, Vienna, the capital city, experienced a cultural and intellectual renaissance that was the envy of all Europe. A brief list of the names associated with Vienna in the first decade of the century includes the philosopher Ludwig Wittgenstein, the composers Gustav Mahler and Arnold Schonberg, the writers Arthur Schnitzler, Karl Kraus, and Hermann Broch, the artists Gustav Klimt and Egon Schiele, the architects Otto Wagner and Adolph Loos, and, most important, Sigmund Freud, whose pioneering work made Vienna synonymous with the new science of PSYCHOANALYSIS.

Politically, however, the empire was in its last days, symbolized by its aging emperor, Franz Joseph (1830–1916), whose long rule was coming to a sad ending with the assassination of his wife, Elizabeth (1898), and the suicide of his son and heir to the throne, Rudolph (1899). To the end, the emperor maintained a strict military discipline, rising each morning at 5:00 and performing ceremonial and administrative duties as conscientiously in old age as he had in youth. But he was a dutiful soldier in a time that required an imaginative leader. He deeply distrusted change or innovation of any kind, leaving the essential tasks of government to a vast, moribund bureaucracy.

In 1908, Austria annexed the Balkan state of Bosnia, a move that was to bring about the end of the empire. Six years later, in response to the growth of Serb nationalism, the heir to the Hapsburg throne, Archduke FRANZ FERDINAND and his wife visited the Bosnian capitol Sarajevo, where they were assassinated by a Serbian nationalist. This event triggered WORLD WAR I, the defeat of Austria-Hungary, and the subsequent dissolution of the empire.

THE LITERATURE

The last years of the Hapsburg Empire provide the background for an outstanding novel, Joseph Roth's (1894–1939) *The Radetzky March* (1932; trans., 1933; new trans., 1995). *The Radetzky March* begins with a key anecdote. During the battle of Solferino (1859), Lieutenant Joseph Trotta saves the life of the young Hapsburg emperor, Franz Joseph, by pushing him aside and taking a bullet in the shoulder. As a result, Trotta is knighted and glorified as the "Hero of Solferino," his deed, mythologized in elementary school textbooks. Basically a simple peasant at heart, he lives the rest of his life uneasy and unhappy with his fame and with his new status as a gentleman. His son, Franz, adjusting more readily to the new status, becomes a provincial district commissioner, a position of some importance in the far-flung Hapsburg Empire.

The Austrian military ideal is epitomized by "The Radetzky March"—a stirring march, composed by the elder Johann Strauss, that celebrates an Austrian field marshal who captured Venice in 1849. This tune, played every Sunday afternoon in the village where Franz resides, represents the glory and splendor of the empire and the military heroism that sustains it.

The major figure of the novel is Franz's son, Carl Joseph, who is commissioned in the army in the years immediately preceding 1914. Carl Joseph has no particular gift for, or interest in, army life. He is merely following his father's wishes. For a young officer, the prewar military world is one of meaningless drills, dissolute living, and mindless adherence to an outmoded code of behavior that involves heavy drinking, erotic escapades, and participation in duels of honor. Contrasted to the ideal depicted by "The Radetzky March" is the tawdry, stagnant reality of an empire and an army in dissolution. That contrast is further embodied in the figure of Franz Joseph himself, the divinely anointed sovereign, now a tired, unhappy, forgetful octogenarian with a runny nose.

When the war breaks out, Carl Joseph is killed during a battle in which he attempts to secure water for his troops. He dies "holding not a weapon but two pails." His heartbroken father, who has never been able to express his love for his son, comes to Vienna, waiting outside the imperial Schoenbrunn palace until he hears the news of the emperor's death. He returns to his village to die shortly after. At Trotta's funeral, his friend, Dr. Skowronneck, makes the novel's final point:

> "I would have liked to have added," said the mayor, "that Herr von Trotta could not outlive the Kaiser. Don't you agree, Doctor?"
> "I don't know," Dr. Skowronnek replied. "I don't think either one of them could have outlived Austria."

As these lines suggest, the novel balances a clear-eyed critique of an empire whose end was inevitable with a sense of loss, felt all the more powerfully when the novel was written in 1932, with the threat of Nazism looming on the horizon. As that threat grew nearer, Roth, who was Jewish, became increasingly committed to the imperial ideal. He died in Paris in 1939, a refugee from his native land and a despairing but vehement supporter of the return of the Hapsburgs.

FURTHER READING

Arthur May's *The Passing of the Hapsburg Monarchy, 1914–18* (2 vols., 1966) is a highly informative, detailed account; Sidney Rosenfeld's *Understanding Joseph Roth* (2001) emphasizes the theme of displacement, the loss of the homeland, in Roth's work.

HARLEM RENAISSANCE

See JAZZ AGE.

HIROSHIMA (1945)

In the first half of the 20th century, Hiroshima was a major military industrial city in southwestern Japan. On the morning of August 6, 1945, a specially equipped American B-29, the *Enola Gay*, dropped an atomic bomb that detonated some 1,800 feet above the city. The blast devastated four-fifths of all the buildings within seven square miles of the center. The single bomb claimed 78,000 lives, but that figure does not include the effect no one had sufficiently anticipated: The explosion created a mushroom cloud that turned into a "black rain," pouring radioactive fallout on the stricken city.

Immediately after the bombing, the United States demanded the surrender of Japan. The Japanese made no response, and on August 9 the Americans dropped an atomic bomb on the city of Nagasaki, killing 40,000 people and destroying 40 percent of its buildings. Six days later Japanese emperor

Hirohito delivered a radio address to the nation in which, without ever mentioning the word *surrender*, he called upon the people to accept the terms of a forthcoming peace treaty.

Seven years later the United States exploded a hydrogen bomb off the island of Eniwetok in the Pacific. It was 200 times more powerful than the bomb dropped on Hiroshima. The world had entered the infinitely dangerous nuclear age.

THE LITERATURE

Black Rain (1966; trans., 1969) by the Japanese novelist Masuji Ibuse (1898–1993) is an extraordinarily powerful novel dealing with the Hiroshima bombing. Cast in the form of several diaries, particularly that of Shigematsu Shizuma, a midlevel executive in a factory that manufactures army uniforms, the novel offers a straightforward, unvarnished account of the city on that fateful day. Avoiding any direct attempt to comprehend the full extent of the disaster, Ibuse focuses on individual experiences, counterpointing these often hideous descriptions with imagery from the natural and animal world. The novel opens four years after the bombing. Shigematsu has begun reading the diary he kept at the time in the hope that it will reveal some important information concerning his niece, Yasuko, who was exposed to radioactive waves and, as a result, is shunned as an eligible marriage partner.

As the diary records it, Yasuko is not in the city on August 6, but she returns the following day and is exposed to the "black rain," the contaminated rain that fell on Hiroshima on August 7. Shigematsu struggles with a sense of guilt for not protecting his niece, although he realizes no one could have foreseen that the aftereffects of the bomb would prove as deadly as the immediate destruction. The novel's title reinforces this theme of the perversion of nature—that rain, the source of rebirth and regeneration, should become the agent of death, as if to say that the human mastery of the physical world had unleashed an evil that is out of control.

Shigematsu's description of "A Mass for the Dead Insects," a traditional Buddhist ritual commemorating the insects whom human beings have unknowingly killed as they go about their business, provides a searing parallel to the human "insects" so casually annihilated. The last diary entry is dated August 15. In the novel's quiet ending, Shigematsu walks away from a crowd that is listening to the emperor's radio address and finds a nearby stream, where baby eels are battling their way upstream—a promise of rebirth in the midst of defeat and despair. Now four years after the bombing, it is clear that Yasuko will almost certainly die of radiation poisoning, but Shigematsu refuses to succumb to despair. He has experienced a purifying fire and acquired a tragic wisdom. In 1989 the novel was adapted to the screen by the Japanese director Shohei Imamura.

Among other notable works evoked by the Hiroshima bombing are John Hersey's (1914–84) nonfictional report *Hiroshima* (1946) and Alain Resnais's memorable film *Hiroshima, mon amour* (1959), the screenplay for which was written by Marguerite Duras (1914–).

FURTHER READING

Jane Claypool's *Hiroshima and Nagasaki* (1984) briefly describes the bombing and discusses the controversies that have arisen regarding the use of nuclear weapons. Anthony Liman's "Black Rain" is a critical study in *Approaches to the Modern Japanese Novel*, edited by Kenya Tsuruta and Thomas Swann (1976).

HISS-CHAMBERS CASE (1948–1950)

Alger Hiss (1904–96) was a career U.S. State Department official who served as an adviser to Franklin Delano ROOSEVELT at the Yalta Conference (where in 1943 Winston Churchill, Roosevelt, and Joseph STALIN planned the defeat of Germany) and as temporary secretary-general of the United Nations in 1946. Later he became head of the Carnegie Foundation for International Peace. Whittaker Chambers (1901–61) was a journalist who joined the Communist Party in 1923, serving as a member of a Communist spy ring until the mid-1930s when he broke with the party. In 1948, Chambers testified before the House Un-American Activities Committee that Hiss had been a fellow spy in the 1930s. Hiss sued Chambers for slander. During the trial, Hiss denied ever having met Chambers.

Chambers then produced State Department documents (Chambers had hidden them in a pumpkin, on his farm, giving rise to their popular description as "the pumpkin papers"), asserting that they had been given to him by Hiss to pass on to Soviet agents. Hiss was indicted for perjury. The first trial ended in a hung jury. In the second trial in 1950, the jury found Hiss guilty. Sentenced to five years in prison, Hiss was released in 1954 and continued to proclaim his innocence until his death in 1996. Hiss's prominence made the case a cause célèbre, contributing to already growing American postwar anxiety over the threat of communism that was reflected in the emergence of MCCARTHYISM. Subsequent evidence, recorded in a heavily researched study of the case, Allen Weinstein's *Perjury* (1978), suggests that Hiss was the highly placed American diplomat referred to in secret Soviet files as "Ales."

THE LITERATURE

Chambers was the model for a major character in *The Middle of the Journey*, a novel published in 1947 by the distinguished literary critic Lionel Trilling (1905–75). The date of publication is particularly significant because it predates by at least a year Chambers's testimony before the House committee. As Trilling explains in his introduction to the 1975 reprint of his novel, he had no prior knowledge of the case. Trilling had never known, or even known of,

Hiss, but he had been an acquaintance, not a friend, of Chambers for 20 years. He chose Chambers as his model for the ex-Communist character Gifford Maxim because "Chambers was the first person I ever knew whose commitment to radical politics was meant to be definitive of his whole moral being, the controlling element of his existence." That commitment had led Chambers to become an espionage agent; his later defection caused him both mental agony and physical fear. The fear grew out of his expectation that in quitting the party, he had put his life in jeopardy.

In *The Middle of the Journey*, John Laskell, a young man recovering from a serious illness, leaves New York for a recuperative vacation in the Connecticut countryside, near his married friends Arthur and Nancy Croom. The visit culminates in a tragic accident whose consequences intensify ideological confrontations between Laskell, the Crooms and Gifford Maxim, the ex-Communist in fear of his life, who exposes the shallowness of the Crooms' flirtation with Marxism. More challenging is the conflict between Laskell's liberal humanism and Maxim's newly acquired religious conservatism, reminiscent of the famous exchanges between Leo Naptha and Settembrini in Thomas Mann's *The Magic Mountain* (1924; trans., 1927). In this debate Trilling's antipathy for Maxim's ideas are clear, but he does full justice to the power and cogency of Maxim's argument.

As a historical novel, *The Middle of the Journey* represents an acutely perceptive attempt, in the author's words, "to draw out some of the moral and intellectual implications of the powerful attraction to communism felt by a considerable part of the American intellectual class during the Thirties and Forties." As a psychological novel, it offers a penetrating account of a man's attempt to come to terms with the fact of death. It is a measure of the novel's significant achievement that it merges the historical and the psychological elements seamlessly.

FURTHER READING

Whittaker Chambers's autobiography *Witness* (1952) is a fascinating account of the man and his time. In his memoir *Recollections of a Life* (1988), Alger Hiss maintained his innocence. Another revelation confirming Chambers's testimony appeared in Elinor Langer's biographical account of the novelist Josephine Herbst (*Josephine Herbst: The Story She Could Never Tell*, 1984). Herbst was married to the writer John Hermann, who was a member of a secret Communist cell in Washington. Herbst knew Chambers at the time and knew that Hiss and Chambers had met, but she did not reveal this fact in order to protect Hermann.

HITLER, ADOLF (1889–1945)

Adolf Hitler was born in a small town in Austria, Braunau on the Inn. His father was a customs official; his mother had been a maid in the Hitler household. As a young man, Adolf moved to Vienna to pursue a career as an artist, but the Vienna Academy of Fine Arts rejected his application, and in 1913 he moved to Munich and joined the German army. During WORLD WAR I, he was wounded and sent to a military hospital. While he was still a patient there, the armistice was declared, an act that he viewed as a betrayal of Germany, the result of the machinations of Jews and Marxist revolutionaries. He became a political instructor for the army, a post that put him in touch with other dissident military figures. His skill as an orator soon led to his assuming the leadership of what was to become the National Socialist (Nazi) Party. In 1923, he led an attempted coup, the MUNICH PUTSCH, the failure of which led to his imprisonment. While in prison, he dictated a book containing his political and racial theories, *Mein Kampf* (1925–26; trans., 1933). After his release, the National Socialist Party gained power steadily; so by 1933 he assumed the post of chancellor.

Once in power he suppressed all opposition, assumed dictatorial powers, and began his persecution of Jews and other minorities. He also inaugurated a massive rearmament campaign that took Germany out of the depression and prepared the way for a series of aggressive incursions into Austria, the Sudetenland, and Czechoslovakia. In an attempt to appease him, the British and French governments signed the MUNICH PACT in 1938, which only whetted his appetite for further aggression.

In September 1939, he ordered the invasion of Poland, setting off WORLD WAR II. His initial success in the war led him to invade the Soviet Union in 1941, a move that was to bring about his eventual downfall. In 1944, he survived the JULY 20 PLOT on his life, but within nine months, with virtually all of Germany in ruins, he was a shattered wreck, huddled in his bunker as the Russian army stormed into Berlin (see BERLIN, FALL OF). On April 30, 1945, four days after his 56th birthday, he committed suicide along with his mistress, Eva Braun, whom he had married the evening before.

The facts of Hitler's life offer clues but no answers to the questions raised in journalist Ron Rosenbaum's provocative *Explaining Hitler* (1998), mainly "who he was, who he *thought* he was, and why he did what he did." These questions have elicited a range of responses from experts who have researched and analyzed every known aspect of his life. Their answers suggest that, in looking for explanations, the experts are digging a bottomless well. Rosenbaum characterizes one Hitler theory as "Hitler as Hamlet," a view he dismisses. However, in a sense there is an appropriate parallel between the prince of Denmark and the führer of the Third Reich: Despite commentary that would fill libraries, no one has been able, as yet, to "pluck out the heart" of their mysteries.

THE LITERATURE

In English alone, there are more than 50 novels in which Hitler plays a prominent role. Many of these are designed to capitalize on the hypnotic fascination their subject holds for so many. In *Imagining Hitler* (1985), the critic Alvin Rosenfeld (1938–) examines the negative implications of this fascination and concludes on a despairing note: "[N]o representations of Hitler, highbrow or low, seem adequately to present the man or satisfactorily to explain him." Rosenfeld sees Hitler fiction as guilty of either demonizing or domesticating its subject, most of it designed to capitalize on the perverse fascination the führer holds for so many. He argues that even those novels with a more serious purpose, either to capture a particular point in his evolution or, more ambitiously, to explore questions about the meaning or nature of human evil, end up allowing Hitler to escape from the reality of history into the sphere of myth.

An example of a novel with the modest aim of capturing a particular phase of Hitler's life is Beryl Bainbridge's (1933–) *Young Adolph* (1978). Young Adolph, 23 years old, flees possible conscription in the Austrian army to visit his half brother, Alois, and his brother's wife, Bridget, who are living, in a working-class section of Liverpool, England. Adolph turns out to be an unwanted guest, moody, hostile, clumsy, and lazy. In Bainbridge's hands, the future führer exemplifies not so much "the banality of evil" as the banality that precedes evil. When his relatives have had enough of him, they buy him a ticket back home. Hitler's departure strikes the one menacing note in the novel. As the train pulls out, he leans out the window, calling out a German phrase to his brother, causing Alois to swear. Bridget says to her husband, "What's wrong? He only said you'd get what he owed you."

"It has a double meaning," Alois tells her angrily. "It was a threat. He meant I'd get what was coming to me."

In an authorial afterword, Bainbridge explains that the plot is based upon an entry in what was reported to be Bridget Hitler's diary, claiming that Hitler had visited them in 1912. While it is true that Alois and Bridget Hitler were living in Liverpool at the time, historians have rejected the notion that the young Hitler visited them. But to the novelist, the fact that Hitler may have lived in the very neighborhood in which she grew up was an irresistible opportunity to see those surroundings in a new way. Hitler served as a catalyst, enabling her to pay homage to the neighborhood and the conduct of its people during World War II. In that sense, the book is less about Hitler than it is about Mr. Browning, a local, heroic air raid warden who does not even appear in the book.

Another novel capturing Hitler at a certain phase of his development is Ernst Weiss's (1882–1940) *Eyewitness* (1939; trans., 1977). Weiss was a Jewish physician and novelist, forced into exile early in the Nazi years. He settled in Paris, where he lived a hand-to-mouth existence, finally committing suicide when France fell to the Germans. While in Paris, Weiss met Dr. Edmund Forster, a German psychiatrist who had treated Hitler at Pasewalk, the military hospital where he was a patient near the end of the First World War.

This section of *Eyewitness* deals with A. H., a soldier confined in a military hospital during World War I, suffering from blindness, presumably the result of a poison gas attack. The psychologist treating him puts him under hypnosis, making the suggestion that he must recover his sight since he is destined to become the savior of the German people. The suggestion works. Hitler recovers his sight, convinced that his recovery signifies the strength of his own iron will. Some historians accept the probability of this story, although any records relating to Hitler's stay in Pasewalk have long since been destroyed.

Two novels dealing with the Hitler of the 1920s are Richard Hughes's (1900–76) *The Fox in the Attic* (1961) (see MUNICH PUTSCH) and Ron Hansen's (1947–) *Hitler's Niece* (1999). Hansen's work deals with the relationship between the future führer and Angelica ("Geli") Raubal, the daughter of Hitler's half-sister, Angela. In *Hitler's Niece*, Hansen depicts Hitler's growing compulsion both to adore and dominate Geli. As depicted in the novel, his attraction to his niece begins in her infancy (she was born in 1908, when Hitler was 19). As he becomes more powerful throughout the 1920s, the psychopathic underside of his attraction becomes increasingly evident. As the petty, spoiled, self-involved loser, who fell apart in the Munich Putsch, steadily gains power and prestige, he attracts his share of female admirers, but that does little to deflect him from his obsession with his niece. Their less than healthy relationship gradually degenerates into sexual abuse.

Geli, early on a willing captive of her famous uncle, becomes increasingly unhappy, and by 1931 the 23-year-old announces her desire to return to Vienna and pursue a singing career. A quarrel ensues, during which Hitler, after breaking her nose with his fist, shoots her: "And then he was sure that Angelica Raubal was dead, and there was nothing further to do but cry with self-pity for his loss and love and misfortune." His aides, generally pleased to have her out of the picture, fabricate a story, depicting Geli as having committed suicide.

As with so many of the major questions surrounding Hitler's personal life, his murder of his niece remains a conjecture, but one that has also been advanced, independently of Hansen's novel, in a nonfictional study, Ronald Hayman's (1932–) *Hitler and Geli* (1998). If the hypothesis proves to be true, it suggests an alternative possibility to Rosenfeld's pessimism about Hitler fiction, one in which the historical fact and the fictional imagination converge and confirm each other.

Another woman in Hitler's life, his mistress and, on the eve of their death, wife, Eva Braun, is the subject of Alison Gold's *The Devil's Mistress* (1997). Cast in the form of Eva Braun's diary (including a surviving fragment from an actual diary Braun kept in 1935), the novel offers only an indirect insight into Hitler's character, since the source of direct knowledge is Eva, a self-involved airhead who accurately describes herself as a "dumb, Bavarian blonde." As the story develops, coarsened by the people surrounding her and by her own self-indulgence, she becomes more assertive and more selfish, but no more aware of the historical forces at work around her than she was at the age of 17, when she first met Hitler. Nevertheless, as the end nears, she recognizes that her fate and that of the Kanzler (chancellor), as she constantly refers to him, are inextricable. Ordered to remain in the relative safety of Bavaria, she returns to Hitler's bunker, determined to die by his side. Touched by her loyalty, he decides to marry her prior to their mutual suicide. The day after the ceremony, as the novel imagines it, Eva shoots him at his request, immediately after he has bitten into a cyanide capsule. Before killing herself, she replaces the picture of Hitler's mother that he had placed on his chest with one of herself. Having displaced her rival, she dies content, "a thirty-three-year-old widow."

In her author's note concluding the novel, Alison Gold adopts the tone of one who is washing her hands after a dirty deed. She asserts that the novel makes no claim to historical accuracy; it is "a thick soup of speculation . . . [whose] morally reprehensible, soulless ingredients" are nevertheless based upon considerable research. Despite the titillation suggested by the title, *The Devil's Mistress* emerges as a depressingly realistic novel. The author's denial of historical accuracy notwithstanding, the reader has the feeling that her depiction of Eva Braun captures the spirit, if not the literal facts, of the woman's life. As for Eva's significance to Hitler, she appears to be an afterthought in his life, somewhat on a par with Blondi, his favorite dog.

At a considerable remove from Geli Raubal and Eva Braun was Gertrude Weisker, Eva's cousin, whom Eva invited to the Obersalzberg (Berchtesgaden), Hitler's house in the Bavarian mountains, outside of Munich. Gertrude's experiences that summer form the basis of *Eva's Cousin* (2000; trans., 2002), a novel by the German novelist Sibylle Knauss (1944–). The setting is the summer of 1944. Of the 22 boys who took the school-leaving exam with Marlene (Gertrude), 10 are already dead. But Marlene, with the unshakeable confidence of a 20-year-old, knows that she has "a most favored person clause in the contract of life." What more proof would she need than this opportunity to live in the house of the führer. At first, although put off by Eva's condescension, Marlene is thrilled by the excitement and splendor of the retreat. But as the summer wears on and she becomes more intimately acquainted with her older cousin, sharing the life Eva leads, she sees the tacit contempt, in which the others, even some of the servants, hold her cousin.

Marlene also begins to understand the nature of the relationship between her cousin and the führer. Eva is among those people who are "brilliant in their timidity. They are looking for a master, and, once they have found him, they can hold him by a degree of self-abnegation that even the most experienced men of power . . . would scarcely think possible. And sometimes a bond develops between the timid and their masters that looks like the bond of love, yet is something quite different, such a perfect interplay of command and obedience . . . that the submissive partner acquires as much power as the dominant partner." But this is a recollected observation by the mature Marlene, looking back. At the time of the novel, she is simply caught up in the luxury, ease, and sense of power that comes from the feeling of living at "the center of the world." Soon, however, this sense begins to erode, exacerbated in Marlene's case by her decision to hide an escaped Polish slave laborer in the cellar of a little cottage near the main house. This decision is not a conscious one: "All at once, I myself felt as if I was serving some kind of higher plan, a plan that had been made long ago and without my personal involvement." Like her complicity with Nazism, her rebellion against it is equally unconscious. But she does not look for exemption from guilt. For "We Nazis," she says, "The memory of a spurious emotion is horrible, shameful, humiliating. And hidden down, disguised and camouflaged out of all recognition, the evil of which we were capable lies in the same memory. That is where it hides."

Easily the most perversely brilliant—or brilliantly perverse—of the Hitler novels is the controversial *The Portage to San Cristobal of A. H.* (1981) by the internationally known critic and man of letters, George Steiner (1929–). A plot summary of *The Portage* reads like a conventional popular thriller: the capture of Hitler, now 90 years old, in the heart of the Brazilian rain forest by a group of Israeli Nazi hunters. The action focuses on the squad's efforts to bring their captive back to their home base through the densely packed jungle during the rainy season. The Israelis remain in radio contact with their leader, Emmanuel Lieber, a man who has dedicated his life to the capture of Hitler. Other chapters provide satirical, if not exactly comic, relief in their description of the English, French, Russian, and American reactions to the news, each nation responding to type.

Plot aside, the high points of the novel are two chapters that stand in vivid, dynamic contrast to each other. One takes the form of a lengthy radio message Lieber sends to his younger subordinates, warning them not to be seduced by Hitler's rhetoric, "the night side of language, a speech for hell. Whose words mean hatred and vomit of life." He commands them not to let Hitler speak, or to stop their ears if he does, and instead to remember what he did. There follows an extraordinary four-and-a-half-page sentence, a catalogue of individual atrocities suffered by Jews in the various countries where the HOLOCAUST took place. The complexity of the novel's perspective is evident here in that Lieber's injunction to focus on the actions, not the words, occurs in a profoundly rhetorical sentence whose linguistic power matches Hitler's.

The most highly controversial chapter is the final one in the novel. Fearful that they will not be able to bring Hitler out alive, the captors decide to conduct the trial in the jungle, and, disobeying Lieber's instructions, allow Hitler to speak in his own defense. The last chapter is that speech, in which

165

he makes his case against the Jews. He argues that the Jews are guilty of three major crimes against humanity, far greater than his. The first is that they, not he, created the myth of the master race—the chosen people—and along with it a tyrannical, vengeful God, who is both immeasurably remote and oppressively present. Second, that the Jews foisted on the world "the white faced Nazarene," who established an impossible ideal for humans to live up to and the terrors of hell for those who failed to do so. Third, the Jews developed the secular version of Christianity, Marxism, burdening the world with another impossible ideal, the just society: "Three times the Jews have pressed on us the blackmail of transcendence . . . infecting our blood and brains with the bacillus of perfection."

In an interview with Ron Rosenbaum, Steiner revealed that he wrote both of these chapters in a "fever dream" in three days while locked in a hotel room. Despite the serious criticism from many that his Hitler speech fuels the flames of anti-Semitism, Steiner stands by the speech, maintaining that Hitler's condemnation is in fact an unconscious tribute to the Jews. As Steiner argues in his memoir *Errata* (1998), anti-Semitism grows out of the fact that Jewish culture constantly reminds us of our failure to achieve the highest standards. The problem for many readers is that, in the novel, the speech goes unanswered.

Unanswered too is the call for the definitive Hitler novel. Perhaps it awaits a 21st-century Dostoyevsky, a master psychologist, with a touch of the demonic.

FURTHER READING

Ian Kershaw's two-volume biography *Hitler* (1998–2000) is commonly regarded as definitive, at least for the present time.

HOLOCAUST, THE (1933–1945)

Although the history of the world is replete with examples of various forms of genocide and mass slaughter, the Nazis' extermination of the Jews marks the first carefully planned, systematic, scientifically assisted attempt to annihilate an entire people. And for these reasons, the Holocaust is historically unique and profoundly troubling in the questions it raises about human nature and Western civilization. Its immediate origins were the inscrutable mind and will of Adolf HITLER, who, in a 1939 speech, "prophesied" that "if the Jewish international financiers succeed in involving the nations in another war, the result will not be world bolshevism and therefore a victory for Judaism, it will be the annihilation of the Jews in Europe." The logical contradiction in this quotation betrays the mind of the speaker: Jewish capitalists are conspiring to create a worldwide communist revolution. However, the rhetorical strategy is clear: When setting up a scapegoat, make it responsible for as much evil as possible.

The more remote cause of the Holocaust was the long-standing tradition of anti-Semitism in the West that ranged from exclusion and segregation to forced conversions to active participation in pogroms to its polite form, a willingness to look the other way when faced with examples of anti-Semitic activity. In the Nazi era, relatively few were heroic enough to aid the Jews in occupied Europe (see PIUS XII) or open-hearted enough in Britain and America, whose governments not only resisted receiving many refugees but tended to cover up the information they did have about the genocide. Nevertheless, the Holocaust represents a quantum leap from traditional anti-Semitism.

The Nazis prepared the way for extermination by a systematic process of trying to dehumanize the Jews, beginning with depriving them of their civil rights, excluding them from many professions, forbidding intermarriage, encouraging Aryans to mistreat them, spreading anti-Semitic literature, forcing them to wear yellow stars, and other acts of humiliation. The goal was to create, in the minds of the German public, images of Jews as less than human, or if human, enemies of the Third Reich, thereby soothing the consciences of those who might raise objections, while providing a rationalization for those looking for one.

When the actual plan to murder all the Jews was put into effect is a matter of some dispute, but it is generally agreed that at the Wannsee Conference in January 1942, the details of the "final solution" were worked out. Instead of mass shootings by mobile killing units (the Einzatsgruppen), such as took place at BABI YAR in the Ukraine, the new plans called for the shipment of millions to death camps, such as AUSCHWITZ and TREBLINKA, where they were efficiently herded into "showers" and gassed to death. The corpses were then cremated or buried in mass graves.

Prodigious efforts of scholarly research and the testimony of survivors have answered many questions concerning the Holocaust. As the historian Yehuda Bauer points out, scholarship, archival sources, and interviews with survivors have explained its how, when, and where, but the unanswered question is why. Bauer rejects the "mystifying" notion that the Holocaust is inexplicable, that it stands apart from history as something "diabolical" or "inhuman." As Bauer reminds us, "Heinrich Himmler . . . was human, and so are we." The effort to explain these events, to discover the reasons why, is a vital one, because if the Holocaust is human, it is repeatable, a truth that subsequent events in Cambodia, Rwanda, and Bosnia have made all too evident.

THE LITERATURE

The question of the Holocaust as a literary subject has been controversial. Some have argued that such literature should be limited to diaries, memoirs, and other firsthand accounts. They maintain that rendering the experience in fictional, poetic, and dramatic forms necessarily transforms the monstrous into a form of aesthetic pleasure, thereby diluting and distorting its reality. They also contend that even when a nonfictional source, such as *The Diary of Anne Frank*, is adapted to the stage and screen, it ends up presenting a universalized portrait (in this case, of adolescence) rather than a specific experience (of a young Jewish girl in the Holocaust). Others maintain that not to inscribe the Holocaust in the history of literature is to turn our backs, to foster ignorance and lack of interest, in effect, to collaborate with the Nazis. The Holocaust can be—and has been—cheapened and exploited by literary hacks, but in the hands of serious writers, its significance can be deepened, not palliated.

Twenty years before Hitler came to power, Franz Kafka (1883–1924), an obscure Jewish insurance clerk in Prague, wrote, but chose not to publish, a series of novels and short stories that would mark him as the literary prophet of the Holocaust. Perhaps the best example of this anticipation is *The Trial* (1925; trans., 1935), a novel whose tone and theme are masterfully rendered in its opening line: "Someone must have been telling lies about Joseph K., for without having done anything wrong, he was arrested one fine morning." The novel goes on to explore the systematic demoralization of the protagonist during his trial. Desperately trying to discover the reason for his arrest, Joseph K. becomes enmeshed in the seemingly mindless, bureaucratic legal machinery that leads inexorably to his conviction and execution. All of his efforts to find a rational explanation for his situation result in experiences of frustration that have come to be called Kafkaesque. He is condemned to death not for what he has done, but for what he is—without ever learning what that *is* is. His last words—"like a dog"—underscore the lack of meaning that his fate exhibits. Of course, Kafka is not predicting an historical event, but trying to capture a universal human condition. In this respect, his work also anticipates the philosophical mood of EXISTENTIALISM. But since the emergence of existentialist thought occurred in the wake of the Holocaust, it may be a pardonable exaggeration to suggest that the latter is a particular and terrible manifestation of the condition meditated on in the former, that the questions of death, nonbeing, negation, choice, and absurdity hover over the Holocaust. Dying at the age 41, Kafka did not live to see this conjunction of idea and event. Had he lived longer, he might have easily become one of the Prague Jews sent to Theresienstadt and later transported to Auschwitz. In any event, the wonder is, as the Israeli novelist and Holocaust survivor Aharon Appelfeld (1932–   ) put it, "How could a man who had never been there know so much, in precise detail, about that world?"

The fiction of the Holocaust may be divided into those novels and stories that deal directly with the ghetto experience, such as John Hersey's (1914–93) and Leon Uris's fictional accounts of the WARSAW GHETTO, or those focusing specifically on the extermination camps, such as the unspeakable brutality captured by Tadeusz Borowski (1922–51) in his collection of short stories, *This Way for the Gas, Ladies and Gentlemen* (1948), or the nonfictional memoirs of Elie Wiesel (1928–   ) (*Night*, 1958) and Primo Levi (1919–87) (*Survival in Auschwitz*, 1947), and those, undoubtedly influenced by Kafka, that approach the subject indirectly or metaphorically, as in Aharon Appelfeld's *Badenheim, 1939* (1980), in which affluent, assimilated Austrian Jews at a summer resort live in denial until the moment when the resort is turned into a concentration camp.

The most impressive, both in scope and emotional power, of direct renderings is the French novelist André Schwarz-Bart's (1928–   ) *The Last of the Just* (1959; trans., 1960). Placing the Nazis' annihilation of Jews in the historical context of European anti-Semitism, the novel outlines the history of the Jewish myth of the "thirty-six just men," who, often unwittingly, take upon themselves undeserved suffering, which, without their sacrifice, would lead to the end of the human race. In one version of the myth, in each generation, it falls to one member of the Levy family to be one of the just men. After outlining the history of the Levy clan from the 12th to the 20th centuries, the story focuses on young Ernie Levy, a schoolboy who comes of age in Germany in the 1930s. Intuiting his special role early on, he discovers, as a result of beatings by classmates and his Nazi teacher, the reality of the "just man's" fate. His first reaction is to avoid it by attempting suicide. His body is saved, but a profound despair overtakes his soul. Despite his sense of the apparent indifference of God, he nevertheless commits himself to the struggle against Hitler. After the family escapes to France, Ernie joins the French army, only to see its defeat and the deportation of his family. On the brink of despair and self-hate, he goes through a period in which he thinks of himself, and acts (coincidentally echoing Kafka's Joseph K.), "like a dog."

Returning to Paris he meets and falls in love with Golda, a handicapped young Jewish woman. After an idyllic day spent walking around the city without their yellow stars, they make love and consider themselves married. The following day, Golda is sent to a transit camp at Drancy. Ernie follows, determined to join her. Their beautifully understated reunion occurs before they are shipped to Auschwitz. In the nightmarish scenes that follow, Ernie, despite his own despair over God's silence, rises to his sacrificial role as one of the just. He brings comfort and hope to the terrified children and many of the adults huddled together in the boxcars carrying them to the death camp. And when they disembark and he is selected to be one of the laborers, he chooses to stay with Golda and the children, destined for the gas chamber. In the chamber itself, as the gas hisses out over them, Ernie "leaned out into the darkness toward the children even at his knees, and he shouted with all the gentleness and all the strength of his soul, 'Breathe deeply, my lambs, and quickly.'"

A final paragraph suggests that the spirit of Ernie lives on, but there is little in the novel, which is filled with a sardonic, often comic anger, to justify such optimism. Many readers prefer the celebrated penultimate paragraph, in which, interspersed amid the repeated incantation, "And praised be the Lord," are the names of the extermination camps: "And praised. *Auschwitz, Be, Maidanek.* The Lord, *Treblinka."* Whether these juxtapositions are intended to be ironic or deeply religious is left for the reader. But the ending is true to the sense that what happens to Ernie is less important than who he is—a just man.

Among the indirect renderings is Jerzy Kosinski's (1933–91) *The Painted Bird* (1965), a novel that its author originally claimed was a nonfictional account of his childhood in World War II. Later he backed away from this claim, responding to the objection that as nonfiction, the story lacked credibility; as a novel, however, it creates a surrealistic world of violence and brutality, and it constitutes an important metaphor of the human capacity for sadistic cruelty that issued in the Holocaust. *The Painted Bird* traces the experiences of a young boy—six years of age at the story's beginning—sent by his parents from a large city to a remote village in an unnamed country (clearly intended to be Poland) right after the Nazi invasion in 1939. After the death of the old woman with whom he is sent to live, the unnamed boy wanders from village to village. Since his looks indicate that he is either a Jew or a gypsy (gypsies were also victims of Nazi racial ideology), he is treated like a pariah, partly because of the traditional racism of the peasants and partly because of the peasants' awareness of the penalties for harboring a member of either group. Beaten, starved, and treated like an animal, the boy experiences a series of horrors, which include witnessing a jealous husband gouging out the eyes of a young man who had been flirting with his wife.

In the novel's nightmarish world, the boy is a traveler through hell, learning the lesson that evil, embodied in the beautifully pressed black uniform and shining boots of a German SS officer, is always triumphant. Eventually the boy's reaction is to lose the power of speech, to reject the distinguishing feature of the human animal, so as not to be further contaminated by the stigma of belonging to the human race. In the end, he recovers speech and reunites with his family, but his faith in the human potential for good has been irretrievably lost. He now feels like a painted bird, one that, having been painted, is no longer recognized or accepted by his own flock. As a result the flock attacks and kills it. As a realistic novel, *The Painted Bird* strains credulity and is crude and often violent for violence's sake, but it is a powerful indictment of the human capacity for evil and, as such, an important reminder that the Holocaust is an all-too-human creation.

The most recent and, in the view of many critics, the most successful attempt to represent what might be called the aftershock of the Holocaust— the collateral damage it has wrought in shaping the inner life of millions—is W. G. Sebald's (1944–2003) *Austerlitz* (2001). The framing story is told by an anonymous narrator who forms a relationship with Jacques Austerlitz, based upon their mutual interest in forms of architecture. But it is the inner story narrated by Austerlitz that constitutes the core of the novel. When not quite five years old, Austerlitz becomes part of a group of young Jewish children transported to Great Britain from Europe in 1939. Adopted by a Calvinist minister and his wife, he grows up in a remote village in Wales, having been given the name *Dafydd Elias.* The minister, a hellfire preacher who only comes alive in the pulpit, and his wife, a completely passive, unexpressive woman, living in a house where "they never opened a window," leave the boy emotionally frozen. Coming of age in this world with people who never refer to his past or to the war raging in Europe, he loses any memories of his earlier life.

His search to regain his past begins when he is sent to a prep school, where he discovers that his real name is Jacques Austerlitz, about the same time that he learns in his history class about the battle of Austerlitz in 1805, in which Napoléon Bonaparte defeated the Russian and Austrian armies. As a result of this nominal association, for the first time, he sees himself as having a place in history. His subsequent search to learn the fate of his parents and his own identity—"illustrated," as in all of Sebald's novels, by photographs of places and people—takes him from the Liverpool Street railway station in London to the new, electronically wired, soulless Bibliothèque nationale in Paris, to an apartment in Prague where he discovers Vera, his nursery maid when he was a child and his mother's closest companion. From her he learns of the fate of his parents, his father a political figure who fled to Paris when the Germans marched into Czechoslovakia, his mother an opera singer who stayed behind, deported to the so-called model ghetto at Theresienstadt, a place where in 1944 the Nazis invited a visit from the International Red Cross to show how well the Jews were treated. The novel records with passionate intensity the reality behind this Nazi showcase. One of the most moving sequences in the novel is Austerlitz's description of his visit to Theresienstadt, now a virtual ghost town, with its Ghetto Museum. Eventually he is able to find a picture of his mother.

As the novel ends Austerlitz is still pursuing his past, trying to discover his father's fate. But the search, however painful, has brought him back to life. In Jacques Austerlitz/Dafydd Elias, the Holocaust had claimed another victim. He is emotionally crippled, suspended in time; the roots of his life had been cut, as illustrated when the possibility of a relationship with a warm, intelligent woman seems lost as a visit with her to the famous spa at Marienbad ends not in romance but in an unexplained anxiety attack. Later, as a result of his search, he discovers the source of that anxiety. In the summer of 1938, he and his parents had visited that resort.

But learning the past, with all the suffering it entails, even the mental breakdown it engenders, is liberating. The end of the novel finds him not only searching for his father, but for the woman he lost at the spa in

Marienbad. Early in the novel, Austerlitz's history teacher remarks, "Our concern for history . . . is a concern with preformed images already imprinted on our brains, images at which we keep staring while the truth lies elsewhere . . . somewhere as yet undiscovered." *Austerlitz* is a record of that discovery.

In a literal sense, this is a difficult novel to read. It has no paragraph breaks, and so the reader may easily get lost in the narrative. There is also the frequently unnecessary repetition of the phrase "Austerlitz said," occurring so often that it becomes an incantation. However, those obstacles somehow don't impede and instead probably intensify the novel's hypnotic power.

The best known of the poems inspired by the Holocaust is Paul Celan's (1920–70) "Death Fugue." Imprisoned in a forced labor camp in his native Romania, Celan called on poetry to "design for [himself] a reality" that could match the experience of the camp, where "death comes as a master from Germany." The poem contrasts the life of the prisoners, drinking the "black milk of daybreak," with that of the "master"—who will later "hunt us down with dogs"—writing love letters to his golden-haired German lover, Margarete. The contrast between the world of the master and the slaves is intensified by the contrast within the master himself, a product of German high culture (the name *Margarete* is a reference to the heroine of Goethe's *Faust*), who is also the monster who will hunt men down with dogs.

FURTHER READING

Yehuda Bauer's *Rethinking the Holocaust* (2001) is an admirable summary and analysis of the essential questions confronting students of the subject. Lawrence Langer's *The Holocaust and the Literary Imagination* (1975) and Daniel Schwarz's *Imagining the Holocaust* (1999) are excellent studies, treating individual works in the context of the larger theoretical question about the legitimacy of fictionalizing the Holocaust.

HUNGARIAN UPRISING (1956)

In WORLD WAR II, Hungary fought on the side of Germany. In 1944, Soviet troops invaded and occupied the country and continued to maintain a military presence after the war. The Soviet Union helped to set up a communist state, headed by Mátyás Rákosi, first secretary of the Communist Party and a devoted Stalinist, whose regime imitated his master's. Highlights of Rákosi's oppressive reign included his imprisonment of the Hungarian Catholic primate Cardinal Joseph Mindszenty and the execution of his rival László Rajk. With Joseph STALIN's death in 1953 and Nikita Khrushchev's policy of de-Stalinization in effect, Rákosi's regime became increasingly untenable. On orders from the Kremlin, Rákosi stepped down, replaced by Imre Nagy, who instituted a series of reforms, aimed at gradually moving Hungary out from under Soviet domination. However, Rákosi and his supporters, securely entrenched in the Hungarian bureaucracy, continuously undermined Nagy's "New Course." In 1955, Nagy was expelled from the ruling party. But Nagy's brief reign had given the Hungarian people a glimpse of new possibilities and loosened the old regime's grip of terror.

When in 1956, Khrushchev delivered his speech attacking Stalin and stressing the value of national sovereignty, Hungarian university students actively demonstrated, calling for a broader civil rights and the reinstatement of Nagy. Fighting broke out in October. A cease-fire went into effect on October 28. Nagy became prime minister and withdrew Hungary from the Warsaw Pact, the Eastern European equivalent of the North Atlantic Treaty Organization (NATO). As a result, Soviet troops invaded Hungary, where they were joined by János Kádár, Nagy's minister of the interior. With Soviet support, Kádár formed a new government, initiating a series of reprisals that included the execution of Nagy in 1958. The intervention of Soviet troops proved to be a public-opinion disaster for the Soviets, causing defections from communist parties around the world and the alienation of an even greater number of formerly sympathetic people, such as the highly influential writer/philosopher Jean-Paul Sartre.

THE LITERATURE

Robert Ardrey's play (1908–80) *Shadow of Heroes* (1958) is a documentary drama of the revolt and of the major events leading up to it. A character, simply called the Author, somewhat in the manner of the Stage Director in Thornton Wilder's *Our Town*, narrates the action at transitional moments. The play opens in 1944, when Lászlo Rajk and his wife, Julia, leaders of the anti-Nazi Hungarian resistance, are captured, interrogated, tortured, and sent on a death march to Belsen concentration camp just as the war comes to an end. Act 2 takes place in 1949. Rajk, now the minister of the interior in the postwar Hungarian Communist government, falls out with his colleagues over his refusal to accept the luxurious living quarters that other high-ranking government officials are enjoying, making the rest of them look bad as a result. He finally consents because his wife has just given birth to a new baby. Nevertheless, as Act 2 ends, he is arrested, as is his wife a few days after. Act 3 takes place six weeks later. All attempts to force Rajk to sign a false confession have failed. János Kádár, Rajk's trusted friend and successor as minister of the interior, visits him in his jail cell and convinces him that he will be allowed to live with his wife and child in the Soviet Union if he signs a false confession. Rajk agrees and shortly after his trial is hanged. In Act 4, Kádár visits Julia, recently released from prison, and confesses that he betrayed Rajk for the good of the party. When the news of Khrushchev's denunciation of Stalin at the 20th Congress reaches Hungary, the government decides to rehabilitate the memory of Rajk. Julia insists that he be given a public state funeral.

173

Despite the government's efforts not to publicize the funeral, 250,000 people attend, triggering the events that culminate in the uprising. Julia is warned by friends that she will be targeted in the Soviet reaction, but the temporary success of the new Nagy government blinds her to the coming Soviet oppression. When Kádár becomes the new premier, replacing Nagy, Julia takes refuge in the Yugoslav embassy. Kádár's promise of amnesty, his final treachery, convinces her, Nagy, and the other refugees to leave the embassy, whereupon they are all arrested. As the play ends, the Author announces that Julia is still a prisoner of the Russians.

Shadow of Heroes had its premiere in London in 1958. Critics praised the play and its outstanding cast, which included Dame Peggy Ashcroft as Julia, but such realistic drama was not popular with theatergoers. Later productions in Germany and New York had similar disappointments at the box office, leading author Robert Ardrey to conclude that there was no longer an audience for plays that engage the political and social issues of their times. Nevertheless Ardrey was able to take pride in one of the play's achievements: "On October 18, 1958, eleven days after the [London] opening, Radio Budapest announced that Mrs. Rajk had been released from prison and had returned with her son to Budapest."

FURTHER READING

François Fejtö's *A History of the People's Democracies and Eastern Europe since Stalin* (1971) contains an excellent account of the uprising. Robert Ardrey's comments on the reception of *Shadow of Heroes* appear in the preface to his *Plays of Three Decades* (1968).

I

INDOCHINA WAR (1946–1954)

From the late 19th century until 1950, the term *Indochina* referred to three states, Laos, Cambodia, and Vietnam, all formerly under the control of a French colonial government. During WORLD WAR II, in the wake of France's early defeat, the Japanese army, while never formerly occupying Indochina, used it as a staging area for military operations. The strongest opposition to the Japanese presence came from a group of guerrilla fighters, known as the Vietminh, led by the charismatic communist commander Ho Chih Minh. The Vietminh enjoyed considerable success against the Japanese, and in August 1945, after the formal defeat of Japan, they marched into Hanoi, proclaiming the northern section of the country the Democratic Republic of Vietnam. In so doing, they deposed the traditional ruler, Emperor Bao Dai, who fled to Hong Kong. Meanwhile the French authorities returned to restore their colonial government in the South. At first France agreed to recognize the North as a "free state," but as negotiations continued, the French took an increasingly hard line. In response the Vietminh staged a preemptive attack on French forces in Hanoi and began to engage in guerrilla warfare. As the war developed, in 1950, the French appealed to the United States for arms and other aid, which in the nervous atmosphere of the early years of the COLD WAR, the Americans supplied in abundance. Nevertheless the French military discovered that jungle warfare against a trained guerrilla group with a strong base of popular support and supplied with arms by the Chinese Communist government was more than they could handle.

The climactic event in the war occurred in the spring of 1954, when, after a two-month siege, an outnumbered French garrison at Dien Bien Phu, a strategically critical outpost bordering on Laos, surrendered to Ho Chih Minh's forces. This decisive Communist victory preceded by a few days the Geneva Conference, the terms of which divided the country into two nations, North and South Vietnam. The conference also contained an agreement that allowed for a face-saving French withdrawal from their former colony. Remaining in the South, however, were the American military advisers and government officials, in what would develop in the next decade into the quagmire known as the VIETNAM WAR.

THE LITERATURE

In Graham Greene's (1904–91) *The Quiet American* (1955), the narrator is Thomas Fowler, an English journalist covering the war in Saigon. There he meets the American Alden Pyle, who has just arrived in Vietnam as an official of a program supposedly designed to benefit the victims of the war. But Pyle exhibits a dangerous innocence: "[H]e was determined . . . to do good, not to any individual person, but to a country, a continent, a world." Complicating their relationship further, Pyle falls in love with Fowler's Vietnamese mistress, Phuong, promising to marry her and bring her back to the United States. Phuong accepts his proposal and moves in with him. The political parallel is clear to the always confident Pyle: The Americans will win, in war as well as love, in Southeast Asia, where the older colonial powers, Britain and France, have failed, because America comes "with clean hands" and the best intentions.

Pyle sees the solution in arming a "third force," an independent anticommunist private army of General The. As a result, he becomes involved in supplying The's army with weapons that cause the death of Vietnamese citizens. Convinced that Pyle is a menace, all the more dangerous because he is acting out of good intentions, Fowler reveals information that leads to Pyle's death.

Fowler has become another Pyle: doing something evil for a good motive. Fowler and Pyle are mirror images of each other. At the conclusion, Fowler is reunited with Phuong, whom he plans to marry. The last words of the novel are Fowler's: "Everything had gone right with me since he [Pyle] had died, but how I wished there existed someone to whom I could say I was sorry." Fowler needs to confess, but, an absolute atheist, he has denied God's existence. In the paradoxical theology of Graham Greene, guilt frequently turns one toward God.

When *The Quiet American* was published in 1955, many critics accused Greene of being anti-American. Twenty years later the American experiment in Vietnam an acknowledged disaster, he was proclaimed a prophet. Still later the release of a 2001 filmed version of the novel was postponed for a year in the wake of the attack on the World Trade Center, a decision testifying to the story's continuing capacity to evoke controversy.

FURTHER READING

Justin Wintle's *The Vietnam Wars* (1991) examines both the Indochina War and the Vietnam War in relation to each other.

INDONESIAN UPRISING (1965)

Indonesia is an island nation consisting of more than 13,000 islands stretching across 3,000 miles of the Pacific Ocean. Formerly a Dutch colony, which during WORLD WAR II had been occupied by the Japanese, Indonesia gained independence in 1949 under the leadership of Achmad Sukarno. Beginning with a democratic government, President Sukarno introduced significant reforms in health and education, but he grew increasingly autocratic and corrupt over the years. In 1963, he precipitated an unsuccessful military "confrontation" with the newly independent state of Malaysia, which generated dissent in the Indonesian army. In the meantime, economic failures created severe suffering among the poorest section of the population, further agitated by a strong Communist Party. Caught between the military right and the Communist left, Sukarno wavered and appeared weak.

On September 30, 1965, the Communists, fearful that the military was planning a coup, attempted a preemptive coup (apparently with the tacit consent of Sukarno). In the middle of the night the rebels attacked the homes of seven important army generals, killing three of them and capturing three others, who were also killed the next day (the seventh evaded capture). Responding rapidly with effective force, the military, under the leadership of General Hadji Suharto, quelled the abortive coup and forced Sukarno to accept their dominance in the political life of the nation. Once in power, they proceeded to unleash a series of reprisals that amounted to massacres in areas where the Communist influence was strongest. In the meantime, Sukarno's prestige and power slowly eroded. In June 1966, the national parliament rescinded Sukarno's title "President-for-Life," and one year later he was removed from office, replaced by Suharto, who remained in power until forced to resign in 1998.

THE LITERATURE

The uprising and the crisis leading up to it form the background of C. J. Koch's *The Year of Living Dangerously* (1978). The title refers to the official name for the year 1965 as proclaimed by Sukarno, who was a dictator with a touch of the poet about him. Guy Hamilton, a journalist for an Australian television network and his dwarfish, highly sensitive cameraman Billy Kwan form a successful team in covering the chaotic events leading up to the preemptive coup. Through Billy, Guy meets Jill Bryant, an official at the British Embassy, and they fall in love, despite Guy's awareness of Billy's unrequited love for Jill. Billy is also an ardent admirer of Sukarno, for whom he develops a deep affinity: "Sometimes I feel we share the same identity . . . I could have been him." Billy keeps dossiers on public figures as well as on his friends. As the love affair grows in intensity and Sukarno's efforts to control events betray his dictatorial impulses, the strain on Billy grows greater. He begins to lose his grip. At the same time, Guy alienates Jill when he betrays her confidence about the Communists smuggling arms. Feeling abandoned by the people who mean the most to him, Billy attends a Sukarno rally, unfolds a large banner reading "SUKARNO, FEED YOUR PEOPLE," and is killed by Sukarno's men. Guy is wounded the night of the coup, but he is rescued and ultimately reunited with Jill.

A high point of the novel is a performance of an Indonesian puppet show that Guy attends. The description suggests the appeal of the traditional culture in contrast to the menace that dominates the political scene. Pervading the novel is the author's love of Indonesia, raising the story beyond the level of a simple action-adventure novel to show the complex and beautiful culture that underlies the political chaos and bloodshed, rendering the violence all the more tragic.

Peter Weir's 1982 exciting film adaptation of the novel is especially noteworthy for the director's brilliant decision to assign the role of Billy to a woman, Linda Hunt, whose performance won an Academy Award for best supporting actress.

FURTHER READING

Robert Cribb and Colin Brown's *Modern Indonesia* (1995) is an excellent history of Indonesia from 1945 to 1987.

INTERNMENT OF JAPANESE AMERICANS (WORLD WAR II)

In the aftermath of the attack on PEARL HARBOR, the tide of American resentment toward the "treacherous" Japanese quickly flowed over into animosity toward Japanese Americans, a relatively small group (approximately 100,000 people) concentrated largely on the West Coast. Reflecting and responding to this phobia, in February 1942, the United States government ordered the internment of all Japanese Americans in what were termed "relocation centers," camps in the Californian desert and other remote areas. As a result, the Nisei (the term for Japanese Americans) were forced to dispose of whatever property they owned and report for evacuation to the camps. Although the Nisei were not actively mistreated, they were isolated, confined to primitive medical and educational facilities, and denied the chance to work. The internment policy was upheld in a Supreme Court decision in 1944, shortly before the government ended the practice.

One of the striking features of this policy was its exceptionalism. No comparable policy was instituted among German Americans or Italian Americans. The conclusion seemed inescapable that racism played a role in the decision to focus on the Nisei. Internment was particularly galling and humiliating to a community whose industry and skills had brought them a sizable measure of success. However, despite this treatment, the young men of the community formed a Nisei army contingent that served admirably in the European theater during the war.

THE LITERATURE

David Guterson's (1956–   ) novel *Snow Falling on Cedars* (1994) explores the near-tragic ramifications of the internment on one family on the island of San Piedro, off the coast of Washington State. The story opens in 1954 with a murder trial. Kabuo Miyamoto, a World War II Nisei veteran and member of San Piedro's very small Japanese-American enclave on the island, has been charged with the murder of Carl Heine, a local fisherman, whose drowned body reveals the possibility of foul play. Testimony at the trial reveals that in 1934 Carl Heine's father had agreed to sell seven acres of land to Kabuo's father, but, since the law at the time forbade land ownership by any Nisei not born in the United States, the land was be held in trust for Kabuo until he reached the age of 20 in 1942, contingent upon the Miyamotos' meeting the mortgage payments over a period of eight years. After having worked the land for more than seven years, Kabuo's family is sent to a relocation camp, where, not being able to work, they fail to make the final payments. Carl's father dies in 1944, and his mother sells the land to someone else. When the second owner decides to sell the plot in 1954, Carl repurchases it just ahead of Kabuo.

During the trial, the prosecution argues that this long-standing dispute constitutes Kabuo's motive for murdering Carl. The story of the sale rekindles the memories of the war years and the treatment of the Nisei. It also evokes in Ishmael, the son of the editor of the town newspaper, the painful memory of his secret, teenage love affair with a Japanese girl, Hatsue, which ended when she, under pressure from her family, rejected him. Now Hatsue is the wife of Kabuo, and Ishmael, still in love with her, is covering the trial for his paper. Ishmael uncovers evidence that will help to exonerate Kabuo, leaving him with an intense moral dilemma: Should he reveal the evidence that will free the one man who stands as an obstacle to his happiness? After a day's delay, he makes the moral choice, which leads to the conclusion that Carl Heine's death was an accident, caused by his boat being overturned in the wake of a larger ship.

Snow Falling on Cedars is an unusual novel. Within the framework of a murder mystery, it interposes a lyrical style, set against a historical background that touches on themes of prejudice, war, and unrequited love. This seemingly odd combination makes for an effective and moving story.

FURTHER READING

Bill Hosokawa's *Nisei: The Quiet Americans* (1969) is a history of the internment.

IRAN-CONTRA SCANDAL (1985–1987)

By the mid-1980s, the Iran-Iraq War (1980–88) had ground to a stalemate, leaving both sides with heavy casualties and economic disaster. At that point officials in the Israeli government informed the Reagan administration that they had been approached about the possible sale of arms to Iran. In exchange for the sale, the Iranians would use their influence with the Shiite Islamic terrorist group, Hezbollah, to free seven American hostages being held in Lebanon. Someone in the administration then came up with the suggestion that the money earned by the weapons sale could be secretly used to help fund the contras, the insurgent guerrillas trying to overthrow the leftist Sandinista regime in Nicaragua.

While selling arms to Iran was a politically risky move in the aftermath of the IRANIAN REVOLUTION, it was not illegal, but the secret funding of the contras without consent of the Congress clearly was. Among the officials involved in both activities were the director of the CENTRAL INTELLIGENCE AGENCY (CIA), William Casey, who was dying of cancer at the time; the national security director, John Poindexter; and his assistant, directly in charge of the operation, U.S. Marine lieutenant colonel Oliver North. He set up secret bank accounts to purchase arms for the contras. The deal came to light in October 1986, when a plane, carrying weapons for the contras, was shot down by the Sandinistas. The pilot confessed that he was part of an American government campaign to aid the contras. A month later, a Lebanese magazine exposed the arms-for-hostages deal. The story was confirmed by the Iranian government, who publicly gloated over having successfully outwitted the Americans.

Following the report of a special committee, Congressional hearings conducted in 1987 resulted in the indictments of Poindexter, North, and Defense Secretary Caspar Weinberger. North and Poindexter stood trial and were convicted, but the convictions were overturned on appeal. Weinberger was pardoned before his trial began. The overriding question throughout the hearings and trials related to the extent of President Ronald Reagan's knowledge and approval of these actions. Since a large number of documents had been destroyed by Oliver North before the hearings were underway, there was no evidence of the president's involvement, but the question was to haunt the remainder of the Reagan era: "What did he know, and when did he know it?"

THE LITERATURE

Joan Didion's (1934–   ) *The Last Thing He Wanted* (1996) explores the covert arms trade and the government's menacing collusion in it. Elena McMahon, having walked out of a loveless marriage to a wealthy man, finds herself caught up in her semisenile father's deal involving the shipment of arms to contra rebels. Standing in for her father, she flies in a plane bearing weapons to Costa Rica and from there to an unnamed Caribbean island. By this time, she has been tricked into traveling under a false passport, has learned that her father is dead, and realizes that she has been set up to take the fall in the event of an investigation. While on the island, she meets Treat Morrison, a trouble-shooting ambassador-at-large. The two become lovers, but their attempt to rescue her from her situation leads to tragic consequences.

Like the heroine of Didion's best-known novel, *Play It as It Lays* (1970), Elena McMahon exhibits a passivity that seems to emerge from a profound despair about the possibility of taking any meaningful action. She is drawn deeper into the mystery behind the arms deal, motivated at the risk of her life simply by the desire to know what's really going on. What she does not discover, but what the novel reveals, is that this action, like all of history in Didion's view, is governed by chance and accident. As Treat Morrison explains to the anonymous reporter/narrator of the novel, "You think you have it covered and you find out you don't have it covered worth a goddamn."

A swiftly paced story and a searing indictment of the corruption within and without official government circles, *The Last Thing He Wanted* is a powerful reminder of the danger of a government that steps outside the law to achieve its goals.

FURTHER READING

Lawrence Walsh's *Iran-Contra: The Final Report* (1994) is the definitive account of the incident by the special prosecutor assigned to investigate it.

IRANIAN REVOLUTION (1979)

In 1956, the shah of Iran, in response to widespread discontent, initiated his "White Revolution," a reform movement aimed at modernizing Iran's economy while promoting the country internationally by establishing its role as the "arbiter of East and West"—that is, as a diplomatic mediator between the Arab world and the West. However, in the course of pursuing these goals, he attempted to weaken the hold of Islamic culture, encouraging, for example, large numbers of students to study abroad and giving greater rights to women, including the right to wear nontraditional clothing. These reforms drew the fire of many Muslim clergy. In response, the shah's regime became increasingly intolerant of dissent. His secret police achieved international notoriety for their brutality and torture, while the number of people imprisoned grew to nearly 50,000. Throughout this period the shah was a staunch defender and ally of the United States, who played a role in maintaining him in power. By 1978, fueled by the preaching of the Muslim clergy, in particular the exiled Ayatollah Khomeini, discontent had reached a feverish pitch. In 1978, the shah's police fired on a group of demonstrating seminarians. As a result, millions of Iranians began to participate in demonstrations, leading to a critical strike by workers in the oil fields. The shah placed the country under military rule, but the protests continued unabated. On January 16, 1979, the shah was forced to flee to Egypt. The following month the Ayatollah returned from exile welcomed by delirious crowds, proclaiming the Islamic Republic of Iran.

The Iranian Revolution was a remarkable success, but even more remarkable was its nature. Instead of the usual right-wing or left-wing coup that was the mark of every other major 20th-century revolt, this was a religious revolution, establishing a theocratic government with ultimate control in the hands of the Ayatollah.

THE LITERATURE

Among the better-known novels dealing with the revolution is James Clavell's (1924–94) *Whirlwind* (1986), which takes place at the height of the revolt, between February 9 and March 4, 1979. Clavell's story centers on a group of European and American helicopter pilots, reluctant to leave Iran because of their emotional commitment to the land or to their women (two of the pilots have Iranian wives). In the background as well is the ownership of the helicopter company that faces financial ruin. As the action develops and the anti-American and European furor intensifies, the most memorable scenes are those in which frenzied mobs overpower anyone or anything that represents the West, particularly the "great Satan," the United States, such as members of minority religious groups and Iranian women not wearing chadors (veils). Adhering closely to the tradition of the adventure story, *Whirlwind* depicts a world peopled with brave men, fanatical hatred, romantic love, and the intrigues of the corporate world. In one episode, Clavell effectively depicts a women's march in Tehran against the rescinding of their rights by the new regime, thousands of women filling the streets, bearing signs such as "No Enforced Chador." In the cities, the marchers appear to be successful, but in the small towns and villages, the marchers are intimidated, some are whipped, and the movement fails. The novel concludes with hints of the hostage crisis and the Iran-Iraq War: "The whole Gulf's poised to explode." Business is business, however, and the company has opted for a highly risky plan that requires the willingness of the pilots to stay a month longer. In its depiction of the intensity, revolutionary fervor, and upheaval, *Whirlwind* lives up to its title.

The Persian Bride (2000; originally published in 1997 under the title *A Good Place to Die*) by the English novelist James Buchan (1954–) brings to life the culture of modern Iran, the source both of unspeakable terror and great beauty. The story begins in 1974 when John Pitt, a young English hippie, accepts a post teaching English in the city of Isfahan and falls in love with a beautiful Iranian student who happens to be the daughter of a prominent general in the shah's army. The two elope knowing that if they are caught, they will be killed. They hide out successfully during the period of the overthrow of the shah. Shirin, Pitt's wife, gives birth to a baby girl, and the two plan to leave Iran, but shortly after they are arrested by the new regime. Pitt is tortured and interrogated in the belief that he is an English spy. After more than 10 years in prison, he is released in order to serve in the army during the Iran-Iraq War. Later he finds himself in Afghanistan on the eve of the takeover by the Taliban in 1996. All the while, John has never wavered in his determination to reunite with his wife. He knows that she and their daughter have been in prison for many years, but their fate remains a mystery. He returns to Isfahan, where the story comes to a moving and graceful end.

James Buchan, the grandson of John Buchan (1875–1940), the espionage novelist—author of *The Thirty-Nine Steps* (1915)—has taken his heritage a step further. In his hands, the adventure story, of which *Whirlwind* is a perfectly good representative, moves into the realm of serious literature (reminiscent of the "entertainments" of Graham Greene [1904–91]) without losing its romantic and passionate essence. In *The Persian Bride*, the people and the culture of Iran emerge as complex and fascinating, alternately terrible and beautiful. For the Western reader, the powerful appeal of Islam appears less of a mystery, although, in its treatment of women, no less of a problem.

FURTHER READING

Shaul Bakhash's *The Reign of the Ayatollas* (1984) offers an eyewitness account of the revolution.

IRISH CIVIL WAR (1922–1923)

The Anglo-Irish treaty that ended the IRISH WAR OF INDEPENDENCE passed the newly formed Dail Eireann (Irish Parliament) by a narrow margin (64–57) on January 7, 1922. The antitreaty forces, led by the Irish president Eamon De Valera, withdrew from the new government, arguing that the treaty betrayed the ideal of an independent, united Ireland. The Treaty created an Ireland that was, strictly speaking, neither independent nor united, an "Irish Free State" with de facto independence, but still a part of the British Commonwealth. It also provided for the partitioning of Ireland into two separate entities, establishing six northern counties in the province of Ulster as

NORTHERN IRELAND. Michael Collins, one of the signatories to the treaty, who had been the leader of the Irish Army in the war against the British, became the head of the Free State Army, bringing about half of the soldiers who had fought in the War of Independence along with him. But the other half, known as the "Republicans," or "the Irregulars," formed a militant guerrilla force determined to resist the partition. In June 1922, the Republicans occupied the Four Courts building in Dublin, destroying official records dating back to the middle ages, but they surrendered to Collins's troops two days later Outside of Dublin, the Republicans had more success, conducting guerrilla activities in the western counties. In August in County Cork, they ambushed a car carrying Michael Collins, killing the government leader, but their fortunes waned from that point on. As in most civil wars, the conflict became increasingly bloody and bitter, with friends and relatives pitted against each other. In May of 1923, the Republicans surrendered, bringing to an end the civil war, but they continued to exist as an underground group, the IRISH REPUBLICAN ARMY (IRA). Eamon De Valera, having lost the support of the IRA, formed his own party (Fianna Fail) and was elected prime minister in 1932. In 1948, Ireland became a totally independent republic. Northern Ireland remained a part of the United Kingdom of Great Britain.

THE LITERATURE

Sean O'Casey's (1880–1964) comitragic drama *Juno and the Paycock* (1924) is an indictment of the civil war and the folly that precipitated it. The play focuses on the Boyle family, dwelling in a Dublin tenement. The father, "Captain" Boyle, an irresponsible roisterer, spends his time in the local pubs, accompanied by his sly, parasitical buddy, Joxer Daly. Boyle's wife, Juno, the play's long-suffering, sharp-tongued heroine, struggles mightily against her husband's fecklessness and the impoverished conditions in which they live. Her two adult children are a source of additional anxiety. John is an IRA veteran, who has lost an arm and had his hip shattered, along with his nerves, fighting for the Irish cause. The daughter, Mary, is on strike, protesting a fellow worker's firing. Both children are fierce believers in "principle," but Juno's response to her son summarizes her basic pragmatism: "Ah, you lost your best principle, me boy, when you lost your arm. Them's the only sort of principles that's any good to a workin' man."

When the family receives news of a legacy left to them, life seems to be taking a turn for the better. But the legacy turns out to be illusory; Mary is impregnated and abandoned by her lover, and John is killed by his Republican comrades when it appears that he has informed on a friend. In the final scene Juno and Mary leave the flat, from which creditors have removed all the furniture, as Juno, devastated by the death of her son, delivers her anguished plea: "Sacred Heart of Jesus, take away our murtherin' hate and give us Thine own eternal love." Her exit is followed by the drunken return of Boyle and

Joxer, where the captain delivers his famous curtain line, "I'm telling you, Joxer, th' whole worl's in a terrible state o' chassis."

The "chassis" of the civil war looms in the background and, in the killing of Johnny, the foreground of the play, but the war's malevolent presence is subsumed under a larger purpose. As the Irish writer James Stephens expressed it, the play "is an orchestrated hymn against all poverty and hate."

Julia O'Faolain's (1932–   ) *No Country for Young Men* (1980) is an ambitious attempt to see the civil war as part of a recurring pattern in Irish history and mythology. The story contains two plots: one set in 1921–22, on the brink of the civil war, and the other in 1979, when the political repercussions of "the Troubles" of Northern Ireland are echoing throughout all of Ireland. The connecting link between the two intricately interwoven plots is Judith Clancy, an ex-nun with a history of mental disease. Released by her order, the aged Judith has come to live with Grainne and Michael O'Malley, married cousins, both of them related to Judith. An Irish-American group sympathetic to the IRA is planning to produce a documentary film about the fate of an Irish American, John (Sparky) Driscoll, who was murdered in Ireland in 1922. Driscoll had been sent over by an Irish-American group to monitor the impending war and to advise them as to which side the group should support. During his stay, Driscoll was a frequent visitor to the family of Judith Clancy. In 1979, James Duffy arrives to do background research for the film. A top priority for him is to interview Judith about her knowledge of Driscoll's fate. Another cousin, Owen Roe O'Malley, a prominent member of the Irish Parliament is concerned that Judith's interview will tarnish the memory of his father, Owen O'Malley, who fought on the side of the Irregulars and later, like Eamon De Valera, became prime minister.

The parallels in the plot become even more pronounced when we learn, through the flashbacks experienced by Judith, that Judith's sister, Kathleen, had fallen in love with Driscoll during his visit, just as, almost 60 years later, Grainne O'Malley begins a passionate love affair with the American visitor, James Duffy. The parallelism extends to the tragic resolution of the two plots and to their convergence in the tortured mind of Judith.

The title *No Country for Young Men* is an allusion to the opening line of William Butler Yeats's celebrated poem "Sailing to Byzantium": "This is no country for old men." The allusion ironically states an important theme of the novel, the role of women in Irish society. The key figures are Judith, Grainne, and Judith's sister, Kathleen. The three are trapped in a society where church, state, and culture combine not only to subordinate the woman but to characterize her as the source of evil. The novel suggests that the oppressed condition of women extends back to Celtic mythology, reflected in the ancient story of Grainne and Diarmuid, lovers whose affair led to war, for which Grainne is then held responsible. In the same myth, *Cormac* is the name of Grainne's father; in the novel he is Grainne's teenage son, who has already been indoctrinated into the world of the IRA. Cormac is an example of the young men, conditioned for violence and bloodshed, who will continue the seemingly endless conflict. Grainne is the representative woman, for whom there seems to be no place but exile. Both *Juno and the Paycock* and *No Country for Young Men* conclude with women leaving, implying the need for them to disassociate themselves from the heritage of violence.

FURTHER READING

Calton Younger's *Ireland's Civil War* (1968) gives a detailed objective account of the significant events. David Krause's *Sean O'Casey: The Man and His Works* (1960) is an excellent critical study.

IRISH REPUBLICAN ARMY (IRA)

The forerunner of the IRA was the Irish Republican Brotherhood, a secret group of militants, founded in 1858 and supported to a large degree by immigrant Irish in the United States. With the coming of WORLD WAR I in 1914, the brotherhood, together with elements from two smaller groups, the Irish Citizen Army and the Irish Volunteers, planned an uprising sometime during the war to take advantage of England's focus on the European front. In 1916, they staged the EASTER RISING, a quixotic attempt to set up an Irish republic. The rising was easily squelched, but the extreme British reprisals, which included the summary executions of the leaders of the revolt, had the effect of creating martyrs of the rebels. Out of the ashes of defeat and anger emerged the Irish Republican Army and its political wing, Sinn Féin, whose name means "ourselves alone" in Gaelic. As disaffection with British rule intensified, Sinn Féin's popularity grew. In 1918, running on a platform of refusing to take seats in the British Parliament, Sinn Féin scored a landslide victory and proceeded to set up its own parliament (Dáil Éireann) in Dublin, which voted for a declaration of independence. Meanwhile the IRA was taking form as a guerrilla army under the brilliant leadership of Michael Collins. In addition to intimidating the national police force (the Royal Irish Constabulary), Collins infiltrated the British intelligence division, enabling him to anticipate his enemy's moves.

The British responded by recruiting ex-soldiers, known by their unusual uniforms as the Black and Tans, to aid the regular troops. The Black and Tans soon developed a reputation for brutal reprisals in the ensuing IRISH WAR OF INDEPENDENCE. After the war was over and a peace treaty signed, the IRA split down the middle: on the one side were those who supported the treaty with England, led by Michael Collins; on the other were the militant "new IRA," determined to continue the fight for a united Ireland, including the six counties of NORTHERN IRELAND, which remained under British control. In the ensuing IRISH CIVIL WAR, the new IRA was defeated. It was outlawed by the Irish government in the 1930s and reduced to a minor role in Irish politics.

In the aftermath of WORLD WAR II, another generation of IRA leaders arose with the intention of focusing on Northern Ireland, but with little success. By the 1960s, the leadership, heavily influenced by Marxist theory, played only a peripheral role in the struggle in which Catholics staged civil rights demonstrations. In December 1969, the Belfast Brigade and other northern units of the army broke away from this "official" IRA, forming the Provisional IRA ("Provos"). In the unrest following the 1972 "Bloody Sunday" massacre of 13 civil rights workers, the Provos were seen by the Catholic community as their only defenders. Waging guerrilla activities against local Northern Ireland authorities and the occupying British forces, the Provos, under the leadership of Gerry Adams and Martin McGuinness, became the de facto official IRA.

In 1981, worldwide attention was brought to bear on the hunger strikes of a number of IRA members held in British prisons, garnering both publicity and support for the organization. In the late '80s, the IRA began to make small but significant peace overtures. This shift was accompanied by defections from hard-line militants, but Adams and McGuinness maintained control over the organization. In 1994, a cease-fire led to peace talks, which succeeded, with considerable help from the Clinton administration, in setting up a power-sharing arrangement (the "Good Friday" agreement) in the Northern Ireland government, contingent upon the IRA's willingness to disarm. The precise terms of the disarmament clause are still the source of serious disagreement, but the power-sharing arrangement continues to be in effect.

THE LITERATURE

As the oldest continuously active guerrilla army in Europe, the IRA has always attracted the attention of writers. Two early novels were later made into classic films, Liam O'Flaherty's (1896–1984) *The Informer* (1925) and F. L. Green's (1902–53) *Odd Man Out* (1945). More recent years have seen a wave of thrillers and espionage novels focusing on IRA activities. One excellent example is James Hynes's *The Wild Colonial Boy* (1990), which takes as its point of departure the 1986 decision of Sinn Féin's leadership to revoke its policy of abstention from the Republic of Ireland's Parliament. Prior to that year, Sinn Féin representatives would run for office in the South but would refuse to take their seats when elected. This new policy, a departure from strict IRA tradition, was seen as initiating a political, nonviolent phase in their strategy, and it met with a fierce minority opposition from hard-liners within the organization.

In the novel, Brian Donovan, a young Irish American, brings over a $10,000 donation to the IRA from his grandfather, an old IRA veteran. He delivers the money to the husband of his cousin, not realizing that the man, Jimmy Coogan, is part of a renegade IRA faction, determined to undermine the Sinn Féin efforts to pursue a political strategy. Coogan convinces Brian to carry an explosive to Great Britain, which is later detonated in London's National Gallery. When Coogan is killed by British police, the reaction within the Sinn Féin/IRA inner circle almost succeeds in aborting the new political initiative. Brian, meanwhile, in an effort to save the life of a young Irish-American woman he has unwittingly implicated in the bombing, turns himself in to the British authorities.

A similar plot is put to a different use in Katharine Weber's (1955–) *The Music Lesson* (1998), which examines the ensnarement of an Irish-American woman in what she assumes is an IRA plan. Patricia Dolan is a 41-year-old art historian, suffering from the recent death of her kindergarten-age child. A surprise visit to her workplace, the Frick Museum in New York, by a distant Irish relative leads to a passionate affair. Slowly her lover Mickey reveals that he wants to use her expertise as an art historian to help steal a priceless Vermeer painting, *The Music Lesson*. While the theft is taking place in the Netherlands, she rents a remote cottage on the west coast of Ireland, where the painting will be hidden during the ransom negotiations.

Only after the theft does she learn that Mickey is a member of a break-away IRA group, the "Irish Republican Liberation Organization," determined to continue the use of violence in the North. When a moment of carelessness on her part results in the death of an innocent neighbor, Patricia awakens to the reality of her situation and Mickey's murderous nature. Managing to eke out a victory of sorts over Mickey and his group, she returns to the United States, knowing that she will live out her life alone: "[I]f life has to be a series of small losses, I still choose life."

Both novels depict naïve Irish Americans who become involved without really knowing whom they are dealing with. Of the two, *The Wild Colonial Boy* is closer to the straight action-adventure story. *The Music Lesson* emphasizes the psychological experience of its chief character, with very little reference to the political dimension of the plot.

Impressively integrating the inner life of its characters and political reality is Edna O'Brien's (1932–) *House of Splendid Isolation* (1994), in which an old country home comes to stand for Ireland, a house divided against itself. The owner is Josie O'Meara, an old woman who has survived an unhappy marriage and plans to live the rest of her life in "splendid isolation." But McGreevy, a notorious IRA gunman, escaping from the police, finds his way to her house and holds her prisoner as he tries to evade a nationwide dragnet. In the five days that the two remain together, the old woman and the young rebel come to understand each other. McGreevy is a man of the North, Josie a woman of the South. She sees the bombings, robberies, and other IRA activities as the degradation of a once noble rebellious tradition. He, having known nothing but the humiliation and oppression of the minority in the North, sees his cause as just. But gradually they come to see each other as wounded individuals. She makes no attempt to betray him to the police, and he endangers himself in an effort to help her. In the end, the house is destroyed, but the land remains and with it the possibility of ending the bloodshed that has "seeped into the soil, the subsoil."

FURTHER READING

J. Bowyer Bell's *The IRA, 1968–2000* (2000) is not a history of the organization but an analysis of its internal structure and goals.

IRISH WAR OF INDEPENDENCE (1919–1921)

In the wake of the EASTER RISING of 1916, nationalist fervor in Ireland intensified. Attempts to negotiate a form of home rule foundered on the question of the exclusion of six counties in the northern province of Ulster from the newly proposed government. In the general election of 1918, Sinn Féin, the most aggressive of the Irish parties, won a significant victory, but instead of joining the English Parliament to which they had been elected, they set up their own parliament, the Dáil Éireann, in Dublin. Meanwhile Michael Collins, a veteran of the Easter Rising and member of the Dail, organized and led a guerrilla army, to be known from 1919 on as the Irish Republican Army (IRA). Collins's guerrillas targeted members of the Royal Irish Constabulary, the government's police force. The IRA conducted many successful forays, attacking police barracks and outposts throughout the country. In response the English government dispatched soldiers and a new group, the Black and Tans (so-called because of the colors of their uniforms), to engage in counter-guerrilla actions. The brutality of the Black and Tans proved to be a public relations embarrassment for the British government, at the time presiding over the dissolution of the Russian, Austrian, and Ottoman Empires, while still exerting traditional imperial repression on their doorstep.

On July 9, 1921, the English government called for a truce, offering Ireland dominion status comparable to that of Canada. The Irish rejected the offer but agreed to negotiate a treaty. The treaty that resulted called for a partition in which the six Ulster counties would retain a separate identity as the Province of NORTHERN IRELAND. The treaty created a heated controversy in the Dáil, finally passing by a narrow vote, but setting the stage for the IRISH CIVIL WAR.

THE LITERATURE

In 1923, Dublin's famous Abbey Theatre introduced a new playwright, Sean O'Casey (1880–1964), whose tragicomedy *The Shadow of a Gunman* (1923) was the first of three plays dealing with pivotal events in recent Irish history. (The other two plays are *Juno and the Paycock* and *The Plough and the Stars;* see EASTER RISING.) *The Shadow of a Gunman*, set in a Dublin tenement during the war, takes as its satirical target the romanticizing of heroism. Its protagonist, Donal Davoren, sees himself as a poet, but his neighbors are convinced that he is an IRA gunman, hiding out from British forces. Once he realizes that the other tenants, particularly the young, attractive Minnie Powell, see him as a hero, he does nothing to dispel their illusions. His deception is matched by his self-deception, for Donal is no more a poet than he is a gunman. Like many of the other residents in his building, he indulges in verbal fantasies, keeping at arm's length the reality of the guerrilla war raging in the streets. But Donal's impersonation comes home to roost when a real IRA gunman hides a bag of bombs in his room. When the Black and Tans come to search his room, Minnie moves the bombs into her room, and she is arrested and killed trying to escape.

Like his predecessor at the Abbey Theatre, J. M. Synge (1871–1909), whose *Playboy of the Western World* satirized the Irish predilection to hero-worship outlaws while recording the colorful language of common people, O'Casey adds a serious note to his work—an expression of his socialist creed meant to show that the working poor are the real victims of the war. As one of his characters puts it, "the gunmen [are] blown' about dyin' for the people, when it's the people that are dyin' for the gunmen."

In *The Last September* (1929), the novelist Elizabeth Bowen (1899–1973) offers a view of the war from a distinctive perspective, that of the Anglo-Irish gentry, a class to which Bowen herself belonged. The Anglo-Irish, English by manners, religion, and custom but Irish in their love of the land and their own sense of national identity, recognize that they are a dying breed but remain in denial of that fact because they see the alternative—relocation—as unimaginable. Their world centers on the "big house," the gracious manors that dotted the Irish countryside, symbolizing their hegemony. In *The Last September,* the big house is the home of Sir Richard and Lady Naylor and their ward, Lois, the central figure of the novel. Caught in the conflict between the brutal Black and Tans and the equally brutal IRA, their position is summed up by one of them as "our side—which is no side—rather scared, rather isolated." The ambivalence is embodied in Lois, engaged to a British officer garrisoned in the area and drawn to a fugitive rebel hiding out in an abandoned mill on the estate. The novel concludes with the inevitable burning of the beautiful house, a deed that is seen as both terrible and liberating for Lois, who has known all along that the house, and the world for which it stood, is gone.

Thomas Flanagan's (1923–2002) *The End of the Hunt* (1994) opens in 1919. Within a wide range of historical and fictional figures, the novel focuses on Janice Nugent, a young Irish Catholic widow of an officer who has been killed in GALLIPOLI, and Christopher Blake, a trusted aide of Michael Collins, the charismatic leader of the Irish rebels. Christopher and Janice fall in love, creating a moral crisis for Janice, who abhors the violence surrounding them, but cannot deny her love for a man who helps to orchestrate a significant portion of that violence. Flanagan skillfully maneuvers her story in order to recreate Collins's successful military campaign and his fatal decision to participate in the 1921 Anglo-Irish Treaty talks in London. The decision is fatal because at the bargaining table the Irish are overmatched by the British threat that if they do not accept the treaty, it will mean all-out war. Collins, knowing better than anyone the completely weakened condition of his troops, agrees to sign, but acknowledges: "I may have signed my actual death-warrant." Collins's words prove to be prophetic in the Irish civil war that ensues. The treaty negotiations are skillfully rendered, particularly the portrait of Collins, who emerges as an imposing, courageous, ultimately tragic figure. Tragic too is the sense that the consequences of the events of the novel continue to be played out in the Troubles of Northern Ireland today.

The End of the Hunt completes the author's trilogy covering modern Irish history, beginning with the best-selling *The Year of the French* (1979), which dealt with the 1798 uprising, followed by *The Tenants of Time* (1988), which covered the period from the 1860s to the early years of the 20th century.

FURTHER READING

Joseph Coohill's *A Short History of Ireland* (2000) not only provides a brief, useful account of the war, it also summarizes differing historical interpretations of key issues surrounding it.

ITALIAN CAMPAIGN (WORLD WAR II) (1943–1945)

After the success of the campaign in North Africa, the Allies—British forces under the command of General Bernard Montgomery, Americans led by General George Patton—invaded Sicily in July 1943. By the beginning of September, Sicily was in Allied hands. On September 3, British troops landed in the toe of the Italian boot and proceeded up the eastern coast along the Adriatic Sea. Five days later the Americans landed at Salerno on the west coast, south of Naples. By this time the Italian dictator Benito Mussolini had been deposed and imprisoned by the new government of Marshal Pietro Badoglio. In September, the same month as the landings on the mainland, Badoglio negotiated an armistice with the Allies. On September 16, in a daring raid, the Germans freed Mussolini, allowing him to set up a new government based on FASCISM in northern Italy. German forces disarmed and imprisoned many Italian troops and recaptured thousands of Allied prisoners, who had been freed after the armistice. The Italian troops were shipped north to work in slave labor camps.

Meanwhile the Allies experienced considerable difficulty trying to penetrate the Gustav line, spread across the mountainous width of the lower Italian peninsula. An American attempt in January 1944 to bypass the Gustav line by invading Anzio Beach, 30 miles south of Rome, was eventually successful, but at the cost of a great number of casualties. At the center of the line, the Allies encountered fierce opposition around the monastery fortress of Monte Cassino. The controversial bombing of the monastery only contributed to the intensity of the German defense, who dug in among the ruins. In May, thanks to the mountain-scaling skills of North African troops and the fierce bravery of a corps of Polish fighters, the Allies captured Monte Cassino, thus opening up the road to Rome. In June 1944, the American forces entered Rome and, two months later, Florence. Meanwhile the Germans retreated north to form the Gothic line along the River Po. From there they slowly retreated, successfully delaying the Allied advance. It was not until May 2, 1945, that the German army in Italy formally surrendered. On balance, the Italian campaign hardly qualifies as an Allied success. The decision to launch a counterattack in Europe through Italy (the British choice) as opposed to landing in Northwest Europe (the American preference) probably prolonged the war, but a Northwest campaign was a riskier proposition and, as the NORMANDY INVASION a year later demonstrated, not easy.

THE LITERATURE

One of the most accomplished American novels of WORLD WAR II, Harry Brown's (1917–86) *A Walk in the Sun* (1944) begins with the American landing at Salerno in September 1943. During the landing, an infantry platoon loses its commanding officer and one of its sergeants. Isolated from the rest of their company (in the infantry, a company consists of four platoons), the platoon leaders move toward a vaguely described goal, a farmhouse some six miles inland, which they are to occupy, if empty, and overcome, if the enemy is within. As they move toward their goal, they lose their remaining two sergeants—one from a nervous breakdown—leaving a corporal in charge and reinforcing the men's fear that they are operating in the dark. Eventually they discover that their task involves subduing the enemy in the farmhouse and blowing up a nearby bridge.

One of the outstanding features of this novel is its quiet, understated tone, conveyed in a clear, clean prose style. Like the soldiers he chronicles, the author goes about his business, building dramatic tension, highlighting the down-to-earth dialogue of the men, and conveying the underlying sense of fear that the wisecracks try to disguise. Brown makes no attempt to probe the men in depth. He sees them not as individuals but as a functioning platoon, a group of men with a job to do, which they successfully perform—theirs not to reason why. In this, Brown captures a basic truth of soldiers under fire and shows how they maintain their sanity by focusing on the task at hand. A fine film version of *A Walk in the Sun*, directed by Lewis Milestone, who also directed *All Quiet on the Western Front*, appeared in 1945.

FURTHER READING

Eric Morris's *Circles of Hell: The War in Italy, 1943–45* (1993) discusses the details of this difficult campaign. Trumbull Higgins's *Soft Underbelly* (1968) details the conflict between the Americans and the British over the choice of Italy for the Allied invasion in 1943.

JAZZ AGE (1919–1929)

During the 1920s, America appeared to be moving in opposite directions simultaneously. On the one hand, a conservative, even reactionary, tide emerged in the wake of WORLD WAR I that stressed isolationism and intolerance, evident in the U.S. Senate's rejection of Woodrow Wilson's proposal for a LEAGUE OF NATIONS; in the reemergence of the Ku Klux Klan; in the Red Scare, epitomized in the SACCO-VANZETTI TRIAL; and in the passage of the PROHIBITION amendment. On the other hand, the era also saw the passage of the women's suffrage amendment, a stock market boom, the development of technological advances, and the mass production of the automobile—a form of transportation that would revolutionize the social and cultural mores of the country. It also produced the reaction against Prohibition: The wild, intoxicating "roaring twenties," in which the speakeasies and the gangsters who ran them demonstrated that while traditional, puritanical values might still reign in the hinterlands, the days of those values were numbered in an increasingly urbanized America.

One expression of this divided sensibility was the African-American musical form jazz. Combining syncopation and improvisation, jazz seemed both to mirror and create the new spirit of individual freedom that swept the urban areas. New Orleans, Chicago, Kansas City, and New York all became jazz centers, a list to which a short while later would be added Paris and London. Generally acknowledged as the greatest jazz musician, Louis Armstrong was also a representative one. Born in New Orleans, he was sent, at the age of 12 to a reform school, where he learned to play the cornet. In 1922, he joined

193

King Oliver's Creole Jazz Band and soon became famous for his superb trumpet playing. With musicians of Armstrong's caliber, jazz earned the respect of serious, classical composers, who began to include jazz passages in their works. The composer who celebrated jazz most extensively was George Gershwin. His *Rhapsody in Blue* (1924) introduced a new form, "symphonic jazz." At the same time, jazz set off a powerful negative reaction. Conservative forces—black as well as white—railed against this "devil's music," seeing in it an occasion of sin.

The emergence of jazz coincided with the Harlem Renaissance, the flowering of African-American literature, music, and dance that took place in New York's Harlem district in the 1920s. Nightclubs like the Cotton Club, reserved for white patrons only, and dance halls like the Savoy, frequented by local Harlemites, were just two of the hundreds of places in Harlem where jazz could be heard. It formed the background of the creative achievements of young African-American artists who had found their voice in this era of "flaming youth."

THE LITERATURE

By common consent, the greatest novel of the jazz age is *The Great Gatsby* (1925), just as its author, F. Scott Fitzgerald (1896–1940), is the best-known embodiment of the age. He was, like many of the characters in his work, both beautiful and damned. A midwesterner by birth, Fitzgerald was irresistibly attracted to the world of glamour, excitement, and wealth that he encountered in the East, first as a student at Princeton University and later as the popular chronicler and member of that world. The titles of his earlier collections of short stories, *Flappers and Philosophers* (1920) and *Tales of the Jazz Age* (1922), illustrate his laserlike focus on his times, but *The Great Gatsby* transcends its subject, looking beyond the bright lights, the music, and the parties to the tragic realm of unrealized ideals.

The story is narrated by Nick Carraway, a midwesterner living in New York who has become friendly with the millionaire Jay Gatsby, the source of whose wealth is both mysterious and suspect. On his Long Island estate, Gatsby throws fabulous parties, designed to lure into his world Daisy Buchanan, to whom he had been engaged five years earlier. Daisy is now the bored, restless, unhappy wife of Tom Buchanan, a wealthy man but a feckless, unfaithful husband. Gatsby's estate in West Egg is situated on the bay directly across from the Buchanan home in East Egg. For Gatsby, Daisy is the incarnation of an ideal that Gatsby has devoted his life to realize. The product of an impoverished, midwestern family, James Gatz (his real name) became the disciple of a self-made man, Dan Cody, from whom he learned how to succeed by engaging in morally dubious, shady business deals. But Gatsby's accumulation of wealth is solely for the purpose of winning Daisy. To that end, he persuades Nick, Daisy's cousin, to help reunite them. Meanwhile Daisy's husband, Tom, has been carrying on a sordid affair with Myrtle, the wife of a local garage owner. When Myrtle is locked in by her jealous husband, she tries to escape but is accidentally run over by Daisy, driving Gatsby's car. Myrtle's husband traces the car back to Gatsby and shoots him. At his funeral, the hundreds of so-called friends who attended his lavish parties are noticeably absent.

Many critics have pointed out that the ideal Daisy embodies in the novel is the original idea of America, corrupted by materialism in the modern age. The vision of America as a "virgin land," which had propelled the first settlers and those who later expanded the frontier, had become a "waste land." T. S. Eliot's poem of this name had been published in 1922 (see WORLD WAR I: AFTERMATH). In the novel the wasteland takes the form of "the valley of ashes," the land between the Long Island mansions and New York City. Thus both on its glittering surface—its parties, its drinking, its music—and its dark underside of lost innocence, *The Great Gatsby* captures the spirit of the 1920s, just as its author both observed and participated in it.

The parallel between Fitzgerald and his age continued through the 1920s and into the sobering reality, the "morning after" that was the GREAT DEPRESSION. As he grew older, the price of the good times increasingly became due. His heavy drinking, the mental illness of his wife, Zelda, and financial difficulties marked the sad second act of his life. He recounted this decline in the novel *Tender Is the Night* (1934), in which he attempted "to show a man who is a natural idealist . . . in his rise to the top of the social world, losing his idealism, his talent, and turning to drink and dissipation." In the story of Dick and Nicole Diver, characters who exhibit a more than passing resemblance to Scott and Zelda, we see two people attempting to make living well an art, but who in fact are heading for a fatal crack-up.

Toni Morrison's (1931–) *Jazz* (1992) opens and closes in the 1920s, but the body of the work moves back in time to the years following the Civil War, chronicling the odyssey of black Americans through various forms of social injustice, from simple snobbery to burning and lynching. Stylistically, the novel takes the jazz form as its model, establishing its major theme and providing individual variations on that theme. Thus the novel's remarkable opening sentences summarize its central event:

Sth, I know that woman. She used to live with a flock of birds on Lenox Avenue. Know her husband too. He fell for an eighteen-year-old girl with one of those deepdown spooky loves that made him so sad and happy that he shot her just to keep the feeling going. When the woman, her name is Violet, went to the funeral to see the girl and to cut her dead face they threw her to the floor and out of the church. She ran, then, through all that snow, and when she got back to her apartment she took the birds from their cages and set them out the windows to freeze or fly, including the parrot that said, "I love you."

In *Jazz*, the innovations on this "melody" include the stories of Violet, her husband, Joe, and the woman he murdered, Dorcas. Violet and Joe have come to Harlem from their sharecropper's farm in Virginia, seeking the freedom that jazz music expresses. But they are rooted in a tragic, repressed past. It is the past of slavery and postslavery so memorably captured in Morrison's masterpiece *Beloved* (1987). In fact *Jazz* is a kind of unofficial sequel to *Beloved:* The mysterious ghostlike figure that is Beloved reappears here in the character Wild, a truly wild woman living in the woods and the cane fields. Wild is Joe's mother, the mother he can never make contact with. Dorcas is a "wild" girl in the gin-drinking, jazz-loving, 1920s sense of the word. In killing her, Joe murders the mother who has rejected him. If Wild is in fact Beloved, the child whom her own mother murdered rather than have her returned to slavery, the novel continues to examine the ongoing, self-destructive impact of racism on American blacks. But this time the story ends happily, with an affirmation of the mature love that Violet and Joe achieve in the relative freedom of Harlem in the 1920s.

Jazz contains some of Morrison's most beautiful prose, passages that soar and dive like an alto saxophone in the hands of a jazz master, as in her description of young musicians on the rooftops overlooking Lenox Avenue: "[P]laying out their maple-sugar hearts, tapping it from four-hundred-year-old trees and letting it run down the trunk . . . slow, if it wished, or fast but a free run down trees bursting to give it up." The novel has been criticized for being excessively lyrical, but its achievements are as real as those of the 1920s Harlem Renaissance itself.

FURTHER READING

Kathy Ogren's *The Jazz Revolution* (1989) analyzes the impact of the music on the culture of the 1920s. J. Brooks Bouson's *Quiet As It's Kept* (2000) discusses the importance of shame and trauma as themes in Toni Morrison's fiction. In *Jazz Modernism* (2002), Alfred Appel, Jr., offers a convincing argument that sees jazz as part of "celebrity modernism" in literature and art.

JULY 20 PLOT AGAINST HITLER (WORLD WAR II) (1944)

On July 20, 1944, Colonel Claus von Stauffenberg, a German staff officer, placed a suitcase containing a bomb under the conference table in Adolf HITLER's headquarters at Rastenburg in East Prussia. The attempt to kill the führer was the key element of a plot in which a group of German officers and other individuals, including the theologian Dietrich BONHOEFFER, planned to take over the German government and presumably arrange a peace with the Allies, bringing to an end a war they knew they could not win. Unhappily, while many of the others in the room were killed, Hitler suffered only slight wounds. (Someone had moved the suitcase away from him shortly before the bomb detonated.) Von Stauffenberg, who had left the room after setting the fuse, was 200 yards from the headquarters when he witnessed the explosion. Confident that the assassination had succeeded, he flew to Berlin, where he assured his fellow conspirators of his success. Although the issue was still in doubt, they proceeded with their plan to wrest power from the Nazis, using their troops from the War Ministry, the headquarters of the plot, to surround government buildings, including Gestapo headquarters.

For a number of hours the issue was unclear, causing many to vacillate, uncertain as to which side to support. Eventually the truth emerged and the roundup of the plotters began. Von Stauffenberg was immediately executed by a firing squad. Among those peripherally involved was the renowned Field Marshal Erwin Rommel, who, although not part of the conspiracy, had given the impression that he would view the overthrow of Hitler as desirable. Because of his distinguished record, the Nazis allowed him to commit suicide. Rommel was one of more than 5,000 Germans, some of them killed because they were relatives of the conspirators, who died as a result of their connection to the conspiracy. Added to that are the millions who died in the last nine months of the war, people who might have survived had the plot succeeded. However, the historian Michael Beschloss argues that President Franklin Delano ROOSEVELT, among others, did not relish the prospect of a post–Hitler German government, particularly one in which the military played a prominent role. Such a government might have interfered with Allied plans for a Germany, as Beschloss explains, "so transformed that it would never threaten the world again."

THE LITERATURE

The popular German novelist Hans Hellmut Kirst (1914–89) offers a detailed, complex account of the plot in *Soldiers' Revolt* (1965; trans., 1966). Kirst's central character is Count von Brackwede, a witty, cool, clever staff officer who is the key figure in the plot. In a postscript to the novel, Kirst declares that he based von Brackwede on Count Fritz-Dietlof von der Schulenberg, scion of a Prussian military family, who joined the National Socialist (Nazi) Party in 1932 but gradually came to see the Nazis as a menace to his country. Schulendorf developed a circle of like-minded officers, most of them German aristocrats, increasingly appalled by Hitler and his cohorts. In the novel, Brackwede is a risk taker, going so far as to bring the Gestapo officer investigating him in on the plot. Once he realizes that the plot has failed, he maintains his cool, rational manner, very nearly succeeding in the takeover of the government even though Hitler has survived. When finally captured, he refuses to implicate anyone else, despite the most brutal tortures the Gestapo can devise. Kirst gives to Brackwede the actual words uttered by Schulenberg at his trial: "We assumed responsibility for this act in order to save Germany from a terrible misfortune. I fully realize that I shall be hanged, but I do not regret the part I played. I hope that, at a more auspicious moment, another man will complete our work."

A more imaginative depiction of the plot is Paul West's (1930–) *The Very Rich Hours of Count von Stauffenberg* (1980). Von Stauffenberg, Hitler's would-be assassin, was, like von der Schulenberg, an aristocrat, determined to rid Germany of the monstrous *Führer*. The book's title refers to the novel's structure as a "book of hours," a medieval prayer book, the layperson's equivalent of a priest's breviary. A book of hours is designed for particular times of the day and includes sections providing the opportunity to reflect and meditate. Among typical sections in a book of hours are sacred texts, such as the life of the Virgin; a section on one's own guilt and sinfulness; a memento mori section in which one considers one's own death; and a section describing the suffering of saints and martyrs. West arranges the relevant aspects of his story in similarly prearranged categories. For example, the penitential section of the novel focuses on Stauffenberg's guilt and self-recriminations for his enthusiastic participation in the invasion of Poland in the first months of the war.

As the novel opens, Stauffenberg lies wounded in the North African campaign, where he lost an eye and seven of his 10 fingers. While recuperating, he reflects on his past and begins to reexamine his values. He sees clearly now that Hitler is a mad fanatic who will lead Germany to destruction. He conspires in the failed plot and is executed, but he continues to narrate the story even after his death, which focuses on the aftermath of the attempt, when the vicious retaliation against the conspirators, their friends, and their families continues unabated right up to the end of the war.

What emerges in this novel, particularly in its analogue to the book of hours, is that this plot that ended so badly represented a moral triumph for its chief conspirator, a righteous man.

FURTHER READING

Harold Deutsch's *The Conspiracy against Hitler in the Twilight War* (1968) is an authoritative study; Michael Beschloss's argument regarding Roosevelt's intentions appears in his *The Conquerors: Roosevelt, Truman and the Destruction of Hitler's Germany, 1941–1945* (2002). David Madden's *Understanding Paul West* (1993) offers an informative account of *The Very Rich Hours of Count von Stauffenberg*.

K

KENNEDY, JOHN FITZGERALD (1917–1963)

John F. Kennedy, the 35th president of the United States, was born in 1917 and assassinated, presumably, by LEE HARVEY OSWALD, in Dealey Plaza, Dallas, Texas, on November 22, 1963. Kennedy came from a powerful Boston Irish clan, headed by Joseph P. Kennedy. In the family, Kennedy was the frail and sickly second son overshadowed by his robust older brother, Joseph Jr. Joseph Kennedy, Sr., intended that his eldest son should be president, but Joe died in WORLD WAR II, and the mantle fell to JFK.

Kennedy, himself a hero in the war for his experiences commanding a PT boat in the Pacific, served in the House of Representatives before winning a seat in the Senate. JFK's senatorial achievements were few. However, his good looks and quick wit and his opponent's somber plainness helped him narrowly defeat Richard M. NIXON in the presidential campaign of 1960. It was the first such campaign in which television, via the Nixon-Kennedy debates, played a decisive role.

Kennedy's brief presidential administration saw, in foreign affairs, the failed Bay of Pigs invasion, the Cuban missile crisis, and a noted summit showdown in Vienna with Soviet premier Nikita Khrushchev in the summer of 1961. When, shortly afterward, Krushchev ordered the Berlin Wall to be built, JFK endeared himself to the citizenry of what was then West Germany by declaring to them, "Ich bin ein Berliner." The signal went out that the United States would defend West Germany. In domestic affairs, Kennedy's "New Frontier" legislative program established the Peace Corps, gave impetus to the space program with a presidential vow to reach the moon in 10 years' time, and initiated a successful tax investment credit. Wishing to delay sending to Congress a forceful bill on civil rights until his second term, Kennedy nevertheless invoked his highest powers in sending federal troops to desegregate the University of Mississippi and to enforce school desegregation orders issued by the courts in Alabama. Despite these successes, the pundits evaluated his administration at the time of his death with mixed grades. He was thought to have made a poor showing on the international stage with Khrushchev, and his actions in increasing the United States' involvement in Vietnam drew criticism. Some saw his record on the economy as not having gone far enough. Others criticized his hesitant stand on the CIVIL RIGHTS MOVEMENT.

Nevertheless, his death by assassination shocked all Americans deeply. The glamour of his presidency veiled his flawed performance as president, and his death ushered in a period of adulation and idealization. Americans were at first grief stricken, but in the end they were bedazzled by television imagery: pictures of his widow, bloodied and mournful, but immensely digni-fied and beautiful as she accompanied his casket and watched Lyndon B. Johnson take the oath of office in Air Force One, and of his brother Bobby, mournful and stricken, his boyishness made more poignant by his brother's sudden death. A sense of nostalgia for a golden age swept the country, and the period of his presidency came to be known as "Camelot."

The Camelot image was somewhat tarnished when journalists made it clear that Kennedy, had been an incorrigible womanizer, whose staff sneaked women into the White House. His affairs or supposed affairs with, among others, Marilyn Monroe and the girlfriend of the notorious mafioso Sam Giancana, also became matters for public speculation and delectation. How-ever, this tarnished image has been superseded by a living mythology about him and his death.

THE LITERATURE

Both *Flying in to Love* (1992), by D. M. Thomas, (1935–) and *I, JFK* (1989), by Robert Mayer (1939–) agree on the mythical nature of Kennedy's life and death; display his charm, wit, and womanizing; and suggest that he died at the hands of a shadowy conspiratorial clique.

D. M. Thomas's novel is a charged, poetic meditation that takes the immediate circumstances of the assassination and expands those minutes in time and space. Before the narrative concludes with Kennedy's death in Dealey Plaza, it moves the reader back and forth in time, and it speculates on what might have happened had JFK not been killed. In the novel, the real shooters, the ones on the grassy knoll, are arrested before they can do their work, and thus after Dealey Plaza, the president takes a tour of Austin and arrives at the Texas ranch of Vice President Lyndon B. Johnson. Thomas gives each moment of the Kennedys' visit here and in Dallas temporal depth, such that he can explore motive and character: Jackie's sadness over the recent loss of her infant son and her well-documented dignity, cultural credentials, and beauty; JFK's uncertainties about policy and his surprising habit of saying his prayers before bedtime. One motive for his womanizing—at least while Jackie is away—is that he hates to fall asleep alone.

Parallel to these temporal and spatial expansions in alternating chapters is the life story of Sister Agnes, a young nun who teaches at the Sacred Heart Convent in Dallas. JFK spots her as his motorcade makes its way to Dealey Plaza, and he stops his car and thanks her for turning up to cheer him on. She says she's proud that a Catholic has become president. JFK shakes her hand and proceeds on his way, thinking of her. He takes from the encounter a powerful sexual attraction to the attractive young nun. She feels the same—though at first she will not acknowledge it. After his death, Sister Agnes becomes wholly obsessed with his image, founding and maintaining a journal, *November 22*, and a November 22 Museum. The story of her life, taken to 1990, includes her family's story. JFK, in his World War II role in the navy, had instructed her father in PT boat operations. JFK remembers the connection—and at the conclusion of the novel recalls that "Teach" Mason had been dismissed from PT boat training for making improper advances to black kids whom he was teaching to read.

Thomas interweaves with this material the narrative of the conspiracy to assassinate the president. The narrator makes it clear that the real shooters were on the knoll, and a giant coverup concealed all the evidence of this conspiracy. Thomas has sections devoted to Lee Harvey Oswald and Marina Oswald; David Ferrie, the New Orleans District Attorney; Jack Ruby; J. D. Tippit; and, finally, one of the shooters, a gruff, uneducated man named Wayne.

In 1990, Wayne comes to Sister Agnes in the museum to confess what he has done and to ask her forgiveness—nobody else to whom he tells his story will believe him. She accedes to this request, and now the proof is at hand. When Sister Agnes realizes that Wayne is telling the truth, she is elated. She has believed all along that the conspiracy existed.

That night she dreams that she has had sex with Wayne. When she wakes up later, she has lost the ability to read. She drinks a bottle of whiskey and swallows many painkillers. Just in time, one of the other nuns finds her and takes her to Parkland Memorial Hospital. All the players in the Kennedy drama "were inside her, assassins and victims alike . . . The drama had taken up residence in Sister Agnes's mind, and every moment of her life was the moment between firing and impact."

Sex and death are pervasive motifs of the novel. JFK interrupts his breakfast on November 22 to visit Beth Pulman, the wife of one of his party stalwarts who has just had a mastectomy, at Parkland Memorial Hospital (where Kennedy is later pronounced dead). He asks her husband to go to the cafeteria for a cup of coffee and then instructs his Secret Service detail to let no one into the room. Once inside, he undresses and gets into bed with the patient. She is delighted; she had slept with him at the 1960 convention. Years later, on her death bed, she tells all to her daughter, Jane, a student of Sister Agnes's, who had been in the nun's class taking a test on November 22, 1963. Now a Ph.D. in psychology, Jane writes a shrewd paper on JFK's sexuality—printed as a chapter of the novel.

Throughout, Thomas's narrative emphasizes both the human frailty and inwardness of JFK and the powerful imaginative impressions he left behind. But Sister Agnes's response to the death of the president is the central element in the novel's mythologizing of the man and his death. The effect on her represents the effect on the country. Ironically, "Jack," the man whose emotions—so inward, so heavily invested in himself and his role as president and as a Kennedy—make him incapable of real love, lands, on the last day of his life, at Love Field, the Dallas airport where his body is loaded onto *Air Force One*. Dying, he flies into the mythos of Agnes's (America's) love.

Robert Mayer's *I, JFK* is narrated by JFK in what he describes as an "emotional mosaic." This is a richly comic work, powered by the verbal wit of the narrator, who deploys farce, parody, burlesque, caricature, and travesty. The real presidential assassin was none other than JFK's half-brother, a midget named Arthur King, the illegitimate child of Joseph P. Kennedy and a Hollywood starlet. In the Texas Book Depository, King is stationed on Lee Harvey Oswald's shoulder and his phenomenally accurate shots do the work. The midget is also a multiple agent—employed by the CENTRAL INTELLI-GENCE AGENCY (CIA), the Russians, Castro, and anti-Castro forces—and lives happily ever after on the trust fund set up for him by his father.

The central conceit is that the powers that be permit JFK 25 more years of hindsight from the day of his death. Thus the narrator lives fictionally until November 22, 1988. In the time and space allotted, JFK goes over the familiar ground of his history, including his relations with his brothers Joe, Jr., and Bobby; with his tyrannical father; with his valet, Raymond; with Adlai Stevenson; and, centrally, with Jackie. In addition, in his scattershot manner, he reviews and comments on a dizzying array of topics: Cuba, Russia, Vietnam, and, repeatedly, Lyndon Johnson, over whose country-boy character he scores wittily. In the end, heaven then "assumes" him, and "the rest is silence."

The famous Kennedy wit and rhetorical skill are deftly parodied, and scatology is freely deployed. Johnson asks JFK to see tapes of the president in bed with Inga, an alleged former spy for Adolf HITLER, to which JFK replies, "I never promised you a Berchtesgaden." Again, when Johnson angrily declares that JFK is considered a "grace" and he "a clod," JFK answers: "A myth is as good as a mile, Lyndon Baines." Likening his brother Joe to Tarzan and himself to Hamlet, he remarks: "It's ambition, not conscience, that makes cowards of us all."

Ultimately, Mayer's work is subversive; the book insists that the Kennedy phenomenon—the glamorous and scandalous life and the murky but shocking assassination—is a subject fit for its epigraph by Gene Fowler: *Tragedy is not always veiled in black.* A more apt epigraph might have been a play on Karl Marx's dictum that history is played out twice—once as tragedy and once as farce.

FURTHER READING

A full factual accounting of President Kennedy can be found in Arthur Schlesinger's *A Thousand Days: John F. Kennedy in the White House* (1965), Doris Kearns Goodwin's *The Fitzgeralds and the Kennedys: An American Saga* (2002), and Laurence Leamer's *The Kennedy Men, 1901–1963: The Laws of the Father* (2001).

—*William Herman*

KNOSSOS, DISCOVERY OF THE PALACE AT (1900–)

The unearthing of King Minos's labyrinth, the most dramatic discovery of 20th-century European archaeology, began to unfold along with the century in 1900 and was still offering major surprises decades later. Although Sir Arthur Evans (1851–1941), the keeper of the Ashmolean Museum in Oxford, was not the first to appreciate the possibilities of the mound at Knossos, a few miles south of modern-day Iraklion, Crete, it was he who succeeded in buying the property at a propitious time, when the hold of the Ottoman Turks on the island had been loosed. From the very first day, the finds were spectacular.

Though the myth of Minos was considered a possible echo of a time when Crete was the dominant sea power in the eastern Mediterranean, the story of the labyrinth seemed pure fairy tale. Every nine years, according to the myth, the Athenians were forced to send a tribute of seven young men and seven maidens to King Minos, who would place them in the labyrinth to be devoured by the Minotaur. With the help of Minos's daughter Ariadne, who provided him with a sword and a ball of thread, the hero Theseus killed the monster and escaped with his companions from the island. Evans's crew dug up the ruins of a complex, multistoried building the size of a palace, with a throne room and wonderful frescoes that revealed, he thought, a joyous people, peaceable, fond of spectacle and dance. Among the frescoes was one that seemed to show two young women and one young man engaging in some form of bull vaulting. Many other bull artifacts were uncovered as well, along with a large number of double axes, the name for which in Luvian (or Carian) was *labrys*. Evans derived the name *labyrinth* from these implements and saw the origin of the myth of the Minotaur in the bull games. But the nasty edge of the legend he attributed to propaganda against their enemies by the early Greeks. It was clear from Homer that Mycenaean Greeks had ultimately conquered the island, but Evans argued for as late a date as possible. Increasingly, he felt that in Minoan civilization (for so he named it) were to be found the origins of much of Greek religion, art, and culture in general.

Evans even succeeded in finding the original object of his quest: early script. Excavations yielded clay tablets with three types of writing: hieroglyphic, Linear A, and Linear B. Evans never found the key to reading the tablets; by delaying publication of most of the material until after his death, he frustrated others from succeeding as well. But in 1939 Linear B tablets were discovered on mainland Greece, at Pylos. Evans's loyalists insisted that these constituted pirate booty and had not been created in mainland Greece. But with the aide of these tablets, English mathematician and amateur classicist Michael Ventris was able to "break the code" in 1952; to his surprise, and to the shock of most others, Linear B turned out to be an early form of Greek, making it clear that Mycenaeans had ruled at Knossos much earlier than Evans would have conceded.

Evans has also come under severe criticism for the speculative nature of his ambitious restorations at Knossos. Scholars have challenged even his most basic idea, that the building at Knossos was a palace. Hans Georg Wunderlich, for example, in *The Secret of Crete* (1974), proposes that the ruins are of a vast necropolis. Less idiosyncratically, Rodney Castleden, in *The Knossos Labyrinth* (1990), thinks they are the ruins of a temple. But a pair of excavations conducted separately on Crete in 1979, one near a village named Archanes, the other in the North House at Knossos, dealt still deadlier blows to Evans's vision of the Minoans. The former contained evidence of a human sacrifice, complete with a body lying on an altar, trussed like a sacrificial victim, a dagger among his bones. Even grimmer were the finds at the latter site. There 327 bones that belonged to at least four children were found with the fine knife marks characteristic of a butcher's removal of meat from the bone. Most likely, ritual cannibalism had been performed. The myth of the Minotaur, it turns out, may have had more precise historical roots than Evans ever imagined. Nonetheless, on balance, the excavation of Knossos remains a major achievement, and Evans's flair for the dramatic clearly advanced the study of Bronze Age Greece throughout Crete.

THE LITERATURE

In the novel *Ariadne's Children* (1995), Roderick Beaton (1951–   ), a critic of modern Greek literature, takes as his subject the discovery of Minoan civilization but handles the events in an unusual way. Either to give free play to his imagination or to avoid harsh criticism of a figure still far more revered than reviled, Beaton creates a character, Lionel Robertson, with many of the qualities of Arthur Evans, but who arrives in Crete in 1920, 20 years after Evans unearthed Knossos. Like Evans, Robertson as a young man wanders in Illyria (the former name applied to the Balkan Peninsula, excluding Greece) and ends up in Ragusa (Dubrovnik) under difficult circumstances. Like Evans, he becomes obsessed by the carved gemstones turning up on Crete. He arrives on Crete and discovers not Knossos, for which Evans is given appropriate credit, but a formidable palatial structure nearby called "Ariadne's Summer Palace," located where the Villa Ariadne, which Evans built for his headquarters, actually stands. The finds at this excavation strongly resemble objects unearthed at Knossos. Robertson himself is known as the "old rogue," a term many would have applied to Evans. A bust of him remains on the site, just as there is a bust of Evans at Knossos. And his son, Daniel, meets his fate in combat against the Germans during the occupation of Crete, just as Evans's young assistant, John Pendlebury, author of *The Archaeology of Crete* (1939), did in real life. The novel, which follows the Robertsons and their women through three generations, finally turns on the discovery of bones with butcher's marks, which the elder Robertson declares a hoax and suppresses. Beaton, in this way, captures the essence of suspicions that Evans manipulated data according to his "pro-Minoan" bias, without having to deal with the probably impossible task of proving it.

FURTHER READING

The most well-known account of the life of Sir Arthur Evans, by his sister Joan, is *Time and Chance* (1943). For a more objective approach, see *The Find of a Lifetime* (1981) by Sylvia L. Horwitz. To place the excavations at Knossos in context, see *The Discovery of the Greek Bronze Age* (1995) by J. Lesley Fitton. Finally, Joseph MacGillivray's *Minotaur* (2000) takes a postmodern view of Arthur Evans's archaeological career, emphasizing how many of his views were firmly in place before excavations began and how he is an exemplary figure of the archaeologist-as-creator, rather than discoverer, of the world of his imagination. Although *Minotaur* takes no note of *Ariadne's Children*, it provides an ironic perspective on the novel: Roderick Beaton undertakes the same imaginative recreation of Evans's life as, MacGillivray contends, Evans used to bring the world's eyes to his Minoans.

—*Karl Malkoff*

KOBE EARTHQUAKE (1995)

At 5:46 A.M. on January 17, 1995, an earthquake hit the city of Kobe in western Japan. The quake lasted for only 20 seconds, but it resulted in the destruction of highways, railways, ports, and more than 100,000 buildings. Measuring 7.2 on the Richter scale, the quake left 5,000 people dead and more than 300,000 homeless. Many of the buildings were destroyed by fires, which raged through the city unabated for days, since there was no water in the city's mains to combat them. Survivors, without water, gas or electricity, huddled in remaining public buildings, freezing in the January cold. The elevated Hanshin expressway collapsed, sending more than 1,600 feet of the roadway crashing to the ground. Thousands fled from Kobe on foot, heading for Osaka, the nearest large city, some 20 miles away. Old-time residents had not seen such devastation since 1944, when American bombers raided the city 25 times.

The quake came as a great shock not just to the Kobe but to the entire nation. Historically, Japan has always been vulnerable to earthquakes, but before the Kobe quake, the Japanese had exhibited a growing confidence in their ability both to predict and absorb a major tremor. The carnage in Kobe left many Japanese with a profound sense of anxiety and unease. Two months later, a terrorist gas attack in a Tokyo subway station intensified that unease even more.

THE LITERATURE

The Japanese novelist and short story writer Haruki Murakami (1949–   ), who was raised in Kobe, explores the penetration of the quake into the lives of a variety of characters, none of them residents of the city, in his collection of short stories *After the Quake* (2000; trans., 2002). The stories deal with the spiritual aftershock emanating from the physical disaster. Most of them involve recognitions that lead to, or anticipate, recoveries in the form of renewed entries into life. In "Thailand," a female research scientist from Kyoto takes a holiday, shortly after the quake, at a remote, luxurious Thailand resort. Her guide brings her to an old village seer who sees in her eyes the hatred she harbors for her ex-husband. The former husband lives in Kobe, and the woman has been carrying within her the wish that he and his new family have been killed in the quake. The woman comes to see the connection between that feeling and the death of the woman's father when she was young. In "UFO in Kushiro," a wife deserts her husband after she has spent five days mesmerized by the television coverage of the disaster. She leaves a note, telling him, "You have nothing inside you." A friend sends the distraught husband on a trip, bearing a package, contents unknown. On arrival, he discovers the connection between himself and his package. In the book's longest story, "Honey Pie," set in Tokyo, a four-year-old girl's recurrent nightmare of being visited by "Mr. Earthquake" triggers a seismic shift in the relations of her parents and their mutual best friend, a short-story writer, alienated from his parents, who are living in Kobe. The interaction between the little girl and the writer may remind readers of some of the stories of J. D. Salinger.

Many of these tales bear the characteristic mark of Murakami's fiction—frequent references to Western culture, popular and classical, particularly to American jazz. (Two of the stories make important references to the Errol Garner album *Concert by the Sea*.) He also invokes fantastic and surrealistic effects in the manner of many Western postmodern novelists. In this respect,

Murakami's work, which has made him among the most popular and respected Japanese novelists at home and abroad, represents what some see as an extreme form of the westernizing trend in Japanese culture. But *After the Quake* and Murakami's nonfictional account of the subway terrorist attack, *Underground* (1997; trans., 2000), testify to his continuing attachment to his Japanese roots.

FURTHER READING

David Van Beema's "When Kobe Died," the *Time* cover story (January 30, 1995), offers vivid, insightful coverage of the earthquake.

KOREAN WAR (1950–1953)

At the Potsdam Conference in July–August 1945, the Allies, having already achieved victory in Europe, agreed that, following the impending defeat of Japan, Korea, which had been controlled by Japan since 1910, would be temporarily partitioned, with Russian troops occupying the northern section of the country and Americans controlling the southern portion. The dividing line would be the thirty-eighth parallel, latitude. This temporary arrangement was to be the first step in the formation of an independent, unified Korea. The unification plan soon ran aground as the United States and the Soviet Union could not agree on the form of government to be established. As a result, the northern section became a Communist state (the Democratic People's Republic of Korea) under the leadership of Kim Il Sung, while the South became the Republic of Korea, which elected Syngman Rhee as its first president. Ominously, both states claimed to represent the entire country. In 1949, the American and Soviet occupying forces withdrew from the country.

On June 25, 1950, troops from the North, well equipped with Soviet weapons, crossed the thirty-eighth parallel, easily overcame the disorganized South Korean army, and within four days captured Seoul, the South Korean capital. In response, the American government, acting through the United Nations, initiated a "police action," which enabled president Truman to avoid asking Congress for a formal declaration of war. Under the leadership of General Douglas MacArthur, American troops stationed in Japan (they would later be joined by delegations from a number of UN member nations) successfully rolled back the North Korean troops across the thirty-eighth parallel. A key maneuver in this counterattack was an amphibious landing at Inchon Harbor, which enabled UN troops to bypass the Korean army and recapture Seoul in one stroke.

The UN offensive pushed north, capturing the North Korean capital, Pyongyang, but when the troops approached the area of the CHOSIN RESERVOIR, near the Yalu River, the dividing line between Korea and Manchuria, they encountered a massive force of 1 million Chinese troops. The outnumbered UN forces had been rendered additionally vulnerable by MacArthur's earlier decision to divide his army into two wings, separated by a stretch of impassable mountains running north to south. UN troops on the eastern side of the mountains, made up mostly of U.S. Marines, retreated, fighting all the way, to the port city of Hungnam, from which they were successfully evacuated. In the western sector, the U.S. Eighth Army retreated, evacuating Seoul to set up a perimeter defense further south. From here they mounted another counterattack, recapturing Seoul and setting up a front line slightly north of the thirty-eighth parallel. At this point, President Truman, infuriated by MacArthur's public pronouncements about the conduct of the war, relieved him of command. MacArthur returned to the United States to receive a hero's welcome. His successor was Eighth Army commander General Matthew Ridgway. In April 1951, the Chinese launched another offensive, but this time the UN troops were fully prepared and well supported by heavy artillery and air strikes.

For the next two years, both sides conducted a war of attrition, complicated by an off-again, on-again series of truce talks. The sticking point holding up the talks was the issue of repatriation of prisoners of war, but behind the issue lay the desire of the Soviet Union to keep the United States busy in Korea in order to minimize its impact in Europe. On July 27, 1953, the fighting ended with an armistice that called for a partition along the thirty-eighth parallel, with the addition of a demilitarized zone 10 miles on each side of the border. The common view of the Korean War is that it had no victor, but the subsequent vast disparity between life in South Korea and that in the North suggests that, in one respect at least, the South Koreans won.

THE LITERATURE

One of the unusual and controversial aspects of the Korean War concerned the Chinese and North Korean treatment of prisoners of war. More than 7,000 UN troops were captured in the course of the war, most of them Americans, but some were British and Turkish as well. Many of the captives were subjected to intense propaganda campaigns designed to convert them to communist ideology. In most cases, the conversion attempt was accompanied by promises of better food and shelter and threats of beatings and death. Not surprisingly, a significant minority played along with their captors in order to survive. A much smaller number—21 out of 7,000—were in fact converted and chose not to return to the United States after the war. This situation led to the widely misunderstood charges of "brainwashing," which received much media attention in the 1950s. Richard Condon's (1915–96) inventive thriller *The Manchurian Candidate* (1959) capitalized on the brainwashing craze. In his novel, he creates a character, Raymond Shaw, who is brainwashed while a prisoner of war to the extent that he becomes an unconscious agent of the Communists, programmed to commit crimes at their command. From this wild premise, the novel develops into a highly exciting thriller.

A less sensational, more substantial treatment of this subject is Frederick Busch's (1946–   ) 1989 novel *War Babies*. The story, set in 1984, is narrated by Peter Santore, the son of an American prisoner of war in Korea who was later convicted and imprisoned as a traitor for his active cooperation with his Chinese captors. Peter's mother divorced his father shortly after Peter was born and refuses to speak about him. Haunted by his lack of knowledge of his father's story, Peter visits England in order to meet Hilary Penells, the daughter of his father's polar opposite. Hilary's father had been imprisoned in the same camp as Peter's, the infamous Camp 12.

Camp 12 was known as "the Caves" because the prisoners were jammed into a series of tunnels dug into the side of a hill. The caves were constantly cold, wet, and overrun with lice, and the prisoners were subject to verbal abuse, torture, and beatings. Their jailers divided them into two groups, the "reactionaries," those who refused to cooperate, and the "progressives," those who paid lip service, along with the few who actively supported the Communist cause. On the threshold of death, Lieutenant Penells, Hilary's father, commanded his men to cooperate (his ordering them relieved them of responsibility) as a way to survive, but he himself refused to do so, even though he was beaten and eventually killed by the Chinese.

Hilary's heroic father is as much of a burden as Peter's, only in her case it is not simply psychological. She has to contend with the oppressive presence of Fox, her father's adjutant, a survivor of the camp and a man with a tenacious hold on the past. Fox holds a special hatred for Peter's father, whom he knew in the camp. That hatred is quickly transferred to Peter after Fox guesses that he and Hilary have begun an affair. The conclusion is underscored by the novel's title, *War Babies*. Peter and Hilary discover that they are at war with their dead fathers. Both the traitor and the hero have left their children a legacy of anger that stains everything in their lives, including their love. The novel is set in Dorset, the county in southwest England that Thomas Hardy (1840–1928) used as the basis of his "Wessex" novels. Hardy's *Tess of the D'Urbervilles* plays a thematic role in *War Babies*. Tess's tragic fate foreshadows the novel's unhappy resolution.

The Pennels character is based on real-life Lieutenant Terence Waters, a young British officer. Waters ordered his men to cooperate with the captors, but he refused to do so himself. As a result, his men survived, while he was brutally tortured and killed.

Both for the precision and richness of its style and the authoritative command of its subject, James Salter's (1925–   ) *The Hunters* (1957) is commonly regarded as the most accomplished novel of the Korean War. Salter served as a pilot in a fighter squadron during the war. As he explains in his introduction to the second edition of the novel, the air war was fought using the newly developed jet planes, American F86s, against Russian MIGs. The basic combat element in the American Air Force was a two-plane combination, the leader and the wingman. The job of the less experienced flier, the wingman, was to serve as the lookout for the leader, particularly once contact was made with enemy planes. This fact plays a critical role in the novel, which deals with Pell, a wingman who fails to protect his leader in order to acquire glory as an "ace." As Pell ascends, accruing praise from superior officers, the novel's protagonist, Cleve Connell, an experienced pilot, has a run of bad luck that seems to spell failure or lack of courage to the rest of the squadron. Connell's redemption, known only to himself, comes during an air duel with the enemy's best pilot. Salter's luminous description of the fight captures the beauty of flight, here enhanced by the imminent possibility of death.

FURTHER READING

James Stokesbury's *A Short History of the Korean War* (1988) is a concise, highly readable account of the war; Stanley Sandler's *The Korean War* (1999) examines the war in the light of recently released Soviet documents. Lewis Carlson's *Remembered Prisoners of a Forgotten War* (2001) is an oral history and analysis of the prisoner-of-war experience.

L

LAMBRAKIS, GRIGORIOS, ASSASSINATION OF (1963)

The tensions that produced the GREEK CIVIL WAR did not disappear with the standing down of the KKE (Greek Communist Party) in 1949. King Paul, who had succeeded to the throne upon the death of George II in 1947, supported Constantine Karamanlis as premier in 1955. Karamanlis dominated Greek politics for the following decade, but his support was fragmented and included elements of the far right, which became increasingly difficult to control as leftist forces began to reassert themselves in the country. In May 1963, right-wing goons attacked Grigorios Lambrakis, a deputy of the United Democratic left, at a peace rally; he died several days later. Karamanlis's hold on power was shaken, and he resigned later that year. George Papandreou became premier, but in 1965 was maneuvered out of office by King Constantine, who had ascended to the throne in 1964. As the electorate continued to shift increasingly to the left in revulsion against the right-wing thuggery, a group of reactionary GREEK COLONELS, fearing a leftist landslide in pending elections, successfully staged a coup in April 1967.

THE LITERATURE

The assassination of Grigorios Lambrakis is anatomized by Vassilis Vassilikos (1933–   ) in his novel Z (1966; trans., 1968). In this narrative, the deputy's name is Z. (standing for the Greek verb *zei*, "he lives," used by supporters to designate the enduring power of his martyrdom). We see the events immediately preceding the assassination from a variety of perspectives. The Friends of Peace have scheduled a rally in a theater, but at the last moment its availability is withdrawn, causing a chaotic scene in which it is difficult to protect Z. He is attacked twice and dies a few days later from the blows to his head. The movie made of this novel by Costa-Gavras (1969) provides the sense of a documentary, but the novel, though it accurately captures the energies of its time, has a strong satiric edge. The police who are complicit with the assassins are led by characters with names such as *Autocratosaur* and *Mastodontosaur*. Most of the leading characters have stereotypical roles: the murderers, Yango and Vango; the lawyer and adviser, Matsas; the bodyguard, Hatzis ("the Tiger"); the widow, sexually betrayed but linked to Z. in profound ways; the witness, Nikitas; the reporter, Andoniou; the investigator; and the public prosecutor. Z. stands above all, larger than life, a powerful man who rejects violence and depends on the force of his ideas to win the day. The public prosecutor succeeds not only in identifying the actual murderers, who are offered up as scapegoats by their betters, but also in exposing the echelons of the police who abetted them. By the novel's cynical conclusion, however, those higher up are wriggling off their respective hooks, Matsas and Hatzis are being sued for libel, and the public prosecutor has died, supposedly of a heart attack.

The novel was published in 1966, at a perilous stage of the events set loose by the murder. Karamanlis had been driven out of office; Papandreou was elected and then betrayed in the lost spring of 1965. The Greek colonels' coup was not far away. But the process ultimately worked itself out in ways that Z., or Lambrakis, would have enjoyed. The eventual fall of the colonels in 1974, brought about, first, the return of Karamanlis and, ultimately, the triumph of Andreas Papandreou (son of George) and his Panhellenic Socialist Party (PASOK). And in 1985 the prototype of the public prosecutor, Christos Sartzetakis, who had not in fact died of a heart attack or of any other cause, was elected president of Greece.

FURTHER READING

See appropriate sections in C. M. Woodhouse's *Modern Greece* (1991) and Richard Clogg's *A Concise History of Greece* (1992) for historical analyses. For an account including the takeover of the greek colonels, see C. M. Woodhouse's *The Rise and Fall of the Greek Colonels* (1985).

—Karl Malkoff

LENIN, VLADIMIR ILICH (1870–1924)

The founding father of the Soviet Union, Lenin (birth name: Vladimir Ulyanov) became involved in revolutionary activity as a student at Kazan University. In 1895, he was arrested and sentenced to five years' exile in

Siberia. While there, he published *The Development of Capitalism in Russia* (1899), a work that established his reputation as a formidable Marxist theorist. On his return, he lived in exile in Geneva, publishing his highly controversial pamphlet *What Is to Be Done* (1902), a revision of Marxist theory calling for a revolution led by a core of professionals rather than waiting for the working class to acquire a revolutionary consciousness. This departure from the theories of Karl Marx created a split between the Bolsheviks, the group supporting Lenin, and the Mensheviks, the adherents of the traditional Marxist position. After playing a limited role in the Russian revolution of 1905, Lenin returned in 1907 to Geneva, where he directed various Bolshevik activities, including robbing banks to support the work of the cause.

At the outbreak of WORLD WAR I, he took the position that international socialism should remain neutral in a struggle that was rooted in capitalist/imperialist motives. After the success of the first stage of the RUSSIAN REVOLUTION (1917), he returned to Russia in April of 1917 to direct the second phase, the October Revolution, which swept the Bolsheviks into power, promising peace, land, and bread and using the slogan "All Power to the Soviets (workers' councils)."

Once in control, Lenin lost no time concluding a peace with Germany, the harsh terms of which triggered an anti-Bolshevik reaction within the country and among the Western Allies. The result was the RUSSIAN CIVIL WAR, which devastated the country, but which the Bolsheviks ultimately won. At the same time, Lenin moved to consolidate the power of the Communist Party within the Soviet Union and his own position as the leader of world communism by establishing the Third International. In the wake of the civil war, he introduced his New Economic Policy, designed to restore the ruined Russian economy.

In 1922, he suffered the first of a series of strokes that left him severely handicapped until his death in 1924. Traditionally regarded as a brilliant and audacious theorist and leader, some historians see him as a malign force second only to Stalin, and others imagine him as a figure whose goals were never achieved, whose program ended, 65 years after his death, in failure.

THE LITERATURE

Among Lenin's severest critics is the Russian novelist Aleksandr Solzhenitsyn (1918–   ). His undisguised hatred of Lenin is most passionately on view in *Lenin in Zurich* (1975; trans., 1976), a work consisting of 11 chapters drawn from Solzhenitsyn's historical tetralogy, *August 1914* (see TANNENBURG), *November 1916*, *March 1917*, and *April 1917*. Solzhenitsyn's Lenin is an arrogant, unprincipled opportunist, using people for his immediate advantage, then later coolly looking back at them "like so many signposts, receding from view until they vanished and were forgotten, though sometimes they loomed sharply at a new turning in the road, this time as enemies." The single humanizing exception to his ruthlessness is his genuine feeling for Inessa Armand, the widowed mother of five children, who shared a close relationship with him for more than 10 years. But he will not leave his wife, the slavishly attentive Nadya, so useful to his work, whereas Inessa would be a perpetual distraction.

The one figure Lenin respects (and therefore fears) as his intellectual equal is Alexander Helphand (known as "Parvus" in socialist circles). Parvus is a self-made millionaire and dedicated revolutionary. During World War I, he operates as a German agent, funneling money to Russian revolutionary groups on the assumption that a successful revolution will take Russia out of the war. One of the most interesting sections of the book is the conversation in which Parvus tries to convince Lenin to join in a secret alliance with the German government; in exchange for this alliance, the party would be financially supported for all of its activities. "Money equals power" is the essence of Parvus's argument. Lenin agrees but, faced with the need to act, he exhibits a Hamlet-like indecisiveness, overanalyzing the other's motives until he convinces himself that inaction is the best strategy. Thus Solzhenitsyn paints a picture not only of a cold, humorless ideologue but also a cautious little man, fearful of seizing power when it is offered.

Alan Brien's (1925–) *Lenin: The Novel* (1988) takes the form of a diary written by Lenin from 1886 to 1923, the year before his death. Brien sets out to reproduce the kind of diary Lenin might have written had he kept one. What emerges is a "self-portrait" of a gifted, highly intelligent, and, when the occasion demanded, utterly ruthless individual. Brien convincingly depicts the details of Lenin's life, his probable reactions to specific events, and his feelings toward particular people, for example, his preference for Leon TROTSKY ("my only hope for perpetuation of my policies") over Joseph STALIN ("too crude and domineering") as his successor. Brien has clearly made every effort to authenticate and verify the attitudes and ideas he attributes to Lenin. The result is a very readable and reliable account of the momentous events that gave birth to the Soviet Union.

Lenin: The Novel does not give the reader enough sense of the interior Lenin, the man within the public figure. What we see instead is a perfectly plausible reconstruction of Lenin's thinking, with a curious lack of insight or, as in Solzhenitsyn's case, passion that makes us care about him as a character in fiction. In short, although probably more historically accurate in its representation of its subject than *Lenin in Zurich*, Brien's novel lacks the emotional power, the energy, and the narrative drive of Solzhenitsyn's. One book gives us the facts; the other, not *the* but *a* truth.

FURTHER READING

Lenin: A New Biography (1944) by Dmitri Volkogonov is a recent biography that takes a very negative view of Lenin's place in history.

LEOPOLD-LOEB CASE (1924)

On May 21, 1924, 14-year-old Bobby Franks failed to return home from Harvard Preparatory School, located in a fashionable district on the South Side of Chicago. Later that evening, his parents received a phone call, informing them that their son had been kidnapped and that he would be returned safely if the Franks family carefully followed instructions. The following day, they received a letter, telling them to secure $10,000 in old bills and await another phone call. While waiting for the kidnappers' call, the Franks heard from the police that the body of a boy had been found in a swamp on the outskirts of town. Refusing to leave the phone, Jacob Franks sent his brother-in-law to the mortuary to examine the body. He then received a call from the kidnapper, giving instructions for delivering the money. As Franks was about to leave the house with the money, his brother-in-law called to inform him that the dead boy in the mortuary was Bobby.

Seven days later police arrested Richard Loeb and Nathan Leopold, and soon both confessed to the murder. The two young men (Leopold was 18; Loeb, 19) were scions of two extremely wealthy and respected Jewish families and had achieved outstanding academic records. Loeb was the youngest student ever to have graduated from the University of Michigan, and Leopold was a student at the law school of the University of Chicago. The two had conspired to commit the perfect crime, confident that their intellectual superiority would enable them to outwit police investigators. They derived part of their rationale from the teachings of the philosopher Friedrich Nietzsche and his doctrine of the "superman," which argued that superior individuals lived "beyond good and evil," the moral constraints that governed ordinary people. But their crime was far from perfect. They had committed a number of obvious blunders: Leopold had left his glasses at the scene of the crime, and Loeb had tossed the murder weapon, a chisel, out the window of their car in a place where it might be, and was, easily found.

The nature of the murder and the prominence of the families involved inevitably led to a sensation in the press, with the Chicago papers vying to outdo each other in shocking revelations, concerning "the crime of the century." The seemingly cold-blooded arrogance of the killers created a public outcry for the death penalty. In a desperate attempt to prevent that possibility, the Loeb family hired the famous Chicago defense lawyer Clarence Darrow. Darrow entered a plea of guilty, thereby ensuring a trial before a judge rather than a jury, which, in the general climate of opinion, would have been likely to recommend the death penalty. Darrow reasoned that his one chance lay with an appeal to the judge. He proceeded to argue that the motive for the murder was not the ransom money. Neither of the defendants had any need for it. The plot had been an intellectual game, played by two boys (Darrow was always careful to underscore their youth), who were emotionally abnormal. He then delivered one of the most celebrated trial summations in American legal history. Darrow argued that his clients were facing the death penalty because they were rich, that the prosecution was pursuing a death penalty conviction with a vengeance that undermined the principle of justice, and that the defendants, though technically not insane, were emotionally unbalanced. He maintained that, despite their alleged intelligence, Leopold and Loeb had the emotional intelligence of small children. At the conclusion of his speech, in which he spoke of the need for pity among all human beings, he was so eloquent that he, many of the spectators, and even the judge himself, were in tears.

Leopold and Loeb were sentenced to life imprisonment. The following year, Darrow achieved even greater fame for his participation in the SCOPES TRIAL. In 1936, Loeb was slashed to death in a shower by a fellow prisoner, who claimed that Loeb had made sexual advances to him. In 1958, Leopold was paroled after 33 years in prison. He died in 1971.

THE LITERATURE

The journalist/novelist Meyer Levin was a fellow student of Leopold at the University of Chicago, working on the story as the campus correspondent for the Chicago *Daily News*. Thirty years later, he wrote a fictional account of the case, *Compulsion* (1956), which became a major best-seller. Levin's distinctive contribution to the historical facts lay in his attempt to supply a psychologically coherent explanation for the behavior of Leopold and Loeb, relying heavily on the insights of PSYCHOANALYSIS.

The novel's narrator is Sid Silver, a Levin-like figure, who is a student at the University of Chicago and a part-time newspaper reporter. Taking a novelist's liberty, the author thrusts his narrator further into the action than was actually the case, but the heart of the story closely follows the historical facts. The main figures are Judd Steiner (Leopold) and Artie Straus (Loeb). The two are an odd couple: Artie, the charming, handsome, wise cracking, devil-may-care ladies' man; Judd, the short, bespectacled nerd. No one guesses that the two are not only friends, but lovers. The murder is largely Artie's idea, but Judd, always eager to please Artie, readily goes along with the plan. The novel describes the murder: After luring Paulie Kessler (Bobby Franks) into their car, Artie smashes a chisel into the back of Paulie's head. Judd's contribution is the idea of mutilating the body with hydrochloric acid and jamming it into a cistern in the swamp.

Levin's analysis rests on a Freudian reading of two major elements of the murder: the weapon used and the place of burial, or, as the novel puts it, the penis and the receptacle. The chisel, an obvious phallic symbol, is Artie's choice, a reflection of his weak sense of his own manhood, his compulsive need to dominate, and his wish to do something violent in order to break through the moods and suicidal fits of depression that he is subject to. His fantasy is to be a master criminal who is caught and punished, the self-destructive expression of revenge against his father. The burial place, on the other hand, is the clue to Judd, who chooses the cistern in the swamp, into which they jam the naked body of a child, now neither boy nor girl, since the mutilating acid has been poured on the genitals of the corpse. This choice reflects Judd's disordered sense of sexual identity, the desire to kill the "girl" within him, and his fundamental death wish, a return to the cistern-like womb. The penis and the receptacle are also meant to be seen as a description of the sexual relationship of Artie and Judd.

For many readers in the 1950s this type of analysis was thirst-quenching heady wine, contributing to the book's popularity. The author's wise decision to include in the novel a lengthy excerpt from Darrow's summation added to its appeal. Levin's authorial comment stated his final position: "Whether my interpretation is literally correct is impossible for me to know. But I hope that it is poetically valid, and that it may be of some help in widening the use of available knowledge in the aid of human failings." When in 1958 Leopold's case was before the parole board, Levin testified on his behalf.

Compulsion was adapted to the stage and later, in 1959, to the screen. An earlier play by Patrick Hamilton, based on the case predating Levin's book, was also adapted to the screen, by Alfred Hitchcock as *Rope* (1948).

FURTHER READING

Hal Higdon's *Leopold & Loeb: The Crime of the Century* (1976) is an excellent account of the case. Nathan Leopold's *Life Plus 99 Years* (1958) is a memoir of his prison years. Kevin Tierney's *Darrow: A Biography* (1979) offers an interesting overview of the lawyer's remarkable career.

LEYTE GULF, BATTLE OF (WORLD WAR II) (1944)

A joint naval and land engagement, the invasion of Leyte in the Philippines in October 1944 and the subsequent naval engagement at Leyte Gulf, the largest naval battle in history, ended in decisive American victories. The Japanese plan of attack included a diversionary tactic to lure the U.S. Third Fleet, under Admiral William Halsey, away from its supporting role in the American invasion of the island. The trick worked insofar as the fleet sailed northward in pursuit of the Japanese decoys, but the few remaining American ships were able to hold their own in the face of a full-scale Japanese attack long enough for Halsey's main force to return to the battle. At its conclusion, the Japanese had lost three battleships, nine cruisers, 10 destroyers, and, most important, four aircraft carriers, the sinking of which virtually eliminated the Japanese naval air force, whose fliers had nowhere to land.

American troops landed on the island of Leyte on October 20, 1944. The Japanese reinforced their position and counterattacked, but they were beaten back. By January 1945, the American forces were in command of the island and preparing for the invasion of the neighboring island of Luzon and its capital city, Manila. Japanese casualties on Leyte amounted to 70,000, while the Americans suffered some 16,000 losses. One aspect of the land war was the fact that scattered Japanese troops, under instructions to "fight to the death," continued guerrilla activities up to and, in some cases, even after, the end of the war in August 1945.

THE LITERATURE

Shohei Ooka's (1909–88) *Fires on the Plain* (1952; trans., 1957), a remarkably realistic account of those driven to extremes, captures the experience of Japanese troops on Leyte. Demoralized and despairing, these men are also starving. The desire for food is their driving force, blunting even the instinct for survival. For the novel's protagonist and first-person narrator, Tamura, an infantry private, the quest for food sets him off on a hunt that becomes a kind of spiritual odyssey.

Diagnosed as tubercular, Tamura has been cut loose both by the military hospital and his own army unit for the same reason—he is seen as just another mouth to feed and therefore is left to fend for himself. Thrust out into nature, accepting his imminent death, Tamura becomes aware of the beauty and power of the natural world. He experiences a brief, edenic peace, which is abruptly ended when he accidentally kills a Filipino woman. Cast out of Eden, he connects with another group of retreating Japanese soldiers, who have been reduced to animals of prey, driven by hunger to cannibalization. Tamura meets his strongest temptation when a dying officer offers him his own flesh. Once the man dies, Tamura begins to dismember the body in order to eat it, but at the last minute he resists this final moral collapse. Later, however, he discovers that he has unknowingly eaten human flesh.

In the novel's epilogue, we learn that Tamura is now a voluntary patient in a mental hospital in Japan, having been repatriated from a prisoner-of-war hospital. He is writing his memoirs on the advice of his psychiatrist. His memoirs conclude with the recollection of prairie fires in the Philippines. Whenever he sees these fires, they serve as omens of some approaching evil. But this time they set the stage for a joyous epiphany, as Tamura remembers and reinterprets his interaction with the officer on the verge of death: "[He] had offered me his own flesh to relieve my starvation. . . . If this was a transfiguration of Christ himself . . . [t]hen glory be to God."

Ambiguity surrounds this Christian resolution to a Japanese novel. Is the final revelation an ironic underscoring of Tamura's schizophrenia, or is it to be taken at face value? If the latter, it may be that Tamura's journey has been a spiritual quest in which the dehumanizing experience of cannibalism has been redeemed and transformed into a form of Christian communion. The interpretive choice is left to the individual reader.

FURTHER READING

Thomas Cutler's *The Battle of Leyte Gulf* (1994) gives a full account of the battle and of the subsequent controversy over Halsey's decision to take the fleet away from Leyte. Frank Motofuji's detailed discussion of *Fires on the Plain* is included in *Approaches to the Modern Japanese Novel,* edited by Kinya Tsuruta and Thomas Swann (1976).

LONG, HUEY (1893–1935)

As governor of Louisiana (1928–31) and U.S. senator from that state (1931–35), Long was a charismatic public speaker and a canny politician. Raised in a devout Southern Baptist home, he was well versed in the Bible, allusions to which formed a powerful rhetorical element in his campaign speeches. One measure of his drive and ability is the fact that he completed the three-year law program at Tulane University in eight months. At the age of 35, he was elected governor of Louisiana and four years later its senator.

The political machine Long created in Louisiana was dictatorial and corrupt, but his administration was responsible for a program of significant achievements that included tax reform, highway construction, and major improvements in public education and medical care. While in the Senate, he promoted a Share-the-Wealth program, which had the effect of forcing the administration of President Franklin Delano ROOSEVELT to adopt a more liberal approach to tax reform. In 1935, at the height of his political power and popular appeal, Long was assassinated by Dr. Carl Weiss, whose father, a state judge and political opponent of Long, had been the victim of a smear campaign conducted by Long.

THE LITERATURE

The career of "the Kingfish," Long's nickname, has formed the basis of at least three novels, including John Dos Passos's (1896–1970) *Number One* (1943), Adria Locke Langley's (1899–1983) *A Lion Is in the Streets* (1945), and, easily the best-known and most highly regarded work drawing on Long's life, Robert Penn Warren's (1905–89) *All the King's Men* (1946). The Long figure in *All the King's Men* is Willie Stark, a self-educated "redneck" from a rural district of a southern state who has risen to become governor. The narrator of his rise and fall is Jack Burden, a failed historian, who serves as Willie's public relations man.

The story is as much about Burden as it is about Willie. Jack is driven to try to understand Willie or, at least, to understand that part of himself that feels a deep kinship with Willie. This drive for understanding governs the development of the story. The quest leads backward in time to the antebellum South, where Jack's ancestors enacted a tragedy that roughly parallels Jack's own loss of Anne Stanton, the woman he loved and lost to Willie. Jack, on

Willie's orders, begins an investigation of Judge Irwin, the fictional equivalent of Judge Weiss. As a result of the revelations of Irwin's past, the judge commits suicide, and Jack discovers that he is Irwin's illegitimate son. The investigation confirms Jack's conviction that we are all born with the burden—the play on his name is deliberate—of history and of a sinful nature, necessarily sinful, for without it there would be no human capacity to differentiate good from evil. Willie is a man who, in the beginning, understands this principle but along the way becomes corrupted by power; he dies knowing he has lost his way, as he acknowledges in his last words: "It might all have been different, Jack."

FURTHER READING

Charles Bohner's *Robert Penn Warren* (1964) offers a lucid analysis of Warren's work.

LONG MARCH (1934–1935)

In October 1934, the Chinese Communist army, surrounded by the nationalist forces of Chiang Kai-shek, broke through the Nationalist lines and began a retreat that was to end one year later, after they had marched some 6,000 miles to Shanxi, the most remote province in northwest China. Constantly pursued by Chiang's army, bombed and strafed by his air force, the Communists suffered severe casualties. Others died from the hardship of the winter and lack of food. Estimates of Communist losses range as high as 170,000 soldiers and civilians. In the course of the march, Mao Zedong was to emerge as the undisputed leader of the Communist forces. Finally reaching their destination, his tattered troops hid in caves, regrouping their strength and preparing for the encounter with a new, even more formidable enemy, the invading Japanese army.

THE LITERATURE

The first few pages of Frederic Tuten's (1936–) *The Adventures of Mao on the Long March* (1971) begin with what appears to be a straight historical account of the march, luring readers into the assumption that what follows will be a traditional, realistic historical novel in the style of James Michener. Instead, they soon find interspersed within this historical account an extraordinary collage of disparate materials that include extensive quotations from Nathaniel Hawthorne's *The Marble Faun* (1860), Walter Pater's *The Renaissance* (1873), parodies of Ernest Hemingway and William Faulkner, and the emergence from a tank of Greta Garbo, come to successfully seduce Mao. At this point, readers may become more conscious of the book's cover design, a reproduction of a lithograph portrait of Mao by the American artist Roy Lichtenstein—for Tuten's novel is the literary equivalent of a pop art painting, in which the scattered fragments of modern civilization are juxtaposed as a way of seeing the familiar from a fresh perspective in a complex spirit of joy and despair that contains satire but is not limited to it. With that goal in mind, the novel gives us a very human, if unhistorical, Mao, who at the end seeks only peace and quiet:

> I'm an old man who wants to dream the remaining days away. Yet I can't take a nice, healthy crap without some fanatic bowing to the stool and singing: "Oh our great Chairman Mao has again fertilized the world." What was all my hard work for, if I can't fill my last hours with serenity and nonproductive contemplation?

The Adventures of Mao on the Long March is, for all its apparent lightheartedness, a serious and provocative political novel.

FURTHER READING

Harrison Salisbury's *The Long March: The Untold Story* (1985) offers a comprehensive view of the march.

LOOS, BATTLE OF (WORLD WAR I) (1915)

In September 1915, the British launched an offensive against the German line near the town of Loos in the Artois district of France. This battle marked the first use by the British of gas as a weapon, an experiment that dramatically failed when the wind shifted, and the gas began to blow back toward the British trenches. But of far greater importance to the outcome was the British tactical blunder, which involved sending men "over the top," in 10 columns closely packed together "as if they were carrying on parade drill." German soldiers could not believe their eyes as their machine guns literally mowed down wave upon wave of English and Scots troops. Eventually the attacking army was forced to retire to its own trenches. When the offensive was finally abandoned, the casualty count for the British was more than 40,000 killed or wounded. The Germans referred to the battlefield as "the corpse field of Loos."

THE LITERATURE

The British soldiers who fought at Loos were part of what was called "Kitchener's army," so-called because they joined the army soon after the declaration of war, inspired by a recruiting poster that featured a picture of Lord Kitchener and a caption reading, "I Want You!" Kitchener, the victorious hero of several African campaigns, symbolized British imperial might, and his appeal stirred the patriotic spirit of many of his countrymen. *The First Hundred Thousand* (1915) is a tribute to these men, written by one of their own,

Ian Hay Beith (1876–   ), who wrote under the name Ian Hay. The novel was originally published in serial form in *Blackwood's Magazine* as a group of chapters designed to capture the experience of the new volunteers as they moved from civilians to battle-hardened veterans. Written while the enthusiasm for the war, both at home and abroad, was still at its high-water mark, it stands in interesting opposition to the literature that was to follow, as the war became increasingly unpopular. The author, describing a unit made up largely of Scots, picks up his narrative from their first days in training camp in September 1914, before they have been issued uniforms, and carries them through to their engagement at Loos. The mood throughout most of the book is resolutely cheerful, frequently comic, aptly depicting men who are lighthearted as well as stout-hearted; it is reflected in the piece of light verse that prefaces the novel:

> But yesterday we said farewell
> To plough; to pit; to dock; to mill
> For glory? Drop it! Why? Oh, well—
> To have a slap at Kaiser Bill.

Once the story moves to a description of the carnage at Loos, the mood alters, but not as radically as the reader might expect. The chipper, stiff-upper-lip tone is still very much in evidence, and although the novel concludes on a doggedly optimistic note, it is a note that has been tempered by the shockingly high casualty rate: "The battle which began upon that grey September morning, has been raging for nearly three weeks. . . . When the final advance comes, as come it must, and our victorious line sweeps forward . . . these sturdy, valiant legions . . . will always be First; but alas! they are no longer The Hundred Thousand."

FURTHER READING

Samuel Hynes's *A War Imagined* (1991) contains a discussion of *The First Hundred Thousand* and its relation to the military fiction of Rudyard Kipling.

LUSITANIA, SINKING OF (MAY 7, 1915)

Early in 1915, the first full year of WORLD WAR I, Germany announced that its submarines (U-boats) would attack all Allied ships, including noncombatant vessels. In May of that year, the British liner RMS *Lusitania*, the world's largest and most luxurious passenger ship, set sail from New York, bound for England. The voyage was uneventful until May 7, 1915, when the ship, rounding the Irish coast, was hit by a torpedo from a German U-boat. A few moments later, a second explosion tore through the ship's bow, this one probably the result of coal gas ignited by the first. This second explosion proved to be fatal, and the ship sank in less than 20 minutes. Of the 1,900 passengers onboard, some 1,200 died, including 128 Americans. One reason for the high fatality rate was the surprising speed with which the ship sank.

The sinking produced an international outcry against the German government. President Woodrow Wilson sent two strong letters of protest, demanding an apology and reparations. The Germans replied that the ship was carrying war materials—an assertion that later proved to be true—and that it was therefore a legitimate military target. As a result, the sinking and the German response played a major role in shifting American opinion away from neutrality toward favoring the Allies. When the United States did enter the war two years later, "Remember the Lusitania" was a recurrent phrase used in recruitment campaigns.

THE LITERATURE

David Butler's (1937–) novel *Lusitania* (1982) embraces a wide range of characters, historical and fictional, while also exploring the military and diplomatic issues related to the incident. The chief figures in the story are the two captains, Will Turner, captain of the ill-fated liner, and Walther Schwieger, the submarine commander. Of the two, Schwieger is the more important, since he is faced with the moral dilemma raised by the opportunity to sink the ship. He also plays a critical role as the unwitting agent in a plot by the German grand admiral, Alfred von Tirpitz. As the author conceives of it, von Tirpitz, unwilling to submit to the subordinate role the navy has assumed in the war, deliberately plans the sinking by placing onboard, as Schwieger's second in command, an officer who uses threats and lies to goad Schwieger into attacking the ship against his will. When he returns to Berlin, Schwieger is berated by the kaiser and abandoned by his fiancée.

Among the passengers on the Lusitania were the millionaire Alfred Vanderbilt and the theatrical producer Charles Frohman, both of whom are depicted going to their deaths with quiet dignity. Chief among the fictional passengers are the members of a Canadian family; the father and daughter die, while the mother and son survive. Their stories and others are related in the course of the voyage. When the story shifts periodically to the United States, it focuses on the conflict between President Wilson and his secretary of state, William Jennings Bryant, who was the most prominent American supporting American neutrality. Wilson, who campaigned in 1916 on the slogan "He kept us out of war," had clung to the idea that a neutral United States could broker an early end to the war. But that hope is seriously damaged by the sinking. His strongly worded rebuke to the Germans results in Bryant's resignation.

Written in the tradition of disaster novels and films, in which quick character sketches and rapidly shifting scenes are designed to build suspense and interest, *Lusitania* provides these generic characteristics and adds some interesting pieces of historical speculation.

FURTHER READING

Diana Preston's *Lusitania: An Epic Tragedy* (2002) reconstructs the voyage and the sinking of the ship. David Ramsay's *Lusitania: Saga and Myth* (2002) sets out "to examine and rebut the many myths of *Lusitania*."

LUXEMBURG, ROSA (1871–1919)

Political theorist and revolutionary leader, Luxemburg was born in Poland and studied political science and law at the University of Zurich, where she received a doctorate in 1898. That same year, she became a German citizen through marriage and moved to Berlin, where she was active in Marxist circles as a writer and teacher. Her brilliance as a thinker and orator brought her to prominence. Together with Karl Liebknecht, she was the cofounder of the Spartacist League, which later became the German Communist Party. Her strong opposition to WORLD WAR I led to her first imprisonment in 1915 and a second incarceration from 1916 to 1918, during which she wrote voluminously. Among her works written there was a sustained critique of the dictatorial character of the Bolshevik government under Vladimir Ilich LENIN.

In 1918, she was released from jail. At that time, in the wake of its defeat in World War I and the kaiser's flight from Germany, the newly established German republic hovered on the brink of anarchy. The country gave strong indications of replicating the Bolshevik RUSSIAN REVOLUTION of 1917. Luxemburg counseled the party members that the time was not ripe for a successful socialist revolution, but she was overruled by Liebknecht and other party members. As a result, the party staged an unsuccessful revolt in January 1919 in which both Luxemburg and Liebknecht were captured and murdered by a right-wing paramilitary group let loose by the government.

THE LITERATURE

Alfred Döblin's (1878–1957) *November 1918* is a two-volume novel (the English translation combines in two volumes the three volumes of the German edition), of which the first is *A People Betrayed* (1948; trans., 1983) and the second *Karl and Rosa* (1950; trans., 1983). Both works deal with events in Germany following the abdication of Kaiser Wilhelm II on November 10, 1918, and climaxing with the murder of Luxemburg and Liebknecht on January 15, 1919.

Within this time frame, the failed revolution takes center stage, but the novel's range includes the peace talks in Paris, the personal struggles of Woodrow Wilson in his failed efforts to secure a just peace, and Rosa Luxemburg's years in prison prior to the revolution. The two volumes explore a number of themes and introduce a wide range of historical (including a passionate and moving portrait of Wilson) and fictional characters. *A People Betrayed* begins, 10 days after the signing of the armistice, in Berlin with a Spartacist attack on a police station, which frees all the prisoners there. Revolution is in the air, fueled by hunger, despair, and fear. Friedrich Becker, a wounded war veteran, returning to his job as a high school teacher, seeks some purpose and meaning in the chaos that surrounds him. Throughout the two novels, he represents the alternative to revolutionary action, the transformation within the individual, the internal revolution that leads one on a spiritual quest. For Becker, social or political action is merely a manifestation of the illusion of control; true control can only emerge in submission to the power of God. Moving steadily to the margins of society, he engages in hallucinatory exchanges with the medieval German mystic Johannes Tauler, who advises him "to sink deeper and deeper into the unnamed abyss, . . . sink [to] where everything loses its name."

Becker's story both parallels and contrasts with Rosa's. *Karl and Rosa* dramatizes her prison experiences, concentrating chiefly on intense, imaginary scenes with her dead lover, Hans Diefenbach. In these scenes, she is depicted not simply as a politically committed intellectual, but as a quasi-religious mystic. She emerges from prison in time to try to prevent the ill-conceived revolution, but her arguments fall on deaf ears. The successful Bolshevik takeover in Russia has lulled everyone into the belief that communism's time has come. Only Rosa perceives the flaws already apparent in the new Soviet Union. Once overruled, however, she commits herself, despite her misgivings, to the attempted coup. Captured by paramilitaries, she is shot, and her body is thrown into the canal.

Like Rosa, Becker undergoes an ignominious death. Their mutual fate may suggest a deep pessimism about the human condition, the futility of any attempt, internal or external, to effect change, or Döblin may be using Rosa and Becker as two extreme cases, their extremism causing their failures. But a third possibility is that both achieve a kind of triumph in the conduct of their lives that is not mitigated by their tragic ends, triumphs reflected in their visionary experiences, so that they stood for was more important than what they achieved.

FURTHER READING

J. P. Nettl's *Rosa Luxemburg* (1966) is a comprehensive two-volume biography. Wolfgang Kort's *Alfred Döblin* (1974) provides an intelligent overview of Döblin's life.

M

MANHATTAN PROJECT (1942–1945)

In 1939, two years before America's entrance into WORLD WAR II, the physicists Albert EINSTEIN, Leo Szilard, and Eugene Wigner wrote a letter to President Franklin Delano ROOSEVELT, warning of the danger of "a nuclear chain reaction in a large mass of uranium" that could lead to "extremely powerful bombs of a new type." The letter strongly recommended that the United States acquire uranium ore. In response, Roosevelt set up a secret commission to investigate possible military uses of these scientific developments. On December 6, 1941, the day before PEARL HARBOR, Roosevelt ordered the establishment of an atomic bomb project. The physicist Enrico Fermi set up a group at the University of Chicago to create a controlled nuclear chain reaction. On December 2, 1942, Fermi's group succeeded in their attempt to induce a chain reaction, completing the critical first stage of the project.

Meanwhile the bomb-building phase, using the code name *Manhattan Project*, had begun under the direction of General Leslie Groves, with Dr. J. Robert Oppenheimer as scientific director. The site chosen for the project was Los Alamos, an area in the New Mexican desert, about 40 miles north of Santa Fe. The property contained a former boys' boarding school, which provided housing for the first group of scientists. As the program expanded, additional housing had to be built, along with laboratories, offices, and storage spaces. Working under strict security, impelled by the strong sense that they were in a race with German scientists, the physicists, engineers, and technical support staff worked feverishly to complete the task. Finally, on July 16, 1945, Oppenheimer's group, using the code name *Trinity*, exploded a plutonium bomb in the desert near Alamagordo. The effect on the observers was overwhelming. General Thomas Farrell wrote: "The whole country was lighted with a searing light . . . golden, purple, violet, gray, and blue. It lighted every peak, crevasse, and ridge of the nearby mountain range." Three weeks later, on August 6, an American bomber, the *Enola Gay*, dropped a uranium bomb on HIROSHIMA, followed, on August 9, by a plutonium bomb dropped on Nagasaki. On August 15, Japan ordered the cessation of hostilities, and it formally surrendered on September 2. On November 1, 1952, the United States exploded a hydrogen bomb on Eniwietok atoll in the Pacific, which was a thousand times more powerful than the bomb dropped on Hiroshima.

An underlying concern during the Manhattan Project's existence was the maintenance of secrecy and security. There were thousands of people involved in the project and leaks were perhaps inevitable. The most important of these emanated from Klaus Fuchs, a refugee German physicist at Los Alamos, who transmitted secrets to the Soviet Union through a courier, Harry Gold. The arrest of Fuchs and Gold in 1950 and the subsequent arrest of Julius and Ethel Rosenberg (see ROSENBERG CASE) led to the attempt to discredit Oppenheimer, particularly when Oppenheimer spoke out in opposition to the development of the hydrogen bomb.

THE LITERATURE

Espionage at the Manhattan Project is the central subject of Joseph Kanon's *Los Alamos* (1997), a novel that combines a first-rate spy story with a vivid recreation of the Manhattan Project on the brink of its completion. The central figure is Michael Connolly, brought in by General Groves to investigate the murder of Karl Bruner, a security officer at "the Hill," as the Los Alamos site is familiarly known. Although the murder took place in town and is being handled by the local police, Groves wants Connolly to find out if any security breach was involved. Connolly soon complicates his investigation by falling in love with the wife of one of the project scientists. He also observes closely the activities of Oppenheimer, who, operating under tremendous strain as the bomb's testing date nears, exhibits extraordinary tact and discipline as he confronts the complex details of the project and the even more complex personalities of the scientists. Connolly's respect for Oppenheimer leads him to solve the murder while covering up the evidence of spying, since the leak has already occurred, and the revelation can only aid Oppenheimer's enemies in the government. The novel's resolution takes place on the evening before Trinity, leaving Connolly the opportunity to observe the test: "Connolly saw, looking out at the cloud in the desert . . . that all those ideas, everything we thought we knew, were nothing more than stories to rewrite insignificance. . . . Now we would always be frightened." The novel concludes with a discussion between Oppenheimer and Connolly, in which the latter expresses his fears, and Oppenheimer his hopes, for the future.

FURTHER READING

Now It Can Be Told: The Story of the Manhattan Project (1962) is General Leslie Groves's memoir of his years as the director of the project. Richard Rhodes's *The Making of the Atomic Bomb* (1986) takes a more critical view of the project.

MAO ZEDONG

See LONG MARCH.

MAO ZEDONG, MADAME (JIANG QING)

See CULTURAL REVOLUTION.

MARNE, BATTLE OF THE (WORLD WAR I) (1914)

In the first weeks of WORLD WAR I, during September 1914, the German army rapidly advanced through Belgium and into France to within 30 miles of Paris, while French and British forces beat hasty retreats. But the speed with which the Germans moved seriously overextended their supply lines and exhausted their troops. When, at the Marne River, the French counterattacked, attempting to surround the invading forces, the Germans were forced to defend their flanks, thus weakening their main line. As a result they failed to press on to Paris, retreating instead to positions north of the Aisne River. This proved to be one of the most fateful decisions of the war. Digging in at their new positions, the opposing forces changed the nature of the conflict from "open" to "trench" warfare. Both sides were to remain stalemated in these positions for the next three and a half years.

THE LITERATURE

A celebrated description of the Marne engagement occurs in a best-selling novel of its period, Vicente Blasco Ibanez's (1867–1928) *The Four Horsemen of the Apocalypse* (1916; trans., 1918). One strain of the novel deals with a love affair on the eve of World War I between a rich, young ladies' man, part French, part Argentinian, Julio Desnoyers, and a married French woman, Marguerite Laurier. Both are rather shallow, spoiled society types, wrapped up in their own desires and completely oblivious to the impending disaster. The war, however, transforms the couple. Marguerite rejects her lover in order to nurse her husband, wounded in the first weeks of the war. Julio enlists in the army as an infantry private, refusing a commission in order to serve as an ordinary soldier.

The other focus of the story falls on Julio's father, Don Marcelo, an Argentine millionaire residing in France. Aroused by the rapid advance of the German army, Don Marcelo returns to a castle he owns immediately north of the Marne to defend it against the invaders. Haughty and overconfident, the older man is used to having his way. He soon learns the first of a series of humbling truths about the nature of modern war. Once the Germans descend on the castle, he is reduced to the status of a servant, an impotent witness to the plunder and desecration of the building, to the murder of his steward and the rape of the steward's daughter. He experiences a brief respite as the German troops move up toward the Marne, but in a short while he sees these same troops in retreat as the castle grounds become a battleground with the French on the attack. The fierce artillery bombardment is seen through Don Marcelo's eyes in convincing, almost overwhelming detail. Eventually he returns to Paris just in time to bid farewell to his son as Julio leaves for the front.

Later Don Marcelo is able through connections to visit his son briefly in the rear trenches, affording another occasion for a powerful rendering of the nature of modern war. What is clear during the visit is that Julio, the former playboy, has become a man of extraordinary courage and generosity. Don Marcelo's love for his son becomes the dominating passion of his life, blinding him to the possibility that Julio could be killed. When he learns of his son's death, Don Marcelo loses the will to live. He has a final vision of the four horsemen from the biblical book of the Apocalypse (Pestilence, Famine, War, and Death): "He recognized them as divinities . . . which had made their presence felt by mankind. All the rest was a dream. The four horsemen were the reality."

The *Four Horsemen* exhibits many of the standard features of popular fiction: a broad canvas ranging from South America to Europe, characters painted in bold strokes with little or no psychological depth, and a clear distinction between good and evil, heroes and villains—in this case, between the French and Germans. Not surprisingly, the novel was made into a phenomenally successful silent film in 1921, starring Rudolph Valentino. But for all its melodramatic limitations, the book's battle scenes are very effective as well as very distinctive, since they are depicted from the point of view of a civilian.

FURTHER READING

S. L. A. Marshall's *The American Heritage History of World War I* (1964) contains a colorful account of the battle.

MAU MAU UPRISING (1952–1959)

When the African nation of Kenya was still a British colony, the colonial administration pursued a policy of expropriating the most desirable land for white settlers, forcing natives off the land and thereby providing a cheap labor force for the new owners. This situation did not go unchallenged, but it was not until the post–WORLD WAR II period that returning native veterans who had fought for Great Britain and militant intellectuals, such as Jomo Kenyatta, began to organize effectively around the issues of landownership and native unemployment. In 1947, Kenyatta became the president of the Kenyan African Union. Shortly thereafter a secret society developed among the Kikuyu, the largest ethnic group in Kenya, based primarily in the central region of the country. The group came to be called the Mau Mau, and they pledged to the violent overthrow of the colonial government.

In 1952, the Mau Mau assassinated a native leader who was a supporter of the colonial government. The government responded by declaring a state of emergency and arresting Kenyatta, charging him with being the leader of the secret society. The charges were unfounded, and the arrest of the popular activist stimulated widespread anger among the native population. The Mau Mau struck back with a series of guerrilla attacks, usually at night, on local police offices and remote farmhouses. Their victims included many more natives, particularly those who were relatively prosperous, than whites. In their efforts to quell the uprising, the British army forced more than a million Kenyans into fortified villages, destroying thousands of homes and interning more than 20,000 Kikuyu in search-and-seizure operations. Eventually Mau Mau forces retreated to a forested area around Mount Kenya, and by 1956 most of the fighting had ended. The final death toll showed more than 11,000 Mau Mau, 1,900 African civilians and soldiers who sided with the British, and only 95 whites, figures that attest to the exaggeration of the reports in the British press at the time of wholesale, savage slaughter of whites by the Mau Mau.

In 1959, Kenyatta was released from prison to become the leader of the entire native population. There was never any credible evidence tying him to the Mau Mau. In 1964, he became president of the newly independent republic, which he governed successfully until his death in 1978.

THE LITERATURE

Ngugi wa Thiong'O (1938–) is a celebrated Kenyan writer who, under the pen name James Ngugi, set his early novels against the background of the Mau Mau revolt. His first novel, *Weep Not, Child* (1964), tells a story of the destruction of a Kikuyu community during the years of the rebellion. Its main character, Njoroge, is a young man who comes of age in the midst of warfare. As a child, he absorbs from his father, Ngoto, a victim of the government's racist land-ownership policy, the importance of education. This becomes his chief source of hope as the situation at home begins to deteriorate. His brother Boro leaves home to join the Mau Mau. When he becomes the only boy in his village selected to go to an exclusive high school, he is overjoyed, but shortly after he is taken from the school to a "house of pain," an interrogation center. Beaten and tortured, he learns that Boro has murdered his father's enemy and that his father has been imprisoned and tortured. The last glimmer of hope recedes with his father's despairing death. As Njoroge moves from innocence to despair, he mirrors his society, ripped apart by long-simmering injustice and the fanatical hatred it breeds.

Weep Not, Child is written in an extremely simple style, appropriate to the consciousness of the child-becoming-a-man that focuses the action. In his third novel, *A Grain of Weat* (1967), Ngugi adapts a more complex, pluralist point of view, as a group of people look back at the period of the rebellion, each individual attempting to come to terms with or evade the past. In it, he suggests the need to accept the violence and inhumanity of the rebellion as a part of Kenya's heritage. Ngugi returned to the rebellion in his play, written in collaboration with Micere Mugo, *The Trial of Dedan Kimathi* (1976), based on the life of one of the Mau Mau leaders.

FURTHER READING

Frank Furedi's *The Mau Mau War in Perspective* (1989) offers an incisive account of the uprising.

MAY 1968 STUDENT REVOLT (PARIS)

On May 2, 1968, students at the University of Paris—first at the Nanterre campus and shortly after at the Sorbonne—began a series of aggressive demonstrations demanding reforms in higher education and in certain social and economic policies of the French government. With each day the demonstrations drew more supporters both from within the university and from the general population, particularly among the liberal professional and intellectual classes. They also grew more riotous and anarchic. The movement soon spread to other campuses throughout France, where it was joined by a large number of organized labor groups protesting low wages.

By mid-May, close to 10 million people were on strike, effectively bringing the nation to its knees. President Charles de Gaulle, on the brink of resigning from office, left the country on May 29, returning the following day to issue a call for a national election. In the meantime the government negotiated favorable pay wages for striking workers, who then withdrew support for the students. This proved to be the turning point of the crisis. The students, lacking any clearly defined strategy, abandoned their occupation of campuses and public buildings. On June 16, Paris police took over the

Sorbonne, evicting the students and bringing the revolt to an end. In the special election, de Gaulle's party was reelected by a large majority.

THE LITERATURE

The American novelist James Jones (1921–77), the author of *From Here to Eternity* (1951) and *The Thin Red Line* (1962), was living in Paris at the time, observing the daily developments of the uprising. In his novel *The Merry Month of May* (1970), Jones describes these events and their impact on a group of American expatriates in Paris. The story is narrated by Jack Hartley, focusing on his friendship with the Gallaghers—Harry, a successful screenwriter, his wife, Louisa, and their son, Hill, a student at the Sorbonne. All four are caught up in the revolt, but only Hartley maintains a relatively detached and objective view. For the others, the riots trigger psychological upheavals with disastrous consequences: Harry becomes sexually obsessed with a young black American woman and deserts his family; Louisa tries to throw off her inhibitions and ends up attempting suicide; and Hill moves from active involvement in the rebellion to drug-induced alienation.

The novel suggests a correlation between the personal and the political that, in the view of many critics, implies a repudiation of the rebellion as destructive and ill-conceived. Others argue that the book is equally harsh in its treatment of the Gaullist government. They see *The Merry Month of May* as a depiction of an American moral and a French political malaise, counterpoised against each other.

FURTHER READING

Leo Weinstein's *The Subversive Tradition in French Literature: 1870–1971* (1989) provides an incisive appreciation of the novel, placing it within a tradition of oppositional writing in French literature.

McCARTHYISM (1950–1954)

In the years following WORLD WAR II, the COLD WAR between the Soviet Union and the West became increasingly intense, generating, particularly in America, fear and anxiety over the goals and tactics of international communism. Chief among the political figures who attempted to capitalize on the fear was Joseph R. McCarthy (1910–58), the junior senator from Wisconsin. who, on the heels of the HISS-CHAMBERS CASE, charged that the U.S. State Department was riddled with Communist agents. In a speech in Wheeling, West Virginia, in 1950, he held up a sheet of paper, which he asserted contained the names of 205 Communists working and "shaping policy in the State Department." Later, he reduced this number to 57, but by that time his campaign to ferret out Communists in government was well under way.

Challenged by a Senate committee to substantiate his charges, McCarthy named Owen Lattimore, a specialist in Far East affairs, but not a State Department employee, as "Moscow's top spy." The committee, headed by Senator Millard Tydings, concluded that McCarthy's accusation was fraudulent. When Tydings ran for reelection, McCarthy, by now a nationally known figure, campaigned heavily against him. Tydings lost the election.

Heading a senatorial subcommittee on investigations, McCarthy conducted a series of hearings that expanded his targets from real or imagined communists to all those who were "soft on communism," a characterization that he applied to the Democratic administration of President Harry S. Truman. In a remarkably short period of time, McCarthy had become an immensely powerful, popular political figure. Without ever proving any of his allegations, he had won the hearts of many working-class Americans, who applauded his attacks on the liberal, elite Northeast establishment.

With the Republican victory of Dwight Eisenhower in 1952, McCarthy's committee, the chief counsel of which was Roy Cohn, turned its attention to communist subversion within the army. The televised hearing of the army investigation reached its climax in June 1952, when the army's special prosecutor, Joseph Welch, responded to a McCarthy attack with the words, "Have you no sense of decency, sir, at long last? Have you left no sense of decency?" Welch's remark was the most dramatic expression of a recognition among Republicans and Democrats that McCarthy had become a menace to American democracy. In December 1954, he received a powerful censure from the Senate, from which he never recovered. Three years later, the always harddrinking senator died of alcoholism at the age of 48. His legacy is the word *McCarthyism*, which describes a climate of intimidation and paranoia, in which unsubstantiated charges go unchecked in the name of patriotism.

THE LITERATURE

Probably the best-known literary work dealing with McCarthyism is the Arthur Miller (1915–) drama *The Crucible* (1953). While ostensibly about the 17th-century Salem, Massachusetts, witchcraft trials, Miller's play clearly targets the "witch hunts" of McCarthy and the House Un-American Activities Committee (HUAC). When a group of adolescent girls in Salem are discovered dancing in the woods at night, they defend themselves by claiming to have been bewitched. The leader of the group, Abigail Williams, identifies as one of the witches Elizabeth Proctor, the wife of John Proctor, with whom Abigail has had an affair. After the arrest of his wife, John Proctor appears in court before the McCarthy figure in the play, Deputy Governor Danforth. In his wife's defense, Proctor brings in a petition, signed by 91 citizens, testifying to her good reputation. Danforth orders the arrest of everyone who signed. When Abigail appears in court, Proctor confronts her, admitting that the two had an affair and asserting that the reason for Abigail's accusation is her desire to have his wife out of the way. Abigail denies the charge and feigns a seizure. When Elizabeth is asked if she had any knowledge of her husband's affair, she answers no, thinking to protect him, but her answer discredits his confession. The Proctors' servant, Mary Warren, to protect herself from charges of witchcraft, denounces Proctor, and he is arrested. Elizabeth is freed, and Proctor is offered a pardon if he will give the names of other witches. He refuses and is hanged along with other innocent citizens.

One of the strengths of the play is the author's ability to reproduce believable 17th-century dialogue, infusing it with poetic passion at critical moments. Its chief fault, in the eyes of many critics, is its one-sidedness. In attacking McCarthyism, Miller took an important and courageous stand in response to a 1950s menace, but weakened his play, in the process, by presenting his prosecutors as evil and corrupt, when, historically, they believed that what they were doing was right. The result is that instead of tragedy, he produced a highly effective melodrama. Another drama that focused allegorically on McCarthyism in the 1950s was *Inherit the Wind* (see SCOPES TRIAL).

FURTHER READING

Richard Rovere's *Senator Joe McCarthy* (1959) is a highly regarded study, written in the immediate aftermath of McCarthy's career Arthur Herman's *Joseph McCarthy* (2000) is a revisionist view, arguing that McCarthy made a positive contribution to the conduct of the cold war.

MENGELE, JOSEF (1911–1979)

The infamous Nazi doctor, known to the inmates of AUSCHWITZ as the "Angel of Death," Mengele, who held a Ph.D. as well as an M.D., became interested in "racial science" in 1934 as a member of the Nazi regime's Hereditary Institute for Biology and Racial Hygiene. He joined the National Socialist (Nazi) Party in 1937, and the following year the S.S. (Schutzstaffel). Assigned to Auschwitz, his duties included organizing the "selection," separating, as they came off the train, the prisoners who would be consigned to barracks from those who would be immediately sent to the gas chambers. He hid his malignant purpose beneath a benign, appealing personality that disarmed his terrified victims. As Grete Salus, an Auschwitz survivor described him, "He stood before us, the handsome devil. . . . He radiated an air of lightness and peacefulness, a welcome contrast to the environs. With utter docility, the people went to the right or the left, wherever the master waved them. Sometimes, a daughter did not want to be separated from her mother, but the words 'You'll see each other tomorrow, after all' would reassure them completely." In addition to the initial selections, he also supervised many of the later selections among the laborers in the camp. The experienced prisoners knew that they had to appear robust and healthy to avoid being sent to the gas chambers. In his memoir *Night*, Elie Wiesel recalls that at one selection, fear sent him racing by Mengele so quickly that the doctor, surprised, just let him pass.

But Mengele's principal interest at the camp was research, such as conducting experiments on pairs of twins and on dwarfs, using them as guinea pigs to test various racial hypotheses. For example, he dripped chemicals into his subjects' eyes to see if they would change color. At the end of his experimentation, he usually killed his subjects by injecting chloroform into their hearts, so that he could then study their internal organs.

When Auschwitz was abandoned by the Germans in January 1945, Mengele moved to the Mauthausen camp in Austria. From there he escaped to Argentina and later to Brazil, successfully evading capture up to the time of his death in a swimming accident in 1979.

THE LITERATURE

In Rolf Hochhuth's (1931) controversial play *The Deputy* (1964), a character based on Mengele plays a prominent role. Unlike the other historical characters in the play, Mengele is known not by his real name, but simply as "the Doctor," an effort, on the author's part, to ascribe to him an allegorical status as the embodiment of evil. Thus Hochhuth makes no attempt to explore the doctor's motivations or inner life. As he indicates in a stage direction introducing the character: "Since this uncanny visitant from another world was obviously only playing the part of a human being, I have refrained from any further effort to plumb its features." Some have questioned this characterization of Mengele on the grounds that the author seems to be shirking his responsibility as an artist to present the doctor as a human being rather than a diabolic figure. In the last act of the play, set in Auschwitz, the doctor debates with the priest-protagonist Father Riccardo Fontana about "the silence of God" over the Holocaust, proof, in the doctor's mind, that no such being exists. He then proceeds to enact the villain's role in the play's melodramatic conclusion. The temptation to turn Mengele into a devil is understandable, but it evades one of the play's most important ideas—an exploration of the individual human being's guilt in relation to the HOLOCAUST. (See also PIUS XII.)

Mengele appears under his own name as a character in Ira Levin's (1929–) thriller *The Boys from Brazil* (1976). A group of former Nazis living in Brazil hopes to establish a "Fourth Reich." The ringmaster is Mengele, who in 1943, according to the book, persuaded Adolf HITLER to donate a half-liter of his blood and a slice of skin from his ribs with the intent of cloning genetic duplicates of the führer. Some years later in his Brazilian hideout Mengele implanted these seeds in the wombs of Brazilian tribeswomen. (No fear of racial contamination here, since the women make no contribution to the embryo, which is "pure Hitler.") As a result the world is now peopled with 94 13-year-old Hitlers scattered around the globe. Not leaving everything to biology, the Nazis are now planning to murder the 94 foster fathers of these boys, thus ensuring a similar psychological makeup as Hitler's, who lost his father at the age of 13. Mengele is eventually run to ground by a Nazi hunter, loosely based upon Simon Wiesenthal. The novel is a far-fetched, entertaining thriller from the author of *Rosemary's Baby*.

A Mengele-type figure, this time transformed into the sadistic dentist, Dr. Szell, appears as the villain of William Goldman's (1931–) *Marathon Man* (1976). Szell leaves his South American hideaway to come to New York in order to recover some precious diamonds. In a memorable scene, he is spotted by a former camp inmate while walking on 47th Street in New York's Diamond District. The woman, becoming increasingly hysterical as he evades her, keeps screaming, "Der weisser Engel!"

Both novels fulfill the requirements of popular literature by having the villain punished. In reality, unfortunately, justice does not always triumph. Mengele died at the age of 68 without having been captured. In the two films made from these books, Laurence Olivier played contrasting roles, appearing in *The Boys from Brazil* (1978) as the Nazi hunter and in *Marathon Man* (1976) as the Mengele character. For each role, the great actor was nominated for an Academy Award.

FURTHER READING

Dr. Miklos Nyiszli, a Hungarian-Jewish pathologist, was deported to Auschwitz in March of 1944, where he became an assistant to Mengele in his experiments. In *Auschwitz: A Doctor's Eyewitness Account* (trans., 1960), Nyiszli describes the experiments in gruesome detail.

MESSINES, BATTLE OF (WORLD WAR I) (1917)

On June 7, 1917, the British army attacked Messines, a fortified ridge near YPRES in Flanders, and captured it within a few hours. Ten thousand German soldiers were killed and some 7,000 taken prisoner. The attack stands as a model of a successfully planned military operation and, in the eyes of some historians, the only one of its kind conducted by the British command on the WESTERN FRONT. Crucial to the success of the action was the simultaneous detonation of 19 underground mines that had been laid under the German positions by British tunnelers working under incredibly difficult and hazardous conditions. These men were drawn from several Welsh units that included many former coal miners. When the 19 packs of dynamite exploded, the noise could be heard across the English Channel in Great Britain. On the heels of this blast, British soldiers swarmed into the breach of the enemy lines, easily overcoming the German forces still reeling from the explosions. This brief battle was the single most effective example of British military strategy during the war. Unfortunately it led the always overconfident British general Douglas Haig to try to duplicate its success at the battle of PASSCHENDAELE—with disastrous results. Later, illustrating once again the seesaw futility of WORLD WAR I, the Messines Ridge was recaptured by the German army.

THE LITERATURE

The Messines offensive plays a major role in Sebastian Faulks's (1953–) *Birdsong* (1993), a novel in which love and war are the central themes. (Faulks employed the same motifs for his novel set in WORLD WAR II, *Charlotte Gray*.) The story opens in 1910 in the French city of Amiens, focusing on a passionate love affair between a visiting young Englishman, Stephen Wraysford, and a married woman, Isabelle Azaire. The two run off together, but Isabelle returns to her home, without telling Stephen the reason, when she discovers she is pregnant. The action moves ahead to the wartime front, where Stephen, still disillusioned over Isabelle's apparent desertion, is an infantry officer in a company that works closely with "sappers," miners who tunnel underground into enemy territory in order to plant and blow up mines. The novel so effectively recreates the miners' experience that it is not recommended reading for anyone prone to claustrophobia. The world of the sappers is harrowing and inhuman, but these very conditions seem to highlight the innate nobility of the men who live in that world. Slowly Stephen loses his detached view of this unit and becomes one of them. Eventually he goes on a brief leave to Amiens where he meets the sister of Isabelle, who tells him why Isabelle left him. Returning to the front in time for the attack on Messiness Ridge, he narrowly escapes death when trapped in a collapsed mine. The last section of the novel is set in the 1970s, in which the granddaughter of Stephen and Isabelle discovers the truth of her mother's birth. This attempt to update the action seriously weakens the impact of *Birdsong*. Fortunately the wound it inflicts is not fatal.

Birdsong also contains a vivid and powerful description of the first day of the battle of the SOMME when the British army had 20,000 men killed and 40,000 wounded.

FURTHER READING

S. L. A. Marshall's *The American Heritage History of World War I* (1964) contains a colorful account of the battle.

MEUSE-ARGONNE OFFENSIVE (WORLD WAR I) (1918)

The final Allied offensive of the war, in September 1918, attempted to break through the Hindenburg line (also known as the Siegfried line), which stretched across the width of the western front. The Allied plan called for British troops to attack on one flank of the line, with Americans on the opposite flank and the French in the middle. American forces under the command of General John Joseph Pershing were assigned the task of penetrating the line in the area between the Meuse River and the Argonne Forest, a heavily fortified sector, where the Germans had been building defenses for three years. It was clear that the Americans were given the most difficult assignment. In addition to the fortifications, the terrain itself was a natural barrier, with a no-man's-land backed by a steep ridge in one area and the Argonne Forest, intersected with jagged ravines, impassable for heavy guns and trucks. In the first six days of fighting, troops in the forest were able to advance a mere five miles. In the area outside the forest, the American attack bogged down when it encountered heavy German fire well beyond the front line. Adding to the Americans' problems were the mismanagement of the campaign and the failures in communication, supplies, and tactical planning. One victim of the disarray was the famous "Lost Battalion," the First Battalion of the 398th Infantry Regiment, which was surrounded by the enemy for five days as the result of higher command's incompetence. Despite these obstacles, and the heavy casualties they suffered, the American forces eventually succeeded in a six-week-long three-phase series of maneuvers that culminated in a frontal assault on the Kremhilde Stellung, an elevated stronghold to the rear of the front lines. The price paid by the American troops was a casualty list of 117,000 men. Shortly after, the armistice was declared, and the war ended on November 11, 1918.

THE LITERATURE

The offensive plays a climactic role in *One of Ours* (1922), a Pulitzer Prize–winning novel by one of America's great, yet often overlooked, writers, Willa Cather (1873–1947). As in much of her work, the greater part of the novel is set in the Nebraska farmlands, where Claude Wheeler, a sensitive young man, finds himself ill at ease with his life as a successful farmer. Claude feels unsatisfied in his relations with others in his community, particularly with his wife, Enid, a rigid, unloving woman. Her rejection leaves him with his sense of manliness shaken.

The war brings the chance of redemption: Claude begins to experience feelings of challenge and purpose as he becomes an officer in the army. Once in France, he forms a friendship with a fellow officer, David Erhardt, a former concert violinist who has lived in France and speaks the language fluently. Through David, Claude is exposed to French art and culture. In one poignant scene, Claude listens to David playing the violin in the home of a cultured French family and becomes fully aware of what has been missing in his life.

Claude's admiration and envy of David and his camaraderie with the men under his command heighten his commitment to the justice of the war: "I never knew there was anything worth living for, till the war came on. Before that, the world seemed like a business proposition." His newly discovered vitality and confidence produce a psychological transformation, as the hesitant young farmer becomes a skilled and courageous leader of men.

In September 1918, Claude and David's battalion is transferred to the Meuse Argonne front, in preparation for the offensive. When the fighting begins, Claude, now a company commander, is ordered to occupy a critical position where the Germans are expected to counterattack. The designated spot is a former German trench, which the Germans had mined before retreating. Just prior to their counterattack, the enemy detonates the mine, wiping out the American machine guns placed there. With only rifles to defend his position, Claude exposes himself to danger by directing his men's fire, and he successfully holds the line until reinforcements arrive. In the process, however, both Claude and David are killed.

When *One of Ours* was first published, some critics complained that the war served as a kind of deus ex machina, a facile solution to Claude's personal malaise. Others objected to its perceived glorification of war, while still others disliked its depiction of battle. Among the latter, Ernest Hemingway suggested, in a letter to Edmund Wilson, that the battle descriptions were derived from the famous D. W. Griffith film *The Birth of a Nation* (1915). (One should not discount the possibility that such comments were the product of injured male pride over a woman daring to describe a battle scene at all.) On the other hand, the novel was awarded the Pulitzer Prize and became a best-seller.

From the vantage point of the 21st century, *One of Ours* appears to be less about war and more about youthful idealism. As Claude perceives it, just prior to the battle: "Ideals were not archaic things, beautiful and impotent; they were the real sources of power among men. As long as that was true, and now he knew it was true—he had come all this way to find out—he had no quarrel with Destiny." As Claude's grieving mother comes to recognize, if he had survived, Claude would probably have joined the list of war heroes who ended up committing suicide, "the ones who . . . had to hope extravagantly and to believe passionately. And they found they had hoped and believed too much." It is clear that Cather is not interested in the glorification of war, but rather in the tragedy of idealism.

FURTHER READING

S. L. A. Marshall's *The American Heritage History of World War I* (1964) includes a clear, concise account of the offensive. Susie Thomas's *Willa Cather* (1990) interestingly explores the Wagnerian motifs in *One of Ours*.

MEXICAN REVOLUTION (1910–1920)

In 1910, an armed rebellion led by Francisco Madero overthrew the government of Porfirio Díaz, establishing Madero as president in 1911. However, Madero was slow to enact the reforms he had promised, and his two allies, Pancho Villa and Emiliano Zapata, openly rebelled against him. In 1913, Madero was killed by his own chief of staff, Victoriano Huerta, who declared himself president. The forces lined up against Huerta included, along with Villa and Zapata, Venetiano Carranza and Alvaro Obregón.

In July 1914, Huerta resigned, and Venetiano Carranza assumed the presidency. Villa now carried on the fight against Carranza, who forced Villa to retreat to the American border. In 1916, Villa's men crossed the border to raid the town of Columbus, New Mexico. The United States retaliated by sending troops, under the command of General John Joseph Pershing, to pursue Villa across the Mexican border. The Mexican government, although enemies of Villa, vigorously objected to the American military presence, and the troops withdrew. Carranza was assassinated, probably on the orders of his successor, Alvaro Obregón, in 1920.

With the death of Zapata in 1919 and the retirement of Villa in 1920, the revolution effectively came to an end. Although its heritage was mixed, the revolution had at least one remarkable achievement: a policy of distributing land to the peasant population that left a permanent impact on the future development of Mexico.

THE LITERATURE

The Mexican novelist and physician Mariano Azuela (1873–1952) was an active participant in the revolution, serving as a physician with Madero's forces and later with Pancho Villa's army. Between 1911 and 1918, Azuela wrote five novels dealing with the revolution. Of these the most famous and highly regarded is *The Underdogs* (1916; trans., 1929), notable for its vivid, realistic rendering of the revolution from the perspective of rebel soldiers. In sharply etched episodes that appear to have been thrown together haphazardly, *The Underdogs* recreates the confusion, mismanagement, and brutality of the fighting, while nevertheless retaining a respect for the initial impulse toward freedom that inspired the cause. Azuela, fully aware of the self-subverting nature of the revolution, in which victory eventually led to the corruption of power, nevertheless honors the common soldiers—the underdogs—willing to die for liberty.

In 1913, the American writer Ambrose Bierce (1842–1914?), aged 71, disappeared in Mexico while covering the revolution as a reporter for the Hearst papers. In *The Old Gringo* (1985), the Mexican novelist Carlos Fuentes (1928–) creates an imaginative account of Bierce's fate. In the novel, Bierce joins the forces of Pancho Villa. His story is recounted by Harriet Winslow, an American schoolteacher who meets Bierce at the same time that she meets and falls in love with Tomas Arroyo, a general in Villa's army. The central action of the novel is the death of Bierce, who, tired of life, provokes Arroyo into killing him. As a consequence Arroyo is himself killed by Pancho Villa because "when it came to killing gringos, only he, Pancho Villa, would say when and why."

The Old Gringo manages the difficult feat of being both complex and highly readable. On the one hand, it contains exciting action peopled with bold, larger than life characters; on the other, it is a richly sensuous and resonant rendering of the revolutionary spirit with touches of magic realism. Moreover, it stands as an acute study of the interrelation between Mexico and the United States, each tied to the other by history and geography, but divided by history and culture.

FURTHER READING

In addition to Bierce, another well-known American journalist, John Reed, covered the revolution. Reed's reportage was collected under the title *Insurgent Mexico* (1914). Luis Leal's *Mariano Azuela* (1971) is a useful study of that author.

MUNICH PACT (1938)

Soon after the 1938 *Anschluss* (in which Germany annexed Austria without any European opposition), Adolf HITLER turned his attention to the Sudetenland, the northwest area of Czechoslovakia, which, although it contained a large German-speaking population, was awarded to Czechoslovakia in the peace treaty of 1919. Germany announced its intention to annex the Sudetenland, prompting a military buildup on both sides of the Czech-German border. A German invasion seemed imminent, and the Czechs looked to their powerful allies, Britain and France, for support. The British government under Prime Minister Neville Chamberlain, anxious to avoid a military conflict, attempted to pressure the Czechs to make concessions to various German demands. This was an early example of the policy of appeasement that characterized Chamberlain's position in dealing with Hitler. On September 29, Chamberlain and the French prime minister Edouard Daladier flew to Munich to meet Hitler and Benito Mussolini. Britain and France agreed to cede the Sudetenland to Germany in exchange for Germany's promise not to invade Czechoslovakia. The Czech government, not represented at the meeting, was forced to accept its terms.

Chamberlain returned to England, where, before cheering crowds, he announced that he had achieved "peace in our time." Six months later German troops marched into Prague, the Czech capitol, over the vain protests of the Western Allies. Five months after that, on September 1, 1939, the Germans invaded Poland, finally forcing the English and French to declare war. Since that time *Munich* has become a pejorative term, used to describe the diplomatic capitulation of principles in order to avoid military conflict.

THE LITERATURE

In *The Reprieve* (1945; trans., 1947), the second volume of his trilogy *The Roads to Freedom*, the French philosopher and novelist Jean-Paul Sartre (1905–80) examines the reactions of a group of characters to the events surrounding the pact. The main figure is Mathieu, a schoolteacher, whose routine, secure existence at first insulates him from the political events occurring in Europe in 1938. Mathieu and his circle of friends are caught up in the deceptions of others and themselves and the distractions that make up their daily existence. Lacking a true commitment that will lend a form of meaning to their lives, they create an image of themselves, an official portrait, offering the illusion that they are free. As the negotiations in Munich reach their climax, the characters hold their breath, suspended by the fear that they are pawns of history. The exception is Mathieu, who, alone crossing the Pont Neuf in Paris, discovers that the freedom he has been seeking has been there all along. But with freedom comes the anguish of realizing it is freedom to no purpose: "I am free for nothing."

Scenes that shift, sometimes within a paragraph, from one place or group of characters to another also include depictions of the representatives of the nations involved in the Munich Pact negotiations. The close stylistic proximity of the political events to the private lives points up their interconnection, the bad faith that links the self-deception of the individual with the capitulation of Chamberlain and Daladier to Hitler. A memorable sequence near the end of the novel juxtaposes the betrayed Czechoslovakian delegates reading the terms of the agreement with the simultaneous rape of Ivich, a Russian woman who is a friend of Mathieu. The novel concludes with another juxtaposition, a Czech in the Sudetenland regretting that his pregnant wife, in a recent fall, did not have a miscarriage, with Daladier, turning to his aide during his hero's welcome on his return to Paris to exclaim, "The God-damned fools!"

For a discussion of Sartre's sequel to this novel, *Troubled Sleep*, see FRANCE, FALL OF.

FURTHER READING

Donald Cameron Watt's *How War Came: The Immediate Origins of the Second World War, 1938–1939* (1989) is an authoritative account.

MUNICH PUTSCH (1923)

In 1923, German anger and resentment over soaring inflation, defeat in WORLD WAR I, and the subsequent terms of the Versailles Treaty led to widespread opposition to the national government. In the province of Bavaria and its capital city, Munich, resistance took the form of a conservative movement to secede from Germany and reestablish Bavaria as an independent monarchy. But Munich was also the headquarters of the fledgling National Socialist (Nazi) Party, who wanted to see Bavaria not as an independent state but as the base for a revolt that would take over the national government under the leadership of Adolf HITLER. To achieve that goal, Hitler persuaded the distinguished German general Erich Ludendorff to participate with him in a march on Berlin (modeled on Benito Mussolini's march on Rome in 1922), originating in Munich.

The leaders of the local Bavarian government, all secessionists, announced a meeting to take place on November 8, in a large beer hall in Munich where they were expected to announce plans to secede. Hitler decided to take over the meeting, keep everyone there in detention, and proclaim the revolution. Using his SA (Sturmabteilung) troops to surround the beer hall, he entered the meeting, jumped up on a table, and fired a pistol shot in the air. "The national revolution has begun," he shouted. He ordered the three highest leaders of the Bavarian government into a separate room where he attempted to intimidate them into supporting the uprising, but the leaders escaped and organized police and army forces to put down the revolt.

In a last desperate attempt at victory, Hitler and Ludendorff marched at the head of 3,000 storm troopers toward the center of the city. At a critical point, the police opened fire. Sixteen Nazis were killed, along with three policemen. The rest of the protesters dispersed, including Hitler, who went into hiding in an attic. The single exception was Ludendorff, who marched alone straight into the city center.

The putsch, or sudden uprising, was a fiasco, and to all appearances it spelled the end of the Nazi Party and its charismatic leader, who was captured and sentenced to five years in prison. However, Hitler emerged from his trial looking like a true patriot in the eyes of many, and after serving nine months of his sentence, he was released. He had spent much of the time in jail dictating his credo *Mein Kampf.*

THE LITERATURE

The putsch plays a central role in Richard Hughes's (1900–76) novel *The Fox in the Attic* (1961). The year is 1923. Augustine, a young Englishman visiting German relatives in Bavaria, is about to discover that "[i]n England the ending of the war had come like waking from a bad dream; in defeated Germany, as the signal for deeper levels of nightmare." Augustine's older relatives are still steeped in the German military tradition, determined to restore it to its former glory. His cousin is harboring in the attic a homicidal maniac who makes the Nazis look tame. But it is the Nazis themselves and their abortive revolt that really come alive in these pages. The putsch is farcical, an *opera bouffe* as one character puts it, although it comes close to succeeding at one point. Farcical, too, is the picture of Hitler in hiding, another madman in an attic, but like a fox in his wily manipulation of those protecting him.

All of this is lost on Augustine, besotted with love for his cousin Mitzi, who becomes blind and is sent off to a convent. Lurking here seems to be a suggestion that had the events in Munich in 1923 been attended to with more care by England, the events in Munich in 1938 (see MUNICH PACT) might never have come to pass.

FURTHER READING

William Shirer's *The Rise and Fall of the Third Reich* (1960) offers a detailed and interesting account of the putsch.

MY LAI MASSACRE (VIETNAM WAR) (1968)

On March 16, 1968, American troops from the first and second platoons of Charlie Company, First Battalion, Twentieth Infantry Brigade, attacked the South Vietnam village of My Lai. Transported by helicopters to an area outside the village, the Americans, anticipating enemy fire, began shooting as soon as they entered My Lai. After four hours of firing, 504 residents of the village lay dead. With the exception of one self-inflicted wound, there were no American casualties. An exhaustive search of the area turned up only three weapons in this alleged enemy stronghold. The victims included elderly people killed lying in bed, mothers still holding their dead babies, and young women, some of whom had been raped before being shot. As one of the American soldiers described it: "We just rounded 'em up, me and a couple of guys, just put the M-16 on automatic, and just mowed 'em down."

A year later, on March 29, 1969, Ron Ridenhour, a recently discharged Vietnam veteran, wrote a lengthy letter to his congressman, Morris Udall of Arizona, with copies to other government and military officials. In the letter, Ridenhour described conversations he had had with soldiers from Charlie Company, clearly indicating that a massacre had taken place. A subsequent investigation concluded that American troops had been guilty of crimes that "included murder, rape, sodomy, maiming, and assault on non-combatants." Thirteen soldiers, including Charlie Company's commander, Captain Ernest Medina, and the platoon officer in direct charge of the operation, Lieutenant William Calley, were charged with murder. Another tribunal accused 12 divisional and regimental officers of having participated in a cover-up. All were acquitted except for Lieutenant Calley, who was sentenced to life imprisonment. But, by this time, Calley had, in the eyes of many supporters of the war, assumed the status of a scapegoat, the victim of the antiwar movement. After four months in prison, Calley was released by order of President Richard M. NIXON.

The explanations for the cause of the massacre range from the demoralized, rage-filled psychological state of American soldiers in Vietnam to a failure of leadership within the army to a high-level American policy, in which great stress was put on the "kill ratio," that is, determining the success of a military operation by the number of enemy casualties. Consistent with this principle and with the prevalent idea that equated a Vietnam peasant with a Viet Cong supporter, the killing of civilians became a tacitly accepted, if not actively approved, procedure.

THE LITERATURE

The novelist Tim O'Brien (1946–) served in the army in Vietnam and in My Lai itself in 1969, a year after the massacre. In his novel *In the Lake of the Woods* (1994), O'Brien employs the event as a means of exploring the moral complexity in which evil and good coexist within an individual and the destructive effects of failing to come to terms with their coexistence. John Wade, a candidate for the Democratic primary for the U.S. Senate from Minnesota, appears to be a sure winner until the revelation that he was a member of Calley's platoon at My Lai. As the novel opens, he and his wife, Kathy, attempting to recover from a disastrous defeat at the polls, are vacationing at a remote Minnesota lakeside cottage. The My Lai revelation has not only destroyed his political career, it has also brought to the surface the hidden strains and flaws in their marriage. Shortly after their arrival at the cottage, Kathy disappears, presumably after having taken a boat out on the lake. While the search goes on, the novel flashes back to central events in Wade's life, including his experience of the massacre. At My Lai, Wade has killed an old man and a fellow soldier; his explanation in both cases is that firing his gun was a reflex action. Beyond that, his behavior is an inexplicable mystery, but a mystery that has left a haunting, deforming guilt. Wade assumes that he has successfully suppressed that guilt. But "the return of the repressed" has consequences almost as terrible as the incident that provoked it. The novel concludes with a variety of possible endings, which forces its readers to make the final choice as to what really happened.

In an interview about My Lai, Tim O'Brien made the following observation about *In the Lake of the Woods:* "When you're writing about any subject, fiction doesn't depend on what happened in the world. It depends upon what happens in the heart, in the gut, in the spirits of people. I hope that my passages of descriptive writing about My Lai gets to the heart and gets to the gut of readers through make-believe and through invention." O'Brien's distinction between "what happened in the world" and what happens to the reader exemplifies a critical difference between history and literature: Although the facts of My Lai are disturbing enough, the novel draws its readers into the inner life of a participant, where they must determine the degree of their identification with the protagonist—and the moral responsibility that identification implies.

FURTHER READING

Facing My Lai (1997), edited by David Anderson, grew out of a conference at Tulane University. Among the contributors were the psychologist Robert Jay Lifton, the historian Stephen Ambrose, journalists David Halberstam and Seymour Hersh, and Tim O'Brien.

N

NANKING [NANJING], RAPE OF (1937)

In the early years of the Sino-Japanese War, the Japanese army entered the undefended city of Nanking and perpetrated one of the worst massacres in modern history. With no attempt to disguise their actions, roaming groups of soldiers and their officers conducted mass executions, beheading and disemboweling their victims, raping and subsequently murdering thousands of Chinese women. In *The Rape of Nanking* (1997), Iris Chang lists the following types of torture and death inflicted by Japanese forces: live burials, mutilation, incineration, forcing naked prisoners to leap into frozen water, and burying prisoners to their waists so that they could be attacked by German shepherds. This campaign of terror persisted for seven weeks and would have continued were it not for the presence of foreign nationals, who created an international safety zone, provided protection to some of the population, and alerted the world to the massacre. To this day, the Japanese government, similar to the Turkish government's response to its connection to the ARMENIAN GENOCIDE, continues to deny the massacre.

THE LITERATURE

In Paul West's *The Tent of Orange Mist* (1995), Scald Ibis is a 16-year-old Nanking girl, bred to gentility. When Japanese soldiers, along with their commander Colonel Hayashi, break into her home, they behead her brother, rape and bayonet her mother, and then proceed to rape her. Her life is spared by Colonel Hayashi, who notices her special appeal and develops other plans for her. He converts her home into a local "pleasure house" for Japanese officers that he calls "the Tent of Orange Mist." Able to adjust to the horrors surrounding her, she is eventually elevated from prostitute to geisha, serving high-ranking military figures. In the meantime her father, who had been serving in the Chinese army, returns to the house disguised as a servant. Seeing his daughter reduced to performing unspeakable acts, he strangles Colonel Hayashi and is himself beheaded and quartered by Japanese troops. Always the survivor, Scald Ibis replaces Hayashi as the manager of the brothel until the end of the war. Having become by this time more Japanese than Chinese, she moves to Japan, where she spends the rest of her life.

Interpolated throughout the novel are excerpts from the journal of a 16th-century, presumably fictional, Jesuit missionary, the relevance of which is obscure at best. There are also some self-indulgent exercises in literary style that come across as authorial showing off. But the novel's strength lies in its depiction of individuals, caught in a vise of historical horror and faced with the choice of being slaughtered or adapting to the point of becoming the enemy. Scald Ibis chooses the latter path. Whether survival is worth the price she pays is left for the reader to determine.

FURTHER READING

Iris Chang's *The Rape of Nanking* (1997) is a powerful indictment of the Japanese army.

NEW DEAL

See GREAT DEPRESSION; ROOSEVELT, FRANKLIN DELANO.

NEW FEMINISM

See FEMINIST MOVEMENT.

NIGHT OF THE LONG KNIVES (1934)

During the 1920s, the private army of the National Socialist (Nazi) Party, the SA (Sturmabteilung), popularly known from the color of its uniform as the "Brownshirts," grew with such rapidity that the regular German army viewed the SA as a threat. In 1934, Adolf HITLER, now the German chancellor and in need of the cooperation of the military establishment in his plans to rearm Germany, recognized the danger represented by the SA and its powerful commander, his longtime associate Ernst Röhm. Röhm had, in fact, expressed a desire to have the regular army subsumed into the SA, a move that would have left Röhm as powerful as Hitler. In the early morning hours of June 30, 1934, Röhm and more than 150 SA leaders were accused of plotting a rebellion, arrested, and executed. The operation was carried out by the SS (Schutzstaffel), the internal police of the SA, under the leadership of Heinrich Himmler.

THE LITERATURE

Richard Hughes's (1900–76) novel *The Fox in the Attic* (1961) deals with the MUNICH PUTSCH. Its sequel, *The Wooden Shepherdess* (1973), concludes with a long section, "Stille Nacht," focusing on the Night of the Long Knives. It is June 1934, and Chancellor Hitler uneasily awaits the expected demise of President Paul von Hindenburg, at which time he will become head of state. In the novel's version of the relevant events, Hitler is troubled by the behavior of the SA, 2 million undisciplined, rowdy "arrogant bullies," not content with a peaceful, orderly accession to power. The only figure who can keep them in control is their leader, Ernst Röhm. Before leaving on a state visit to Benito Mussolini's Italy, Hitler dispatches his minister of propaganda, Joseph Goebbels, to keep Röhm in check. In the meantime two of Röhm's intraparty enemies, Hermann Göring and Heinrich Himmler, are concocting a plot to convince Hitler that Röhm is planning a coup. When Hitler returns from Italy to prepare for a meeting with the SA leaders on June 30, Göring and Himmler try to convince him that Röhm intends to assassinate the führer at the meeting. Hitler does not believe their theory, but after a cautious delay he decides to act as if it were true, a supposition that will enable him to purge the entire leadership of the SA.

On the evening of June 29, he flies to Munich to institute the first phase of the operation, neutralizing SA headquarters in the city. From Munich he proceeds to the resort town of Wiessee, where the meeting is set for noon the next day. There, in the early morning hours, he arrests Röhm and the rest of the leadership as they arrive for the meeting. After they have been rounded up, they are brought to the prison yard in Munich, where they are machine-gunned to death. Röhm is put in a cell with a loaded pistol and told he is expected to commit suicide, but he refuses to do so and is executed. In the midst of the roundup, it suddenly occurs to Hitler that this would be a good occasion to rid himself of various other enemies, unrelated to the SA, so the purge is extended even further.

In his "historical note" appended to the end of his novel, Hughes states that although he has striven for factual accuracy, the fact that "the Nazis destroyed all official records bearing on the Blood-Purge of 1934" and "surviving contemporary sources tend to be the work of known liars on both sides" means it is up to the reader to determine how much of his historical reconstruction to accept as true. The historical facts notwithstanding, Hughes's ability in these two novels to align the rise of the Nazis with the fates of ordinary people provides a fascinating account of the interactions of individuals with history.

FURTHER READING

Ian Kershaw's *Hitler* (1998–2000) contains a complete account of the purge.

1948 PRESIDENTIAL CAMPAIGN

The death of President Franklin Delano ROOSEVELT in 1945 elevated to the highest office his little-known vice president, Harry S. Truman. To many citizens, Truman appeared to be a small-town Missouri "hick," entirely incapable of following in the footsteps of his world-famous, charismatic predecessor. Within a few months of taking office, he had to participate in the critical Potsdam Conference, matching wits with Winston Churchill and Joseph STALIN, and to make the final decision to use the atomic bomb against Japan (see HIROSHIMA and MANHATTAN PROJECT). Working with a resistant Congress dominated by a coalition of Republicans and southern Democrats, he made a number of controversial decisions, including desegregating the armed forces.

In 1948, Truman faced a serious political challenge when his nomination for a second term was bitterly contested, resulting in the breakaway of a group of southern Democrats who formed their own party, the Dixiecrats. Still another splinter group, this time on the left, formed around Henry Wallace, Truman's predecessor as vice president under Roosevelt.

With the Democrats split into three factions and facing a Republican challenger, Thomas E. Dewey, who had run a spirited campaign against Roosevelt in 1944, Truman appeared certain to lose. The polls, the leading newspapers, and the great majority of political pundits predicted a Dewey landslide. Unfazed by the prophets of doom and with bulldog determination, Truman embarked on a series of whistle-stop campaigns, speaking from the back of a train in all 48 states, taking his case and his fighting spirit to the people. Dewey, on the other hand, conducted a listless campaign that consisted largely of avoiding controversy. On election night, a leading anti-Truman newspaper, the *Chicago Tribune*, published an early edition of the next day's paper with the headline, DEWEY DEFEATS TRUMAN.

The final tally revealed a different story: Truman, 24,105,812 (303 electoral votes); Dewey, 21,970,065 (189 electoral votes). On his return trip to Washington after his reelection, someone handed Truman a copy of the *Tribune* headline. Holding it above his head, he told a cheering crowd, "Don't believe everything you read in the papers."

THE LITERATURE

The *Tribune*'s headline serves as the title of Thomas Mallon's (1951–) 1997 novel, set in Owosso, Michigan, Dewey's birthplace. *Dewey Defeats Truman* approaches its subject with a mixture of warm nostalgia and gentle irony.

Owosso is a Frank Capra-esque small town, busily preparing to bask in, and cash in on, its impending fame. One local entrepreneur has proposed a 1948 version of a theme park celebrating the various phases of the hometown hero's life. The central plot concerns Anne Macmurray, a recent arrival in town, and her two suitors, Peter, an aspiring Republican politician, and Jack, an organizer for the United Auto Workers, heavily committed to Truman. Paralleling, but opposite to, the political story, Jack, the Democratic lover, is the clear front-runner, and the Republican Peter is the underdog. But Peter is a confident, Trumanesque figure, taking big risks in the face of imminent defeat, while Jack is a shade too sure of himself. Anne's dilemma is neatly reflected in the fact that she loves Owosso (Jack), but she also loves Truman (Peter).

In an author's note at the conclusion of the novel, Mallon reminds us, "Nouns always trump adjectives, and in the phrase 'historical fiction' it is important to know which of the two words is which." His point—the novelist should always be free to take liberties with the historical facts in order to reach another type of truth, the truth of the imagination—is well-taken, but perhaps unnecessary in this novel, which is fairly scrupulous in its fidelity to its historical time and place. Even the fictional plot of *Dewey Defeats Truman* is completely true to the spirit, if not the letter, of the historical event it commemorates.

FURTHER READING

David McCullough's acclaimed biography *Truman* (1992) offers a thorough, discerning account of the campaign.

NIXON, RICHARD M. (1913–1994)

Nixon, a good part of whose success as a politician lay in his image as a simple, self-made man, was born in Yorba Linda, California, but the family soon moved to the nearby town of Whittier. There Richard attended the First Friends Quaker Church, worked in the family grocery store, and later went to Whittier College. He served in the navy during WORLD WAR II and was elected to the House of Representatives in 1946, the same year as his future rival, John F. KENNEDY. As a congressman, he played a prominent role in the HISS-CHAMBERS CASE, which led to his election to the Senate in 1950, after a campaign in which he misrepresented his opponent, Helen Gahagan Douglas, as a "pink lady." In 1952, he became the running mate of Dwight Eisenhower, serving as vice president until 1960, when he was defeated by Kennedy in an extremely close presidential election. When he lost the race for governor of California in 1962, he announced his retirement from politics, telling assembled reporters, "You won't have Dick Nixon to kick around anymore."

While pursuing a private law practice, he kept his hand in Republican politics and in 1968 ran again for president, this time successfully in the midst of national turmoil over the CIVIL RIGHTS MOVEMENT and the VIETNAM WAR. After the election, he withdrew 500,000 troops from Vietnam, but he expanded the war with bombing campaigns in Laos and Cambodia. In a surprise move, he visited China and opened up trade relations with the Communist government there. Three months later he went to Moscow to sign a treaty banning the deployment of new antiballistic missiles by the United States and the Soviet Union.

In the 1972 election, he carried 49 of the 50 states. But not long after, persistent stories concerning a break-in at the offices of the Democratic National headquarters in the WATERGATE hotel/office complex began to reveal a pattern of conspiracy and money-laundering within the White House. In 1973, the Senate began an investigation of the role of the White House in the break-in and the ensuing coverup of information. A year later, Nixon resigned from office and was granted a pardon by his successor, President Gerald Ford.

One of the most complicated and conflicted people to ever hold presidential office, Nixon elicited enormous enmity throughout his lifetime. His ability and his aspirations to be a great president were continually undercut by his incipient paranoia, the impulse to exact personal revenge, deeply rooted insecurity, and his willingness to step outside the law in order to achieve his ends.

THE LITERATURE

Robert Coover's (1932–   ) *The Public Burning* (1977) is ostensibly about the execution of Julius and Ethel Rosenberg in 1953 (see ROSENBERG CASE), but the novel, written in the wake of Watergate, is more directly concerned with its unlikely chief narrator, Vice President Richard Nixon, and his symbolic status as the embodiment of COLD WAR America. Fully utilizing the techniques of magic realism and postmodern fiction, Coover makes no attempt to represent actual events. Instead he employs a wide range of styles, mixing historical fact with popular culture, myths, parodies, and fables. The result is a massive collage that adds up to a satiric indictment of American culture, with Nixon as its representative. But despite the polemics that dominate the work, Coover manages a portrait of Nixon that is not entirely lacking in compassion.

The novel begins with the announcement that following the final rejection of their appeal, the Rosenbergs' fate has been "sealed, and it is determined to burn them in New York City's Times Square on the night of their 14th wedding anniversary, Thursday, June 18, 1953." Against this background, Nixon narrates his life story in a candid, self-revealing fashion. He speaks, for example, of his difficulty in connecting with other people, epitomized is his description of his relation with his wife Pat: "Without having to say a thing, she became my arbiter, my audience, guide, model, and goal. Sometimes she felt that she did have to say something, but it was usually better when she kept quiet." He is acutely conscious of the fact that President Eisenhower, like most people he knows, doesn't particularly like him. But the resentment he feels serves as fuel for his ambition.

In his analysis of the Rosenberg trial, he displays his sharp lawyer's intelligence, but he also finds himself increasingly wondering about the two spies, comparing them to himself: "I was the Vice President. . . . They were condemned to burn as traitors. What went wrong?" He becomes particularly interested in Ethel. As the execution date nears, he makes a desperate attempt to prevent it by going to Sing Sing Prison with the intention of getting them to confess. But when he confronts Ethel, he is swept up in a passion for her, a passion she requites. The two repressed people have a wild sexual encounter just prior to the entrance of the executioner. Nixon narrowly escapes, with his pants around his knees.

At the public execution in Times Square, a frenzied Dionysian blood sacrifice, Nixon makes an appearance, pants still around his feet. Faced with howls and cackles from the manic crowd, he engages in a meaningless rant invoking the sacred clichés of political life. Finally, the audience takes up the chant, "PANTS DOWN." Everyone begins to drop their pants as the Rosenbergs are led to their deaths.

Not surprisingly, many publishers turned down the manuscript of *The Public Burning*, fearing the lawsuits that it might provoke. Some also questioned the taste of what seemed to many reviewers the author's adolescent humor. Others maintain it to be a postmodernist classic. Thus the controversy that surrounded the man in his lifetime continues in the reaction to the literature he evoked.

FURTHER READING

Richard Reeves's *President Nixon* (2001) is an exhaustively researched study of his presidency. Garry Wills's *Nixon Agonistes* (1970) offers a psychological portrait at the outset of his presidency.

NORMANDY INVASION (WORLD WAR II) (1944)

The Allied invasion of Normandy on D day, June 6, 1944, was the largest, most complicated military action in history. Operation Overlord, as it was named, involved more than 4,000 ships, transporting men and shelling the Normandy shore; 10,000 aircraft, providing protection and carrying airborne divisions; and 130,000 American, British, and Canadian troops, a figure that, within a month, rose to 1 million. The event itself was preceded by months of diplomatic and political negotiations, strategic and tactical planning, and the critical guessing game, played with the enemy, as to when and where the landing would take place. The deception that led the Germans to assume the invasion would occur at Pas de Calais, the closest port to England, or even as far north as Norway, proved to be a great advantage because Allied bombing of roads and railways made the quick shift of German reinforcement troops intensely difficult.

The Normandy invasion began in the predawn of June 6. The Allies landed on five beaches—code-named Sword, Juno, Gold, Omaha, and Utah—while airborne divisions were dropped farther inland to protect the flanks of the beaches against enemy counterattacks. The worst Allied casualties occurred at Omaha Beach, where the Germans, ensconced in fortified positions overlooking the beach, directed fierce fire at the landing vessels and pinned the American troops right at the edge of the water before they could make their way to the protecting shelf that rose from the beach. But Omaha proved to be the single exception in an attack with comparatively light casualties that saw the Germans confused and demoralized. At the end of the day, the Allies had secured the beaches and moved steadily inland, piercing the Atlantic wall with relative ease.

In the planning and rehearsal phase of the operation, security was a continuing concern. With so vast a collection of men and machines, complete secrecy and effective deception appeared to be an impossible goal. One source of apprehension occurred in late April, about six weeks prior to D day. During a rehearsal of the invasion off the small English coastal village of Slapton Sands, German E-boats slipped by the ships guarding the bay and torpedoed two transports. More than 700 men were lost. Serious as the incident was, it raised an even more ominous specter for the Allied high command: the possibility that the E-boats might have picked up survivors capable of leaking information.

THE LITERATURE

This incident forms the jumping off point of John Harris's (1916–   ) *The Fox from His Lair: A Novel of D-Day* (1978). In Harris's fictionalized version of the incident, 10 officers with top secret clearances are among the missing, jeopardizing the entire invasion plan. Assigned to trace the missing men is an American security officer, Colonel Linus Iremonger, who soon teams up with his British equivalent, Major Cuthbert Pargeter (true to their names, the two are stereotypical American and British officers). Pargeter is investigating the separate murders of two British officers, who turn out to have been British intelligence agents. The two investigations converge on an elusive figure who is disguised as an American officer currently named Fox, although he changes his name regularly. Eventually Iremonger and Pargeter determine that the elusive "Fox" is a German spy, Ebert Reinecke. On the eve of D day, they track him down to a company that is among the first wave to hit Omaha Beach. Reinecke is carrying with him critical details of the Allied plans following up the landings. (As if that were not enough, he is also carrying secrets regarding the ULTRA decoding process.) In order to prevent him from reaching the German lines, the two allies commandeer an amphibious vehicle participating in the Omaha landing and find themselves in the midst of the most severe enemy fire. They catch up with their wounded prey just as he is about to cross over into German territory.

The Fox from His Lair is fairly standard spy-thriller fare, featuring the bluff, hearty American, the mild-mannered Englishman with the heart of a lion, and the devilishly clever, resourceful Nazi. It rises above that level in its account of the landing on Normandy, capturing on paper, as Steven Spielberg's *Saving Private Ryan* would later do on film, the living hell of the first-wave landing.

FURTHER READING

Stephen Ambrose's *D-Day, June 6, 1944* (1994) combines an authoritative account of the invasion with the recollections of veterans on both sides, providing a human face to the historical event.

NORTHERN IRELAND (THE TROUBLES)

The Anglo-Irish Treaty in 1921, which officially concluded the IRISH WAR OF INDEPENDENCE, established the Irish Free State as a virtually autonomous nation. One provision in the treaty, however, radically undermined the nature of the new state: Ireland was to be partitioned, with six counties in the northeast section of the country remaining a part of the United Kingdom, to be known as Northern Ireland. In these six counties, the majority—approximately two-thirds—were Protestants, vehemently opposed to assimilation with the overwhelmingly Catholic South. These religious differences, in effect since the late 17th century, when England established Protestant settlements in the North, were underscored by economic ones: Northern Ireland had a relatively industrialized economy, as opposed to the largely agrarian South. The dispute over partition and other issues of the treaty deeply divided the South, resulting in the IRISH CIVIL WAR in 1922.

In the decades that followed, long-standing discrimination, de facto segregation, and physical repression (the Royal Ulster Constabulary [RUC], the Northern Irish police force, was more than 95 percent Protestant) against the Catholic minority in the North led to increased dissension. In 1967, the Northern Ireland Civil Rights Association was formed to promote equality in such areas as public housing and employment. The organization organized a protest march in 1969 that was violently suppressed by the police. The police action was caught on television, triggering a negative reaction against the RUC and the local government in both England and Ireland. In 1969, the British army was called in to keep the peace, an action that was applauded by the Catholic minority, since the British soldiers were now seen as their protectors. That view soon changed as the British army conducted house-to-house searches for weapons in a rude and offensive fashion that alienated the Catholic population. At this point, the Northern branch of the IRISH REPUBLICAN ARMY (IRA), which had been dormant for a number of years, began a reorganization that by 1971 resulted in a bombing campaign aimed at, among others, British soldiers. The government retaliated with a policy of "internment," arrest and imprisonment without charges for an indefinite period. The violence escalated further on Sunday, January 30, 1972, when British troops fired on a peaceful civil rights demonstration in the city of Derry (Londonderry), killing 13 civilians. This "Bloody Sunday" set off further demonstrations as the violence steadily increased. Two militant Protestant groups, the Ulster Volunteer Force and the Ulster Defence Association, matched, and often exceeded, the IRA in terrorist activity.

Tensions increased in 1981 when 10 IRA prisoners died on a hunger strike, but in 1984 an accord between the English prime minister Margaret Thatcher and the Irish prime minister Garrett Fitzgerald was welcomed by the moderate political parties, although condemned by extremists on both sides. The agreement recognized the right of the majority of people in Northern Ireland to determine their form of government, while calling for the protection of the minority's civil liberties. This cooperation between Great Britain and the Republic of Ireland constituted the first step in the slow development of the peace process, which got under way again in 1994. The on-again, off-again peace discussions finally bore fruit on April 10, 1998, when the "Good Friday" agreement allowed for a power-sharing arrangement in the Northern Ireland government. The old animosities continued to plague the new government, however, causing Britain to suspend the Northern Ireland Assembly in 2002.

THE LITERATURE

Set in Belfast in the 1970s, Eoin McNamee's (1961–) *Resurrection Man* (1994) is a novel in which the pathology of the Troubles is embodied in the mind of the central character. Vincent Kelly is a Protestant and a Catholic—that is, he is a Protestant with a Catholic last name, a condition that in the sectarian madness of Belfast at this period constitutes a fusion of opposites that can only combust into violence. With a fantasy life nurtured by American gangster films, and coming of age during an internecine war, Vincent succeeds in becoming a murder artist, carving his victims as if they were religious statues or "graven images." Taking bloodletting to a new level, Vincent forms a group of killers who prey on randomly selected people, who, they assume, are Catholics. They come to be known as "Renaissance Men," after a gang from an earlier time, which was in the business of murdering people and selling the corpses to medical schools. Vincent's group is overseen, unbeknownst to them, by the mysterious McClure, who moves in the higher circles of Protestant paramilitarism and the British secret service and who determines when the group's excesses will become counterproductive. McClure lures a newspaperman, Ryan, into investigating the group, but Ryan, recently divorced and relying heavily on liquor to get him through his day, is never able to penetrate the conspiracy in which Vincent unwittingly plays a part.

In her critical study *Plotting Terror* (2001), Margaret Scanlan offers an incisive summary of the historical basis of *Resurrection Man*. The model for Victor Kelly is Lenny Murphy, whose group, known as the "Shankhill butchers," was responsible for the murders of more than 20 people, most of them from multiple stab wounds. The character of McClure is based to some degree on William McGrath. Arrested in 1980 on charges of molesting and recruiting boys as homosexual prostitutes at a state-run home for boys, where he was a social worker, McGrath was also the founder of a group dedicated to taking over the Northern Ireland government in the event of a British evacuation and to subsequently invading the Irish Republic. Investigations led to the charge that McGrath had been an agent of MI-5, the British internal security office. In the novel, McClure arranges parties, where "well spoken English gentlemen in suits" and various paramilitary figures are provided with boys for the evening. The author departs from the facts in depicting a direct connection between the two figures based on Murphy and McClure. Nevertheless the historical record does indicate some degree of collusion between the British and the Protestant paramilitaries, at least in the 1970s.

FURTHER READING

John McGarry and Brendan O'Leary's *Explaining Northern Ireland* (1995) is a balanced and perceptive study.

O

OCTOBER 3, 1951

On this date, the United States announced that the Soviet Union had exploded its second atomic bomb. The story in the *New York Times*, the following day, called it an "atom blast." Obsessed with COLD WAR secrecy, the White House withheld the time and place of the explosion.

The Soviet test had taken place on September 24 at the Semipalatinsk nuclear weapons site. The bomb exploded was a 40-kiloton Joe-2, an improved plutonium weapon that, in the test, yielded 38 kilotons. An earlier model, Joe-1, or "First Lightning," with a smaller yield, was detonated in 1949. These early tests led to rapid Soviet progress in their development of nuclear weapons, including at the last a 400-kiloton thermonuclear device, the Joe-4. Doubtless, the designation *Joe* stood for Joseph STALIN. All these models are on display in the Russian Atomic Weapon Museum located at Sarov, 400 kilometers east of Moscow. No one has yet determined the extent or the degree of the fallout produced by any of the Joes.

On the same date as the announcement of the Soviet test, the New York Giants baseball team and their crosstown rivals, the Brooklyn Dodgers, played the third and last of a three-game playoff series for the National League pennant at the Polo Grounds, home of the Giants. That such a series was taking place seemed to baseball fans a miracle: The Dodgers had led the National League for most of the season, and then the Giants, 13 and a half games behind, charged to the fore and matched the Dodgers in games won and lost in the regular season—hence the playoffs.

On this date, the three-game series was tied, one game apiece. The decisive moment of this game came in the bottom of the ninth inning, with the Giants trailing 4–2, Ralph Branca pitching for the Dodgers and Bobby Thomson at bat. Two men were on base, the count 0–1, when, with one mighty swing, Thomson sent the next pitch into the left-field seats. Russ Hodges, the startled play-by-play radio announcer, then uttered the now-immortal repetition in a hoarse scream: "The Giants win the pennant! The Giants win the pennant! The Giants win the pennant! The Giants win the pennant." Sportswriters would call Thomson's home run "the shot heard round the world."

Thomson and Branca achieved the status of legendary figures in a mythic event. For years they traded on the moment. Every baseball fan in America burned the occasion into memory.

THE LITERATURE

The 60-page prologue of Don DeLillo's (1936–   ) *Underworld* (1997), "The Triumph of Death," depicts the day with the panoramic gusto of a visionary.

The novel begins with Cotter Martin, a high-school student who lives in Harlem, sneaking into the game. Cotter is shrewd and resourceful, with the reflexes and athleticism to evade the police and get a seat in the left-field stands. There an older fan, Bill Waterson, strikes up a conversation with the boy and becomes friendly enough to buy Cotter a bag of peanuts. Bill is a staunch Giants fan—never losing faith—while Cotter, also a Giants fan, despairs as the end nears.

In these seats, Cotter gains possession of Thomson's home-run ball, but only after a wild melee on the cement floor and under the cramped green seats. Very close to the end of the prologue, Bill stalks Cotter deep into Harlem, demanding the ball, calling on their comradeship during the game, until at the last Cotter taunts him by holding the ball out and then snatching it away, and Bill, realizing he's in Harlem, retreats.

The narrative of Bill and Cotter threads through the depiction of the game, along with changing foci on players, the fans as a whole and singly, and, most important, a group occupying Giants' manager Leo Durocher's field-level box: Frank Sinatra; Jackie Gleason, the great comedian; and Toots Shor, a self-described "saloon keeper." Shor's restaurant was famous for the famous, especially athletes, who showed up there regularly. The fourth occupant is J. Edgar Hoover, the notoriously secretive, celebrity-loving, ultrahygienic, and sexually perverse director of the Federal Bureau of Investigation. In the course of the game, the first three, especially Gleason and Shor, become drunker and more obscene, while Gleason, an unrestrained eater, also gorges himself on enough ballpark food to throw up loudly, partly onto Sinatra. Hoover is silently disapproving and moves discreetly away from the vomit-spewing.

A series of contrasts and themes are embodied in the narrative: celebrity and anonymity, the overt and the covert, history on a grand scale and the singular attraction to baseball of ordinary people, which constitutes a smaller, but no less significant, history. Hoover gets a message during the game that the Soviet Union has conducted an atomic test, and he "fixes today's date in his mind. . . . He stamps the date." The message stirs in him more secrets and at the same time a memory of a great event, PEARL HARBOR, only 10 years earlier.

Paper plays a large role in the prologue. It wafts down from the upper stands in shreds, rolled-up balls, whole pages torn out of magazines. This aimless, directionless fall of detritus suggests the upredictable, fallout from a nuclear explosion. Thus the Soviet atomic test and Thomson's home run are tied together: two shots heard round the world.

The prologue's depiction of an enormous canvas of individuals and movements attests to DeLillo's notion that all of history is arbitrary and unexpected and that the memorable moments of baseball—"it changes nothing but your life"—are also simply arbitrary triumphs and failures. The large canvas invites us to think of an interconnected set of people and events, a terribly significant conspiracy, initiated by no one, uncontrolled, uncontrollable.

FURTHER READING

The complete story of "the shot heard round the world" from the participants' perspective can be found in Bobby Thomson's *The Giants Win the Pennant! The Giants Win the Pennant!* (1992; afterword by Ralph Branca). On the bomb, see David Holloway, *Stalin and the Bomb: The Soviet Union and Atomic Energy, 1939–1956* (1994).

—*William Herman*

OCTOBER REVOLUTION

See RUSSIAN REVOLUTION (1917).

OSWALD, LEE HARVEY (1939–1963)

The man generally recognized as the assassin of President John Fitzgerald KENNEDY was born in New Orleans. He and his mother, a widow, lived in several cites as he was growing up. At the age of 17, he joined the U.S. Marine Corps, serving for three years before receiving a dishonorable discharge. After leaving the service, he moved to the Soviet Union with the intention of becoming a citizen. While there, he married a Russian woman, Marina, and shortly after the birth of a daughter, the family returned to the United States in 1962. Sometime prior to November 22, 1963, he began working at the

Dallas Book Depository, a building that overlooked the presidential parade route. According to the official report of the Warren Commission, he fired two shots from a window of the depository, killing the president. He was apprehended later that day in a Dallas movie theater after killing a policeman. Two days later, while being moved from the Dallas police station, he was shot and killed in full view of television cameras, while surrounded by local and federal police officers. His assailant was Jack Ruby, the owner of a disreputable local nightclub. The killing of Oswald while in police custody and evidence supplied by an amateur photographer's picture of the assassination have created considerable doubt that Oswald was the only assassin.

THE LITERATURE

Don DeLillo's (1936–   ) *Libra* (1988) recreates the assassination through a series of complex and compelling perspectives designed to capture the event as a truly American tragedy. The title refers to Oswald's birth sign, suggesting that he was a classical "negative Libra," in that he lacked a real sense of his identity. DeLillo tells his story, alternating it with the author's account of a conspiracy instigated by some renegade CENTRAL INTELLIGENCE AGENCY (CIA) operatives designed to set up an attempted assassination of the president that could be made to look like a Cuban plot. Their aim is to create a groundswell of popular feeling for the invasion of Cuba that would topple Castro. Their allies in this plot are members of the exiled Cuban community and a New Orleans mafioso, who longs for the return of Havana's prerevolutionary days when the hotels and casinos were mob-owned (see CUBAN REVOLUTION). For the conspirators, Oswald's availability as a "lone gunman" figure is a happy accident, providing them with a convenient fall guy. In fact, in the novel's construction the bullet that actually kills Kennedy comes not from Oswald's gun but from one fired from the nearby grassy knoll.

However, the bulk of the novel concentrates on the character of Oswald, the ultimate outsider in search of a script in which he will play the major role, that of presidential assassin, as the critic Frank Lentricchia points out. His death on television is the perfect conclusion to a life in which print and electronic media have replaced actual reality, giving a narrative shape to an otherwise meaningless existence.

FURTHER READING

Introducing Don DeLillo, edited by Frank Lentricchia (1991), includes the editor's trenchant comments on *Libra*.

P

PASSCHENDAELE, BATTLE OF (WORLD WAR I) (1917)

Passchendaele is the name of a small village in Belgium, as well as the popular name for the third battle of YPRES, which lasted from July to November 1917. Passchendaele Ridge, a fortified elevated position that the Germans had captured in 1914, overlooked the front line near Ypres. The British commander General Douglas Haig regarded it as the key point in the overall Ypres battle. As usual, preparations for the battle consisted of a massive artillery attack that, in addition to giving the Germans prior notice of British intentions, turned the rain-soaked battlefield into a sea of mud. Advancing British soldiers found themselves waist-deep in the mud, and many actually drowned. They could move only by laying down planks and lifting them to lay them down ahead as they advanced. Such a procedure left them totally exposed to enemy fire. The casualty lists grew on both sides. Finally, the British succeeded in capturing the ridge. They had gained five miles of territory at a cost of 275,000 men. The following year, the Germans recaptured the ridge. For the inhuman conditions its soldiers endured, coupled with its strategic insignificance, this battle came to signify both the horror and the mismanagement of the war.

THE LITERATURE

A description of the battle highlights a significant episode in *Fifth Business* (1970), a novel by the Canadian author Robertson Davies (1913–95). *Fifth Business* takes the form of a memoir written by Dunstan Ramsay, who is retiring, after teaching in a private boys' school for 45 years. Angered over the condescending portrait of himself recorded in the school newspaper, he writes to set the record straight. Although outwardly a harmless old pedant, he has in fact played a critical role in the lives of other people. He has been the *Fifth Business*—an insider's term in drama and opera denoting the character who, while not the star performer, is essential to the resolution of the plot. A critical example is provided in the opening pages of the novel. In 1908, as a young boy in a small Canadian village, Ramsay dodges a snowball intended for him. The snowball hits Mrs. Dempster, a pregnant woman, causing her to give birth prematurely and leaving her with a simplicity of mind that people regard as madness, but Ramsay alone perceives as literal saintliness.

With the outbreak of WORLD WAR I, Ramsay enlists in the Canadian army and is sent to France. At Passchendaele, he is wounded by shrapnel during an attack on a machine-gun nest. Lost in the dark, he drags his body to a piece of jagged masonry, the remains of a wall of an old church. While propped up against it, he is convinced he is about to die when the bombardment suddenly ceases and a flare illuminates the sky:

> By its light I could see that the remnant of standing masonry in which I was lying was all that was left of a church. . . . As the hissing flame dropped, I saw there about ten or twelve feet above me on an opposite wall, in a niche, a statue of the Virgin and Child. . . . I thought in a flash that it must be the Crowned Woman in Revelation—she who had the moon beneath her feet and was menaced by the Red Dragon. But what hit me worse than the blow of the shrapnel was that the face was Mrs. Dempster's face.

Despite this overtly religious symbolism, the novel does not suggest a specifically Christian theme. Rather it sees religion as belonging to the same order of human experience as myth, magic, and art, manifestations of the presence of the miraculous and the mysterious in life and of the magical elements hidden beneath the surface of the everyday. Ramsay is searching for the marvelous in life. In this quest, he performs his role as Fifth Business with diligence and integrity.

The many admirers of this novel point to its Dickensian richness of character and plot and its celebration of the arcane and mysterious, the magic and mythic aspects of life. One example is its transformation of the hell of Passchendaele into a visionary redemption.

FURTHER READING

In *Passchendaele: The Untold Story* (1996), Robin Prior and Trevor Wilson argue that "the delusions of the military and the waywardness of the political leadership" combined to create the disastrous results.

PEARL HARBOR CONTROVERSY (1941)

The day after the Japanese attack on Pearl Harbor on December 7, 1941 (see WAR IN THE PACIFIC), the United States declared war on Japan. Two days later, Germany and Italy declared war on the United States. Suddenly, the domestic opposition to American participation in WORLD WAR II all but disappeared. But to some critics of President Franklin Delano ROOSEVELT, it seemed all too convenient. Prior to December 7, the president had been frustrated by the popular opposition to American involvement in the war then raging in Europe. Disillusioned by the results of WORLD WAR I, which had been billed as a mission to "save the world for democracy," but which had left Europe worse off than it had ever been, the majority of Americans generally held to the doctrine of "no foreign entanglements." Even the possibility of containing the scope of war to the Japanese evaporated when, a few days after Pearl Harbor, Adolf HITLER committed his second great folly of 1941 (the first had been his invasion of the Soviet Union) by declaring war on the United States.

During the war years, criticism relating to Pearl Harbor was muted as Americans rallied behind the president, but after the war journalists and historians, such as Charles Beard, raised questions about the failure of American military intelligence to anticipate the attack, given the fact that the United States had already broken the Japanese code. The official version laid much of the blame on the army and naval commanders at Pearl Harbor, General Walter Short and Admiral Husband Kimmel, for having taken insufficient precautions when ordered to put their troops on alert the week before the attack. The commanders had interpreted their orders to refer to the possibility of sabotage, not to an air attack. But the critics called attention to the failure of headquarters in Washington to relay intercepted messages to Japanese agents, asking for specific information about the deployment of ships at Pearl Harbor. For most Americans, the notion that the president would put his entire fleet in mortal jeopardy seems to be incredible, particularly since the attack would have resulted in war in any case.

A lesser and, for many, more credible version of the allegation argues that Roosevelt set out to provoke the Japanese into the attack by creating an oil embargo, prohibiting the sale of iron, steel, scrap metal, and other materials to Japan, freezing Japanese funds in the United States, and insisting that Japan withdraw from the territory it had conquered in China. Those rebutting this charge maintain that Japan's aggressive, militaristic government had become a major threat to the entire Pacific area, in addition to being an ally of Hitler. The economic measures Roosevelt had taken against this government were thus entirely justified. Apologists admit that there were serious mistakes made before and during December 7, such as a junior officer's ignoring a critical radar warning. In any case, it does not now appear that either allegation will ever be satisfactorily proven or disproven.

THE LITERATURE

One of the best-known proponents of the Pearl Harbor conspiracy theory is the novelist, playwright, and man of letters Gore Vidal (1925–). His novel *The Golden Age* (2000) covers the period from 1939 to 1954. As early as page 4, one of his characters, speaking of Roosevelt, declares, "He's going to get us into this thing. He thinks he's another Wilson, as if the original wasn't bad enough." The setting is Washington, D.C.; the characters are historical and fictional Washington insiders for whom gossip and rumors are meat and drink. As in his other historical novels, Vidal supplies a rich menu of both. For example, there is here the story that the Republican convention of 1940 has been manipulated by British agents, whose "dirty tricks" include the murder of the Republican in charge of credentials at the convention. The reason is that the next in line for the job was a Wendell Wilkie-supporter; the plot thereby helped to ensure Wilkie's nomination, rather than that of his rival Republican isolationists. Regardless of whether Wilkie or Roosevelt won the election, though, the American government would continue to support aid to Britain and eventual entry into the war.

Another example of the blending of history and fiction comes from the conversation of the fictional character Caroline Sanford, publisher of a major Washington paper, and the historical Harry Hopkins, Roosevelt's highly influential special assistant. Speaking of Japan's intentions before Pearl Harbor, Harry asserts, "We think they'll attack Manila, and if by some miracle they should manage to blow up that horse's ass MacArthur, our cup will truly runneth over." Later, Caroline speaks again to Harry, this time shortly after the attack:

> 'But you knew last night they would attack.'
> 'Attack yes, but not Pearl Harbor. Somewhere. In the southwest Pacific was my guess.'
>
> Caroline knew that every word her friend was telling was being said for the record, for history—for the defense?

Without accepting the author's ideas, one can still enjoy the cleverness and wit of his presentation.

Another view is available in Martin Cruz Smith's (1942–) novel *December 6* (2002). Set in Tokyo, the novel centers on Harry Niles, son of American missionaries in Japan, educated in Japanese schools, but a wild boy who grows up to be quick-witted and cynical. He is the owner of a gin joint, called the Happy Paris, to which everyone seems to flock. The Happy Paris has a beautiful Japanese woman who sits next to the jukebox, moving sinuously to Duke Ellington or Rodgers and Hart tunes. She is Harry's mistress, and she has made it clear that she would rather kill him than let him go. But Harry sees just around the corner the inevitable war that will render him an enemy alien.

Harry is approached by some Japanese school friends looking for information. Always two steps ahead, Harry misleads them into believing that there are oil storage tanks hidden in the hills beyond Pearl Harbor. On December 6, Harry sees General Tojo, Japanese prime minister, in a local park, dressed in tweeds, being photographed for the local newspapers. He guesses that the attack on Pearl Harbor will begin tomorrow. He goes to a friend at the American embassy to give a warning about the imminent attack, but no one believes him. The following day, the Japanese realize that they passed up the oil storage tanks in full view at Pearl Harbor in order to go on a wild goose chase. Harry's trick, and the fact that the American aircraft carriers were away from Pearl Harbor, means that the attack failed. Instead of killing Harry, his Japanese friends commit ritual suicide. As the novel comes to a close, Harry, always the gambler, calculates the odds of his surviving in wartime Japan and thinks he stands a chance.

December 6 does not take a stand on the Pearl Harbor controversy, although it suggests that one should never discount the role of bureaucracy and incompetence in major historical events.

FURTHER READING

Hans Trefousse's *Pearl Harbor: The Continuing Controversy* (1982) offers a concise, judicious introduction to the debate.

PERÓN, EVA (1919–1952)

An illegitimate child never recognized by her father, Maria Eva de Duarte (her maiden name) displayed early on an independent spirit that gave her a reputation for being wild. She came to Buenos Aires as a teenager and established herself as a radio actress when she met Colonel Juan Perón. The couple were married in 1945. A year later he was elected president, and Eva threw herself into the role of first lady, setting up charitable foundations for the poor and the elderly that she personally directed. She also became an outspoken supporter of women's rights.

Quickly she gained the adoration of the common people. Their devotion reached its zenith during Perón's second inauguration in 1949, when millions of *descamisados* ("shirtless ones") marched on the capital to demand that she be named vice president. By the time of her early death from cancer in 1952, she had assumed the status of a saint in the minds of the common people.

According to her biographer Alicia Ortiz, Evita left behind three myths about herself that continue to the present day: The first is the myth of the secular Blessed Mother, the all-loving, compassionate matriarch interceding with the powerful on behalf of her children, the *descamisados*. The second, popular among the Argentine upper classes, is that of the Scheming Whore, who slept her way to the top. Both of these are variations of the virgin/whore dichotomy that is a familiar feature of patriarchal societies, in which women are represented as belonging in one of the two extreme categories, regardless of reality. The third myth is that of the Red Evita, which developed among the generation coming of age in the 1960s. These young radicals enlisted her name on behalf of socialist politics, claiming that the connection to her semi-Fascist husband was an accident of history and a distortion of her true self.

THE LITERATURE

In *Santa Evita* (1995; trans., 1996), Tomás Eloy Martínez plunges with skill and daring into the life, death, and afterlife of Eva Perón. Martínez chooses a difficult path, opting not to de-mythologize Evita, but, if anything, to add to her legend, while never losing the worldly, ironic tone that pervaded his fictional treatment of JUAN PERÓN in *The Perón Novel*. After Eva's death in 1952, Perón had her body embalmed and put on public display, thus reinforcing the popular view among the poor and working class that she was a saint. Crowds flocked to pray before her casket. When the military cadre overthrew Perón in 1955, they faced in Eva's corpse a daunting symbolic enemy. As one official in the novel puts it, "That woman is more dangerous dead than she was alive." The government assigns Colonel Moori Koenig of the intelligence corps to dispose of the corpse. The first thing he learns is that there are not one but four "corpses"—the original and three identical plastic copies. The colonel, a ruthless rationalist, undeterred by the unforeseen, devises a plan to eliminate all four simultaneously. In a series of absurd, irrational accidents, in which a mysterious group called the Commando of Vengeance plays a menacing role, the plan goes haywire, and the colonel finds himself storing the real corpse in his office. Inexorably, he develops a passionate obsession with the dead body. When he is transferred to Germany, he arranges to have the corpse smuggled abroad. It becomes clear that the colonel is losing his mind. Shortly before his death, while watching the moon landings on television, he becomes convinced that the astronauts are burying Evita's coffin on the moon.

The colonel joins a long list of those who come under the spell of Evita, not the least of whom is the author himself. At various points in the novel, Martínez injects himself as author/narrator, relating his strenuous research efforts and his growing involvement with the mythic Evita as he attempts to pluck out the heart of her mystery. In the course of this effort, he relates his frustrated, near despairing, virtually religious awe, when he discovers, but does not reveal to the reader, the "truth." And what might that be? Has Martínez elevated magic realism to a new level, or is there something really miraculous about her corpse—is the *Santa* in *Santa Evita* quite literally the case? In his review of the novel, the Peruvian writer Mario Vargas Llosa (1936–) testifies to the dilemma in which the novel places the typical "enlightened" reader: "[I]n the course of reading, I picked up bad habits and betrayed my most liberal principles. . . . *Santa Evita* should be banned . . . or read without delay."

FURTHER READING

Eva Perón (1995; trans., 1996) by Alicia Ortiz is a balanced, comprehensive biography.

PERÓN, JUAN (1895–1974)

Educated at a military school, Perón received a commission in the army in 1914. In 1930, he was appointed professor of military history at the Argentine Staff College. In the late 1930s, he visited Italy in order to observe the operations of Benito Mussolini's government. He came away deeply impressed by the efficiency and popular appeal of Italian FASCISM. In 1943, he played a key role in an army coup that overthrew the existing government. His reward was the appointment as secretary of labor in 1944, the year in which he met his future wife, EVA PERÓN. Together Juan and Eva built a strong constituency within organized labor, which formed the core of his victorious campaign for the presidency in 1946. During his first term, his policies in support of the urban working class and domestic industries at the expense of the landowning aristocrats, reinforced by Eva's powerful personal appeal, led to an overwhelming victory in the 1951 election. However, in the following year, Eva Perón died of cancer, and Perón's policies became increasingly arbitrary and ineffective. Ousted by a military coup in 1955, he moved to Spain, where he lived for the next 18 years. But the Peronist party soldiered on in his absence. In 1973, after a period filled with social and economic crises, the Peronists were victorious in the national election, and the aged dictator returned to power. Within a year of his return, he died and was succeeded by his third wife, Isabelita, whose indecisive and incompetent regime led to another military coup in 1976.

THE LITERATURE

Tomás Eloy Martínez's (1934) *The Perón Novel* (1985; trans., 1987) is a sophisticated, ironic portrait of the man whose stature as a mythical figure was eclipsed only by that of his wife. But whereas time has enhanced the Eva Perón myth, it has eroded the stature of her husband. The novel opens and concludes on January 20, 1973, the day that marks Perón's return to power. The plane from Spain bearing Perón, his wife Isabelita, his powerful, devious secretary, José López Rega, and assorted members of their retinue is kept in a holding pattern over the Buenos Aires airport, caused by a shoot-out between the old-guard Peronists and the revolutionary-minded Peronist Youth. The decision to land at an alternative airport comes not from Perón, now a confused, weary 77-year-old man, but from López Rega. The story then opens up, moving back in time from the memoirs that the old general is dictating to López Rega to the investigations of Perón's past by a journalist to the activities of Perón's humble followers to the opponents of Perón's return. What emerges is a picture of a politician gradually assuming the role of dictator, modeled on the career of Mussolini (without making Mussolini's mistake in becoming embroiled in major wars). The result is a book in which facts intermingle with fiction and, on occasion, with fantasy to deliver a portrait of a man who could and should have been much better than he was.

FURTHER READING

Joseph Page's *Perón: A Biography* (1984) offers a careful analysis of the general's career.

PIUS XII (1876–1958)

Born Eugenio Pacelli in Rome, he was ordained a priest in 1899 and shortly after became a member of the Vatican diplomatic corps. He served as papal nuncio to Bavaria in 1919 during the short-lived Communist takeover of the government there. At one point members of the Bavarian Red Guard burst into his office, threatening him at gunpoint. The incident added to his conviction that the greatest danger to the Catholic Church and to the world in the 20th century was communism. In 1920 he was appointed Papal Nuncio to Germany and in 1933 arranged the concordat between the church and Adolf HITLER's National Socialist (Nazi) government, in which the Nazi government permitted the practice of Catholicism in exchange for the church's non-involvement in political matters. Elected pope in 1939, he led the church throughout WORLD WAR II.

After the war, he was severely criticized for not speaking out against the persecution of the Jews. Pius's defenders point out that in his Christmas address in 1942, he alluded to "those who, without any fault of their own, sometimes only by reason of their nationality or race, are marked down for death or gradual extinction." But, as the Catholic writer Garry Wills has pointed out, the address makes no specific mention of Jews or Germany.

THE LITERATURE

One of the most controversial plays of the 20th century is *The Deputy* (1963; trans., 1964) by the German playwright Rolf Hochhuth (1931–). *The Deputy* focuses on Pius XII's failure to condemn publicly the Nazi genocide of the Jews. Productions of the play in Europe and the United States set off a storm of protest and defense. When the *New York Times Book Review*, in a front-page article, treated the published version of the play in 1964, it ran two reviews side by side, "a Catholic and non-Catholic" response.

Written in the traditional style of a German tragedy, the play uses blank verse. As written, the play is extremely long—more than six hours playing time—so that all productions have been selective adaptations. Its chief character is Father Riccardo Fontana, a Jesuit priest, a member of a prominent Italian family, and a member of the Vatican diplomatic corps. He joins forces with an SS (Schutzstaffel) officer, Kurt Gerstein, to pressure the Pope to condemn the Nazi extermination of the Jews, which by the time of the play, 1942, was well known in the Vatican.

The key controversial scene occurs in Act 4. Set in the Vatican in 1943, the scene begins with the pope expressing his concern over the possible bombing of Rome. Confronted with a report of Fontana's behavior on behalf of the Jews, the Pope states his view: "Whoever wants to help must not provoke Hitler / Secretly . . . silently, cunning as serpents / that is how the SS must be met." Summoned to Pius's presence, Fontana passionately petitions the pope to speak out even as Italian Jews are being rounded up beneath the windows of the Vatican. The pope's response is less that of a priest than of a seasoned diplomat. He enumerates the reasons why he has chosen not to condemn the Nazi atrocities or the HOLOCAUST. The principal reason is that he wishes the Vatican to preserve a neutral image, enabling it to serve as the mediator of a future peace treaty, the possibility of which has already been seriously damaged by the Allied insistence on "unconditional surrender." If Franklin Delano ROOSEVELT and Winston Churchill insist on taking this hard-line position, Pius maintains, we will witness a postwar world in which a victorious Soviet Union menaces the whole of Europe. In the pope's view, Hitler, as terrible as he is, is the lesser of two evils.

Then, appearing to change his mind, Pius begins to dictate a proclamation condemning the deportation of Italian Jews, which is going on at that moment. But the proclamation contains nothing but intentionally vague, empty, diplomatic language, containing no direct references to Jews. As the dictation proceeds, Fontana takes out a yellow star, pins it to his cassock, and exits, declaring, "God shall not destroy His Church / only because a Pope shrinks from His summons." Act 5 takes place in AUSCHWITZ, where Fontana has joined a shipment of Italian Jews, as the "representative of the Church." Here he meets "the Doctor," modeled on the notorious Dr. Josef MENGELE, who conducted experiments on the inmates while maintaining his smooth, likable demeanor. Hochhuth describes him as representing "Absolute Evil." In a debate with Fontana, the doctor argues that the pope's silence is merely the symbol of a greater void, God's silence. Thus Act 5 bears the title, "Auschwitz, or Where Are You, God?"

In a long historical supplement, "Sidelights on History," Hochhuth maintains that the pope's intervention might have at least inhibited the Nazis or saved the lives of the Italian Jews being deported in 1943. Defenders of Pius argue that it is equally probable that condemnation would have unleashed even more bloodletting, onto both Jews and Catholics. What is clear is that the pope, for a variety of motives, chose to appease Hitler, just as the English and French governments had in the era of the MUNICH PACT.

Critics have on the whole found serious problems with *The Deputy* as an example of dramatic art, particularly the hasty, opportunistic, American production in 1964. But all agree that it addresses a serious moral question boldly and powerfully.

FURTHER READING

Garry Wills' *Papal Sin* (2000) takes a critical view of Pius XII. *The Storm over The Deputy*, edited by Eric Bentley (1964), is an excellent selection of essays on the play by drama reviewers, historians, literary critics, and philosophers.

PROHIBITION (1919–1933)

The Eighteenth Amendment to the U. S. Constitution made the production, distribution, and consumption of alcoholic beverages a federal crime. The crusade against alcohol began in the 19th century, spearheaded by the Women's Christian Temperance Union and the Anti-Saloon League, and it gained momentum in the first decade of the 20th century, when the Progressive movement adopted it as a plank in their platform. Aside from those who supported Prohibition for religious or moral reasons, there were some powerful people with less altruistic motives. Henry Ford, Andrew Carneigie, and other industrial leaders were convinced that it would increase worker productivity. The amendment was submitted for ratification by the states (a two-thirds majority being necessary), which was secured by 1919. Congress then passed the Volstead Act, designed to ensure enforcement of the new law.

The amendment proved to verify the proverb that the road to Hell is paved with good intentions. Instead of producing an abstemious, religious, and sober society, Prohibition fostered a lack of respect for law and created an angry divide between the citizens of large urban areas and those in small towns. More important, it abetted one of 20th-century America's most unfortunate developments, organized crime. From the very beginning, gangsters were conscious of the potential profits to be reaped from smuggling or manufacturing liquor. Smugglers had little fear of capture since they were operating on coastlines thousands of miles long. In addition to the imported variety of liquor, there was also the homegrown version, bathtub gin. Speakeasies sprang up everywhere, featuring not just liquor, but the equally intoxicating new musical form known as jazz. The reaction to Prohibition produced a wide range of social and cultural changes, summarized in the term *JAZZ AGE*.

THE LITERATURE

Smuggling liquor during Prohibition is the central subject of *The Devil Is Loose!* (1984; trans., 1987), a richly comic novel by the French-Canadian writer Antonine Maillet (1929–   ). Set in Acadia, on Canada's eastern seaboard, the story focuses on a legendary figure—the novel is told as a piece of local folklore handed down from one generation to another—of Crache-à-Pic ("Spit in your Eye"), "a long-legged girl with a turned-up nose, a mane of windswept blonde hair, and a pair of blue eyes that would take your breath away." Restoring and reclaiming an old wreck of a schooner, *The Sea-Cow*, she, along with a truly motley crew, plunges into the smuggling business. She soon proves to be the bête noire of the chief smuggler in the area, Dieudonne, outwitting him at every turn. In a series of episodes that include hijacking a Dieudonne shipment of wine and cognac destined for the island retreat of the president of the United States and disguising herself as a nun in order to cross the border, Crache-à-Pic soon wins over the local population as a champion of the underdog.

She meets her match, however, when the handsome, clever Quicksilver arrives in the village as the new constable. The two engage in a battle of wits that barely conceals their strong attraction for each other. Although the quarreling lovers appear to be headed for the predictable romantic ending, fate takes a different turn. Dieudonne is at sea, awaiting a rendezvous with Al Capone's men, when he sees bearing down on him *The Sea-Cow*. Thinking Crache-à-Pic is at the helm, he fires a shot that kills Quicksilver, who has commandeered the schooner in order to arrest the smuggler. The rest of the novel is devoted to Dieudonne's farcical trial, where the anarchic, opinionated population forces the frustrated judge to declare a mistrial. But Crache-à-Pic finds another way of bringing Dieudonne to justice. In the end, in the best tradition of folklore, Crache-à-Pic brings blessings to her native village. The narrator's concern is an accurate representation of Prohibition, as a time "when our mothers and fathers, denied drink by the laws of man, had to appeal to God, who raised up for them, among the marsh weeds and the dune hay, a bold and joyful race of smugglers."

FURTHER READING

Frederick Lewis Allen's classic account of the 1920s, *Only Yesterday* (1931), includes a vivid picture of Prohibition.

PSYCHOANALYSIS

Originally a method of treating mental disorders derived from the theory and practice of Sigmund Freud (1856–1939), psychoanalysis precipitated a mode of thinking about human behavior and motives that had a profound effect on the culture and thought of the 20th century. Among the powerful ideas that Freud generated was the concept of the unconscious, the theory that a major portion of the human psyche lies hidden from the conscious mind. The mind in its totality, according to Freud, is divided into three major areas: the "ego," the rational, though partly unconscious, governing principle; the "id," the force of instinctive energy; and the "superego," another unconscious element, the censoring voice of parent and society. The task of psychoanalysis, according to Freud, is "to strengthen the ego, make it more independent of the superego . . . and so to extend [the ego's] organization [so] that it can take over new portions of the id. Where id was, there shall ego be." A central concept in classical psychoanalysis revolves around the Oedipal conflict, the theory that at a certain stage of infancy, very young children experience an intense love for the parent of the opposite sex and a consequent hatred and fear of the other parent, whom they view as a rival. The Oedipal conflict is a prime example of repressed material, unwanted memories that have been excluded from the conscious mind.

In treatment, psychoanalysts frequently rely on clues in a patient's free associations, slips of the tongue, and, particularly, dreams. In this process, the analyst anticipates and frequently receives resistance from the patient.

THE LITERATURE

Italo Svevo, the pen name of Ettore Schmitz (1861–1928), was a native of Trieste at a time when that city was a part of the Austro-Hungarian Empire. In the 1890s, Svevo published two novels, both of which were ignored by critics and the general public. As a result, he gave up writing and entered his father-in-law's paint business. In 1907, he hired the young émigré James Joyce to tutor him in English. The two showed each other their writing. Spurred on by Joyce's encouragement, Svevo began writing again during WORLD WAR I. The novel that resulted, *The Confessions of Zeno* (1923; trans., 1930), which Joyce helped publicize, created a great stir in literary circles, and Svevo began work on a sequel, incomplete at the time of his death in an automobile accident in 1928. *The Confessions of Zeno*, newly translated under the title *Zeno's Conscience* (2002), stands as the first psychoanalytical novel. The bulk of the novel takes the form of the memories of a patient, Zeno Cosini, a well-to-do, middle-aged married man. Written at the request of his psychiatrist, just prior to Zeno's entering analysis, the memoir opens with an account of Zeno's lifelong attempts to give up smoking. His failed technique consists of designating the date of a "last cigarette." The wall of his room is covered with dates commemorating his failed attempts to quit. The problem is that the "last cigarette" tastes too good, since while smoking it the pleasure is enhanced by the "sense of victory over oneself and the sure hope of health and strength in the immediate future." As a result, although he could give up smoking, he could never give up the pleasure of the "last cigarette." It is clear that, like his namesake, the Greek philosopher Zeno of Elea (495–430 BCE), he is a master of the paradox.

Zeno proceeds in his memoir to recount the death of his father, his lack of fidelity to his wife and how (another paradox) this has strengthened his marriage, and his business partnership with his rival, Guido, who seemed superior in all things and turns out to be a pathetic loser. The final chapter, dealing with the analysis itself, begins a year later, shortly after the start of World War I. Zeno begins by asserting that much of what he has written in the earlier chapters is untrue: "But invention is a creative act, not merely a lie." While in therapy, he recovers different, dreamlike visions of the past, but his therapist casts everything, as he claims, within "the grand conceit that allows him to group all the phenomena of the world around his theory. . . . I was in love with my mother and wanted to murder my father." Zeno rejects psychoanalysis as a "stupid illusion, a foolish trick." He goes back to being a businessman, profiting from the conditions created by the war.

There are at least two levels of irony (or paradox) at work in his account of psychoanalysis. On the one hand, the narrator repudiates the practice as a fraud and waste of time; on the other, we see the impact of therapy on his behavior. But in the final view, the author abandons paradox and asserts directly that "we need something more than psychoanalysis to help us," for the law of nature has been replaced by the law of the machine. The result, in this often comic, but very disturbing, novel is a painfully recognizable prophecy of nuclear disaster:

> [A] man . . . will invent an explosive of such potency that all the explosives in existence will seem like toys beside it. And another man . . . will steal that explosive and crawl to the center of the earth with it, and place it just where he calculates it would have the maximum effect. There will be a tremendous explosion, but no one will hear it and the earth will return to its nebulous state and go wandering through the sky, free at last of parasites and disease.

This strange, apocalyptic vision suggests a profound pessimism, not simply about the efficacy of psychoanalysis, but about human destiny.

Part 3 of D. M. Thomas's *The White Hotel* (1980) takes the form of a case history "Frau Anna G.," written by Sigmund Freud. For a discussion of this novel, see BABI YAR.

FURTHER READING
B. A. Farrell's *The Standing of Psychoanalysis* (1981) considers the current status of the practice. P. N. Furbank's *Italo Svevo: The Man and the Writer* (1966) is an admirable critical and biographical study.

PURE FOOD AND DRUG LAWS (1906)

Responding to the growing public furor over revelations of unsanitary food and dangerous medicines, the U.S. Congress passed the Pure Food and Drug and the Meat Inspection Acts. The laws attempted to safeguard the public from the machinations of the so-called Beef Trust, the large meatpacking companies centered in Chicago, and of the various patent medicine companies whose products contained significant amounts of alcohol or drugs, such as cocaine and laudanum. Public outrage had been fueled by the discovery that during the Spanish American War, more American soldiers had died from eating diseased, canned beef than had been killed in battle. Nevertheless the food industries made strenuous efforts to suppress the bill. They might have succeeded were it not for the publication in February 1906 of Upton Sinclair's novel *The Jungle*.

THE LITERATURE

The protagonist of *The Jungle* is Jurgis Rudkus, who, with his wife Ona and 10 relatives, emigrates from Lithuania, lured by the promise of freedom and economic opportunity. Fired with optimism and the desire to work, he finds a job in Packingtown, Chicago's stockyard district. The working conditions are brutal and dangerous, but Jurgis's tenacious willingness to "work harder" enables him to overcome one hardship after another. However, the accumulation of additional tragic developments, culminating in the deaths of his wife and child, causes him to succumb to the cynical, self-interested world around him. He passes through a number of jobs that leave him increasingly alienated until, finally, he regains his faith in humankind by becoming a militant socialist.

Despite the enormous success of the book, the reaction disappointed the author. Sinclair (1878–1968) felt that the book's socialist theme had been overwhelmed by the graphic descriptions of the meat packing industry: "I aimed at the public's heart, and by accident I hit it in the stomach." In fact, it is generally acknowledged that the weakest part of the novel from a literary standpoint is in the socialist redemption of its hero. *The Jungle* marked the beginning of Sinclair's career as a prolific, indefatigable advocate for social justice (see SACCO-VANZETTI TRIAL).

FURTHER READING

For a discussion of the legislation, see Sean Cashman's *America in the Age of the Titans* (1988).

R

ROOSEVELT, FRANKLIN DELANO (1882–1945)

The 32nd president, who held the office longer than anyone else (1933–45), Roosevelt guided the country through two critical periods, the GREAT DEPRESSION and WORLD WAR II.

A member of a prominent New York Family, he was the fifth cousin of President Theodore Roosevelt. Early on FDR showed a taste for politics and government. He served as undersecretary of the navy in the administration of Woodrow Wilson, whom he used as a model for his own career. In 1921, he contracted poliomyelitis, which left his legs paralyzed, but he learned to artfully disguise this fact when in public. In 1928, he was elected governor of New York, and four years later he ran for president on a platform that promised a "New Deal" for the American people. Elected in 1932, he took office when the country was at the lowest point of the Great Depression. With enormous vigor, he set about realizing the New Deal in concrete programs. He created a number of "alphabet agencies" (including the Works Progress Administration [WPA], the Tennessee Valley Authority [TVA], and the Federal Deposit Insurance Corporation [FDIC]) designed to create jobs and instill confidence in the economy. His administration strengthened the banking system, provided relief to farmers and the unemployed, established the Social Security system, encouraged the growth of labor unions, and provided federal loans for businesses.

Despite conservative critics who deplored his activist government as "creeping socialism," his popularity was such that he was reelected in 1936 by the greatest majority in American history. But for all his efforts, the effects of the depression lingered on until the end of the decade. The economy finally rebounded with the onset of World War II, putting the country to work on a wartime basis, supplying aid to Great Britain and the Soviet Union, and building up American military strength in the event of war. War came on December 7, 1941, with the Japanese attack on PEARL HARBOR, an attack that, in the view of some historians, FDR provoked and may have had prior knowledge of.

Although suffering from continuously failing health, he proved to be an effective wartime leader, using his considerable gifts as a communicator to uphold the morale of both the military and civilian populations. He died on the eve of victory in April 1945, mourned by most of the country as a source of inspiration. In this respect he was equaled by his wife, Eleanor Roosevelt (1884–1962), an articulate, idealistic, and tireless defender of the downtrodden. Her outspoken liberal views, particularly her support of African Americans, made her a highly controversial but very effective first lady who later served as the United States ambassador to the United Nations.

THE LITERATURE

Dore Schary's (1905–80) play *Sunrise at Campobello* (1958) is the moving drama of FDR's three-year struggle to overcome the crippling effects of polio and to reenter the political arena as a viable candidate. The play opens on August 10, 1921, in the Roosevelt summer home at Campobello, New Brunswick, Canada. After a strenuous day sailing and swimming with his children, FDR feels a sudden pain. When we next see him, he is being carried out to an ambulance. The two scenes of Act 2 take place in 1922 and 1923. FDR, confined to a wheelchair, resolves to make a mark in the world, despite his permanently crippled legs, over the objection of his formidable mother, Sara, but with the encouragement of his wife, Eleanor, and his devoted aide, Louis Howe. The third act takes place in 1924. At the Democratic Convention, FDR prepares to give the nominating speech for Al Smith, the speech that marked his return to political life. As the curtain comes down, FDR, the braces on his legs buried beneath his trousers, moves to the platform.

Sunrise at Campobello does not set out to be a major play probing the depths of its characters. Its ambition is modest: to give an account of a man overcoming an ordeal and in the process developing the strength of character that played a key role in his extraordinary success as a world leader. In this it succeeds. It is a poignant and often humorous drama that pays its subject the tribute that is his due. In 1960, the play was made into a successful film, directed by Vincent Donehue.

Jerome Charyn's (1937–   ) *The Franklin Scare* (1977) provides a somewhat humorous and affectionate portrait of FDR in his last year, seen from the perspective of Oliver Beebe, a young navy barber, who becomes the president's personal barber and the guardian of the president's dog Fala. The year is 1944 and the ailing president is running for reelection. FDR comes increasingly to rely on this simple, direct, totally loyal figure. Beebe's "insider status" is a source of concern to the Secret Service, whose investigation of him reveals certain dubious facts, but it has little impact on the relationship between the two men. The sailor accompanies the "boss" on his trip to the Yalta Conference, where Beebe has a humorous exchange with Joseph STALIN, but where the growing weakness of the president is painfully obvious. Beebe is also present at FDR's death in Warm Springs. Under Beebe's influence, FDR exudes a simple warmth that may or may not have had some factual basis, but that as fiction is credible, since it skirts, but never lapses into, sentimentality.

FURTHER READING

James MacGregor Burns's *Roosevelt: The Lion and the Fox* (1956) is a classic analysis of FDR as a leader.

ROSENBERG CASE

In 1950, Julius Rosenberg, his wife, Ethel, and her brother, army sergeant David Greenglass, were arrested in New York City, charged with having transmitted secret military information to the Soviet Union. Their arrests followed the arrest in England of Klaus Fuchs, an English physicist who had worked on the development of the atomic bomb in Los Alamos (see MAN-HATTAN PROJECT) and that of a Philadelphia chemist, Harry Gold. Both Fuchs and Sergeant Greenglass had passed on atomic secrets to Gold, a courier, who in turn transmitted them to the Soviets. Greenglass testified that his brother-in-law had persuaded him to steal the secrets. On the strength of the testimony of Greenglass and his wife, the Rosenbergs were found guilty and sentenced to death. They appealed to the Supreme Court, but the appeal was denied. The death sentence created an international outcry, similar to the reaction 30 years earlier to the SACCO-VANZETTI TRIAL. Despite appeals on their behalf, the Rosenbergs were executed on June 19, 1953, a time when the spirit of MCCARTHYISM was at its zenith. Although it is now generally accepted that Julius Rosenberg was guilty of spying and that Ethel knew of his activities, it is equally true that the death penalty, particularly for Ethel, was an extreme punishment, inextricably involved in the politics of the period. A measure of the severity of the sentence is evident in the sentences of the two spies who actually stole the secrets: Fuchs served 14 years in prison, while Greenglass was sentenced to 15 years.

THE LITERATURE

In E. L. Doctorow's (1931–) *The Book of Daniel* (1971), Daniel Isaccson Lewin, whose parents were executed as spies in 1954, is a graduate student at

Columbia University. The time is 1967, when the campus protest movement is nearing its peak. Rather than working to complete his doctoral dissertation in his library carrel, Daniel attempts to quell his inner rage over the fate of both his parents and his younger sister, now suffering from mental illness, by trying to discover the truth about the case. After reading all the books and available records on the trial, he interviews the widow of his parents' defense attorney and his foster parents. Descriptions of the interviews are interspersed with his childhood experiences before and during his parents' imprisonment and execution. Another narrative feature of the novel are short accounts of the cultural and political atmosphere of the early 1950s. Near the end of the novel, Daniel flies to California to interview Selig Mindish, the friend of his parents, whose testimony convicted them. He meets Mindish in Disneyland, but the old man, completely senile, can only respond to Daniel by kissing him.

Daniel concludes his account with the death of his sister. As he finishes his story, student rebels invade the library to "liberate" it. This final ironic note is consistent with the bitter, angry tone of the novel, but it also suggests an underlying conflict within Daniel about his parents' political commitment and the price that he and his sister paid for it.

Millicent Dillon's (1925–) *Harry Gold: A Novel* (2000) focuses on the courier who transmitted the information and, to a lesser extent, on Fuchs. The eldest child of poor Russian-Jewish immigrants, Harry Gold comes of age in the GREAT DEPRESSION. Although he excelled in science, he has to go to work right after high school to support his parents and siblings. Eventually he attends college in the evening, graduating from Xavier University with a degree in chemical engineering. Like many people suffering in the depths of the depression, he concludes that capitalism is in its death throes and communism the best hope for a more equitable society. But he has no use for the Communist Party—he never joins it—with its endless wrangling and hairsplitting, theoretical discussions.

As presented in the novel, Harry is a simple man, whose principal motive for spying is a desire to help the people of Russia, like his parents. He is a man doing the wrong thing for the right reasons, a man with a very weak sense of self-esteem, thus easily persuaded to do someone else's bidding. As a recruiter of other spies, he is clumsy and inept, but he is somewhat more effective as a courier, although he comes to hate the drab, boring, lonely life it generates. His dislike changes somewhat when he is assigned to Klaus Fuchs, for whom he has immense respect as a distinguished physicist and refugee from Nazi Germany. But the meetings with Fuchs are very few, though important.

When the news of the arrest of Klaus Fuchs breaks, Harry assumes that his days are numbered. Offered the opportunity to escape to the Soviet Union, he realizes that he is an American at heart. Interviewed by the Federal Bureau of Investigation (FBI), and stalling for one or two sessions, he suddenly confesses, finally unburdening himself of his secret life and the guilt it engendered. At his trial, his behavior impresses his lawyer, John D. Hamilton, who, in his summary, describes Gold as "the most extraordinarily selfless person I have ever met in my life." Gold finds both peace and purpose in prison, where he trains other inmates as medical technicians and performs original chemical research for the U.S. Health Service. Paroled in 1966, he becomes chief biochemist at Philadelphia's John F. KENNEDY Memorial Hospital, where he serves until his death in 1972.

As a fictional character, Harry bears a resemblance to another spy, the protagonist of Maxim Gorky's (1868–1956) *The Life of a Useless Man* (see RUSSIAN REVOLUTION [1905]). But Millicent Dillon approaches her subject with more compassion than Gorky. She imagines an inner life for Harry that strikes a sympathetic but entirely unsentimental note. The result is a painful and moving story of a man in search of a cause larger than his own self-interest, who in deceiving others never deceives himself. He looks at his motives in a ruthlessly unsparing light: "He had done what he had done because at his core was a being, hard, sharp, demanding, and willful." Ironically, the feature of Harry the spy that stands out most prominently in the novel is his honesty.

The Rosenberg case plays a significant role in Robert Coover's *The Public Burning* (see NIXON, RICHARD M.).

FURTHER READING

Ronald Radosh and Joyce Milton's *The Rosenberg File* (1983), based upon government files and scores of interviews, concludes that Julius Rosenberg was in fact a Soviet spy and that Ethel was aware of her husband's activities but not directly involved. The authors also argue that it was in the interest of the FBI, the KGB, and some supporters of the couple to see the Rosenbergs executed: "[W]hile the Rosenbergs were not the victims of a frame-up, they were the hapless scapegoats of a propaganda war."

RUSSIAN CIVIL WAR (1918–1921)

In the wake of the RUSSIAN REVOLUTION, the new Communist government sued for peace with Germany. The terms they were forced to accept in the Treaty of Brest Litovsk (March 3, 1918) were so unfavorable that many of the moderate groups joined with the pro-czar factions to overthrow the Bolshevik regime. Operating in the provinces, particularly in Siberia, the Ural Mountains, the Ukraine, and the region near the Don River in South Russia, the anti-Bolsheviks constituted a formidable enemy. Among their ranks were a group of 40,000 Czech former prisoners of war who opted not to return to the Austro-Hungarian army in which they had unwillingly served. They agreed to fight against the Bolshevik regime in exchange for the promise of Czech independence after the war. This group effectively tied up the Trans-Siberian railroad and inspired other dissident groups to rebel.

Added to these enemies were the European Allies, who viewed the Soviet capitulation to Germany as a betrayal. In 1918, an Allied force that included British, French, and American troops landed at the port of Murmansk, a vital seaport that the Allies wanted to secure from a potential German takeover. But the Russian anti-Bolshevik forces, known as the "White Guard" (as opposed to the Communist "Red Guard"), lacked a unifying central control and lost a number of key battles. The Allied force withdrew in 1919, and by 1921 the war was over, the reign of Vladimir Ilich LENIN firmly established, the reign of Joseph STALIN a specter on the horizon.

THE LITERATURE

The First Cavalry Army, under the leadership of General Semyon Budenny, played a crucial role in the Red Guard victories in the civil war and in the unsuccessful invasion of Poland in 1920. Among these rough-riding Cossacks, notorious for their anti-Semitism, was a bespectacled Jewish writer and intellectual, Isaac Babel (1894–1941), who served as an information officer, disseminating propaganda among the cavalrymen, most of them proudly illiterate. Babel used his war experiences as the basis of a collection of acutely ironic short stories, some of them brief anecdotes, published in 1926 (trans., 1929) under the title *Red Cavalry*. Most of the stories are narrated by Lyutov, a stand-in for the author, who records his ambivalent feelings, a mixture of attraction and repulsion, for his comrades-in-arms, men for whom violence and death were the ordinary stuff of life. His ambivalence is caught in the story "My First Goose." The newly assigned Lyutov is treated with disrespect by the Cossacks, and, as a result, by the landlady of the house where they are billeted. Frustrated, he takes a sword, kills her pet goose, and orders her to cook it for him. Immediately, his comrades welcome him as a real man. That night he has erotic dreams, "But my heart, stained with bloodshed, grated and brimmed over." Such an ironic cast of mind could never survive Stalin's GREAT TERROR of the 1930s. In 1939, Babel was arrested; in 1941, while still in prison, he died, according to the official report, "of unspecified causes."

The publication of the English-language edition of Boris Pasternak's (1890–1960) *Doctor Zhivago* in 1958 was the major literary event of that year. The novel had been banned in the Soviet Union and denounced by Communist officials for exhibiting a "spirit of non-acceptance of the socialist revolution." When Pasternak was awarded the Nobel Prize in 1958, he was forced to turn it down. Thus the English edition actually preceded the Russian original. The latter did not appear until 1992, after the fall of the Soviet Union, at which time Russian readers expressed amazement that such a non-political book could ever have been banned.

The central figure of the novel is Yuri Zhivago, a physician and poet. Orphaned at an early age, he is brought up by a benevolent university professor, Alexander Gromeko, and his wife, Anna. On completing his medical studies, he marries Tonia, the daughter of the Gromekos. Called out on an emergency one evening, he encounters a mysterious young woman, Lara, to whom he is drawn but does not pursue. When the First World War breaks out, he joins a medical unit at the front, where he is wounded. He wakes to find that his nurse is Lara; upon his recovery, the two work closely together. With the war's end, they separate, and Yuri returns to his wife and child in Moscow, only to find that the revolution has made life there intolerable.

With his family, he retreats, on an extraordinary train ride that is one of the highlights of the novel, to an old family summer house in the Ural Mountains bordering Siberia. There he discovers Lara living in a nearby village. They begin a passionate, secret affair that is interrupted when he is forcibly conscripted into a Red Guard brigade as its medical officer. This section of the novel deals with the civil war directly. The area in which Yuri's brigade operates is controlled by the Whites, forcing the partisans, as the Red forces are known locally, into constant movement, alternately attacking and retreating. Although sympathetic to the aims of the Red forces, Yuri sees the war itself as undisguised barbarism on both sides. Eventually he deserts, discovers that his family has been deported, and returns to Lara. The two experience an idyllic retreat from the world, while Yuri writes the beautiful poems that are appended to the novel. But the couple is forced to separate in order to save Lara's life. Yuri returns to Moscow a broken man, eventually dying of a heart attack.

The real significance of *Doctor Zhivago* lies neither in its plot nor in the fate of its characters. As the first of Zhivago's poems ("Hamlet") suggests, tragedy is the novel's mode of existence, one in which the time is profoundly "out of joint." *Doctor Zhivago* is, as the philosopher Stuart Hampshire notes, a philosophical novel, testifying to the triumph of the inner experience of the individual, who has wrung from the depths of suffering and pain a transcendent vision of life as rich and meaningful. In this context, the novel ultimately asserts a value that rejects the humanistic impulse lying at the roots of Marxist ideology in favor of a spiritual apprehension of life, caught in Lara's recollection of their love as she mourns Yuri's death:

> Never . . . were they unaware of a sublime joy in the universe, a feeling that they . . . were part of the whole, an element in the beauty of the cosmos. This unity of the whole was the breath of life to them. And the elevation of man above the rest of nature, the modern coddling and worshipping of man, never appealed to them. A social system based on such a false premise, as well as its political application, struck them as pathetically amateurish.

Little wonder that the Soviet authorities suppressed this profoundly "nonpolitical" work.

FURTHER READING

Pasternak: A Collection of Critical Essays, edited by Victor Erlich (1978), contains a number of penetrating essays on *Doctor Zhivago* and on Pasternak's poetry.

RUSSIAN REVOLUTION (1905)

At the beginning of the 20th century, the Russian Empire covered a vast land area and boasted the largest army in Europe. But beneath this powerful surface lay seething discontent, nourished by the heavy-handed, autocratic rule of Czar Nicholas II and the emergence of a Marxist intelligentsia determined to shape the urban working class into a revolutionary power base. The Russian defeat in the Russo-Japanese War (1904–05) provided the catalyst for long-standing unrest across a broad spectrum of Russian society. In January 1905, government troops fired on a peaceful workers' demonstration outside the czar's winter palace in St. Petersburg. Bloody Sunday, as it became known, triggered a series of violent protests throughout the empire. Beginning in the large cities, the uprisings soon spread to the rural areas where the long-victimized Russian peasants gave vent to their anger and frustration. In October, the czar appeared to yield to the popular will by promising to create an elected national parliament, the Duma. Eventually government troops suppressed both the urban and rural revolts, but some reforms were instituted. With the establishment of the Duma, it appeared that Russia would be following the path of the Western powers, moving toward a constitutional monarchy. But subsequent events, particularly the onset of WORLD WAR I, would lead Russia to a more radical fate (see RUSSIAN REVOLUTION [1917]).

THE LITERATURE

Joseph Conrad's (1857–1926) *Under Western Eyes* (1911), set in the years immediately prior to the revolution, contrasts the terrorist activities of a revolutionary group to the passionate struggle within an individual "Russian soul." In his preface, the author announces his intention to approach the political struggle with "scrupulous impartiality" and to depict "senseless desperation provoked by senseless tyranny." The story focuses on the dilemma of Razumov, a student at the university in St. Petersburg, who discovers a fellow student hiding in his apartment. The student, Victor Haldin, assuming that Razumov shares his political views, reveals that he has just assassinated a particularly brutal government official and asks Razumov to help him escape. After some initial hesitation, Razumov, resentful of Haldin's presumption and fearful of the authorities, decides to betray his fellow student, who is arrested and killed by the police. Razumov is then forced to become a secret agent for the government, for which purpose he moves to Geneva, the headquarters in exile of the revolutionaries. Filled with loathing, self-contempt, and a nihilistic despair, he is nevertheless admitted into the conspirators' world. There he encounters Haldin's sister, Natalia, with whom he falls in love, which only intensifies his anguish. He finally confesses his guilt to the revolutionaries, is punished and accidentally injured, and ends his life in a wheelchair.

With its emphasis on the tormented inner life of the protagonist, *Under Western Eyes* bears a strong relationship to Fyodor Dostoyevsky's (1821–81) *Crime and Punishment* (1866). Like Dostoyevsky's great work, Conrad's novel offers a masterly psychological and moral analysis of a mind wracked with guilt. Ironically, Conrad saw Dostoyevsky as a powerful but malevolent force: For him, the Russian novelist stood for passion and disorder, for a mysticism inherent in the Russian character that leads to the extremes of czarist autocracy or revolutionary terrorism. Conrad's rejection of both seems to leave a political vacuum, which, in the words of the revolutionary leader in the novel, "can never be bridged by foreign liberalism. . . . Bridged it can never be. It has to be filled up." The one hopeful figure, Natalia, suggests another possibility: "[T]hat the future will be merciful to us all. Revolutionist and reactionary, victim and executioner, betrayer and betrayed, they shall all be pitied when the light breaks on our black sky at last." Whether this represents Conrad's conviction or simply his hope remains an open question.

A novel dealing directly with the revolution is Maxim Gorky's (1868–1936) *The Life of a Useless Man* (1907; trans., 1971). Gorky focuses on one figure, Yevsey Klimkov, a man defeated by life from his earliest years. Orphaned at the age of seven, he is raised by relatives who alternately bully and ignore him, instilling in him a pervasive sense of fear and a desire to be told what to do. As an adult, he is recruited to become a government spy in a provincial city, a task he performs with little initiative and even less effectiveness. When, during the early months of the revolution, he finally does infiltrate a radical group, he betrays them because he has been rejected by a woman in the group. As the revolution develops and appears to succeed, he begins to see the justice of the fight against the government, but he is so overwhelmed with fear that his behavior attracts attention; he is identified and hunted down as a government informer. In his panic, he throws himself under a train, but even in this act he equivocates. Trying at the last second to avoid the train, he shouts the words that summarize his life, "I will do anything you say—I will, I will!"

In his portrait of a "useless man," Gorky appears to be describing those who "lack all conviction," who submit to authority unthinkingly, out of a desire to escape the burden of free choice. Conrad's hero is the more complex figure, being neither slave nor rebel, but a man caught between "senseless desperation" and "senseless tyranny," who in suffering achieves at least a personal salvation.

FURTHER READING

Eloise Knapp Hay's *The Political Novels of Joseph Conrad* (1963) and Avrom Fleishman's *Conrad's Politics* (1967) contain conflicting, but equally admirable, studies of *Under Western Eyes*.

RUSSIAN REVOLUTION (BOLSHEVIK REVOLUTION; OCTOBER REVOLUTION) (1917)

In February 1917, shortages of food, economic hardships, dissatisfaction with Russian military failures in WORLD WAR I, and the persistent refusal of Czar Nicholas II to conciliate his subjects led to angry mobs in the streets of the Russian capital, St. Petersburg, demanding reform. Soon the military garrison stationed in the city joined forces with the revolutionary crowd. In March, Czar Nicholas II agreed to abdicate the throne. Thus Russia ceased to be a monarchy. A provisional government was established under Price Lvov, but the situation grew worse. The army continued to suffer reversals, peasants engaged in open revolt against landlords, and urban workers agitated for control of industry. In July, the Menshevik (that is, moderate socialist) leader Alexander Kerensky became prime minister, but the situation deteriorated further as the Russian army suffered additional setbacks at the hands of their German enemies. Kerensky's vacillation led to an unsuccessful uprising by the Bolsheviks in July. In September, the commander in chief of the Russian military forces, General Lavr Kornilov (1870–1918), attempted a failed coup against the Kerensky government that further divided the army. Kornilov was arrested for treason, thus eliminating the major obstacle to a Bolshevik takeover.

Promising a program of peace, land, and bread, and employing the slogan, "All Power to the Soviets (workers' councils)," the Bolshevik leader Vladimir Ilich LENIN, returning to Russia from exile, launched what became known as the October Revolution, deposing Kerensky and assuming the title of chairman of the Council of People's Commissars. Lenin's Red Guards, commanded by his aide, Leon TROTSKY, occupied key government buildings, railway stations, and telegraph offices in St. Petersburg. In March 1918, the new government, having transferred the capital to Moscow, concluded a peace treaty with Germany, which cost the government heavily both at home and abroad. The discontent at home led to the outbreak of the RUSSIAN CIVIL WAR. In July 1918, Bolshevik guards, on instructions from Moscow, murdered Czar Nicholas II and his entire family. The following month, an unsuccessful assassination attempt on Lenin's life resulted in a campaign of terror carried out by the Cheka, the Bolshevik secret police.

The aim of the revolution was to transform Russian society not simply politically but in every sphere. The revolutionaries set out first to eliminate private property. All deeds of ownership were destroyed. But the power that Lenin had promised to the Soviets, the workers' councils, existed in name only. Actual power was vested in the leadership of the Bolshevik Party, which in 1918 assumed the name *Communist Party*. The long-anticipated Marxist revolution proved to be, consistent with Lenin's revision of the theories of Karl Marx, the triumph of a radical elite whose interests and goals were far removed from the will of the Russian people.

THE LITERATURE

The best-known fictional rendering of the period of the revolution and its aftermath is Mikhail Sholokhov's (1905–84) *And Quiet Flows the Don* (1928–32; trans., 1934), the first part of a two-part novel, set in the Don River area of southwestern Russia. The story focuses on the conflicting loyalties of the local Cossacks at the time of the revolution and during the civil war that followed it. The principal protagonist is Gregor Melekhov, a young Cossack, but this is a panoramic novel, peopled with a broad cast of characters, reminiscent in some respects of Count Lev Nikolayevich Tolstoy's great epic *War and Peace* (1864–69). Indeed, the major subdivisions of Sholokhov's novel bear the titles, *Peace*, *War*, *Revolution*, and *Civil War*. In the first section, set just before World War I, Gregor causes a major scandal within the Cossack village by conducting an affair with a married woman, Aksinia. Gregor and Aksinia leave the village to work on the nearby estate of retired General Listnitsky. Shortly after Aksinia gives birth to a baby girl, Gregor leaves to join the army. While he is gone Aksinia has an affair with Eugene Listnitsky, the son of the general. Home on leave, Gregor discovers the affair and returns to his home in the village, where he is reunited with his wife.

Once war is declared, Gregor, after undergoing a crisis of conscience for having killed a man, becomes an efficient, somewhat hardened warrior. In the revolution section of the novel, the scene shifts to the Cossack regiments' reactions, first to the overthrow of the czar and, later, to the Bolshevik victory. The war has left the army completely demoralized. This is less true of the Cossacks with their proud military tradition, but even here there is trouble, as the Bolsheviks among them foment dissension. In July, Eugene Listnitsky's Cossack regiment is assigned to Petersburg, the capital, to guard government offices. When General Kornilov is appointed commander and chief by Kerensky, Listnitsky's fellow officers vow to support Kornilov in what they anticipate will be an army coup, but in September Kornilov and his conspirators are arrested and imprisoned by the provisional government, paving the way for the successful Bolshevik takeover the following month. Listnitsky's company is ordered to guard the Winter Palace, but once there the men listen to the pleas of a Bolshevik envoy and march away from their posts.

On the front lines, a Cossack regiment, in retreat from the advancing Germans, learns of the successful Bolshevik revolt in Petersburg and immediately entrains to return home to the villages on the Don. Gregor, ambivalent and unclear as to which side to support, becomes an officer in the Red Guard, fights in a losing battle against the White Guard, and retires to his village. When the village is threatened by a Red Guard attack, he joins his fellow villagers to repel the advancing army, but when they arrive at their destination, they find that the Red forces have already been defeated. Although sympathetic to the Bolshevik position, Gregor realizes that his first loyalty is to his region and his identity as a Cossack.

Part 2 of the novel, published in English in 1940 as *The Don Flows Home to the Sea*, recounts the eventual victory of the Red Guard over the Whites, but it does not, as the Soviet government would have wished, conclude with Gregor's conversion to communism. In that respect, the novel does not conform to the doctrine of "socialist realism," the rigid code that transformed most Soviet literature into propaganda. Although in every other respect, throughout his career, Sholokhov was a conforming Stalinist, in *And Quiet Flows the Don* and, to a lesser extent, *The Don Flows Home to Sea*, he was primarily an artist, depicting characters in their full humanity, not as exemplary representations of the peasant or the proletarian. As a result, he brought to his readers in their darkest times the life-affirming spirit of great literature.

Sholokhov's ability to evade the censors is a measure of the enormous popularity the novel enjoyed among its readers, who were starved for genuine literature. Even the title ushers in a consistent, nonsocialist, realist motif throughout the novel, the contrast between nature and human affairs. In the background of cataclysmic events—world war, revolution, civil war—the silent Don flows imperturbably out to sea, a reminder of the grandeur of nature, indifferent to human history. In this respect, Sholokhov's theme resembles that of another great Russian novel, Boris Pasternak's *Doctor Zhivago* (see RUSSIAN CIVIL WAR).

FURTHER READING

Alexander Rabinowitch's *The Bolsheviks Come to Power* (1976) is a detailed, reliable account of the revolution. Harold Shukman's *The Russian Revolution* (1998) offers a readable short history. Edward Brown's *Russian Literature since the Revolution* (1963; revised edition, 1982) is a definitive study of its subject.

S

SACCO-VANZETTI TRIAL

In May 1921, two Italian immigrants, Niccola Sacco and Bartolomeo Vanzetti, were brought to trial for the murders of two employees of the Rice Hutchins Shoe Company during a robbery of the company's payroll in South Braintree, Massachusetts. Both Sacco and Vanzetti were dedicated anarchists at a time when the federal government had made a concerted effort to rid the country of "reds" of any type.

Despite numerous witnesses who testified to the defendants' having been miles away from the scene of the crime, the jury convicted the pair, a verdict that had been strongly implied in the charge it received from Judge Webster Thayer. For the next seven years, the case was appealed, first to Judge Thayer and later to the Massachusetts State and the U.S. Supreme Court. In the meantime the defendants had galvanized support throughout the nation and the world, but despite the efforts of a powerful legal team, the original decision was upheld and the date of execution set for August 22, 1927. Demonstrations involving thousands of people took place throughout the major cities of the world while the two immigrants were electrocuted. Fifty years later, Massachusetts governor Michael Dukakis proclaimed August 22, 1977, as "Sacco-Vanzetti Memorial Day" and described the trial as a miscarriage of justice.

THE LITERATURE

The case has been the source of numerous novels, poems, and plays, almost all of them written to protest the xenophobia, legal corruption, and social injustice underlying the arrest and trials. The earliest of these is Upton Sinclair's (1878–1968) *Boston* (1928). The protagonist of Sinclair's two-volume novel is Cornelia Thornwell, a member of the Boston upper class and, as the novel opens, the recent widow of the former governor of Massachusetts. The death of her husband frees the 60-year-old widow from the triple bonds of a loveless marriage, her mercenary children, and the stifling snobbery of Brahmin Boston. Under an assumed name, she moves into a working-class neighborhood where she meets Bartolomeo Vanzetti, depicted here as a humble, wise, saintly figure, but nonetheless a dedicated anarchist. With Vanzetti's arrest, Cornelia becomes actively involved in the formation of his defense, and consequently her identity is revealed.

The rest of the novel deals with Cornelia's education as she tries to apply the basic ethical principles she has subscribed to all her life to the social-political reality underlying the case. A critical moment occurs when the defense attorney tries to persuade her that she can save Vanzetti if she is willing to perjure herself and testify that he was with her at the time of the robbery. She refuses, but not without a painful self-examination of her motives and values.

Boston is thus an ironic "coming of age" novel chronicling a grandmotherly woman's movement from innocence to knowledge. Cornelia's advanced age enables Sinclair to underscore her symbolic status: She represents 19th-century America coming to grips with the corruption and injustice that had become an inescapable aspect of the nation's growth and power.

Probably the best-known literary use of the case is Maxwell Anderson's (1888–1959) drama *Winterset* (1935), a tragedy in verse describing the efforts of a young man, Mio, to vindicate his father, Romagna, an Italian working man and anarchist, executed for a crime he did not commit. In a desolate urban area beneath a bridge, Mio encounters Judge Gaunt, the conscience-stricken and deranged judge who tried the case; Garth, an accomplice in the original crime who, out of fear, never came forth to testify, and Trock, the actual murderer. He also meets Garth's sister, Miriamne, and the two fall in love. Mio acquires proof not only of his father's innocence but also of the man's idealistic and forgiving nature. In the play's conclusion, both Mio and Miriamne are murdered by Trock.

Anderson's play received the New York Drama Critics' Circle Award for the best play of 1935, which cited "its unusual poetic force, realizing a drama of rich meaning." Subsequent criticism has been less enthusiastic in its judgment of the play's language and characterization. From the perspective of the 21st century, *Winterset* appears to be a well-intentioned period piece, representative of the politically committed literature of the 1930s, but lacking the complexity of character and theme that mark significant drama.

FURTHER READING

Before becoming a U.S. Supreme Court justice, Felix Frankfurter published a judicious, dispassionate analysis of the trial, *The Case of Sacco and Vanzetti* (1927).

SCOPES TRIAL (1925)

In March 1925, the governor of Tennessee signed into law the Butler Act, which specified "that it should be unlawful for any teacher in any of the universities, normals [teachers' colleges], or schools of the State . . . to teach any theory that denies the story of the divine creation of man as taught in the Bible, and to teach instead that man is descended from a lower order of animals." Shortly thereafter, the American Civil Liberties Union (ACLU) announced their intention to support any Tennessee teacher willing to challenge the new law. The ACLU's goal was to bring the case to the state appeals courts or to the U.S. Supreme Court, where they were confident the law would be ruled unconstitutional. Seeing the opportunity to bring publicity and prosperity to their small town, a group of civic leaders in Dayton, Tennessee, prevailed upon John Scopes, the local high-school biology teacher, to test the law by having himself arrested.

No small part of the notoriety of the trial derived from the celebrity of the two lawyers who argued the case. The chief counsel for the prosecution was the famed orator, former secretary of state, and three-time Democratic candidate for president, William Jennings Bryan. Heading the Scopes defense team was Clarence Darrow, the country's best-known defense attorney, fresh from his triumph in the LEOPOLD-LOEB CASE. Billed as the confrontation between fundamentalist religion and godless science, the case attracted international attention under its popular name, the "Monkey Trial." The highlight occurred near the trial's conclusion when the defense called Bryan to the stand as a hostile witness. Darrow's remorseless grilling revealed Bryan's lack of knowledge of science and theological naïveté, after which the defense rested, asking that the jury deliver a guilty verdict, thereby ensuring an appeal. The verdict of guilty resulted in a fine of $100. The appeals court upheld the statute but overturned the conviction, thereby making a further appeal impossible. Neither side had won. In 1967, the Tennessee legislature voted to overturn the Butler Act.

THE LITERATURE

Thirty years after the trial, Jerome Lawrence (1915–   ) and Robert E. Lee's (1918–94) drama *Inherit the Wind* (1955) opened on Broadway. Although the incidents of the play were heavily indebted to the Scopes trial, the authors, in their introduction to the text, were at pains to clarify the distinctions between the play and its source:

> *Inherit the Wind* is not history. The events which took place during the scorching July of 1925 are clearly the genesis of this play. It has, however, an exodus of its own.

Beneath the biblical references of this announcement lies the suggestion that the "exodus" is the mid-1950s, the era of MCCARTHYISM. Like the

Arthur Miller (1915–   ) drama *The Crucible*, which uses the Salem witch-hunts to comment on the near-hysterical congressional hunt for subversives, *Inherit the Wind* emphasized the threat to freedom of speech and thought represented by the Butler Act and its relevance in the McCarthy era.

To underscore their poetic license, the authors gave their characters fictional names that approximate those of the real figures. Thus the Bryan character is called Matthew Harrison Brady, Darrow is Henry Drummond, and Scopes is Bertram Cates. Dayton has become Hillsboro, and the time according to the authors "is not 1925." The stage directions set the time as "Not long ago. It might have been yesterday. It could be tomorrow." Other changes involve the addition of a fictional fiancée for Cates/Scopes to add a romantic interest. But the play's chief departure from the historical record lies in its one-sided melodramatic treatment of the two major characters and the issues they represent. Bryan is represented not simply as wrong but as a menacing figure, his threatening behavior more appropriate to McCarthy; Darrow is not only right but righteous, a selfless crusader, not the sharp and often sharklike lawyer he was.

But as time has passed and the McCarthy threat faded, the play and, to an even greater extent, the 1960 film version directed by Stanley Kramer have fixed in the popular mind an image of the trial that has become part of American folklore, a process that has been intensified by a development the authors never anticipated—the growth of Christian fundamentalism. A significant aspect of this renewal is creationism, the argument that the divine creation of the world and humankind is a scientifically valid hypothesis. Thus there are at least two ironies surrounding the Scopes trial and *Inherit the Wind*: One is that the trial itself was instigated as a commercial proposition, designed to bring prosperity to the town. The second is that many critics of the original production objected to the equation of fundamentalism with McCarthyism as being unfair to the fundamentalists. However, when the play was revived in 1996, critics ignored the McCarthy connection and saw the play as a comment on the increasing power of the "Christian Right." In short, a play designed to use the original issue—religious fundamentalism—in the trial as a metaphor for another issue—McCarthyism—now seems relevant because of the rebirth of interest in the original issue.

FURTHER READING

John Lawson's *Summer for the Gods* (1997) is an even-handed, judicious account that demythologizes both the trial and *Inherit the Wind*.

SCOTTSBORO TRIALS

In 1931, in the town of Scottsboro, Tennessee, nine young African-American men were arrested for, and convicted of, raping two white women. Eight of the nine defendants were sentenced to death. Liberals and radicals, including the American Communist Party, created a storm of protest, resulting in a reversal of the conviction by the U.S. Supreme Court. A subsequent conviction was also overturned. Eventually five of the nine were convicted and served time, but within 10 years of their convictions all but one had been released from prison. The case, and the Supreme Court decisions related to it, drew the nation's attention to the determinations of all-white juries, particularly in the South, on verdicts related to racial issues.

THE LITERATURE

Langston Hughes's (1902–67) *Scottsboro Limited: Four Poems and a Play* (1932) represents an early and impassioned response to the trials. A more distant but even more powerful presentation of the issues in the case is Harper Lee's (1926–) *To Kill a Mockingbird* (1960). In Lee's novel, a black man, Tom Robinson, is falsely accused of raping a white woman. As in the Scottsboro case, there is an attempted lynching of the defendant and the testimony of the plaintiff is contradictory and unclear. And like the lawyers for the Scottsboro men, Tom Robinson's lawyer, Atticus Finch, delivers an eloquent plea for the principle of equality before the law:

> We know that all men are not created equal in the sense that some people would have us believe. . . . Some people are born gifted beyond the normal scope of most men. . . . But there is one way in this country in which all men are created equal—there is one human institution that makes a pauper the equal of a Rockefeller, the stupid man the equal of an Einstein, and the ignorant man the equal of any college president. That institution, gentlemen, is a court.

FURTHER READING

Dan T. Carter's *Scottsboro: A Tragedy of the American South* (1969) examines the case from a historical perspective. Claudia D. Johnson's *To Kill a Mockingbird: Threatening Boundaries* (1994) is a critical study of the novel.

SHANGHAI INSURRECTION (1927)

In the 1920s, in an effort to combat the anarchy created by the rule of the WARLORDS, Sun Yat Sen, the president of the Chinese republic, formed a coalition of his Nationalist Party (the Guomindang) with the Chinese Communist Party. Both the Communists and the Nationalists viewed Shanghai as the key to the eventual control of all of China. After Sun's death in 1925, the fragile coalition began to come apart. Under the leadership of Chiang Kai-shek, the Guomindang began a campaign to eliminate warlord control in northern China. The Communists, still ostensibly Chiang's allies, staged a successful uprising in Shanghai, leaving this strategically located commercial city essentially in their hands. The Communist insurrection took place on March 21, 1927, first as a general strike, later as an armed struggle against the warlord Sun Ch'uan-fang. The strike, involving 600,000 workers, brought the city to a standstill. The insurrectionists then took over police headquarters, cut power lines, and seized railway stations. Six days later, Chiang entered the city and singled out the Communist-dominated unions for particular praise. Shortly after, he met secretly with leaders of the local business community and the representatives of foreign business interests. On April 12 special units of his forces, dressed in civilian clothes, attacked various union headquarters throughout the city, rounding up Communist leaders, many of whom were summarily executed. Chiang's deception was the first of a series of early victories over the Communists that was to culminate in the LONG MARCH.

THE LITERATURE

The French novelist and, later, statesman André Malraux (1901–76), 25 years old at the time, participated in the insurrection, using it as the setting of his most famous novel, *Man's Fate* (1933; trans., 1934). The opening chapters describe the successful uprising, focusing on three Communist leaders of the revolt: Kyo, half French, half Japanese; Katov, a Russian; and Chen, a young terrorist. The bulk of the story deals with the reactions of these three and a number of diverse minor characters awaiting the arrival of the Nationalist army and Chiang's demand that the Communists surrender their arms and their control of the city to him. All three protagonists, defying the orders of the Chinese Communist Party, which takes its orders from Moscow, refuse to submit. Chen is killed while trying to kill Chiang, and his rash assassination attempt triggers a brutal repression by the Nationalists. Kyo and Katov are arrested; in the novel's most powerful scene, they are taken to a school hall to await execution by being thrown into the boiler of a locomotive. Kyo has secreted three cyanide pellets, one of which he gives to Katov. At the last minute, he gives away the remaining pellets to two young, frightened prisoners next to him. He is left to face a horrible death alone, but a death that has given meaning to his life.

Man's Fate is a political novel with a rich philosophical and moral relevance. The three major characters and the half-dozen other minor figures are all haunted by, and grappling with, the profound awareness of the human condition (the French title of the novel is *La Condition Humaine*), the fact that the movement into death that we call life is a solitary journey. However, this inevitable, final isolation is at least partly overcome when one dies for an ideal. Kyo's sacrifice elevates him to the stature of a tragic hero, whose death affirms the possibility of human transcendence in an otherwise meaningless world.

FURTHER READING

Jonathan Spence's *The Search for Modern China* (1990) provides a clear, detailed account of the uprising. Axel Madsen's *Malraux* (1976) is a fascinating study of the author's rich life, containing a perceptive discussion of *Man's Fate*.

SOMME, BATTLE OF THE (WORLD WAR I) (1916)

In the summer of 1916, in an effort to relieve French forces in the battle of VERDUN, Douglas Haig, commander in chief of the British expeditionary force in France, convinced of the efficacy of a full frontal attack on entrenched enemy forces, developed a plan that relied heavily on an intense preliminary bombardment of enemy positions. As a result, British artillery dropped more than 1 million shells into the German lines, along a broad front on the Somme River, in an effort to destroy their trenches and cut the barbed wire protecting them. On July 1, the British infantry began its advance only to discover that the Germans, secure in their 30-foot-deep dugouts, had been relatively untouched by the bombardment and their barbed wire remained uncut, rendering the infantry easy targets for German machine guns. The result was the most appalling single day in British military history: approximately 20,000 dead and 40,000 wounded.

The offensive continued for the next four months, introducing at one point one of the earliest examples of tank warfare, but for the most part the stalemate that the offensive was designed to break remained intact. At the formal conclusion of the offensive on November 19, 1916, the casualty figures for both sides amounted to more than 1 million men killed and wounded for what turned out to be a small patch of ground. Many British soldiers and civilians were reminded of the lines of Shakespeare's Hamlet, speaking of the deaths of thousands of soldiers who:

> Go to their graves like beds, fight for a plot
> Whereon the numbers cannot try the cause,
> Which is not tomb enough and continent
> To hide the slain.

THE LITERATURE

Frederic Manning's *Her Privates We* (1930) provides a powerfully realistic account of a company of British soldiers during the course of the Somme Offensive. Unusual for war novels, *Her Privates We* focuses less on men in battle than on soldiers in reserve, recovering from or preparing for front-line combat. Its chief character is Private Bourne, an educated, cultivated man—and therefore, in the clearly demarcated class distinctions of British society, "officer material." But Bourne prefers the company of the privates and non-commissioned officers, and it is this group that the author brings to life with such fidelity to "how things really were." These men are neither heroic nor unusual. They live without hope or belief or any of the ideals they may have brought with them into the war. They have no respect for their officers and nothing but contempt for the high command, but they obey orders. They slog through freezing mud, their nerves strained to the breaking point, anticipating the inevitable day when they are either killed or wounded—either way, out of the war. That day arrives for Bourne when his captain, jealous of Bourne's imperturbability, sends him on a dangerous raid. Consistent with the novel's honesty, Bourne's death is ignominious: As the Shakespearean epigraph to the final chapter puts it, "[T]here are few die well who die in battle."

When the novel was first published, its author was listed as "Private 19022," Manning's army serial number. Much of the material is autobiographical. Manning served as an infantry private on the Somme front in 1916, after which his continual drinking bouts (in the novel alcohol serves as a major source of relief for the protagonist) rendered him unfit for service. He died in 1935. Among those who held this novel in the highest regard was Ernest Hemingway, himself the author of one of the great World War I novels, *A Farewell to Arms* (see CAPORETTO).

The original version of the novel bore the title *The Middle Parts of Fortune*, published in 1929 in a limited edition. The following year an edition with the title *Her Privates We* was published in expurgated form, without the soldiers' obscenities that appeared in the original. The uncensored 1930 text has now been reissued in paperback as *Her Privates We* by the Serpent's Tail Press (1999) with an introduction by William Boyd. Both titles are taken from an exchange between Hamlet and Rosencrantz and Guilderstern in Act 2 of *Hamlet*.

FURTHER READING

For an analysis of the Somme Offensive and a portrait of the character of General Haig, see John Keegan's *The First World War* (1999).

SOWETO REVOLT

Soweto is an acronym for South Western Townships, a suburb of Johannesburg, South Africa, reserved for blacks in that country's rigidly segregated APARTHEID era. Following WORLD WAR II, to meet the growing demand for black labor in the city, the government constructed vast rows of shacks, lacking running water or electricity, to accommodate close to 1 million people. But the immediate occasion of the revolt was not a social but a cultural issue. On June 16, 1976, 15,000 junior-high-school children in Soweto staged a peaceful protest against a government policy requiring that instruction in certain subjects be conducted in the Afrikaans language. Government troops opened fire on the children, killing two of them. What followed was a revolt, extraordinary in its being primarily conducted by teenage children, directed as much against the passivity of the older generation of blacks as it was against the oppressive state.

Equally extraordinary was its rapid spread from Soweto to the rest of black South Africa, raging like an out-of-control forest fire. By the time the revolt was finally quelled, more than 500 teenage children and young adults had been killed and some 2,400 wounded, but the consciousness of blacks and some whites had changed. Among the victims was the Black Consciousness leader Steve Biko, whose brutal treatment at the hands of the police resulted in his death in prison. The suppression of the revolt constituted a pyrrhic victory for the government, resulting in international condemnation and isolation, both for the initial police action and for its subsequent brutal behavior. The African National Congress, the leading native African political party, continues to celebrate the initial anniversary of the protest. Soweto proved to be a turning point in South African history, bringing to the nation a new generation of black militants who now recognized their collective power.

THE LITERATURE

The Soweto revolt plays a key role in Nadine Gordimer's (1923–   ) *Burger's Daughter* (1979). Rosa Burger is the daughter of a prominent South African Communist who has died in jail after communism has been outlawed. Growing up as the child of a man who had devoted his life to ending white supremacy in South Africa, a man who had been not only politically correct, but a genuinely loving, life-affirming person, Rosa feels no trace of racism in her conscious self. But what she discovers in the wake of the Soweto revolt and the growth of the black consciousness movement is the presence at an unconscious level of white paternalism. In order to achieve this awareness she has first to give priority to her private life, to cease being her father's daughter by rejecting the primacy of the political over the personal.

She goes to Europe to extricate herself from the consuming problems of South Africa. In Europe she falls in love and begins the sense of self-discovery she has been seeking. However, in London she encounters a black South African militant, whom she had known in childhood. In fact, the boy had lived at her house, and the two of them had been like brother and sister, or so she thought. The militant rejects that past, including her father's paternalistic attitude and the fact that the white heroes of the antiapartheid movement are the most celebrated. The shock of this attack results in Rosa's decision to return to South Africa, taking a post as a physiotherapist in a hospital in Soweto. There she treats children with congenital, crippling diseases, until "the second half of 1976 when the children who were born deformed were joined by the children who were shot." In the aftermath of the revolt, she joins the resistance, is arrested, and, like her father, imprisoned. The novel ends with Rosa still in prison, but having achieved a kind of serenity, accepting the limitations of the white person's role in the struggle that the Soweto revolt has transformed.

Banned by the South African authorities soon after its publication in 1979, *Burger's Daughter* is now recognized as an important contribution to the clarification of the gap that emerged in black/white relations in South Africa in the 1970s, the implications of which are still apparent. But the novel also stands on its literary merits, particularly its capacity to capture the relationship between the personal and the historical.

FURTHER READING

Gail M. Gerhart's *Black Power in South Africa: The Evolution of an Ideology* (1978) explores the significance of the Soweto revolt. Stephen Clingman's *The Novels of Nadine Gordimer: History from the Inside* (1986) offers both an acute reading of the novel and an insightful account of recent South African history.

SPACE EXPLORATION

In October 1957, the Soviet Union surprised the world by announcing that it had launched a satellite vehicle, *Sputnik*, that was circling the earth at a speed of 18,000 mph. The satellite, a steel ball about 22 inches in diameter, contained four radio antennas. On November 3, the Soviets sent a second *Sputnik* into orbit, six times larger than the first, with a little dog on board, wired to send back information about the physiological effects of space travel. In America, the reaction was a mixture of anger, humiliation, and fear of its COLD WAR rival. Attention turned to the American school system and its weaknesses in providing an adequate scientific education for its children.

In 1961, Russian cosmonaut Yuri Gagarin became the first human being to travel in outer space, orbiting Earth once in one hour and 29 minutes. In that same year newly elected President John Fitzgerald KENNEDY, whose "New Frontier" presidential campaign had given the space program high priority, ordered a stepped-up American program, resulting in John Glenn's successful triple orbiting of the Earth in February 1962. At the time, Kennedy predicted that the United States would put a man on the moon by the end of the decade. His prediction was validated on July 20, 1969, when Neil Armstrong stepped out onto the lunar surface, declaring, "That's one small step for a man, one giant leap for mankind."

Notable developments since the moon landing include the employment of reusable orbital vehicles and the establishment of the first space station, Mir, by the Soviet Union in 1986, leading, in 1998, to the first phase of a projected international space station. On the negative side, the space shuttle *Challenger* exploded shortly after lift-off in 1986; 17 years later, in 2003, the *Columbia* shuttle crashed during its reentry, leading some to question the wisdom of continuing manned space flights.

THE LITERATURE

Thomas Mallon's (1951–   ) *Aurora Seven* (1991) is set on May 24, 1962, the date on which astronaut Scott Carpenter orbited Earth three times, narrowly escaping disaster before landing safely in the Pacific Ocean. The central figure in the novel is 11-year-old Gregory Noonan, living with his parents in a Westchester County suburb. He is deeply absorbed by the space program; as a result, he becomes alienated from his father, a glove salesman. In addition to Gregory and his parents, the supporting cast includes, among others, a Mary McCarthy–esque writer and intellectual, a Catholic priest having difficulty controlling his sexual feelings, a young Puerto Rican man interviewing for a job as an elevator operator, and a New York City cab driver—all of them are orbiting the city, looking for a safe landing. Interpolated into the accounts of the characters are excerpts from the text of air-ground voice communications among Carpenter, the Control Center at Cape Canaveral, and the various tracking stations he was in touch with. Also true to life are the words of Walter Cronkite's reporting of the flight for CBS, preserved at the Museum of Broadcasting in New York.

After spending the morning in school, surreptitiously listening to radio reports of the flight, Gregory impulsively plays hooky at lunchtime and hops a train to New York to join the crowd watching the television coverage of the event on the giant monitors in Grand Central Station. His mother becomes alarmed when she spots him on television among the crowd. His father, who works in the Grand Central area, also happens to be among the crowd, but the two do not meet. After the landing, Gregory sets out for his father's workplace. On the way, he has a near-fatal mishap, involving the cab driver, the novelist, and the young man, leading to a reunion with his father. The confluence of his and Carpenter's narrow escapes reinforces the boy's conviction that there is a design at work in human history, however obscure and clouded.

Gregory had pondered the question of history's design earlier in the day; Participating in a school rehearsal of a pageant about the Civil War, he objects to the fact that his teacher has Union and Confederate soldiers joining in a dance during the war. His teacher invokes the phrase "historical license" by way of explanation. "History is history," thinks Gregory. "If you play with it, it is no longer true. Any tampering could make the world veer off its course . . . keeping it from going where it is supposed to be going, which eventually . . . is back in the palm of God, a small sphere, returning, like a baseball to the pitcher." The small sphere returning to its home is a good description of the plot as a whole: the return of the satellite, the reconciliation of the boy and his father, and the great globe itself, spinning off course regularly, courting extinction, but eventually making its way back, at least for the time being.

FURTHER READING

Space Exploration, edited by Christopher Mari (1999), considers possible future developments in the space program. Tom Wolfe's dazzling *The Right Stuff* (1979) captures the spirit and ambition of the original astronauts. Thomas Mallon alludes to *Aurora Seven* in "Writing Historical Fiction," included in his collection *In Fact: Essays on Writers and Writing* (2001).

SPANISH CIVIL WAR

In July 1936, Spanish army troops in Morocco, led by General Francisco Franco, staged an insurrection against the recently elected left-wing "popular front" government. (*Popular front* was a term for an international communist policy advocating communist participation in coalition governments threatened by the rising tide of FASCISM in Europe.) The Nationalists, or Falangists, as Franco's supporters came to be known, were backed by large landowners, the clergy, and eventually by increasing numbers of the middle class. The Loyalists, defenders of the elected republican government, drew their support from urban areas and the peasant class. Both sides looked to foreign governments for external support. Franco received military aid from the two reigning fascist governments, Italy and Germany, while the Loyalists, or Republicans, were supplied with arms by the Soviet Union. In addition, more than 40,000 men and women from around the world formed Loyalist "international brigades" to fight "the good fight," as the war was known in leftist circles. Among these groups was the American ABRAHAM LINCOLN BRIGADE, a force of 2,800, approximately one-third of whom were killed in action.

Initially Franco's forces made rapid advances, reaching the suburbs of Madrid in early November, but the Republicans held the city, despite continued aerial attacks, and followed it up with a victory at the battle of Guadalajara. In February 1937, a sustained battle on the Jarama River, southeast of the capital, resulted in severe losses for the Republicans. By June, Franco's army had captured the important city of Bilbao in the Basque region. Its victory in the Basque country had been preceded by the notorious attack by German bombers and fighter planes on the civilian population in Guernica, the old Basque capital. As the subject of Pablo Picasso's magnificent mural, the bombing of Guernica has come to stand as the symbol of the inhumanity of modern warfare.

In 1938, the failure of the Loyalist attempt to capture and hold the city of Teruel in the Aragon province left the loyalists in a desperate position. They attempted a last-ditch counterattack at the battle of the Ebro River in November 1938 but were beaten back. Shortly after, in January 1939, Barcelona was captured, and in March of that year Madrid fell to the Nationalists. On April 1, 1939, General Franco declared victory. His dictatorial regime would rule Spain until his death in 1975.

The retrospective significance of the Spanish civil war is that it proved to be a prelude to WORLD WAR II. At the beginning of the war, all of the other European nations agreed not to intervene in this internal struggle, but within a very short time, Germany, Italy, and the Soviet Union became active participants. The Italians supplied as many as 50,000 troops; the Germans bomber pilots fought on the Nationalist side. The Soviets contributed to the Republicans arms, men, and mischief—the latter in the form of their treacherous attempt to eliminate anarchist and other left-wing factions on the Republican side. The betrayal of these groups is memorably recorded in the classic memoir *Homage to Catalonia* (1938), by George Orwell (1903–50).

THE LITERATURE

Like the war it responded to, the literature of the Spanish civil war had an international character. To the various international brigades flocked scores of politically committed writers, the large majority sympathetic to the Republican cause, although a small number of conservatives sided with the Falangists. Even larger numbers on both sides remained at home writing and participating in fund-raising drives. Among the writers on the left were the British poets W. H. Auden (1907–73), George Barker (1913–91), and Stephen Spender (1909–95); the French poets André Breton (1896–1966), Louis Aragon (1897–1982), and Paul Eluard (1895–1952); and the American poets Archibald MacLeish (1892–1982), Kenneth Rexroth (1905–82), Langston Hughes (1902–67), and Edna St. Vincent Millay (1892–1950). Among the writers supporting the Nationalists were the French poet and dramatist Paul Claudel (1868–1955), the English poet Roy Campbell (1901–57), and the French novelist Pierre Drieu La Rochelle (1893–1945).

Best known of the poems on the civil war is Auden's "Spain" (1938), which deals with the country's past, present, and future, in which the "present" (the civil war) is the necessarily "murderous" time that will usher in a Utopian future. In later years, after he had returned to the Anglican faith of his birth, Auden repudiated this poem as pure propaganda.

Among the novelists who drew on the experience of the war are Andre Malraux (1901–76) (*Man's Hope*), the German Communist Gustav Regler (1898–1963) (*The Great Crusade*), and the prolific American novelist John

Dos Passos (1896–1970) (*The Adventures of a Young Man*). Based closely on Malraux's experience as the leader of an international squadron of fliers in the first year of the war, *Man's Hope* (1937; trans., 1938) covers the first eight months of the war, when Republican hopes are high, to Franco's victory at Toledo, the Republicans' successful defense of Madrid, and victory at Guadalajara. Concluding the novel on a victorious note reinforces the theme of hope, alluded to in the title. Regler's *The Great Crusade* (trans., 1940) also concentrates on the opening months of the war, when the international brigades scored a number of victories. The novel provides a group portrait of a particular brigade made up of men from various European countries. As the war develops, the bonds linking the different nationalities become increasingly strong. Eventually, however, doubt and the sense of betrayal weaken their resolve. In Dos Passos's *Adventures of a Young Man* (1939), Glenn Spotswood, an early convert to communism, comes to realize, while working as a union organizer in America, that the party is using the workers merely to support its own goals. Branded as a heretical Trotskyite, he joins an international brigade. In Spain, he meets an old anarchist friend only to learn later that the friend has been executed as a traitor. He himself is jailed and, when released, sent on a virtual suicide mission. In this novel, Dos Passos records his disillusion with the Stalinist mentality that fractured the Republican movement and betrayed the thousands of people who had invested their lives in what they believed to be a just cause.

The best-known novel of the war is Ernest Hemingway's *For Whom the Bell Tolls* (1940). Hemingway (1899–1961), who served as a war correspondent in Spain, had been a tireless enemy of the Falangists, having written a play, *The Fifth Column*, and a number of short stories that were essentially antifascist propaganda. But by the time he came to write *For Whom the Bell Tolls*, immediately after the war, he harbored few illusions about the political leadership of the Loyalists. What informs his novel is not an ideological position but a hatred of fascism and a love of Spain and its people, reflected also in his first novel, *The Sun Also Rises* (1926), and in his book on the mystique of bullfighting, *Death in the Afternoon* (1932).

The action takes place over four days in a mountainous region northwest of Madrid. Robert Jordan, a young American, comes to the camp of a band of Loyalist guerrillas with an assignment from general headquarters to blow up a strategically important bridge. The leader of the group, Pablo, has lost his nerve and is uneasy about the mission. Not so Pablo's fiery woman, Pilar, who is totally committed to the cause. Pilar is nursing back to health the young Maria, who has been raped and had her head shaved by Nationalist troops. She and Jordan fall in love almost immediately. Jordan's carefully worked out plan is sabotaged by Pablo, who destroys Jordan's detonator before deserting the band. Jordan now has to use a hand grenade to set off the explosion, but he successfully carries out the mission, although he is wounded in the process. As the novel ends, he lies alone in a forest, a gun within reach, awaiting the enemy as the rest of the band makes its escape.

A number of flashbacks adds depth and dimension to the main characters, as does the novel's title, taken from a sermon by John Donne: "No man is an island . . . any man's death diminishes me. And therefore never send to know for whom the bell tolls; it tolls for thee." The novel's language, although recognizably in the famous Hemingway style, takes on a more lyrical, even romantic tone compared to his earlier works. In this respect, the style reflects the theme. In place of a stoic acceptance of an "unfair" world, such as one sees in *A Farewell to Arms* (*see* CAPORETTO, RETREAT FROM), the author seems to be affirming here the possibilities of meaningful, heroic sacrifice and a common human bond.

The Cypresses Believe in God (1953; trans., 1957) by the Spanish novelist José Maria Gironella (1917–   ) is the first, and better known, of a two-part novel that deals with events before, during, and immediately after the civil war. *The Cypresses* opens in 1931, the first year of the new Spanish republic, in the city of Gerona, where Ignacio Alvear, a young law student, lives with his parents, his sister, Pilar, and his brother, Cesar, who is studying for the priesthood. The novel records the family's responses and reactions, particularly those of Ignacio, to the events leading up to the war. As the political and ideological conflict erupts in strikes, violence, bombings, and assassinations, the family, middle class and apolitical, becomes inexorably involved. Ignacio struggles to discover his responsibility in the chaos, attending meetings of both the Falangists and the Communists, weighing his decision. The novel concludes with the execution of Ignacio's brother Cesar, a victim of the widespread anticlericalism among the Loyalist forces.

The second volume, *One Million Dead* (1961; trans., 1963), covers the period of the war itself, from 1936 to 1939. Ignacio, now rejecting the forces that murdered his brother, enlists as a medical orderly in the Nationalist army. He finds work at a hospital in Madrid, while his family remains in Gerona, which is controlled by the Loyalists. As the war draws to an end, the family members are reunited, still mourning the death of Cesar. In his preface to this volume, Gironella speaks of his struggle to achieve "the necessary impartiality," but the relatively impartial treatment of both sides is finally broken, near the end of the novel, in a tribute to Franco, praising his strength and military genius. Nevertheless, whereas the novels of Dos Passos and Hemingway are memorable reconstructions of civil war, Gironella's works recreate the *Spanish* civil war.

FURTHER READING

Hugh Thomas's *The Spanish Civil War* (1961) is an excellent, authoritative history: Frederick Benson's *Writers in Arms* (1967) offers a useful overview of the literary history of the war.

STALIN, JOSEPH (1879–1953)

Born Josef Dzhugashivili in the Russian province of Georgia, Stalin was an able student, admitted in 1893 to the orthodox seminary in Tiflis. In 1899, he was expelled from the seminary for his radical political views. Arrested for revolutionary activity in 1902, he was sent to Siberia, from which he later escaped. By 1907, he had come to the attention of the party leader Vladimir Ilich LENIN, who secretly endorsed his policy of robbing government banks to support the revolutionary party. At this point, the party leadership viewed him as a thuggish but effective hard-liner with considerable administrative skills. He played only a small role in the 1917 RUSSIAN REVOLUTION but by 1922 had risen in the ranks of the leadership to become general secretary of the Communist Party. The position offered him an ideal place from which to rise to succeed Lenin, who shortly before his death had called for Stalin's removal from power. Stalin overcame the opposition of Leon TROTSKY and his followers by pursuing a policy that reinforced the centrality of the Communist Party in the new government and the rejection of the goal of world revolution in favor of developing communism within the Soviet Union.

Once in control, he instituted plans to develop the nation into an industrial power and to collectivize all agriculture. Industrialization proceeded with remarkable success in a relatively brief span of time, but collectivization met with strong opposition, to which he responded with characteristic brutality. In 1934, he unleashed the GREAT TERROR, his ruthless purge of the Communist Party, the military, and the professional class, intending to rid the nation of Trotskyism and any evidence of bourgeois influence. By the time of the last "show trial" in 1938, he had absolute control. His nonaggression pact with Adolf HITLER in 1939 enabled the Soviet Union and Germany to carve up pieces of Poland, but it counted for little else, as Hitler demonstrated in 1941 by attacking the Soviet Union (see BARBAROSSA). With the successful conclusion of WORLD WAR II, Stalin displayed adroit diplomacy at the Yalta and Potsdam Conferences, leading to Soviet control of Eastern Europe and the onset of the COLD WAR. During the last years of his life, his rule became even more repressive, adding anti-Semitism to his list of offenses.

Despite his record, second only to Hitler in its murderous, dictatorial impact, he was a hero in the eyes of many when he died in 1953. The tide turned suddenly, however, in 1956 when his successor Nikita Khrushchev condemned Stalin at the 20th Congress of the Communist Party. Five years later, his embalmed corpse was removed from its place of honor in Lenin's tomb and buried elsewhere. By the end of the century, the novelist Joseph Heller's characterization of Joseph Stalin as "the worst man who ever lived" seemed only a slight exaggeration.

THE LITERATURE

Richard Lourie's (1940–) *The Autobiography of Joseph Stalin: A Novel* (1999) offers a portrait of a leader whose cool logic successfully masks his homicidal paranoia. It is 1938, and Stalin has learned that the man who haunts him like a classical nemesis, Leon Trotsky, is writing a biography of him. Haunted by the fear that in his research, Trotsky will uncover the one fact that could bring about his downfall, Stalin begins to record the events of his life. He writes, not in defense, but in celebration of the supremacy of will that has enabled him to penetrate to the essence of life, which is to say, his sense of the essential nothingness that underlies existence.

He describes his brutal childhood, where his father, a drunken lout, jealous of his son's early academic success, repeatedly beat and humiliated him. From there, Stalin records the central event of his adolescence: his challenge to God to prove his existence by taking his soul immediately. When the challenge goes unanswered, the young seminary student is confirmed in his atheism, free to pursue power untrammeled by conscience.

His rise in the revolutionary party is assured when he convinces Lenin that he is the man to initiate the policy of "expropriation" (organized robberies) to support the work of the party. The novel ends with Stalin's crowning achievement, his carefully orchestrated assassination of Trotsky at his home in Mexico. It comes just as Stalin's worst fear has been realized: Trotsky has discovered that Lenin did not die from a series of strokes as was generally believed, but rather he was poisoned on the orders of Joseph Stalin.

FURTHER READING

The English title of Trotsky's biography of Stalin is *Stalin: An Appraisal of the Man and His Influence* (trans., 1941).

STALINGRAD, BATTLE OF (WORLD WAR II) (1942–1943)

In the late spring of 1942, after the winter stalemate in the German invasion of the Soviet Union (see BARBAROSSA), Adolf HITLER renewed his offensive against Leningrad in the north and Moscow in the center, but this time he divided his attack in the south into two fronts, one designed to capture the Soviet oil fields in the Caucasus and the other to capture the important industrial city of Stalingrad (now Volgograd). This dispersal of German strength over four fronts proved to be disastrous.

Stalingrad was a modern city, built in the 1930s as a model of the "workers' paradise," its factory complexes balanced by parks and small detached houses, each with its own garden. It was particularly important to the ego of the man for whom it was named, Joseph STALIN. Fighting began on August

23, by which time the Soviet army had been heavily reinforced. The battle proved to be fierce and costly for both sides, as every building in the city was bitterly contested, often in hand-to-hand fighting. By November, fighting within Stalingrad still raged, but on November 19 the German Sixth Army found themselves encircled in a brilliant counterstroke by the Russian commander, Marshal Georgi Zhukov.

In two pincer movements, one from the north and another from the south, the Soviets completely surrounded the German forces in the city. The only logical German strategy was to try to break through the encirclement and retreat to the west, but Hitler, who by this time had become obsessed with Stalingrad, insisted that the army remain in place, promising that they would be relieved by additional German forces and that supplies would be flown in by the German air force. Neither promise was kept, and the Sixth Army, already exhausted by the bitter struggle for the city, now faced starvation and another Russian winter. Finally, with his own headquarters overrun, the German commanding officer, General Friedrich von Paulus, surrendered. After 164 days of savage, brutal warfare, the fighting formally ended on February 2, 1943. German losses—dead, wounded, and captured—amounted to an astonishing 1.2 million. The German army never fully recovered from this defeat, which ranks as one of the fiercest battles in the history of modern warfare.

THE LITERATURE

Theodor Plievier's (1892–1955) *Stalingrad* (1945; trans., 1948), regarded by many as the finest battle novel of WORLD WAR II, is a powerful, often nightmarish account of the conflict. It offers a graphic picture of the suffering, death, and destruction of the men of the German Sixth Army, senselessly slaughtered by the will of one man. Its cast of characters ranges from the commanding general, Frederich von Paulus—appalled by the increasing horror of his situation, but paralyzed by the specter of the führer's wrath, his fear betrayed in a facial tic—to the lowly Private Gnotke, reduced to the position of gravedigger in a world where thousands of bodies lie unburied. Gnotke, like his prototype, the gravedigger in Shakespeare's *Hamlet*, is a common man speaking the truth about power in direct contrast to Paulus and the general staff, whose guiding principle is "Never contradict the Fuhrer."

The novel's central figure is Colonel Vilshofen, a courageous and resourceful tank officer, representing the best of the German military tradition, in which personal honor and rationality are highly prized. The author reserves his greatest scorn for the general staff, once proud exemplars of the Prussian military heritage, who sacrifice their honor as soldiers in cowardly obeisance to, and fear of, Hitler. Their inability to stand up to his wanton destruction of the men under their command amounts to "military criminality."

Plievier was a German Communist who fled his country in 1933 and served in the Soviet army. The harrowing details of battle, hunger, and extreme fatigue that he presents in the novel came from eyewitness accounts of German prisoners of war whom he interrogated, which helps to account for the book's intensely realistic focus. Settling in Germany after the war, Plievier eventually became disenchanted with Soviet communism and moved to Switzerland. *Stalingrad* is the first volume of a trilogy that also includes *Moscow* and *Berlin* (see BERLIN, FALL OF).

FURTHER READING

Edwin Hoyt, Jr.'s, *199 Days: The Battle for Stalingrad* (1993) vividly recreates the battle, maintaining that it marked the turning point of the war. In *"Stalingrad* and My Lai," an article in *Critical Inquiry* (summer 1979), Strother Purdy argues that the absence of a novel on the My Lai massacre that might be comparable to *Stalingrad* exemplifies a "retreat from moral responsibility" in the literature of the late 20th century. In 1994, Tim O'Brien's *In the Lake of the Woods* represented precisely the type of novel Purdy was implicitly calling for (see MY LAI MASSACRE).

STALINIST PURGES

See GREAT TERROR, THE.

STOCK MARKET CRASH (1929)

On September 3, 1929, the American stock market rose to an all-time high. Six weeks later, at the closing bell on October 29, the New York Stock Exchange lay in ruins, the result of history's greatest stock market disaster. In that period of time the market had lost $30 billion, the equivalent of almost half the national debt. The most critical day was "Black Thursday" (October 24), in which desperate investors in a wild panic began dumping their stocks in an effort to salvage what they could. Attempting to reassure the investing public, a group of prominent bankers, led by J. P. Morgan, pooled more than $200 million, using it to buy stocks. For a few days, the strategy worked, but on "Black Tuesday" (October 29), panic-selling of stocks occurred on a massive scale, dwarfing the decline of the previous Thursday. By mid-November, the loss had mounted to more than $30 billion. Three years later, the figure had risen to $75 billion. People who had been riding high in the "boom market" found themselves back at the starting line. Newspapers began to be filled with daily accounts of suicides. The dizzying ride of the 1920s had come to an end.

The collapse of the market was the culmination of years of a stock market boom fueled by rash speculation in which large numbers of investors had bought "on margin," paying only a portion of the full price of the stock, gambling money they didn't have. But the crash itself would not have been so significant if the economy had been basically sound. In the boom years of the 1920s, the nation's industries had responded to the demand for consumer goods by increasing production and building more factories. As production outstripped consumption, inventories of unsold goods rose to a dangerously high level. Meanwhile agricultural prices plunged, leaving farmers destitute (see DUST BOWL). The crash exposed not simply the foolishness of the stock market but also the decayed state of the national economy.

Fifty-eight years later, in October 1987, the stock market experienced a similar sharp decline. This time, however, the fundamentally sound economy withstood the excesses of Wall Street, allowing for a significant recovery in a relatively brief time. However, the full markets of the 1990s experienced a "soft landing" recession at the turn of the new century.

THE LITERATURE

Although it takes as its subject America in the 1920s, the culminating event of *The Big Money* (1936), the last volume of John Dos Passos's (1896–1970) *U.S.A.* trilogy, is the crash. *The Big Money* portrays a society in which economic collapse is mirrored in the personal deterioration of its characters. The entire trilogy is notable for its experimental narrative techniques, which include a large number of fictional characters whose life stories are interwoven with "newsreels"—collages of headlines, speeches, and songs ironically juxtaposed as comments about the contemporary world; biographies of prominent public figures (including William Randolph Hearst, Thomas Edison, and J. P. Morgan); and "camera eye" sections, which, in stream-of-consciousness narratives, present Dos Passos's own response to events. The final "newsreel" in *The Big Money* bears the title "Wall Street Stunned" and intermingles such headlines as "Market Sure to Recover from Slump," "Decline in Contracts," "Red Pickets Fined for Protest Here," and "President Sees Prosperity Near." Dos Passos suggests that, just as the executions of SACCO AND VANZETTI represent the death of America's attempt to achieve social justice, the market collapse represents the inevitable result of commercial corruption and excess.

The crash figures as the critical turning point in the lives of some of the characters in Anita Shreve's (1947) *Sea Glass* (2002). Honora and Sexton Beecher marry in June of 1929 and move into an abandoned house on the beach, near a New England mill town. There, in lieu of rent, the young couple will act as caretakers and fix up the property. Sexton is a typewriter salesman, filled with go-getter enthusiasm about the future, confident of his ability to be a success in business. His sales increase substantially in the summer of 1929, so much so that when offered a chance to buy the house they are living in, he seizes it, even though it means going into debt. While Sexton is at work, Honora spends time collecting sea glass that has washed up on the shore. Here she meets Vivian, a socialite from Boston, who is living in a nearby cottage, owned by her lover, Dickie, a member of her social set.

When the crash occurs, Dickie loses everything, and Vivian, whose wealth is not affected by the market, buys the cottage. Sexton loses his job and, defaulting on a loan, his car, the key to his identity as a salesman. Plunged in despair, he takes a job at a local cotton mill. Sexton becomes involved with a major strike of the mill in town, and the house becomes the headquarters for the strike leaders. The strike action pulls everyone together, except Honora and Sexton, as their relationship deteriorates further. Meanwhile Honora and McDermott, another of the strike leaders, fall in love, although neither acknowledges feelings for the other. In McDermott's care is a boy, Alphonse, a waif trying to help his widowed mother. The strikers' victory proves to be short-lived, as the mill closes. In the violent conclusion, Sexton's irresponsibility triggers a tragedy, leaving Honora, Vivian, and Alphonse to put together the pieces of their old life, like the shards of sea glass on the beach.

FURTHER READING

John Kenneth Galbraith's *The Great Crash: 1929* (1955) is an analysis by a noted economist.

SUEZ CRISIS (1956)

In 1956, Egyptian president Gamal Abdel Nasser, responding to the failure of the Western nations to help finance the building of the Aswan Dam on the Nile River, nationalized the Suez Canal, a private company owned primarily by British and French shareholders. In retaliation, the British and French governments, while keeping their American ally in the dark, fell back on an earlier agreement stipulating that in the event of an Israeli-Egyptian war, British and French troops would occupy the canal zone. Acting in collusion with the British and French, Israel invaded Egypt, occupying the Sinai Peninsula. The ploy fooled no one. The United States stated that it would support Egypt if it was subject to aggression. The Soviet Union warned the three invaders that unless they withdrew immediately, they would be targeted by Soviet missiles. Such international condemnation of their actions, along with powerful opposition at home, forced the British and French to withdraw within a month. The following year, Israel withdrew from the Sinai.

The ignominious defeat of Britain and France—they had not only failed, they had looked foolish in the process—seriously damaged their prestige and power in the Middle East. As a result, the Eisenhower administration, operating at the height of the COLD WAR, feared a vacuum of power, into which the Soviets would step. The president therefore promulgated the Eisenhower Doctrine, asserting the determination "to protect the territorial integrity of . . . nations requesting such aid from any nation controlled by International Communism."

THE LITERATURE

The malaise created by the Suez crisis is poignantly captured in John Osborne's (1929–) 1957 drama *The Entertainer*. Its main character is Archie Rice, a veteran music hall comedian, whose act, wearing thin for years, is now painful to behold. The old music halls have gone, and Archie is reduced to appearing in a kind of burlesque show. The play, which is structured not in acts, but in 13 parts, alternates scenes of Archie on stage, mixing jokes with tired song-and-dance routines, and Archie at home with his family, wife Phoebe, aging father Billy, daughter Jean, and son Frank. Archie's other son, 19-year-old Mick, is serving in the army at Suez. Archie learns that Mick has been taken prisoner in the fighting, but Archie prides himself on being untouchable, an unloving, unfaithful husband, indifferent parent, completely cynical about himself and his world. This façade begins to crumble as his anxiety about his son takes hold. In Part 8, he reminisces drunkenly about the night he sat in a bar listening to "the most moving thing I ever heard . . . an old fat negress getting up to sing about Jesus. . . . I wish to God I could feel like that old black bitch and sing. If I'd done one thing as good as that in my whole life I'd have been all right."

Shortly after this moment, the family receives the news that Mick has been killed. Archie, whose signature song has always been "Why should I care / Why should I let it touch me" collapses and begins to moan a blues spiritual slowly, "O Lord I don't care where they bury my body . . . 'cos my soul's going to live with God." But in Part 13, Archie has recovered his old cynical self. He plans to rescue his career by bringing his father back to the stage, but his father dies, and Archie now faces jail for income tax evasion. Cynical to the end, his final exit is to the tune of "Why should I care / Why should I let it touch me."

Following on the heels of his first great dramatic success, *Look Back in Anger* (1956), *The Entertainer* established John Osborne as the foremost representative of the *Angry Young Men*, the term used for the young British writers of the 1950s who attacked the rigid class structure and values of the ruling English establishment. Without belaboring the parallel, Osborne clearly intends Archie as a symbol of Suez-era England, a nation whose "act" is hopelessly outdated, reduced to a shabby second-rate status (see BRITISH EMPIRE, END OF). In the play, England is now living off its past, as Archie tries to live off Billy, while sacrificing its future, Mick, in a pathetic attempt to maintain the illusion of its imperial power and the mask of stiff-upper-lip impregnability. Making this metaphor work requires acting of the highest order, which is precisely what the original production and the 1960 film version received from Laurence Olivier in the lead role.

FURTHER READING

Keith Kyle's *Suez* (1991) looks at the crisis from a variety of perspectives.

TANNENBERG, BATTLE OF (WORLD WAR I)

In August 1914, the first month of WORLD WAR I, the Russian army, scoring an early success against German troops on the eastern front, advanced well into East Prussia. Near the town of Tannenberg, the Germans counterattacked after having secretly encircled the Russian forces. When the Russians tried to retreat, they found themselves trapped. More than 135,000 were captured and some 30,000 killed, including the Russian commander, General Aleksandr Samsonov, who committed suicide. Shortly after, the Russians suffered another defeat at the battle of Masurian Lakes. What clearly emerged from these battles was a theme that was to be repeated throughout the war on the Allied side: unprepared but courageous soldiers led by incompetent commanders. For the Russians, these demoralizing defeats intensified the growing dissatisfaction with the war in particular and with the czar's regime in general. In retrospect, the defeat can be seen as an early harbinger of the 1917 RUSSIAN REVOLUTION.

On the strength of their win, the two victorious German generals, Erich Ludendorf and Paul von Hindenburg, became national heroes and later the joint heads of the German supreme command for the remainder of the war. In 1925, Hindenburg was elected president of the German Republic and reelected in 1932, narrowly defeating Adolf HITLER, who became chancellor. When Hindenburg died in 1934, he was buried in the National War Memorial at Tannenberg, the scene of his greatest victory.

THE LITERATURE

Aleksandr Solzhenitsyn's (1918–) novel *August 1914* (1971; trans., 1972) is devoted in large part to the battle of Tannenberg and its significance. Conceived as the first of a series of four novels covering Russian history from events preceding World War I through the revolution, *August 1914* is written with the passion, wide learning, and fiery indignation that has distinguished all of Solzhenitsyn's work. The core of the novel is a meticulously detailed account of the battle, framed by a description of events leading up to the war and intercut with excerpts in the form of newsreels, much in the manner of John Dos Passos's *U.S.A.* The central character is Colonel Vorotyntsev, a member of General Samsonov's staff, through whose eyes we see the mendacity and ineptitude of certain high-ranking Russian officers. The theme of the individual accepting or evading his or her share of individual responsibility for collective action plays a critical role in the novel. General Samsonov is depicted as having been victimized by the bungling of his superiors, the general staff, and by the jealousy and incompetence of his corps commanders. The general staff's chief blunder lies in their decision to take the offensive with an army that is woefully unprepared for combat. At the conclusion of the novel, Vorotyntsev tries to convince the general staff of the need to learn from their mistakes. But as soon as he leaves the room, the news arrives of a Russian victory on the Polish front and the defeat at Tannenberg is quickly forgotten. *August 1914* is infused with its author's passionate love for his country. Thus, although the novel devotes a large share of attention to the bumbling efforts of its commanders, it is unstinting in its praise of the common Russian soldier.

An expanded, revised edition of *August 1914* appeared in 1989. This version, with a new English translation, adds more than 300 pages, most of which concern Vladimir Ilich LENIN and had been separately published as *Lenin in Zurich*. Other additions relate to Peter Stolypin, the Russian premier assassinated in 1911, an event Solzhenitsyn views as having catastrophic consequences for Russia. Critics have been divided in their reactions to the new edition, some complaining that the added material makes the already large book a tedious reading experience; others have seen traces of anti-Semitism in the description of certain characters, such as Stolypin's assassin.

FURTHER READING

Tannenberg occupies an important place in Winston Churchill's *The Unknown War: The Eastern Front* (1931). D. M. Thomas's *Alexander Solzhenitsyn: A Century in His Life* (1998) is a passionate and eloquent biography of the author.

TET OFFENSIVE (VIETNAM WAR) (1968)

On January 31, 1968, the first night of Tet, the Vietnamese New Year celebration, troops of the National Liberation Front (Viet Cong) launched attacks on nearly 100 cities and villages in South Vietnam, including its capital, Saigon, and the strategically critical air base at Da Nang. Communists troops captured the city of Hue and proceeded to execute 2,800 civilians. In Saigon, the Viet Cong blasted through the walls surrounding the American embassy and also took control of the radio station. Quickly, the Americans launched a counteroffensive, beating back the attacks, eventually securing a victory in the strictly military sense. While winning a propaganda victory abroad, the Communists suffered severe casualties. As a result of the Hue massacre, they also alienated many South Vietnam civilians who had been quietly favoring them, but the impact of the offensive on American public opinion proved a devastating defeat for the administration of President Lyndon Johnson.

Across the country, Americans watched televised scenes of savage brutality and American vulnerability that fueled antiwar sentiment. Particularly powerful was the scene of a South Vietnamese officer casually shooting a prisoner through the head without even questioning him. For the first time, millions of Americans were witnesses to war in all its ugliness. The televised scenes of the attack on the embassy also convinced many that their government had been misleading them in their optimistic reports and their confident comments about "light at the end of the tunnel." President Johnson's popularity plummeted to such an extent that two months later he announced his decision not to be a candidate in the upcoming presidential election. The Tet Offensive had proved to be the home-front turning point of the VIETNAM WAR, the realization by the majority of Americans that massive military intervention had been a tragic mistake. (See also MY LAI MASSACRE.)

THE LITERATURE

Gustav Hasford's (1947–93) *The Short-Timers* (1979) is a violent, often savage account of the early days of the Tet Offensive and later of the embattled marine forces at Khe sanh, near the Laotian border. The events are narrated by an enlisted marine named Joker (most of the characters are referred to by their nicknames), whose story begins with a detailed description of the marine boot camp at Parris Island, South Carolina. The aim of boot camp is to turn the raw recruits into killing machines; an important part of that process is to have the recruit "fall in love with his weapon." This section concludes with an incident illustrating the tragic consequences of such training. The novel proper begins with Tet attacks on January 31. Joker, already a seasoned veteran, is assigned as a combat correspondent for the official marine paper to a squad fighting in the street-by-street battle for the recovery of Hue, which had been lost in the first night of the offensive.

In a grippingly realistic, emblematic scene, a North Vietnamese sniper fires on the squad from a group of abandoned buildings. The marines enlist the aid of a nearby tank, which proceeds to demolish the buildings, while the squad searches in the rubble for the sniper. Joker runs across the sniper and, in a split-second recognition, sees that she is a young girl, about 15, but "with the eyes of a grunt." (*Grunt* is respectful military slang for a seasoned combat soldier of any army.) She is immediately shot by the squad, and as she lays dying in agony, Joker kills her out of pity. But the mercy killing sets off a chain reaction among the squad, as each one, vying for the title of "most hard," proceeds to dismember the body. The scene gruesomely recapitulates the entire Vietnam experience: the enormous overkill, using massive, destructive weaponry on small targets; the laying waste of a once beautiful place (Hue had been the ancient capital of the country, the site of the old imperial palace with priceless treasures); and the dehumanizing impact on those involved in the fighting.

Dehumanization, in fact, is the major focus of the novel. As Joker explains when asked for advice by a close buddy, "That sounds like a personal problem to me, Cowboy. I can't tell you what to do. If I was a human being instead of a marine, maybe I'd know." This quotation offers a fair sampling of the complex, comedic character of Joker. In many of his actions, he is just a "marine," a killing machine—referring to the napalmed bodies in Hue as "crispy critters," killing an old Vietnamese farmer because the man looked at him sympathetically. He is a true grunt, but he is also someone struggling to make sense of what happens to him. His is the controlling consciousness of the novel, and in his awareness of who he is, we come to see him as a victim of Vietnam. The term *short-timers* refers to those who have only a short time to serve before being rotated back home. Most of the members of Joker's squad are short-timers, but he realizes that "home won't be there anymore and we won't be there either. Upon each of us the war has lodged itself, a black crab feeding."

In 1987, Stanley Kubrick adapted the novel for the screen, with a screenplay by Hasford, Kubrick, and Michael Herr. The result, *Full Metal Jacket*, is generally regarded as among the finest films of the Vietnam War.

FURTHER READING

Don Oberdorfer's *Tet!* (1971) looks at the offensive as "a classic case study of the interaction of war, politics, the press, and public opinion." Philip Melling's *Vietnam in American Literature* (1990) contains an interesting reading of the *The Short-Timers*.

TITANIC, SINKING OF THE (1912)

Built in the Harland-Wolff shipyards in Belfast, Ireland, the RMS *Titanic* was the largest, most luxurious passenger ship of its day. Its advanced engineering design featured watertight compartments, rendering it virtually "unsinkable" and, as such, a symbol of technology's triumph over nature. When on April

10, 1912, it sailed on its maiden voyage from Southhampton, England, to New York, its passenger list included the names of such prominent American millionaires as John Jacob Astor, Benjamin Guggenheim, Isidor Strauss, George Widener, and his son, Harry Elkins Widener. Another noted passenger was Archibald Butt, President William Howard Taft's military aide, returning from high-level meetings with European leaders.

At 11:40 P.M. on April 14, the *Titanic* collided with an iceberg. One hour later, the lifeboats were lowered into the sea, but there were only enough boats for half the passengers. In the ensuing chaos, in which first-class women and children were given priority over passengers in the lower decks, many of these boats were only half-filled. The result: 705 people were rescued, while 1,503 perished.

Many people, particularly those of a conservative religious bent, viewed the sinking of the unsinkable as divine retribution for an arrogant faith in technological progress. The use of the "women and children first" rule in the evacuation—since it exemplified the tradition of the chivalrous male protecting "the weaker sex"—reinforced the opposition to the women's movement of the time. Similarly, the glorification of the men in first class promoted the image of their clear superiority to the immigrants in steerage. These and many other social attitudes emerging in the aftermath of the disaster lent a kind of mythic status to the ship. A measure of the continued vitality of that myth is the 1998 Academy Award–winning *Titanic*, the most financially successful film of all time.

THE LITERATURE

The disaster produced an outpouring of morally toned, uplifting verse, more interesting to cultural historians than readers of literature. Walter Lord's (1917–2002) best-selling *A Night to Remember* (1955) employs a number of interesting stylistic devices, notably the minute-by-minute account of the actual sinking, but it is basically a nonfictional history. Clive Cussler's (1931–) *Raise the Titanic* (1976) and Danielle Steel's (1947–) *No Greater Love* (1991) are two popular novels that capitalize on the sinking (Steel) and the anticipated raising (Cussler) of the ship.

Jack Finney (1911–95), well known for his time-travel novel of 1880s New York *Time and Again* (1970), uses the *Titanic* as the basis for his sequel, *From Time to Time* (1995). Simon Morley, the protagonist of *Time and Again*, residing happily in the 1880s, is dispatched forward to 1912 in an effort to prevent the disaster. The rationale for the effort is that Archibald Butt, who went down with the ship, was carrying papers back from Europe that would have lead to the prevention of WORLD WAR I. As a matter of principle, Morley is unwilling to attempt to alter the part; it is only the unmitigated catastrophe of the First World War, along with the knowledge that his own son will be killed in that war, that compels Morley to make what proves to be an unsuccessful effort to alter the ship's fate. The ship goes down as recorded in history. The conclusion finds Morley back in the 1880s, battening down the hatches in anticipation of the blizzard of 1888.

One major problem with *From Time to Time* is that much of it is given over to a description of New York in 1912, which makes for diverting reading, but which contributes very little to the novel's plot or the development of its two-dimensional characters. Another is that the novel suffers the fate of most sequels: It lacks the fresh appeal and novelty of its predecessor, the charming *Time and Again*. But in its inventive connection to World War I, it reflects the historical imagination in full flight.

The most accomplished of the *Titanic* novels is Beryl Bainbridge's (1933–) *Every Man for Himself* (1996). The main character, Morgan, known only by his last name, is a young man whose only distinction appears to be that he is the nephew of J. P. Morgan, who, as part of his vast fortune, is the owner of the *Titanic's* Cunard Line. Morgan is the son of his uncle's half-sister-in-law, who, after being deserted by his father, died in poverty three years after the boy's birth. Before being rescued from an orphanage by his relatives, he had been living with a woman who had been murdered. These early experiences, forgotten by the young man, have nevertheless left him with one conviction about himself: "I was destined to be a participant rather than a spectator of singular events." Early on, we witness his destiny working itself out, as a man he passes on a street collapses and dies in his arms, an event that will serve a positive purpose later in the novel.

Morgan, having completed a year's work as a draftsman, working on minor features of *Titanic's* design, decides to take part in the ship's maiden voyage, because the presence of hard-drinking sons and daughters of the rich promises fun and possibly romance. Among the people he encounters, however, is a mysterious, charismatic older man, Scurra, who becomes a father figure for Morgan. It is Scurra who imparts the advice that in this world "it is every man for himself." Scurra himself demonstrates this doctrine, in one instance, to Morgan's intense chagrin.

As the novel moves toward its fatal conclusion, the other characters, though they, like the ship, appear impregnable on the surface, begin to their underlying flaws. In the chaos and despair of the final scene, Morgan confirms his inner sense of himself as one destined to be a "participant rather than a spectator," acting with complete disregard for his own interests, until the very last moment before the ship sinks. His heroism continues in the lifeboat, as he organizes the shocked passengers until the rescue arrives. Even then, he reproaches himself for his happiness at being saved: "[T]hat momentary leap of relief was replaced by unease that deepened into guilt, for in that moment I had already begun to forget the dead." Morgan's maturation suggests that given the arbitrary whim of fate governing life, living for others may be the best form of living for oneself.

FURTHER READING
Steven Biel's *Down with the Old Canoe* (1996) provides an illuminating and engaging cultural history of the disaster and its aftermath.

TOTALITARIANISM

Although autocratic rule—tyranny, despotism, dictatorship—is an age-old type of government, a distinctive form emerged in the 20th century, to which Benito Mussolini, one of its practitioners, gave the name *totalitarianism*. The chief characteristic of totalitarianism is its attempt to control every aspect of the life of its subjects, viewing any sign of independence as treasonous. Although despotically controlled by one figure, a totalitarian state operates through a centralized party, which becomes the instrument of policy, supplanting the older legal, educational, religious, and social institutions with new ones. It also involves a radical reshaping of the country's economy. Among its other distinguishing features is a secret police organization, whose aim is to root out any form of dissidence. Perhaps the most chilling aspect of totalitarianism is its perversion of the democratic ideal by insisting on the active participation, not just the submission, of all citizens in support of its policies. Critical to this goal is a pervasive government propaganda campaign, designed to recruit everyone into the role of informer. At its extreme, this effort extends into the most fundamental and tenacious of the old institutions, the family. In a pure totalitarian system, spying on one's family becomes the sacred obligation of the citizen. All of this produces a climate of purposeless fear—purposeless since fear offers no safeguard against the terror the totalitarian government randomly employs. In Joseph STALIN's GREAT TERROR, for example, today's executioner frequently became tomorrow's victim.

Although Mussolini's Italy represents the first example of a 20th century totalitarian society, it never quite reached its desired goal. The two complete forms of totalitarianism in the 20th century have been Adolf HITLER's Germany and Stalin's Soviet Union. Many would add to this list Mao Zedong's China during the period of the CULTURAL REVOLUTION and Pol Pot's Cambodia during and after the CAMBODIAN GENOCIDE. All of these governments came to power in the aftermath of historical catastrophes, which led to despair on the part of the general population, rendering them vulnerable to a false utopian vision of the just society.

In her masterly analysis of the Hitler and Stalin versions of totalitarianism, the political theorist Hannah Arendt argued that Nazism founded its justification on the law of nature, while communism appealed to the law of history. But underlying both principles is the idea of development, or process. That is, the Nazis appealed to "race laws as the expression of the law of nature in man," just as the Communists looked to "class-struggle as the expression of the law of history." Both beliefs rest upon the Darwinian principle of "survival of the fittest," and both translated this developmental process into the "law" of killing or terror: "In the body politic of totalitarian government, the place of positive laws is taken by total terror, which is designed to translate into reality the law of the movement of history or nature." Thus terror is the essence of totalitarian government. For terror to thrive, there must be isolation, loneliness, the feeling of not belonging. Modern alienation has thus provided fertile ground for the growth of totalitarianism. But, fortunately, totalitarian governments contain the seeds of their own destruction; they are engaged in a battle they cannot win, since every human birth is a new beginning of freedom. Eventually *human* nature overcomes the so-called *law* of nature.

THE LITERATURE

By common consent, the definitive fictional treatment of totalitarianism is George Orwell's (1905–50) *1984* (1949), a work that is less a novel than, as the critic Irving Howe has put it, an "anti-Utopian" fiction, a work in which the emphasis is on ideas and theories and in which normal human relations, taken for granted in ordinary novels, become an unreachable ideal. Published in 1949, the book offers a vision of the world 35 years into the future, controlled by three superpowers, each one with its own ideology, and constantly at war with each other. Warfare, in fact, is the principle on which their economies are based. The superstate Oceania contains the land, formerly known as England, now called Airstrip One. Its society is divided into three classes, the Inner Party, the Outer Party, and, the most numerous group, the Proles. The Inner Party consists of the elite, at the head of which stands the omnipresent figure Big Brother, watching everyone through telescreens in place everywhere. At the bottom of the pyramid are the Proles, who are given a certain latitude because they are so easily manipulated. In the middle is the Outer Party, functionaries who must be tightly controlled, since they contain the people most likely to dissent. Outer Party people, for example, are not permitted to have sex with each other. Winston Smith is an Outer Party member and a secret rebel. His rebellion consists of a hidden diary he has been keeping where he records his hatred of the government. He carries his rebellion a step further when he has a sexual affair with Julia, another Outer Party member. Soon the two are arrested, and Winston undergoes torture and interrogation by the menacing O'Brien, who, in a moment of total candor, explains that the Party is not using power as the means to a better end: "The Party seeks power entirely for its own sake. . . . Power is in inflicting pain and humiliation. Power is tearing human minds to pieces and putting them back together again in new shapes of your own choosing." The last sentence describes precisely what O'Brien does to Winston, who ends up drinking gin and gazing at a giant telescreen, happy in the recognition that, at last, "He loved Big Brother."

One measure of the impact of *1984* is its contribution to the language. Phrases such as "War is peace" and "Big Brother is watching you" and terms such as *doublethink, thinkpol* (Thought Police), and *Newspeak* have been incorporated into the political dialogue of English-speaking countries. Newspeak is particularly important, for Orwell devoted an appendix to the new language, describing its grammar and vocabulary. As he represents it Newspeak would be phased in over the decades so that by 2050 it would be fully assimilated. The process by which this would be achieved is simply "the destruction of words." Words like *honor, justice, morality, science,* and *religion* would be eliminated. Any form of sexual conduct would be called *sexcrime*, except for sex without any pleasure between a man and a woman, for which the term was *goodsex*. With the vocabulary reduced to a tiny portion of Oldspeak, as traditional English was called, it would become impossible to translate the opening sentences of the Declaration of Independence into Newspeak, except "to swallow the whole passage in the single word *crimethink*." Orwell explains that, when the transition from Oldspeak to Newspeak was completed, Newspeak would have achieved its goal: Any thought not approved by the Party line would be "unthinkable."

One of the sources and inspirations for *1984* was a Russian anti-Utopian fiction, Eugene Zamyatin's (1884–1937) *We* (1924), a satiric account of a 26th-century state in which everything is regimented according to sound, rational principles. Everything follows a plan, presided over by the leader, the Benefactor. People no longer have names, only numbers, and there is no sense of the singular individual, only the collective "we." Seemingly, everyone is content, particularly the main character, D-503, a mathematician, perfectly at home in his regimented world. But all that changes for him when he falls in love and begins to show signs of a serious illness: "I know that I have imagination; that is what my illness consists of." Introduced by his lover to a group of rebels, D-503 experiences freedom for the first time, and it frightens him. His cure is a special X-ray treatment that restores him to his former happy state. He watches with perfect equanimity as his lover is repeatedly tortured for her rebelliousness. Orwell applauded *We* for its "intuitive grasp of the irrational side of totalitarianism—human sacrifice, cruelty as an end in itself, the worship of a leader who is credited with divine attributes." Zamyatin inevitably ran afoul of the Soviet authorities and was allowed to emigrate to France, where he died in 1937.

FURTHER READING

Hannah Arendt's *The Origins of Totalitarianism* (1951) is the classic text on the subject. Irving Howe's *Orwell's Nineteen Eighty Four: Text, Sources, Criticism* (1963) includes the novel and Orwell's comments on *We*.

TREBLINKA (1942–1943)

A Nazi death camp, located outside of Warsaw, Treblinka served as the chief extermination camp for the WARSAW GHETTO. In the relatively brief span of time when it was in operation (between July 1942 and October 1943), 870,000 people, the overwhelming majority Polish Jews, were murdered there. The camp was a model of genocidal efficiency, in which most prisoners were taken directly from their train transports to the gas chamber. There were two separate camps at Treblinka. One was a forced labor camp, known as Camp One; the extermination camp, Camp Two, was a short distance away.

In March 1943, the head of the SS (Schutzstaffel), Heinrich Himmler, visited Treblinka and ordered that the bodies buried in mass graves be dug up and burned to eliminate any evidence of the murders. In August 1943, convinced that they were about to be killed, a group of prisoners, first setting fire to the camp, led a revolt, in which more than 600 of them escaped to the nearby forests. Of these, only 50 prisoners survived to describe the horrifying reality of life in Treblinka.

One of the key functions at an extermination camp belonged to the person who operated the gas chamber. At Treblinka, the inmates nicknamed that operator "Ivan the Terrible" because of the zeal and energy he displayed in his job. In 1986, John Demjanjuk, a naturalized American citizen who had immigrated to the United States after WORLD WAR II, was extradited to Israel to face charges that he was Ivan the Terrible. In 1988, after a lengthy trial, he was found guilty and sentenced to death. The Israeli Supreme Court later overturned the decision.

THE LITERATURE

Ian MacMillan's (1941–) *Village of a Million Spirits* (1999) centers on the prisoner revolt on August 2, 1943. In his foreword, the author points out that the public events in the novel scrupulously correspond to the known facts, but that all the major characters are fictional. Among these are Voss, an SS officer who dulls the horrors he witnesses every day with liberal dosages of vodka; Janusz Siedlecki, a Jewish teenager with a mysterious, protective aura who becomes one of the camp "dentists," assigned to extract gold from the teeth of the corpses; and Magda, a local Polish farm girl, impregnated by her lover, Anatoly, a Ukrainian guard at the camp. Their stories are interwoven in a series of nonchronological episodes, whose backgrounds always contain the stench of burning bodies and the screams of helpless victims. And in two early episodes, the background becomes foreground as we move from the freight train, where the deportees' illusions are crushed, to the gas chambers, where uncomprehending disbelief accompanies suffocating, anguished death.

Like many novels dealing with the HOLOCAUST, *Village of a Million Spirits* at times becomes almost too painful, bringing the reader close to despair.

As the author's foreword makes clear, this novel is written from the perspective of the end of the 20th century, when genocide is even more prevalent than in the Nazi era and yet a time when Holocaust-denial continues to surface. Treblinka was in fact an early example of that denial. After the dissolution of the camp in 1943, new housing was constructed on the site, where Ukrainian camp personnel were assigned in order to pretend that they had been living there for years and to swear that they never heard of any "camp" in the vicinity. The novel's coda depicts one Ukrainian living in a house that was built from the bricks of the gas chamber: "[H]e studies the bricks, wondering what this scratch is, that discoloration, that tiny material dried and fringed with a stain as if the material had bled an oil into the porous surface of the brick. . . . Everything would have been right if he had not learned about the bricks." The Ukrainian is haunted by the million spirits who died in Treblinka, as are the readers of this novel.

FURTHER READING

Alexander Donat's *The Death Camp Treblinka* (1979) is an authoritative history. Tom Teicholz's *The Trial of Ivan the Terrible* (1990) focuses on the Demjanjuk case.

TRIANGLE SHIRTWAIST FIRE (1911)

On March 25, 1911, a fire broke out on the eighth floor of a factory building on the edge of Washington Square in New York City. When workers at the Triangle Shirtwaist Company, which occupied the eighth, ninth, and 10th floors of the building, attempted to douse the flames, they discovered that the fire hoses were rusted through and that a few of the fire exit doors were locked. Some of the workers rushed out onto the fire escape, but the rusted old structure separated from the wall and sent them crashing to their deaths. The firemen's ladders extended only to the sixth floor, so the employees on the eighth and ninth had to leap into nets, but their number was so great that the nets gave way. In the end, 146 people were killed, the great majority, composed of young Jewish and Italian women, recent immigrants from Europe. The last survivor of the fire, Rose Freedman, died in 2001 at the age of 107. She escaped by following the company's executives to the roof, where she was pulled to the roof of an adjoining building. Rose never forgave the owners' refusal to unlock the doors and continued to fight for the rights of workers all her life.

One of the consequences of the disaster was the implementation of stricter safety laws in factories and other workplaces. The New York State Factory Investigation Commission was established, resulting in the passing of 57 laws relating to factory inspections and safety. Another outcome was the growth of what eventually became the International Ladies Garment Workers Union, one of the most influential American trade unions for many years.

THE LITERATURE

The title of Kevin Baker's (1958–) *Dream Land* (1999) refers to the fabled amusement park in Coney Island, which coincidentally also burnt down in 1911. In this setting, a recent immigrant, and even more recent gangster, Kid Twist, meets Esther Abramowitz, a seamstress and union organizer at the Triangle Shirtwaist Company. In the course of their love affair, Esther becomes increasingly involved with the garment workers' union, participating in its historical strike in 1910. The love story develops against a background of turn-of-the-century New York that includes supporting characters, both historical and fictional, in the manner of E. L. Doctorow's (1931–) *Ragtime* (1975) and Caleb Carr's (1955–) *The Alienist* (1994). Among the mix of historical and fictional figures in *Dream Land* are gangsters, politicians, sideshow dwarves performing at Coney Island, and Sigmund Freud and Carl Jung, visiting the city prior to Freud's delivering the lectures that introduced PSYCHO-ANALYSIS to America. The novel concludes with a dramatic rendering of the fire in which Esther presumably perishes, although after describing her death, the author indulges in several alternative endings in which she survives, suggesting that although many workers died, they lived on in the memories of others (such as Rose Freedman) who continued their fight.

FURTHER READING

Corinne Naden's *The Triangle Shirtwaist Fire* (1971) examines the fire and its later significance.

TROTSKY, LEON (1879–1940)

Born Lev Bronstein—he adopted the name *Trotsky*—in the southern Ukraine, he became active in socialist causes at an early age and was exiled to Siberia in 1898. Four years later he escaped, eventually arriving in London, where he met Vladimir Ilich LENIN and became a leading spokesman for the fledging Russian workers' party. He participated in the 1905 RUSSIAN REVO-LUTION, which resulted in a second arrest and deportation to Siberia. Again he escaped, this time to Vienna, where he became the editor of the socialist newspaper *Pravda*. During WORLD WAR I. he lived in Paris, an outspoken opponent of the war and the intense nationalism it fostered in opposition to his desire for an internationalist workers' movement. He returned to Russia in 1917 to join Lenin in the Bolshevik triumph over the Menshevik faction of the revolutionary movement during the 1917 RUSSIAN REVOLUTION. During the RUSSIAN CIVIL WAR, he served as minister of war, building the various units of the Red Army into a unified fighting force. After the death of Lenin in 1924, Trotsky lost the power struggle to succeed him (he had been Lenin's choice) to Joseph STALIN. In 1927–28, he was expelled from the

Communist Party and sent into exile. Eventually he settled in Mexico, where in 1940 he was assassinated by one of Stalin's agents. During his exile he was a prolific writer and powerful opponent of Stalinism. In *The Revolution Betrayed* (1936), he analyzed Stalin's regime as one in which a small bureaucracy, governed by a dictator, had usurped the function of a true workers' socialism. He also criticized the Soviet government's failure to respond to the growing threat of Nazism. History appears to have vindicated his position on both issues.

THE LITERATURE

Joseph Roth (1894–1939) was an Austrian novelist, best known as the author of *The Radetzky March* (see HAPSBURG EMPIRE.). His novel *The Silent Prophet* (1966; trans., 1980) is an attempt to see Trotsky both as an individual and as a representative of ideological extremism. *The Silent Prophet* was written in 1928, at a time when Trotsky had just been expelled from the Communist Party and his whereabouts were unknown. Roth's Trotsky figure, Friedrich Kargan, is a stateless man, an inherent outsider, whose commitment to the revolution "has become a passion." An illegitimate child, orphaned at an early age, Kargan, although born in Russia, is raised in Trieste, then a part of Austria. As a young employee of a travel agent, he is sent to the Austrian-Russian border to facilitate the passage of immigrants and army deserters from Russia. There he meets Savelli, the novel's Stalin figure, and becomes involved in the revolutionary cause. Arrested by the czar's police, he is sent to Siberia, from which he escapes at the outbreak of World War I. He travels to Zurich, the headquarters of the Russian revolutionaries in exile, returning to Russia at the outbreak of the revolution. But the success of the revolution turns to ashes in his mouth as he sees Savelli's rise betraying its basic principles.

Kargan is a man with no life outside of his commitment to the revolution. As a young man he falls in love with a Viennese woman, but he rejects her because she is a member of the bourgeoisie. His renunciation letter is a masterpiece of Marxist conviction: "I send you this avowal only because . . . I love you. Or—because I mistrust the ideas bourgeois society supplies us with and the words so often misused in your society—I believe I love you." Years later he and the woman have a brief affair, but it occurs just before his exile to Siberia at the end of the novel. However, it is clear that even if the love affair had been sustained, it would never have altered Kargan's vision of life nor liberated him from the frozen hell within which his emotional life is imprisoned. His total commitment has been to an ideal that is being destroyed before his eyes, but the purity of that ideal remains untarnished in his imagination. The novel succeeds in its presentation of Kargan as a cold-blooded ideologue, but it is this very success that undermines the reader's interest in his fate.

FURTHER READING

Irving Howe's *Leon Trotsky* (1978) analyzes the development of his thought. Sidney Rosenfeld's *Understanding Joseph Roth* (2001) provides a critical overview of the novelist's work.

TRUJILLO MOLINA, RAFAEL LEÓNIDAS (1891–1961)

Dictator of the Dominican Republic from his first seizure of power in 1930 until his assassination on May 30, 1961, Trujillo began as a police captain but got himself elected president six years later. Quickly nicknamed "El Jefe" and "the Goat," he consolidated his power—by way of a docile legislature and judiciary and an efficient SIM, or secret police—and amassed a huge personal fortune along the way.

American interests in Dominican cocoa, bananas, sugar, and coffee and Trujillo's staunch anticommunist foreign policy gained him the approbation and support of American COLD WAR politicians and successive post–WORLD WAR II administrations until his excesses turned the tide. As Cordell Hull, former U.S. secretary of state, put it: "He may be a son-of-a-bitch, but he is our son-of-a-bitch." Under his repressive regime, the support of the Catholic Church faltered, and two bishops issued a Pastoral Letter (in 1960), read in all the island churches, calling on him to "halt the excesses, dry the tears, heal the wounds."

In 1960, the Organization of American States placed sanctions on the Dominican Republic that severely depressed the economy and, finally, caused a small coterie, all closely connected with Trujillo—military adjutants, high-ranking soldiers, and managers of his businesses—to hatch a plot to kill the dictator. The plan succeeded, and four men shot him to death on the evening of May 30, 1961.

THE LITERATURE

Mario Vargas Llosa's (1936–) novel *The Feast of the Goat* (2000; trans., 2001) takes its title from a joyous and satirical Dominican merengue, "They Killed the Goat." The novel shows, in detail, exactly how Trujillo exerted his influence.

The book begins with the arrival home in the mid-1990s of Urania Cabral, the 49-year-old, unmarried daughter of Augustin Cabral, once president of Trujillo's Senate but disgraced and removed from office by Trujillo long before the novel begins. Cabral is now a wheelchair-bound victim of a series of strokes. His story and, as his daughter relives 1960–61, Urania's revelations about her role in his life and her encounter with Trujillo frame the novel. Vargas Llosa returns again and again to the scenes of Urania's unfolding of her story in her father's house, in the presence of her female relatives and barely perceiving father. In between Vargas Llosa brings the reader the events of the final day and year of the Goat's life. The narrative entertains a number of points of view: that of Trujillo himself as he lives out that fatal day in 1961 and that of the four principal assassins as they wait on the road to intercept the Goat's Chevrolet, heading toward one of his pleasure domes. Through these four—the Turk, Amadito, Tony Imbert, and Garcia Guerrero—we see the nature of their involvement with Trujillo and with Dominican society. Each, closely bound to Trujillo, nevertheless has a personal grudge and an accompanying hatred of the dictator.

An epic cast of historical characters appears in the novel: the greedy, drunken and degenerate Trujillo clan, including his wife, Maria, known as the "Bountiful First Lady," and his sons, Ramfis and Rhadames; the much-feared head of SIM, Johnny Andres Garcia; the calculating and dissolute but clever adviser, Senator Henry Chirinos; and Trujillo's cunning vice president and successor, Joaquín Balaguer. Dozens of minor figures, both military and civilian, also populate the work. In a central, ironic gesture, the narrator refers to nearly all with great Hispanic courtesy, giving each full three-part names.

In the Trujillo sections of the book, we learn of his mesmeric gaze, his monstrous ego, and his preoccupation with his potency, even as it fails. A physician who gives him the bad news that he has prostate cancer is summarily executed. We also learn of his vast sense of his own infallibility and his shrewd and tireless work on behalf, as he sees it, of "[his] people." We see his fanatical devotion to his personal hygiene, his contempt for "gringos," and his certainty that he can outwit and outmaneuver the United States.

Following the narrative of the assassins, we see them execute the Goat in a hail of bullets. A plot to achieve a coup afterward depends on their leader, General Pupo Roman, who refuses to rouse the military onto the side of the rebellion before he sees the body of Trujillo. Yet though he is shown the body, he falters at the crucial moment and does not act. Such has been the legendary strength and invincibility of the chief and what Vargas Llosa calls the "mystical consubstantiation" that existed between Trujillo and all Dominicans.

The aftermath of Trujillo's death is bloody and chaotic. Conspirators talk—even when not tortured. Pupo Roman is named, captured, and tortured horribly over a period of four months. The torturers force doctors to keep him alive.

Urania Cabral's revelation is the climactic end of the novel, resolving the novel's central mystery, the Kafka-esque fate of Urania's father. Because Senator Cabral had failed in a mission to moderate the Organization of American States (OAS) sanctions, he has been made into a nonperson by the Trujillo regime. Seeking to understand his guilt, Cabral visits Manuel Alfonso, a self-declared pimp for the generalissimo and patriotically proud of this role. Alfonso suggests, without undue subtlety, that his then-14-year-old daughter,

Urania, be offered to Trujillo. The innocent and trusting Urania, thinking she's going to a party, is driven to Trujillo's mahogany house. There we see in graphic detail the chief's inability to achieve an erection, his digital defloration of Urania, and his sending her away in disgust. For Urania in the mid-1990s, this episode is her father's real disgrace, emblematic of all the excesses of the regime, and her survival—sans marriage or close emotional relations—as her triumph.

The violation of Urania represents the fate of the Dominican people, raped and abused by a series of irresistible dictators but clinging tenaciously to life in spite of this history.

FURTHER READING

Nonfictional accounts of Trujillo and his regime may be found in Jesus de Galindez's *The Era of Trujillo—Dominican Dictator* (1973) and German E. Ornes's *Trujillo: Little Caesar of the Caribbean* (1958).

—William Herman

U

ULTRA

Before the outbreak of WORLD WAR II, German military intelligence adopted a cipher machine, the Enigma, to send and receive messages in code. During the war, the Germans reproduced thousands of these machines. Their small size, portability, and user-friendly operation made it possible to supply every German air base, ship, and army headquarters with one. But its most attractive feature was its inscrutability. Capable of hundreds of millions of transpositions for any given letter, the Enigma was as described by Robert Harris, a "masterpiece of human engineering that created both chaos and a tiny ribbon of meaning." Polish mathematicians had made important contributions to solving the Enigma in the years preceding the invasion of Poland in 1939, and they shared their results with British and French intelligence. In 1940, the British set up a unit at Bletchley Park dedicated to breaking the Enigma codes. The British efforts, operating under the code name *Ultra*, drew on the best mathematical and linguistic brains of Oxford and Cambridge. (Bletchley Park was located midway between the two universities.) The most formidable mind of these was that of Alan Turing, who made a critical contribution to the breakthrough by developing the first computer, the "Colossus," which was capable of quantifications equal to Enigma.

Ultra played a key role in the British victory at EL ALAMEIN, in the Allied invasion of Sicily, and in the thwarting of a German counteroffensive aimed at American troops, following the invasion of NORMANDY. It played an even more significant role in the ongoing Allied battle against U-boats in the North Atlantic.

In 1943, the British pooled their intelligence with the Americans, who had earlier succeeded in breaking the Japanese code. The American code-breaking unit, Magic, had its greatest success in pinpointing Midway as the target of the Japanese naval armada, leading to the critical American victory there. Another code-breaking coup was the information that led to the shooting down of a plane carrying the Japanese chief of naval operations, Admiral Isoroku Yamamoto.

THE LITERATURE

A critical period in the history of Ultra occurred between February 1942 and March 1943, when the Germans altered their submarine code, seriously affecting the fate of Allied shipping in the North Atlantic. This crisis forms the subject of Robert Harris's *Enigma* (1995). The central character is Thomas Jericho, the brilliant disciple of Alan Turing and a leading cryptanalyst in Hut 8, the unit devoted to deciphering the naval Enigma code. Jericho has recently undergone a nervous breakdown, occasioned by intense overwork and his rejection, after a brief affair, by Claire Romilly, a beautiful, free-spirited woman working at Bletchley. The cause of the overwork was a German change in the submarine code "Shark," which Jericho had desperately, but successfully, solved. After a brief recuperation at Cambridge, Jericho is summoned back to Bletchley Park because the Germans have now changed their "short weather code," which Jericho had used to penetrate Shark. Upon his return, he discovers that three major American convoys bearing vital supplies are at sea and in imminent danger from submarines, whose locations Ultra is unable to discover. At the same time, Jericho learns that Claire Romily has disappeared.

As Jericho pursues the two mysteries, the new key to solving Shark and the whereabouts of Claire, he enlists the aid of Claire's roommate, Hester Wallace. Together, the two conspire to uncover the two parallel mysteries that soon prove to be interrelated. One of the most moving moments in the novel occurs when they visit a remote intercept station, where the young women operators studiously copy down every Morse-coded message, "eight hours listening at a stretch taking down gibberish. Specially at night in the winter. Bloody freezing out here." One of these women intercepts Jericho to ask if what they do is important: "I know I shouldn't ask, sir—we're never meant to ask are we?—but well *is it?* Rubbish, that's all it is to us, just rubbish, rubbish, all day long and all night, too. . . . Drive you barmy after a bit. . . . You are making sense of it? It is important? I won't tell." As Jericho reassures her, the scene opens up to include the critical supporting role played by thousands, mostly women, providing the raw material for the cryptanalysts. Andrew Greig's novel *The Clouds Above* records a similar debt to women radar operators (see BRITAIN, BATTLE OF).

The solution to the mystery, as Jericho discovers, has all the elegance of a classical mathematical proof, "inevitability, unexpectedness, and economy."

In this case, it also includes an appropriate tribute to a magnificent achievement of human intelligence.

FURTHER READING

Ralph Bennett's two volumes, *Ultra in the West* (1979) and *Ultra and Mediterranean Strategy* (1989), examine the impact of Ultra in two vital areas of the European campaign.

V

VERDUN, BATTLE OF (WORLD WAR I) (1916)

The longest and most famous of the battles of WORLD WAR I, Verdun was a 10-month-long offensive launched by German troops against the French in February 1916 and continued, with both sides alternating as attackers and defenders, until December of that year. Verdun is an ancient city in northeastern France, ringed by a number of forts built in the wake of the Franco-Prussian War of 1870. Its status as an impregnable fortress symbolized for the French people the invincibility of their nation.

The area around Verdun had seen some heavy fighting in 1914 but was relatively quiet until the Germans launched an all-out attack on February 21. The German commander Erich Von Falkenhayn chose Verdun as much for its symbolic as its strategic value. If the Germans could break through there, it would constitute a crippling blow to the morale of the French, whose soldiers were already exhibiting the war-weariness that would eventually erupt in a full-scale mutiny in 1917. The initial attack was preceded by a furious 12-hour artillery barrage that laid waste the French positions, enabling German troops to make significant gains in the first few days. In an attempt to stop the hemorrhaging, the French high command appointed General Henri Pétain, a defensive specialist, as commander of the French forces. Pétain's managerial skill brought order to the French army, enabling it to push back the invading Germans.

Subsequent fighting raged back and forth for the rest of the year, bringing with it staggering casualties. By the conclusion of the offensive in December 1916, close to 1 million men had been killed or wounded, more than 500,000 French and 400,000 German. Although next to nothing of military value had been gained in the battle, it represented a significant psychological victory for France and a personal triumph for Pétain, who became known as "the hero of Verdun," a title that was to acquire an ironic ring some 20 years later, when he became the head of the Vichy government that collaborated with the German occupation during WORLD WAR II.

THE LITERATURE

The French novelist and dramatist Jules Romains (1885–1972) was the author of an epic cycle of 27 novels (*Men of Good Will*), attempting to capture the spirit of French society from the years 1908 to 1933. By general consent the most successful of these novels are volumes XV and XVI, devoted to the battle of Verdun. The English translation of these volumes was published in one volume under the title *Verdun* (1939).

Verdun begins with an acerbic analysis of the war leading up to the battle. A series of brief, juxtaposed scenes introduces a wide range of characters from every sphere of French society: war profiteers to a factory worker, generals to privates. The description of the battle is marked by meticulous accuracy and carefully observed details of the fighting. The most important single character (as he is throughout all the other volumes in *Men of Good Will*) is Joseph Jerphanion, a young teacher recently married, now serving as an officer at the front. Jerphanion is a sensitive, somewhat detached, skeptical observer of life and society. Much of the action in battle is seen through his eyes and filtered through his sensibility.

Nevertheless Romains's goal is not to render individual experience: He is more interested in focusing on the collective soul, an aim he gave expression to in a manifesto written in 1906; here he coined the term *unanimism* to describe his aim as a writer. Influenced by the then new discipline of sociology, Romains sought to uncover the "single soul," which the etymology of the word *unanimism* suggests. Romains's unanimism looks not at the individual being shaped by his environment, as did his predecessor Émile Zola, but at the dynamics of the environment itself, the crosscurrents created by social interaction, as, for example, in Romains's celebrated description of Paris during the evening rush hour. In *Verdun*, this unanimistic approach enables Romains to create a remarkably lucid and comprehensive account of the Verdun Offensive, capturing the critical importance of the battle in the virtually unanimous response of the French people to this threat to their very identity. In its representation of the collective consciousness of France, and of the psychology of war, *Verdun* stakes a major claim to being the most accomplished novel of World War I.

FURTHER READING

B. H. Liddell Hart's *History of the First World War* (rev. ed. 1970) includes a lively and provocative view of the battle. Henri Peyre's *French Novelists of Today* (1967) offers a discerning evaluation of *Verdun*.

VIETNAM WAR (1965–1975)

American involvement in Vietnam began in 1946 when the United States dispatched supplies to French forces during France's failed attempt to restore its colonies in Southeast Asia (see INDOCHINA WAR). In 1954, the French withdrew under a cease-fire agreement, calling for a two-year partition of the country into North and South Vietnam, after which they were to be united following a general election. In the interim, American military and diplomatic advisers replaced the remaining French troops. By 1956, it was clear that the winner of the general election would be the Communist government in the North, led by the popular Ho Chi Minh. Backed by the United States, the leader in the South, Ngo Dinh Diem, refused to hold the election. Meanwhile Diem's autocratic rule had created widespread discontent that led to the development of a strong Communist group within South Vietnam, the National Front for the Liberation of South Vietnam (NLF), also known as the Viet Cong.

In 1958, a civil war broke out, pitting Diem's troops against the Viet Cong, who were closely allied with and supplied by Ho Chi Minh's forces in the North. By 1963, dissatisfaction with Diem and the conduct of the civil war led to a military coup, implicitly sanctioned by the John F. KENNEDY administration, in which Diem was executed and replaced by Nguyen van Thieu. After Kennedy's assassination in November 1963, President Lyndon Johnson, operating on the so-called Domino Theory—the fear that if Vietnam became communist, all of Southeast Asia would follow—rapidly expanded the American military presence, which included special-forces shock troops known as Green Berets.

In 1964, Vietnamese torpedo boats (subsequent revelations indicated that President Johnson had misinformed Congress about the nature of the attacks and the activities of the destroyers) allegedly attacked two American destroyers in the Gulf of Tonkin, and by a virtually unanimous vote the U.S. Congress passed the Gulf of Tonkin Resolution, which gave the administration a free hand in expanding the war. American combat troops began operations in February 1965 with the bombing of supply lines in North Vietnam. The following month, the first regular (as opposed to Special Forces) ground troops landed. By the end of 1965, their number had increased to 180,000. By the end of 1967, close to 500,000 American troops were in Vietnam, employing the state-of-the-art destructive technology of modern warfare—saturation bombing, chemical defoliation, the use of napalm, and the destruction of villages after "relocating" the inhabitants. All of this proved to have little significant impact on the enemy. In January 1968, the Viet Cong launched the TET OFFENSIVE, attacking more than 40 South Vietnamese cities and towns, including Saigon, and capturing the city of Hue.

The Tet Offensive, portrayed every evening on television news, proved to be the turning point of the war for American citizens at home. More than a year earlier, American college students, conditioned by the CIVIL RIGHTS MOVEMENT, had begun demonstrations, sit-ins, and acts of civil disobedience, assailing the war and the Johnson administration's conduct of it. Fueled by a mixture of idealism and self-interest (they did not want to be drafted to fight the war), the students initiated a national debate filled with passionate intensity, often taking the form of a battle of the young versus the older generations. The Tet Offensive—and, later, the MY LAI MASSACRE—demonstrated not only that the war was not going well but also that American generals and politicians had been lying about its success. Johnson's approval ratings plunged, and he subsequently announced that he would not be a candidate for reelection. The stormy 1968 presidential campaign, which saw the assassination of Robert Kennedy and subsequent division among Democrats, ended with the election of Richard M. NIXON, who campaigned on a slogan of "peace with honor" in Vietnam.

Nixon's strategy consisted of arming and training the South Vietnamese military to enable them to replace the American army in the actual conduct of the war. But this approach involved expanding the war by first bombing, and later invading, neighboring Cambodia, which the Viet Cong had been using as a staging area from which to launch their offensives. In 1971, South Vietnamese troops, with American air support, invaded Laos, but the invaders were repelled. In December 1972, the Americans launched the largest, most destructive bombing campaign of the war, concentrating on Hanoi (the northern capital), Haiphong, and other Vietnamese cities. In January 1973, after five years of negotiation, the warring parties signed a cease-fire agreement, which provided for the withdrawal of American military forces, the return of American prisoners of war, and what proved to be the temporary survival of the South Vietnamese regime. Two years later, South Vietnam fell, the evacuation of the American embassy providing the last and most telling picture of a humiliating American defeat.

The death toll of the 10-year war included more than 1 million Vietnamese soldiers, North and South, and more than 55,000 American troops. The final ironic note was that the Domino Theory proved to be a complete misreading of the situation. Postwar Communist regimes in Southeast Asia spent more time in internecine warfare with each other and in developing forms of a capitalist economy than in spreading the doctrines of Karl Marx or Mao Zedong. In America, the war produced a large segment of alienated and disaffected people, especially among those who had either served in or had bitterly opposed the conflict. Both of these groups developed an enduring skepticism of their government. That skepticism would soon grow even stronger as a result of the WATERGATE investigation.

THE LITERATURE

As might be expected, the growing disillusion with war is reflected in the fiction dealing with it. Many of the early novels took an uncritical attitude toward America's involvement. Robin Moore's (1925–) popular *The Green Berets* (1965), later turned into a jingoistic John Wayne film (1967), is the best-known example. But the novels written after the Tet Offensive take on an increasingly critical tone.

A novel notable for its perceptive analysis of the westerner's inability to comprehend the Asian mind is Takeshi Kaiko's (1930–) *Into a Black Sun* (1968; trans., 1980). Kaiko was a journalist covering the war for a Japanese newspaper in 1964–65, the early years of the conflict, but even then the stench of corruption pervaded the air. The nameless narrator of *Into a Black Sun* is, like the author, a Japanese journalist arrived in Saigon to cover the war. Although sympathetic to and admiring of Americans, he sees the imprint of their presence in the desolation and decay of the city. (Kaiko is particularly skilled in representing the smells of the city and its people.)

Early on, the narrator hears a story by an American captain that encapsulates the tragic farce of American involvement. In a small village, a magic fish in a pond has been the source of a number of miracles. As its fame spreads, people from all over Vietnam have come to partake of the curative powers of the water in the pond. The government, concerned about the spread of superstition, has ordered the military to take action. American Special Forces come and dynamite the pond, machine-gun it, and loose some rockets into it, all to no avail. They find no trace of the magic fish. But in the process of polluting and destroying the pond, they have soon alienated the people of the village, who then go over to the Viet Cong. This is a major motif in the novel: the destruction of a culture and its deepest beliefs by forces entirely ignorant of the people they are trying to "improve." When asked by an American officer for the view of the war held by the average Japanese citizen, the narrator responds, "America has betrayed democracy—that's how they look at it . . . it's an uneven contest and ideology doesn't come into the picture. Charlie Cong is small, poor, and barefoot, and Uncle Sam is huge, strong, and rich."

The narrator succumbs to the moral malaise of Saigon, experiencing a parasitical existence, living off the war, misrepresenting it in the very act of translating it into language: "A lion was an indefinable feral source of fear before it was called 'lion'; once labeled, though no less fierce or frightening, it shrank, became another quadruped and little more."

His self-disgust leads him to volunteer to do his reporting from the front lines. He joins a search-and-destroy mission with a company of South Vietnamese soldiers and three American officers acting as liaisons. The group runs into an ambush, in which most of the men are slaughtered. Looking at the bodies sprawled around him, he notes that "all died silently, without complaint, regardless of which field their chests had burst on, North or South."

The distinctive feature of this novel is its Asian perspective. The novel ulti-mately views the once-admired Americans as culpable, but it is a critique written more in sorrow than in anger.

Considered by many to be the finest novel of the Vietnam War, Tim O'Brien's (1946–) *Going after Cacciato* (1978) is a multilayered story that encloses the war within a theme exploring fact and fiction, the real and imag-ined. In Vietnam, reality as experienced by the soldier or civilian lacked order, clarity, and purpose. O'Brien's novel operates on the assumption that only an act of the imagination could create meaning out of the chaos of the war. Interwoven within its texture are three narrative strands, combining to sur-round the major theme. The first of these is the story of a squad's search for one of its members, Cacciato, who has deserted with the announced intention of walking to Paris, some 8,600 miles from the battle scene. The second is the series of powerful and haunting battle scenes the squad participates in. The last is the Observation Post monologues, in which the authorial voice enters the story. Throughout the novel, the laws of chronology are consistently vio-lated; eventually the reader's clearest guide to when a particular event occurs comes from knowing which of the squad members are dead at that time. The novel opens with a litany of the dead:

> It was a bad time. Billy Boy Watkins was dead and so was Frenchie Tucker. Billy Boy had died of fright, scared to death on the field of battle, and Frenchie Tucker had been shot through the nose. Bernie Lynn and Lieu-tenant Sidney Martin had died in tunnels. Pederson was dead and Rudy Chassler was dead. Buff was dead. Ready Mix was dead. They were all among the dead.

The deaths of these soldiers will be described later in the novel, along with those of other squad members. These scenes and the pursuit of Cacciato are seen through the imagination and consciousness of a squad member, Paul Berlin, who is as divided within himself as the city whose name he bears (see BERLIN WALL). Berlin wrestles with his fear, not only of dying, but of dying like Billy Boy, of fear. In searching for Cacciato, he is really looking within himself. As the pursuit becomes more and more an act of Berlin's imagination, it inspires and is inspired by his recollections of the deaths in battle he has wit-nessed. Recovering these recollections, many of which he had suppressed, enables Berlin to come to terms with his fear and his guilt. The chief source of guilt stems from his participation in the squad's murder of its lieutenant, Sidney Martin. The only squad member who had refused to acquiesce in the murder was Cacciato. This raises another question for Paul: Does he have the courage to desert, to "go after Cacciato," in the sense of following in his footsteps?

At the conclusion of the novel, it is clear that the trek to Paris that absorbs much of the book has been imaginary. After an initial attempt to capture Cacciato, the squad had, in fact, returned to its duties. The rest has been imagined by Paul, but, precisely for that reason, it has shaped and reformed Paul into a soldier who understands himself and what his experiences in the war have taught him: He is not free enough to be a deserter, like Cacciato; he is bound to the other members of his squad in a relationship of mutual responsibility. He could never have achieved that understanding without imagining the pursuit of Cacciato. In his mind he has transformed the chaos of war and the fear of death into an act of self-recognition.

The characters of Ward Just's (1935–) *A Dangerous Friend* (1999) are caught up in a tragic conflict between their ideals and the blindness that idealism can sometimes create. Set in the Vietnam of 1965, the critical moment when American involvement was about to pass the point of no return, the novel tells a specific story that is representative of the whole sorry history of the war. The main character is Sidney Parade, who joins a government-subsidized, foreign-aid group in Vietnam, determined to "win the hearts and minds" of the Vietnamese. Unfortunately, the members of the group operate under two fatal illusions. They see their task as "re-forming" Vietnam, showing its people that what they really want is "to live like a Californian." Their other illusion is that they have enough power to offset the power of the military, although this illusion is not shared by their leader, Rostok, a man who "sees around corners."

The plot turns on the effort to rescue a captured air force pilot, the relative of an important congressman. In bringing about the rescue, Parade inadvertently triggers a military retaliation that wipes out an entire village of neutral civilians and endangers the lives of two friends, a French planter and his American wife, two people whom Parade has come to respect and value. As the title suggests, America proves to be a dangerous friend to Vietnam, all the more dangerous when its intervention is clouded over in a haze of good intentions.

Another of the salient facts of the war, the role of the black soldier, emerged as an offshoot of the CIVIL RIGHTS MOVEMENT. The overlapping of civil rights questions with opposition to the war itself came into play on such issues as the disproportionate number of casualties among black American soldiers, raising the question as to whether they were assigned the more hazardous duty. In John A. Williams's (1925) *Captain Blackman* (1972), a wounded black officer pinned down by enemy fire waits for his men to rescue him. While he waits, he conjures up a waking dream in which the history of the black soldier in America unfolds.

Vietnam was a two-front war. The second front, the battle fought at home, was less visible, its wounds interior. The home-front war itself had two zones, the battle between the prowar hawks and the antiwar doves, and the quieter, more destructive one between the returning veterans and the "folks back home." A particularly effective dramatic rendering of the latter is David

Rabe's (1940–) drama *Sticks and Bones* (1969), in which a blinded Vietnam vet returns to his all-American family (the parents are named Ozzie and Harriet, their two sons, David and Ricky). David, the veteran, blinded in battle, is clearly incapable of returning to the sitcom world of his family (most of the action of the play is set in the "television room"). Haunted by the presence of the Vietnamese woman he left behind and the guilt he feels for the violence the war unleashed in him, David is a remorseless threat to the family's superficial serenity. Finally, intimidated and overwhelmed by David's moral judgment of them, the rest of the family leads him to commit suicide.

Robert Stone's (1937–) novel *Dog Soldiers* (1974) records the corrupting effects of the war on the social fabric of American life. John Converse, a newsman in Vietnam, agrees to a scheme to smuggle two kilos of heroin into the United States. He involves in the plan both his wife and the man functioning as the carrier. Although the story begins in Vietnam, the bulk of the novel takes place in California and deals with the corrosive consequences of the scheme for the three individuals and the society as a whole. The war has spread to the homeland, and heroin is the lethal weapon.

FURTHER READING

Frances FitzGerald's Pulitzer Prize–winning *Fire in the Lake* (1972) examines the war in the context of the history of Vietnam. Philip Beidler's *American Literature and the Experience of Vietnam* (1982) is an insightful study by a Vietnam veteran.

W

WALDHEIM, KURT (1918–   )

Waldheim was a career diplomat in the Austrian foreign service. He served as ambassador to Canada (1958–60) and to the United Nations (1960–68) and as Austrian foreign minister (1968–70), returning to the United Nations in 1970. In 1972, he succeeded U Thant as secretary-general of the United Nations, a post he held until 1981. In 1986, he ran for president of Austria. During the campaign, allegations arose concerning his military record during WORLD WAR II. He had been an officer in the German army occupying Yugoslavia and Greece. In 1942, he served in Yugoslavia in an area where the German army conducted brutal reprisals against partisans and civilians. In 1943–44, he was an intelligence officer assigned to antipartisan activities in the village of Arsakli, near the city of Salonika in northern Greece. Salonika had had a large Jewish population for 500 years. In 1943, all 56,000 Jews in the city were deported to concentration camps. Even closer to Arsakli was the village of Hortiati, where, in retaliation for a partisan attack on a German army medical unit in September 1944, the Germans burned the village to the ground. A large number of villagers who had not been able to escape into the hills, including old men, women, and children, were jammed into the village bakery, where they were burned alive.

THE LITERATURE

Edmund Keeley (1928–   ), a distinguished scholar and writer, best known for his English translations of modern Greek poets, has also written seven novels. The most recent of these, *Some Wine for Remembrance* (2001), focuses on the search for evidence of the involvement of a Walhheim-like figure (referred to in the novel as the "Big O") in the Hortiati massacre. The investigator is Jackson Ripaldo, an American journalist enlisted into the investigation by an Austrian friend who heads a committee determined to discover the truth of the Big O's wartime activities. In Arsakli, Ripaldo discovers a villager who had worked as a cleaning woman at German headquarters. After some hesitation, she reveals that she had had a passionate affair with a German soldier, Corporal Schonfeld. Ripaldo is able to track down the deceased Schonfeld's journal, which reveals that he was part of the medical unit ambushed prior to the Hortiati massacre. Immediately after the attack, Schonfeld's superior officer notified intelligence headquarters at Arsakli. Intelligence then ordered the reprisal that culminated in the massacre.

This is as close to a smoking gun as Ripaldo gets, but it is not enough to pinpoint Big O's specific involvement. In the end, Ripaldo, on the edge of obsession, has to settle for the satisfaction of confronting the Big O directly at the Salzburg Theatre Festival and seeing what he perceives to be the guilt in his enemy's eyes. With that, Ripaldo reluctantly decides "to leave the old sinner to himself."

Some Wine for Remembrance exemplifies another genre of historical fiction, that which brings to light a long-overlooked or forgotten event. As a result, the Hortiati massacre emerges on the historical horizon not simply as another Nazi atrocity but as one which reverberates with memory, love, guilt, denial, and the search for justice.

FURTHER READING

Robert Edwin Herzstein's *Waldheim: The Missing Years* (1988) offers a fair-minded, judicious analysis of Waldheim's career in World War II.

THE WAR IN THE PACIFIC (1941–1945)

At 7:55 on the morning of December 7, 1941, Japan launched a massive attack against the United States as its carrier-based aircraft struck the naval base at Pearl Harbor on the Hawaiian island of Oahu. The attack was so devastating that it appeared to have destroyed America's entire Pacific Fleet. By the time Japanese planes returned to their carriers, they had sunk or disabled 19 ships (including six battleships), killed 2,403 soldiers, sailors, and civilians, and destroyed 180 American aircraft, most of them lined up on the ground at Hickham Field. In one of the most thoroughly planned and well-executed maneuvers in modern military history, Japan also attacked American and British bases in Midway, the Philippines, Guam, Hong Kong, and Malaysia. These coordinated attacks led President Franklin Delano ROOSEVELT to speak of December 7 as "a date that will live in infamy" on the following day, when he asked the Congress for a declaration of war against Japan.

Although the bombing of Pearl Harbor is known in history as a "sneak attack," tensions between the United States and Japan had been growing for more than a decade. Japan's renunciation of the Washington Naval Treaty of 1922 and the London Naval Treaty of 1930 had already put Washington on its guard. But when these were followed by the invasion of China in 1937, the alliance with Germany and Italy in 1940, and the occupation of French Indochina in July 1941, a growing sense that war was inevitable seized both nations—and both were beginning to prepare for that war. In the summer of 1941, the United States froze Japanese assets, embargoed petroleum and other war materials, and virtually severed all commercial relations between the two nations. Even as Japanese planes took off from their carriers, negotiations between Japan and the United States were still in progress. But the Japanese prime minister, Tojo Hideki, had decided on war.

Led by Admiral Isoroku Yamamoto, the Japanese high command had carefully planned the attack on America's Pacific Fleet. Months of intensive planning had led the Japanese military to believe that a well-delivered knockout blow on the Pacific Fleet would prove so devastating that it would force the United States to accept Japanese hegemony over Southeast Asia and the Indonesian archipelago. The Japanese fleet of five carriers, two battleships, three cruisers, and 11 destroyers sailed from Japan on November 26 under great secrecy. Eleven days later, with the fleet 275 miles north of Hawaii, Japan sent 360 planes to attack the American naval and air bases. While damage from the attack was extraordinary, and while it illustrated the laxity of American military planning, the attack still fell short of Japan's objectives. The attacking planes missed what the high command considered the most important target, the three aircraft carriers attached to America's Pacific Fleet. None of the carriers was moored in Pearl Harbor on that Sunday morning.

America's Pacific Fleet would be rebuilt with stunning speed, and the aircraft carrier would prove to be the single most important weapon in the island-hopping war that was to follow the attack on Pearl Harbor. Even more important to the ultimate success of America's war effort was the way the attack on Pearl Harbor became a rallying cry that united the entire country. Antiwar sentiment, which had been running strong and had prevented President Roosevelt from carrying out a more aggressive American role in the struggle against the Axis powers, virtually disappeared overnight. Both Congress and the nation-at-large responded to the attack with a determination that the Japanese had not foreseen. The slogan "Remember Pearl Harbor!" became 20th-century America's equivalent of "Remember the Alamo!," and Roosevelt's request for a declaration of war was passed with only a single dissenting voice, that of Representative Jeanette Rankin of Montana. (The first woman to serve in Congress, she had also been the one dissenting congressional voice in the vote that propelled America into WORLD WAR I.) For a discussion of the ongoing debate about Roosevelt's provocation and fore-knowledge of the attack, see PEARL HARBOR CONTROVERSY.

American industry immediately shook off the lingering effects of the GREAT DEPRESSION and focused the nation's immense industrial might on winning the war. As a people, Americans were more unified than ever, and the nation discovered that its physical resources and industrial power were unmatched.

But for the first six months following the attack on Pearl Harbor, Japan's armies swept through Southeast Asia in a series of lightning conquests. With the fall of the fortified Island of Corregidor in May 1942, the entire Philippines fell under Japanese control. In rapid succession, Singapore, the Dutch East Indies, and Burma were overwhelmed. Even Australia seemed vulnerable to a Japanese assault by late spring of 1942. The Japanese military drive wasn't halted until the Americans defeated Japanese forces at the battle of Midway in June 1942, which cost Japan not only four of its aircraft carriers but the impetus it had possessed to that point. For the first time, the Japanese navy had been forced to retreat. When the battle of Guadalcanal in the Solomon Islands also ended in defeat and retreat for the Japanese, the course of the war had decisively changed. From January 1943 on, Japan was to fight a defensive war. American technical superiority, along with the nation's growing confidence in its military performance, would witness one Japanese defeat after the other.

But the War in the Pacific proved to be as long as it was ugly. Fought on islands and archipelagoes once known only to students of geography, it progressed from bloody battle to bloody battle. Almost as difficult for the military as fighting an island-hopping war against Japan's dedicated troops was the constant struggle against disease and a hostile environment. The fighting on Guadalcanal killed some 1,600 American troops. But far more than that number succumbed to malaria and other jungle diseases. In 1944, the American fleet achieved a narrow but decisive victory over the Japanese navy in the LEYTE GULF, which sparked the army's recovery of the Philippines.

As the war progressed, the United States took possession of islands closer to the Japanese mainland, which were then turned into air bases. At this point, a massive bombing campaign against the Japanese mainland began. Japan's cities were constantly targeted as America waged what the French sociologist Raymond Aron has termed "total war." The bombing campaign didn't end until atomic bombs were dropped on HIROSHIMA (August 6, 1945) and Nagasaki (August 9, 1945). The bombing of Japan was already so massive that more Japanese were killed in a single night's firebombing of Tokyo than at either Hiroshima or Nagasaki. Yet with its navy destroyed, its cities in ruins, and its air force reduced to suicide attacks against the encroaching American fleet, there was still some resistance from the Japanese military to the idea of surrender. But because of the emperor's direct intervention, Japan agreed to the surrender terms on August 14, 1945. An exhausted Japanese nation lay in ruins. The official surrender documents were signed on September 2, 1945, on the deck of the USS *Missouri*.

THE LITERATURE

The War in the Pacific would find its most comprehensive literary expression in three naturalistic novels, James Jones's (1921–77) *From Here to Eternity* (1951) and *The Thin Red Line* (1962) and Norman Mailer's (1923–   ) *The Naked and the Dead* (1948). (The final volume of what Jones intended as his war trilogy, *Whistle*, would be posthumously published in 1978. In its way as vivid as its predecessors, it treats not the fighting in the Pacific but the return to the United States of four wounded marines.) Jones and Mailer are the most successful fiction chroniclers of the War in the Pacific, but the war also serves as the background to Herman Wouk's (1915–   ) novel *The Caine Mutiny* (1951). Thomas Heggen (1919–49) also uses the War in the Pacific as the setting of his comic novel *Mister Roberts* (1946), later adapted into a successful play and film. In neither novel, however, is the war actually a felt experience. It is, instead, used as the setting for one of the war's main themes, the fight against tyranny.

The experience of a Japanese soldier in the later stages of the war is memorably captured in Shoai Ooka's (1909–88) *Fires on the Plain* (see LEYTE GULF). An intriguing view of the Japanese military is found in Mishima Yukio's (1925–70) brilliant story "Patriotism" (1966). Mishima renders the ritual suicide of a young army officer with obvious admiration and empathy. His sympathy for the code of honor that allows *seppuku* (ritual disembowelment) frames a mind-set peculiar to that segment of Japanese society that dominated the military. Although it is a deeply poetic story, "Patriotism" is entirely realistic. After reading it, one understands why, even after Hiroshima and Nagasaki had been destroyed, some members of the Japanese army wanted to continue the war.

The view of the war from the victorious American side is less spiritual. It is also far less triumphal, as neither Jones nor Mailer glorifies the American side in the war or the role of the fighting American. Each views the war from the vantage of the enlisted man, and each sees fighting against the Japanese as a point from which to take a fresh look at America itself. In *From Here to Eternity*, the only combat in the novel occurs at the end, when Pearl Harbor is attacked. Among the accidental casualties is the novel's protagonist, Private Robert E. Lee Prewitt. While *The Naked and the Dead* and *The Thin Red Line* both contain detailed scenes of combat, the Japanese army is somehow absent from the consciousness of Jones and Mailer. These novels engage the reader in the details of the fighting, but they fail to make the enemy as real as the physical landscape. Mailer and Jones view the enemy not so much as Japan or as the jungle terrain in which the fighting takes place but as the American world from which the GI's emerge.

This reflects the traditional writer's view of war in American fiction. The war novel is as much a novel of social commentary as it is a novel about fighting between powers. The model Mailer and Jones each used when they approached the task of writing a novel about a group of soldiers was John Dos Passos's (1896–1970) *U.S.A.*, which looks at American society from the turn of the century to the depression of the 1930s. The men doing the fighting on Guadalcanal (the island in *The Thin Red Line*) and Anopopei (the name Mailer gives to the island in *The Naked and the Dead*) seem to probe the heart of the nation, exploring the most fundamental of American conflicts, the struggle between the individual and society. The men in *The Thin Red Line* are so blended that C-company, the central group of soldiers in the novel, becomes not so much a group as a singular condition of war (this dramatic element was distorted by director Terrence Malick in his 1998 adaptation of Jones's novel, in which there are more than 200 speaking parts). We are focused not on the different men but on the single unit, whose job is to eliminate the Japanese on Guadalcanal. Mailer's platoon in *The Naked and the Dead* is carefully designed so that it can be seen as a microcosm of America. The men bring to the war on Anopopei their vigorous racial and religious hatreds. Separate chapters record the prewar lives of the characters, from the self-absorbed ambitious commanding general to the men of a reconnaissance platoon. Mailer depicts a bitter world in which officers and men on the same side fear and distrust each other more than they do the enemy.

Of the novels under discussion, *From Here to Eternity* is probably most successful in creating characters able to stand as individuals. But that is because Jones was writing about the prewar army of drifters and rootless men, seeking to get away, even when they aren't sure of what it is they want to get away from. And to some extent, Jones's novel suffers from the kind of tough sentimentality that made it such a successful Hollywood film in 1953. (The film received eight Academy Awards.) Using the peculiarly hard-boiled sentimentality that both Hollywood and naturalistic fiction employ, *From Here to Eternity* becomes an indictment of stratified American society rather than of the men who made up the prewar army. And it is a fitting commentary on how the War in the Pacific was viewed in the nation's popular consciousness. During almost four years of intense, unrelenting warfare, many films about the war were produced in Hollywood. And they offer, even when viewed as propaganda, excellent examples of how the enemy in a war is visibly invisible. Even in the best of those films, we are faced with an enemy so dehumanized as to be beyond caricature. In a curious way, serious novelists such as Mailer and Jones, who began their novels about the war as soon as it ended, do much the same thing—only they dehumanize not by caricature but by ignoring the enemy.

Contrary to a good deal of criticism, the novels about the War in the Pacific did manage to depict a nation that had begun to emerge with a new sense of its own power. *The Naked and the Dead* and *From Here to Eternity* share the sense that the depression had ended and that the America that had emerged from the war was the world's dominant power. That neither Mailer nor Jones would depict that America with very much objectivity in their later novels is of little consequence, particularly since objectivity is not a characteristic we usually require of novelists. They were war novelists, and a good deal of their fight was with the nation itself.

FURTHER READING

The number of books about the war in the Pacific is gargantuan. John Costello's *The Pacific War* (1981) and William Craig's *The Fall of Japan* (1967) trace the events that led to Japan's military defeat. Although it was published more than 50 years ago, soon after the war's end in 1950, Herbert Feis's *The Road to Pearl Harbor: The Coming of the War between the United States and Japan* remains of interest. Feis's *The Atomic Bomb and the End of World War II* (1966) tells the story of the cataclysmic event that led to Japan's surrender. An excellent journalist and historian, William Manchester has authored a superb memoir about his life as a young marine and his reaction to what has evolved in the Pacific since the war, entitled *Goodbye, Darkness: A Memoir of the Pacific War* (1980).

—Leonard Kriegel

WARLORDS (CHINA) (1917–1927)

After the successful Chinese Revolution of 1911, Sun Yat-sen, the revolutionary leader, established a republican government. Elected president, he stepped down, replaced by the military leader Yuan Shikai (Shih-k'ai). However, Yuan Shikai tried to set himself up as emperor, a move that divided the nation. When Yuan Shikai died in 1916, he left behind a seriously weakened national government. Into that vacuum stepped the leaders of various personal armies scattered throughout the fledgling republic. These military commanders, known as warlords, had complete control of civilian as well as military operations in their particular provinces. There were more than 100 such figures, many of them interested in expanding their territory, resulting in almost constant warfare with each other. For most of the Chinese population, the warlord era was a period of bloodshed, chaos, and terror. Along with these evils, the warlords also fostered the reintroduction of the large-scale production and use of opium.

In a successful campaign known as the Northern Expedition, Chiang Kai-shek's nationalist army, in coalition with the Communist army, systematically defeated a number of major warlords, while others joined forces with him. After Chiang's break with the Communists (see SHANGHAI UPRISING), he came to depend on warlord support, thereby weakening his efforts to establish a unified rule in China.

THE LITERATURE

Although most of the warlords were little better than roaming bandits, a few were men of honor and principle, dedicated to the preservation of traditional religious and cultural values. Such a leader is Tang Shan-teh, warlord in the northern province of Shandong (Shantung), and the fictional protagonist of Malcolm Bosse's (1926–2002) *The Warlord* (1983). Tang is an intelligent, idealistic, and selfless warrior deeply concerned for the future of China, which appears fated to fall into the hands of a foreign power, Japan in particular. As a follower of Confucius, Tang leads an ascetic life, rooted in respect for his ancestors. The threat to these principles takes the form of the beautiful Vera Rogacheva, a White Russian émigré and survivor of the Bolshevik Revolution (the RUSSIAN REVOLUTION [1917]). Vera is the mistress of Erich Luckner, a German arms dealer, who is selling weapons to Tang. Once Vera and Tang meet, their fates are sealed. Their love affair distracts him sufficiently that he is left open to his enemies. Meeting with Chiang Kai-shek, who is consolidating his power and looking for allies, Tang discovers that he has earned Chiang's enmity, principally because of Vera, who is particularly objectionable to Chiang because she is not only a foreigner, but a Russian. From Chiang's point of view, a Russian is a communist, Chiang's fiercest enemy. Tang faces a series of betrayals, personal and political, including that of a young American soldier in his army who falls in love with Vera. But at the end, Tang recovers his dignity and philosophical calm in the face of death. Vera, pregnant with his child, leaves with the American for the West, as the darkening years of the 1930s loom in China's future.

FURTHER READING

Edward McCord's *The Power of the Gun: The Emergence of Modern Chinese Warlordism* (1993) analyzes the roots and development of the warlord phenomenon.

WARSAW GHETTO (WORLD WAR II)

After the German conquest of Poland in 1939, the Jewish population of Warsaw, which included some 400,000 people, was forced to move into a quarter in the city, which was then walled off. The penalty for leaving the walled ghetto without permission was death. Under the guise of offering a form of self-government, the Nazis set up a Jewish Council (Judenrat) and a Jewish police force. In actuality, both the council and the police were under the total control of the Germans. By 1941, faced with incredibly overcrowded conditions and a chronic shortage of food, Jews were dying of starvation, disease, exposure to cold, or execution at the rate of 4,000 a month. The following year the Germans intensified this pace by regularly rounding up Jews and deporting them to the nearby TREBLINKA extermination camp. Eventually 250,000 Warsaw Jews were murdered in Treblinka.

While these deportations were going on, some ghetto residents formed a resistance group, the Jewish Fighting Organization (ZOB). In January 1943, when the Germans attempted to deport more Jews from the ghetto, the ZOB, armed primarily with pistols, fought back. Taken by surprise, the Germans postponed their operation. When they made their next attempt, in April 1943, they were under orders from the Gestapo chief Heinrich Himmler to eradicate the ghetto completely. Employing only small-arms weapons and Molotov cocktails, the rebels held the invaders at bay, while the remaining Jews, refusing to comply with orders to present themselves for deportation, hid out in bunkers, tunnels, and sewers. The ZOB's strategy involved hit-and-run guerrilla activity that enabled the vastly outnumbered fighters to maintain the struggle for three weeks. When the battle was over, the Germans razed every building in the ghetto.

THE LITERATURE

After visiting the ruins of the Warsaw Ghetto near the end of WORLD WAR II, the novelist/journalist John Hersey (1914–93) became determined to write a novel about the uprising. His chief problem was that all the available sources at the time were written in Polish or Yiddish. His response was to have the source materials, mostly diaries and personal reports, translated not into writing but spoken into wire recorders. Listening to the voices of the translators proved to play a pivotal role in shaping what became his novel *The Wall* (1950). He realized that the story had to be told not by a third-person, authorial narrator, but "by a Jew . . . a person who was there . . . imagination would not serve, only memory would serve. . . . I had to invent a memory." In *The Wall*, that person is Noach Levinson, a composite character of the many diarists who left a record of life in the ghetto.

Levinson's account is a personal history in which he probes the members of his underground group in order to get at the "felt life," the moral and emotional issues, that confront them in the crisis. In effect, his account is a device that enables Hersey to introduce seamlessly into the historical record the material of serious fiction. The result is a gripping, compelling story in which heroism, fear, agony, and rage become daily commonplaces. Two scenes are particularly memorable. In the first, Levinson in the midst of the uprising delivers a lecture in the bunkers on the meaning of Jewishness, as expressed in the work of Yiddish writer Isaac Peretz. In the second, a newborn baby's continuous crying threatens to give away the hiding place of 100 people. Taking the infant from the distraught mother, the leader of the group silences the infant in the only way that seems possible.

Beginning in November 1939, two months after the fall of Poland, and concluding in May 1943, when the remains of the group make their escape to the woods outside of Warsaw, Levinson records the degradation, humiliation, and ultimately the destruction of the Warsaw Jews, while highlighting the individual spirit that somehow manages to assert itself in the face of annihilation. Ironically, no small part of that individual affirmation lies in each member's collective identity as a Jew—as if to say the Nazis' fanatical hatred, rather than exterminating Judaism, gave it a new birth.

Another American novel dealing with the uprising is Leon Uris's (1924–2003) *Mila 18* (1960). The title refers to the address of the ZOB headquarters in the ghetto. *Mila 18* shares some strong similarities with *The Wall*. Both novels rely heavily on the archival sources; both employ fictional diarists, although the diary entries play a much smaller role in Mila 18; and both conclude with the escape of some survivors through a sewer manhole and into a waiting truck.

The chief difference between the two books lies in the fact that *Mila 18* was written for a popular audience. It is a swiftly moving, exciting, highly readable novel, relying, both in style and content, on the devices of melodrama—two-dimensional characters, plots filled with action and intrigue, and strong appeals to the readers' emotions. Certainly these elements are also present in *The Wall*, but there they are subordinated within a more challenging intellectual and emotional texture. Thus, with the precedent of *The Wall* in mind, many critics of *Mila 18* took a negative view of the novel precisely because they felt the subject matter deserved better. The reviewer for *Time* magazine, for example, dismissed it as "the type of theatricality that demeans the subject it was meant to dignify." Countless readers of *Mila 18* (it was a Book-of-the-Month Club selection and has gone through more than 35 printings in the paperback edition) would doubtless disagree. Among the questions that the difference between popular and critical judgments raises for historical fiction are: What impact does each type of treatment have on the "afterlife" of the event itself? How is the event fixed in the minds of later generations?

FURTHER READING

Israel Gutman's *Resistance: The Warsaw Ghetto Uprising* (1994) is an authoritative account.

WATERGATE SCANDAL

In the midst of the 1972 presidential campaign, in the early-morning hours of June 17, five men broke into the offices of the Democratic National Campaign at Washington's Watergate apartment and office building complex. Their intention was to plant wiretaps in the Democrats' office. Police arrested the five along with two others, who had supervised the break-in. Denying any connection with the burglary, President Richard M. NIXON was reelected by a wide margin. Subsequent investigative reporting by two reporters for the *Washington Post*, Bob Woodward and Carl Bernstein, revealed that the interlopers had been on a secret payroll of the Committee for the Re-election of the President (CREEP). Operating with clues supplied by an anonymous White House insider (code-named "Deep Throat"), Woodward and Bernstein began to unravel a pattern of illegality and "dirty tricks," of which the break-in was only one example. In 1973, the burglars went on trial before Judge John Sirica, whose close questioning of the defendants revealed their connections to the president's personal staff. A subsequent televised senatorial investigation, chaired by Senator Sam Ervin, led to the testimony of John Dean, special counsel to the president, which indicated the president's knowledge of the cover-up that followed, although not necessarily of the break-in. Further testimony directly involved the president's chief of staff, H. R. Haldeman, and John Ehrlichman, his domestic adviser, both of whom were forced to resign and later served prison terms for perjury and obstruction of justice.

The next significant revelation in the hearings came when a witness casually mentioned that the president had installed a taping system in his office, which recorded all of his conversations. When the special prosecutor investigating the scandal, Archibald Cox, sued to have access to the tapes, Nixon fired him, whereupon his attorney general, Elliot Richardson, resigned in protest. Forced to name a new special prosecutor, Leon Jaworski, the president continued to deny any guilt, proclaiming at one point, "I am not a crook." In July 1974, the Supreme Court ruled that Nixon had to turn over the tapes to the special prosecutor. Facing impeachment as well as conviction, he relinquished the tapes, some of which implicated him in the cover-up. On August 8, 1974, he resigned from the presidency. A month later, the new president, Gerald Ford, pardoned him.

The Watergate legacy was twofold: On the one hand, the revelations and the subsequent pardon deepened the skepticism of many about the nature of politics and the integrity of government. On the other hand, the scandal also demonstrated the power of a free press, the strength of constitutional law, and the basic stability of a nation that could experience the deposition of its leader without a shot being fired.

THE LITERATURE

The narrator of Herman Wouk's (1915–   ) novel *Inside, Outside* (1985) is Israel David Goodkind, a prominent tax lawyer, hired as special assistant to President Nixon in 1973, just as the Watergate problem is about to reach its boiling point. Goodkind's chief task is to act as an unofficial liaison between the Israeli ambassador and the White House. Thus the frame stories in the novel are the unraveling of Watergate and the 1973 Yom Kippur War between Israel and Egypt (see ARAB-ISRAELI CONFLICT). But the bulk of the novel is given over to to Goodkind's memoirs of his early days in the 1930s, specifically his job as a gag writer, refashioning old jokes that his boss, the charismatic Harry Goldhandler, sells to professional comedians, and to Goodkind's passionate affair with an actress, Bobbie Webb, whom he cannot marry because she is not Jewish.

Since Goodkind has no direct involvement in Watergate, his story sheds light on that time only in its descriptions of Nixon before his fall: "He dwells in a dark hole somewhere deep inside himself, and all the world sees of the real man . . . is the faint gleam of phosphorescent eyes peering from that hole." To Goodkind, as to so many others, the man remains a mystery.

FURTHER READING

Stanley Kutler's *The Wars of Watergate: The Last Crisis of Richard Nixon* (1990) is an excellent study of the scandal.

WESTERN FRONT (WORLD WAR I) (1914–1918)

Adopting a strategy known as the Schlieffen Plan, the German army invaded Belgium on August 3, 1914, and advanced into France, overwhelming retreating Allied troops until they were within 30 miles of Paris. At that point, near the MARNE River, the Allies counterattacked, halting the advance. Had the Germans continued their advance, they almost certainly would have captured Paris, but fearing that their supply lines were overextended, they chose to dig in along a front that formed an arc, eventually stretching from the coast of the English Channel in Flanders to VERDUN, near the Swiss border. It was this site—the western front—that was to be the scene of trench warfare over the next four years, a stalemate in which little ground would be won and many lives would be lost. The front was, in historian Eric Hobsbawm's words, "a machine for massacre such as probably had never before been seen in the history of warfare." The long drudgery of the war, periodically interrupted by major offensives launched at the SOMME, PASSCHENDAELE, LOOS, and Verdun, left the rank and file of both sides demoralized, war-weary, and profoundly suspicious of the authorities, military and political, that were responsible for the bloodletting.

In 1918, having defeated the Russians on the EASTERN FRONT, the Germans risked one more throw of the dice with a massive offensive in what came to be called the second battle of the Somme. They might have succeeded but for the presence of the newest ally, the Americans, who brought overwhelming numbers of fresh troops and arms to the Allied side. The Allies launched their final offensive in the MEUSE-ARGONNE area of the front in the fall of 1918. The offensive was a success, but not enough to end the war. The armistice on November 11, 1918, resulted not directly from the military situation, but from the collapse of the German government on the home front, triggered by the starvation and despair of the mass of German people.

THE LITERATURE

The most famous literary treatment of this sector is Erich Maria Remarque's (1898–1970) *All Quiet on the Western Front* (1929; trans., 1930). Narrated by a 19-year-old German foot soldier, Paul Baumer, the novel depicts the terror, degradation, and death that permeated trench warfare. Filled with patriotic fervor, Baumer and his classmates leave school in his quiet village to join the army. In training camp, they receive their first shock, encountering the mindless rigidity of military life and the petty tyranny of the corporal who oversees them. Once at the front, they are initiated into the butchery of modern warfare and the camaraderie of fellow sufferers in hell. Typical of the style and the experiences recorded in the novel in Paul's description, after a bombardment, of the wounded horses on the battlefield:

> The men cannot overtake the wounded beasts that fly in their pain, their wide-open mouths, full of anguish. One of the horses goes down on one knee, a shot—one horse drops—another. The last one drops itself on its forelegs and drags itself around in a circle . . . in circles on its stiffened forelegs, apparently its back is broken. The soldier runs up and shoots it. Slowly, humbly, it sinks to the ground.

When Paul goes home on leave, he discovers that a chasm has opened up between the simple life he had known and the nightmare reality of the front. Attempting to read some of his favorite books in his room, he exclaims, "I want to feel the same powerful, nameless urge I used to feel when I turned to my books . . . the quick joy in the world of thought. . . . I take one of the books intending to read. But I put it away and take out another. . . . Words, words, words—they do not reach me. Slowly I replace the books back on the shelves."

When he returns, he goes on night patrol and gets lost; when a French soldier falls into the shell-hole in which he is hiding, Paul stabs him. For the next day, still under bombardment, he must stay with the dying man, doing penance for killing not the anonymous enemy, but a man like himself. Later, Paul is wounded, which provides another brief respite from the terror. In the meantime all of his close companions are killed and, with them, any hope for the future. Finally, one month before the armistice, he is killed by a single bullet on an unusually quiet day on the front.

Upon publication in 1928, the novel caused a popular sensation, although it was regarded by the radical left as apolitical and therefore shallow, and by the newly rising Nazi party as a blasphemous libel on the German army and nation. When Hitler came to power in 1933, copies of the book were publicly burned. In the rest of the world, however, *All Quiet on the Western Front* assumed the status of a classic. Millions of copies have been sold in the more than 40 languages into which the novel has been translated. Its popularity was enhanced by the moving film adaptation directed by Lewis Milestone in 1930.

FURTHER READING

Richard Firda's *All Quiet on the Western Front: Literary Analysis and Cultural Context* (1993) looks at the novel from a cultural/historical perspective.

WOMEN'S MOVEMENT

See FEMINIST MOVEMENT.

WORLD WAR I (1914–1918)

The first World War is most notable for its wanton destruction of lives—almost 10 million killed, 20 million wounded. The staggering loss of life resulted primarily from the technological advances of modern warfare—including barbed wire, poison gas, the machine gun, and massive artillery—but no small part of the slaughter grew out of the blindness of military tacticians on both sides who continued to rely on huge infantry attacks, in which waves of soldiers burdened with heavy backpacks went over the top of their trenches to be mowed down on an open plain—no-man's-land—time after time.

But the Great War, as it was known, is even more notable for the catastrophic consequences that followed in its wake. WORLD WAR II, despite its wider impact, remains not just a result of World War I, but an extension of it. At the roots of the Great War were developments that might easily have been avoided. Instead, with what appears to be in hindsight a kind of whimsical carelessness, the great powers plunged Europe into an abyss of suffering and misery, which was then compounded by the cynicism and self-interest that created the terms of the five separate peace treaties in 1919 that concluded the war.

The years preceding the outbreak were marked by relative peace and prosperity, giving the superficial impression of a civilization too advanced for war. However, as with the case of the *TITANIC*, a ship thought too technologically sound to be sunk, there was shaping beneath the surface an iceberg in the form of military buildups fueled by national jealousies and fears. The Germans were envious of the English and French colonial empires in Asia and Africa. The English, in turn, feared Germany's naval development, designed to challenge British supremacy at sea, while the French, still smarting from their loss of Alsace-Lorraine in the Franco-Prussian War of 1870, armed themselves in anticipation of a reenactment of that war. Meanwhile three imperial powers—Austria-Hungary, Russia, and the Ottoman Empire—all teetered on the brink of revolution within their borders, sparked by unrest within the ethnic minority populations they had mistreated for years. As a result, the major nations set up a series of alliances designed to ensure mutual protection. In 1907, Britain, Russia, and France formed the Triple Entente, which led Germany to feel both isolated and "surrounded." In turn, the Germans concluded comparable pacts with Austria-Hungary and the Ottoman Empire.

Thus the fuse was in place; it was lit in Sarajevo on June 28, 1914, when Archduke FRANZ FERDINAND, heir of the Austrian emperor Franz Joseph, was assassinated by a Serbian nationalist. Soon after, Austria declared war on Serbia, and Germany, Austria's ally, declared war on Russia and France, leading Great Britain to declare war on Germany. Joining the German and Austrian empires were the Ottoman Empire and Bulgaria. In 1915, Italy, following a failed attempt to cut a deal with the Austrians on postwar spoils, came into the war on the side of the Allies. In 1917, after considerable soul-searching on the part of President Woodrow Wilson, the United States entered the war, a move that had a decisive effect on the outcome. The war drew to a close amid political chaos and social upheaval. The Russian Empire was transformed into the Union of Soviet Socialist Republics (USSR), while the three empires on the losing side—the Austro-Hungarian, German, and Ottoman—were dissolved, transforming the map of Europe and the Middle East in a way that had, and continues to have, profound consequences for the stability of the continent.

THE LITERATURE

In the beginning, the literature of World War I on both sides was predictably supportive—depicting the conflict as a quasi-religious crusade, calling the nation to its sacred duty, demonizing the enemy, and extolling the nobility of dying for one's country. In England this type of drum-beating patriotism was reflected in the poems of Rudyard Kipling (1865–1936), and Rupert Brooke (1887–1915), the latter a young soldier poet whose early death before seeing action transformed him into a symbol of the glory of English manhood. The religious theme emerged in the journalist Arthur Machen's (1863–1947) *The Angels of Mons* (1915), which reported the appearance of ghostly spirits in the form of old English bowmen, fighting alongside British troops during the battle of Mons. Ironically, this flight of fancy occupied a major role in popular English mythology, sustaining the home front's belief in the war. Some German writers, notably Ernst Jünger (1895–1998) (*Storm of Steel*) embraced the tradition of war in itself as a mystical and spiritual enhancement of human life, a belief that lingered in the mind of at least one German soldier, an obscure corporal named Adolf HITLER. Similarly, in France, the poet and essayist Charles Péguy (1873–1914), who maintained simultaneous commitments to Catholicism, militarism, nationalism, and socialism—all these symbolized in the figure of Joan of Arc—glorified the war as the setting for France's return to greatness. In America, this type of propaganda literature is reflected in Edith Wharton's (1862–1937) *The Marne* (1918), a novel describing America's entry into the war as an irresistible force "powered from the reservoir of the new world to replace the wasted veins of the old."

But when the people who were actually experiencing this new form of mechanized warfare and its attendant slaughter began writing, the war took on a different look and its literature a different language. Heroic ideals and romantic imagery gave way to anger and ironic images rooted in the concrete reality of death and dying. Among the first to experience the war not as a crusade but, in Ernest Hemingway's words, as "the most colossal, murderous, mismanaged butchery that has ever taken place on earth" were the English poets Siegfried Sassoon (1886–1967), Isaac Rosenberg (1890–1918), and Wilfred Owen (1893–1918). Two of these poets, Owen and Rosenberg, were killed in combat. Typical of their poems are Rosenberg's "Break of Day in the Trenches," an ironic ode to the rat, the trench soldier's constant companion, and Owen's "Dulce et Decorum Est," a furious rejection of Ovid's "Dulce et decorum est pro patria mori" ("It is sweet and just to die for one's country"). The great Russian poet Anna Akhmatova (1889–1966), whose work spanned the two world wars and the momentous upheavals within Russia in the 20th century, wrote powerful poems on the war, including the prophetic "July, 1914," in which she foresees "famine, tremors, death all around" as the consequence of the impending war.

Along with these poets were novelists such as the French writer Henri Barbusse (1873–1935), whose *Under Fire* (1916; trans., 1917) offered an authentic voice describing the inglorious reality that gave the lie to official propaganda. Barbusse's dirty, weary, cynical infantrymen, their speech liberally sprinkled with obscenities, want no part of military glory, nor do they hate their German counterparts, whom they see as fellow victims. In this representation of the common soldiers transcending the limitations of nationalism, Barbusse is heavily influenced by his internationalist, communist convictions. In sharp contrast to this social view is the perspective offered in some of the most outstanding English novels emerging from the war, Ford Madox Ford's (1873–1939) tetralogy *Parade's End*, consisting of *Some Do Not* (1924), *No More Parades* (1925), *A Man Could Stand Up* (1926), and *The Last Post* (1928). According to Ford, in these works he assumed "the really proud position" of "historian of his own times." To that end, the tetralogy covers the period from 1912 to the postwar years, depicting the social, moral, and political war-induced changes in England on both the home front and the battlegrounds.

Ford's protagonist is Christopher Tietjens, an old-school Tory landowner, wedded to traditional values, appalled by what he sees as the dissolution of those values. Tietjens is woefully ill-equipped to deal with the emerging modern world, hampered as he is by a stubborn integrity and fidelity to his own sense of honor. His military career is constantly undermined by the machinations of his wife in collaboration with his treacherous commanding officer. Largely regarded as a failure, he is in fact a brave and intelligent officer, qualities that go unrecognized by his crass, careerist superiors. In the end he succumbs to the inevitable: "The war had made a man of him. It had coarsened him and hardened him." Eventually he finds a place in the postwar world for himself and the long-suffering woman he loves. He comes to accept the diminished modern world. The Great War was a catalyst of change to a mechanical, debased world, but still one where "a man could stand up."

Important American novels to emerge from World War I include Ernest Hemingway's *A Farewell to Arms* (1929) (see CAPORETTO), e. e. cummings's *The Enormous Room* (1922), and John Dos Passos's *Three Soldiers* (1921). Of these, *The Enormous Room* is the most unusual both in subject and tone. It is the fictionalized account of Cummings's experience while serving as an ambulance driver for the French forces. In 1917, he and his friend were arrested for treason by French authorities and sent to the Ferté prison, where he was confined for three months. *The Enormous Room* is a protest against the war itself, most pointedly against the intransigence and arbitrariness of the military mind and its ruthless disregard of the individual.

A similar theme underlies *Three Soldiers*. The three soldiers represent three character types from three different social spheres: Fuselli is an Italian American from the West Coast intent on making a success of his military career; Chrisfield is a midwestern farm boy who seeks in war an outlet for his violent nature; and the main character, John Andrews, is a university graduate and aspiring composer who joins the army in an effort to find fulfillment in some vaguely perceived act of self-sacrifice. All three soon fall victim to the bureaucratic constraints and soul-deadening routines of army life. Implicit in the novel is the suggestion that the army is a metaphor for all of modern life, in which the twin forces of mechanization and bureaucratization combine to imprison the individual spirit.

Recent years have seen a revival of interest in the First World War as a literary subject. Among the best of these newer works are two by English women novelists, Susan Hill (1942–) and Pat Barker (1943–), as well as Sebastian Faulks's (1953–) *Birdsong* (see MESSINES). Susan Hill's *Strange Meeting* (1971) is the story of the close friendship between two young British officers in the trenches. John Hilliard, a disillusioned, wounded veteran of the war rejoins his battalion shortly before they are due to return to the front lines. His new roommate, David Barton, is a newcomer to the battlefield, a man of unflagging good humor and open-heartedness. Barton's fundamental goodness helps Hilliard overcome his alienation and sense of despair. Barton, the product of a large and loving family, to whom he writes long and cheerful letters, invites his family to correspond with Hilliard, whose own family is cold and emotionally ungiving. Once exposed to the horrors of the trenches, however, it is Barton whose spirit and nerves need to be strengthened. Hilliard is able to mitigate Barton's suicidal depression, and the two become even closer. In a particularly futile patrol operation, Hilliard is seriously wounded, and Barton is killed. Hilliard is again plunged into despair, but the novel concludes on an optimistic note as Hilliard goes to visit Barton's family with the sense of someone who is at last coming home. *Strange Meeting* is well written, particularly in its depiction of trench life and military combat. Its success in this area puts to rest the canard that women cannot write realistically of war. Harris shows little interest in the social issues associated with the war. Her focus is almost exclusively psychological, and within that sphere she succeeds in capturing the full force of the war's assault on the individual psyche.

On the other hand, Pat Barker's highly acclaimed *Regeneration* trilogy (*Regeneration* [1991], *The Eye in the Door* [1993], and *The Ghost Road* [1995]) is deeply tied to social questions. The three novels focus on three figures, two historical, one fictional. In *Regeneration*, the poet Siegfried Sassoon, after earning the Military Cross for gallantry in action, refuses to return to the front and publishes a statement disowning the war: "I can no longer be a party to prolong these sufferings for ends which I believe to be evil and unjust." Rather than risk the embarrassment of court-martialing a decorated hero, a military tribunal declares him mentally unsound and sends him to Craiglockhart, a hospital for victims of "shell shock." There he is treated by the celebrated psychologist (and anthropologist) Dr. William Rivers, whose task it is to restore his patients sufficiently so that they can be returned to battle.

In the sessions with Sassoon, Rivers finds himself facing a crisis: He is being won over to Sassoon's position. *Regeneration* ends with Sassoon's decision to return to battle to share the fate of the men under his command. In the second novel (*The Eye in the Door*), Sassoon is wounded and returns to England. Meanwhile the focus shifts to the third major character in the trilogy, the fictional Billy Prior, an officer who is also a patient of Dr. Rivers, having become temporarily mute after a traumatic experience in the trenches. Prior is a man caught between two worlds: He is a working-class officer, a rarity in the British army of the time; a bisexual, in a society in which homosexuality is a crime; and a patriot with a moral commitment to pacifism. *The Eye in the Door* explores all of these conflicts against the background of a society torn apart by a mounting body count in a seemingly endless war.

In the last volume of the trilogy, *The Ghost Road*, Prior, Sassoon, and the poet Wilfred Owen, who historically had also been a patient at Craiglockhart, are back in the front lines for the final offensive of the war. One week before the armistice, Owen and Prior are killed. Meanwhile Dr. Rivers, suffering from a mild case of influenza, deliriously recalls his days as an anthropologist living with a tribe of headhunters. The relation of this experience to that of the war insistently imposes itself on his mind, as he treats a dying soldier whose last garbled words are, "It wasn't worth it."

The *Regeneration* trilogy is a work whose implications extend beyond the events of World War I. Barker skillfully weaves into the story the themes of gender and class, both profoundly influenced by the war. Billy Prior, the bisexual officer from a working-class background, becomes involved with Sarah, a working-class woman laboring in a munitions factory, and experiencing, as many women of the time did, their first taste of independence. But Prior is also having sex with a fellow officer from the aristocratic class. Barker sees the war as the opening breach in the clearly drawn lines indicating the status of women, the distinctions of class, and the definition of "manly" behavior. English society was, at great cost, changing. In *Parade's End*, these changes are seen as entirely pernicious, shattering the framework of English society. Writing almost 70 eventful years later, Barker, deploring the destructive madness of the war even more vehemently than Ford, takes the longer historical view that the old order, in its death throes, suicidally induced the war, and (if the word *regeneration* is not being used ironically) that in the boundless suffering of the war, some cleansing took place. Other war novels of note include Frederic Manning's *Her Privates We* (see SOMME), Blasco Ibanez's *The Four Horsemen of the Apocalypse* (see MARNE), Aleksandr Solzhenitsyn's *August 1914* (see TANNENBERG), A. P. Herbert's *The Secret Battle* (see GALLIPOLI), Ian Hay's *The First Hundred Thousand* (see LOOS), Jules Romain's *Verdun* (see VERDUN), and William March's *Company K* (see BELLEAU WOOD). For the best-known novel of the period, Erich Maria Remarque's *All Quiet on the Western Front*, see WESTERN FRONT; for the comic masterpiece of the war, Stefan Zweig's *The Good Soldier Schweik*, see EASTERN FRONT.

FURTHER READING

John Keegan's *The First World War* (1999) is an authoritative, well-written military history of the war. Paul Fussell's *The Great War and Modern Memory* (1975) and Samuel Hynes's *A War Imagined* (1991) are excellent literary studies of the war and its impact on English culture. *The First World War in Fiction*, edited by Holger Klein (1976), is a collection of critical essays on Anglo-American and continental European novels dealing with the war.

WORLD WAR I: AFTERMATH

The political and economic consequences of WORLD WAR I were immense. In the popular view of the Allied nations, Germany would have to pay reparations for the enormous damage the war had created. Realists, like the English prime minister, Lloyd George, recognized that the war had so wrecked the German economy that the new German government would be lucky to survive the political upheaval that followed the war. Revolutions, some attempting to mirror the Bolshevik coup in Russia (see RUSSIAN REVOLUTION [1917]), erupted all over Europe, presaged by the mutinies of soldiers and sailors who simply wanted to go home (see LUXEMBURG, ROSA).

These effects of the war were matched by the social disruption and psychological damage resulting from the 30 million casualties, the dispossession and relocation of ethnic populations, and the disappearance of an established order of life. In 1914, the vast majority of European territory had been controlled by four major imperial powers—Russia, Germany, Austria-Hungary, and the Ottoman Empire. Four years later those governments had disappeared and Europe found it had to invent itself anew. While that invention took a positive, democratic form in many countries, in Italy, Spain, and Germany, it veered in the destructive direction of FASCISM and, in the Soviet Union, communism. In Germany, in particular, the inequities of the 1919 peace treaties provided Adolf HITLER with fertile ground on which to sow his seeds of hatred and revenge.

THE LITERATURE

"It might be possible, Septimus thought, looking at England from the train window . . . it might be possible that the world itself is without meaning." Septimus here is Septimus Smith, the war veteran returning home in Virginia Woolf's (1882–1941) *Mrs. Dalloway* (1925). He is suffering from shattered nerves that eventually lead to his suicide. His perception that the war had called into question whether life had any meaning explicitly echoes a theme that emerged in postwar English and American literature. Its most celebrated poetic expression is T. S. Eliot's (1888–1965) *The Waste Land* (1922), its title possibly suggesting for readers of the period the barren no-man's-land of Flanders and northern France, but certainly underscoring the alienation felt by many during this time. Eliot's poem is a collection of fragmented images and voices, designed to capture a civilization that had been blown apart by the shells of the Great War. Although the poem embraces larger themes of spiritual desolation and the loss of meaning, it is also, in a narrower but authentic sense, a post–World War I poem. It begins with ominous intimations in the prewar world, of sledding dangerously downhill with my "cousin, the archduke," moving to a postwar conversation in a pub about the wife of a demobilized veteran ("When Lil's husband got demobbed, I said, . . . Now Albert's coming back make yourself a bit smart").

The phrase in Eliot's poem that summarizes this disrupted world is "a heap of broken images." The critic Samuel Hynes glosses the phrase thus: "The idea that reality could be described . . . as broken and formless is one that many trench writers recognized, and adopted in their descriptions of the Front. Eliot saw that the war had imposed that vision upon the world after the war." The waste land metaphor also occupies a significant place in a major apocalyptic, satirical drama by the brilliant Austrian satirist Karl Kraus (1874–1936), "The Last Days of Mankind" (1919). For Kraus, the war was both the contributor to, and the definitive expression of, the corruption and decay of European society.

A similar resort to satire is evident in America in two postwar novels of Sinclair Lewis (1885–1951), *Main Street* (1920) and *Babbitt* (1922), wicked dissections of small-town America, its get-up-and-go optimism disguising an empty longing for meaning. Like a trained anthropologist, Lewis examines the myths and rituals of small town society, as it moves from agrarianism to capitalism. In *Main Street*, Gopher Prairie (modeled after Lewis's hometown, Sauk Center, Minnesota) prides itself on its Puritanical morals, conservatism, and distrust of foreigners. Equally critical of American society at large is John Dos Passos (1896–1970), whose *U.S.A.* (1930–36) charts the decline of the progressive spirit of the first two decades of the century into the greed and materialism of the postwar years.

FURTHER READING

Samuel Hynes's *A War Imagined* (1991) is an excellent study of the impact of the war on English culture.

WORLD WAR II (1939–1945)

The Second World War was the child of the first; in fact, the connection between the two is so intimate that many observers see the two wars as one, creating what historian Eric Hobsbawm calls "the thirty-one year war that began in 1914 and ended in 1945." Certainly the social, political, and economic upheavals following the 1918 armistice and the Treaty of Versailles provided the seeds of despair, disintegration, and, in Germany at least, humiliation and the desire for vengeance. All of these conditions played into the hands of the nascent Nazi Party and its charismatic leader Adolf HITLER, who added to this brew a hierarchical racist theory that posited the Aryans as the master race and the Jews as the degraded, virtually subhuman race whose very existence constituted a dangerous threat to Aryan purity. Coming to power in 1933, Hitler transformed Germany from a crippled, dissension-riddled republic into a powerful, menacing fascist state, willing and able to wreak vengeance on its old enemies.

Beginning in 1936 with the occupation of the Rhineland, a demilitarized zone between France and Germany, then moving to the annexation of Austria and the Sudetenland in 1938, Hitler not only extended his power but also tested the resolve of the western Allies. With each uncontested step, he became more firmly convinced of the Allies' fundamental weakness, underscored finally by the MUNICH PACT of 1939, in which the French and British prime ministers, Edouard Daladier and Neville Chamberlain, caved into his demands in exchange for his empty promise to help ensure "peace in our time," as Chamberlain was to proclaim on his return from Munich. Within six months, Germany had browbeaten the Czechoslovakian government into requesting status as a "protectorate" of Germany. As Hitler paraded in triumph through Prague, the Allies declared that any further act of aggression on Germany's part would result in war. Hitler's response was to sign a nonaggression pact with the Soviet Union, giving the Soviets control over the Baltic states of Estonia, Latvia, Lithuania, and a substantial slice of Poland in exchange for their support for a German attack on Poland.

On September 1, 1939, Germany invaded Poland. Great Britain and France immediately declared war, a declaration that did little to deter the German army, which swept over the ill-equipped Poles in less than a month. During the "phony war," the period from September 1939 to April 1940, the Allies hastily rearmed, and the Axis nations (Germany, Italy, Hungary, and Romania) prepared for a spring offensive. It began with the German invasion of Denmark and Norway in April 1940. A month later the Germans initiated their *Blitzkrieg*—"lightning war"—bypassing the Maginot Line, the concrete bunkers placed across the French-German border, and invading the neutral countries of Belgium and the Netherlands, finally crashing into France through the Ardennes forest.

On June 22, 1940, France surrendered (see FRANCE, FALL OF). In the interim, more than 300,000 British and French troops had been trapped near the port city of DUNKIRK. A hastily arranged evacuation prevented the capture of most of these troops, preserving them for the next phase of the war, the battle of BRITAIN. The battle of Britain was an air war, intended by the Germans as a prelude to an invasion. Despite the relentless bombardment of British military targets and major cities (see, BLITZ, THE), the Germans were unable to overcome the skill of the Royal Air Force pilots, the superiority of the spitfire fighter planes, and the new technological innovation, radar.

By 1941, the war had spread to the Balkans and North Africa. Italy had invaded Greece but was beaten back by fierce Greek resistance, forcing the Germans to come to the aid of their Italian allies. Benito Mussolini's army proved equally ineffective in North Africa, needing to be rescued again, this time by the German Afrikan Korps, led by the brilliant strategist Field Marshal Erwin Rommel.

In June 1941, Hitler made a catastrophic decision to open up a new front by invading the Soviet Union (see BARBAROSSA). At first, the unprepared Soviet army, seriously weakened by Joseph STALIN's purge of the general command (see GREAT TERROR), retreated in the face of a three-pronged German onslaught. Only a heroic defense on the outskirts of Moscow prevented the collapse of the Soviet government. When, after a winter stalemate, the fighting resumed in the spring of 1942, the Germans redirected their main efforts to capturing the city of STALINGRAD, in a seven-month battle that resulted in the loss of an entire German army and marked the beginning of the turning of the tide.

Another momentous and mistaken decision was made in December of 1941 when Japan, Germany's Asian ally, unleashed a surprise attack on the American naval base at PEARL HARBOR in Hawaii, dramatically expanding the conflict into a true "world war." See WAR IN THE PACIFIC. Japanese dive bombers and torpedo boats succeeded in sinking 19 American naval vessels, killing more than 2,400 American servicepeople and civilians. America declared war on December 8, and three days later Germany declared war against the United States. The Japanese followed up the attack with invasions of Malaya (now Malaysia), Burma (now Myanmar), and the Dutch East Indies (now Indonesia), all of which, including the island fortress of Singapore, rapidly fell to the invaders. Similar success attended the Japanese invasion of the Philippines, in which the last American outposts, the Bataan peninsula and the small island of Corregidor, fell in April and May 1942.

By June of 1942, the Japanese had experienced astonishing success on land and at sea, Victory seemed to be within their grasp. But overconfidence led them to carelessness in their handling of coded plans for an attack on the American fleet off the Midway islands. The battle that ensued proved to be the turning point of the Pacific war. The Japanese lost four aircraft carriers and from that point on were forced to fight a defensive war. On the strength of this victory, American troops began a series of attacks on Japanese-held islands, some of which became the scenes of particularly fierce battles, eventually won by the Americans.

In 1944, General Douglas MacArthur, the commanding general of the United States forces, fulfilling a vow to "return," launched an attack on Leyte Island in the Philippines. At the same time, the naval battle of LEYTE GULF, the largest battle in the history of naval warfare, took place, with the Americans securing a narrow but decisive victory.

In 1943, following the British victory the previous year over Rommel's forces at ALAMEIN and with joint British and American forces in Tunisia, the Allies now opened up a new front by invading Sicily in July and mainland Italy in September. The ITALIAN CAMPAIGN proved to be long, arduous, and relatively ineffective. What was required was a wholesale assault on western Europe, designed ultimately to catch the German armies in a pincer movement between the Russians in the East and the British and American forces in the West. Such an assault occurred on June 6, 1944, with the D day NORMANDY INVASION in northern France. Despite fierce resistance, the ensuing campaign, combined with the relentless and overwhelming Soviet army's offensive in the East, eventually brought Germany to its knees. The Nazi defeat was finally signaled by the suicide of Hitler in April 1945 and the formal end of the war in Europe on May 8, 1945 (see BERLIN, FALL OF).

Four months later the United States dropped the first atomic bomb on the Japanese city of HIROSHIMA, followed three days later by a second nuclear bomb on Nagasaki. The devastation caused the Japanese government, previously committed to fight to the bitter end, to sue for peace.

THE LITERATURE

The literature of the First World War can be generally divided into two simple categories: works that supported the war, invoking patriotism and demonizing the enemy, and works that powerfully protested the war as an assault on human values, growing out of the direct participation in trench war. In World War II, the literary categories became more complex, partly because of the nature of the war itself, which was larger in scale, economically, militarily, technologically, and, most important, humanly. In World War II, the distinction between citizen and soldier was virtually erased. The bombing of Guernica and other cities during the SPANISH CIVIL WAR proved to be dress rehearsals for the overpowering onslaught directed at noncombatants, which achieved its ultimate expression at Hiroshima. The other example of the civilianizing of war came in the form of the staggering idea that all Jews, infants as well as their great-grandparents, were enemies that had to be not just defeated, but exterminated, in what came to be known as the HOLOCAUST.

This expanded definition of the war gave birth to an expanded view of war literature. Thus, for example, one of the best-known and celebrated "war novels" is Günther Grass's (1927–) *The Tin Drum*, which takes place entirely on the "home front." The home front in this case is, of course, Nazi Germany, explored in a satiric, discordant, semiallegorical diagnosis of the disease that infected everyone (see DANZIG). Similarly, the Italian novelist Natalia Ginzburg's (1916–91) *All Our Yesterdays* (1952; trans., 1956) captures two families' experiences in Italy as the war moves from the distant background to the oppressive and overwhelming foreground. In America, Saul Bellow's (1915–) *Dangling Man* (1944) explores the existential crisis of a young man in Chicago, waiting to be drafted and meanwhile trying to determine the purpose of his life, not unlike the hero of Jean-Paul Sartre's (1905–80) *The Reprieve* (see MUNICH PACT).

The obvious candidate for the first important literary response to the war is W. H. Auden's (1907–73) poem "September 1, 1939," written within a week of the Nazi invasion of Poland. The poem captures the demoralizing fear, anger, and confusion of most people at the prospect looming before them. Auden's apprehension was echoed in other poetry, notably C. Day Lewis's (1904–72) "Ode to Fear," which gives explicit voice to the emotion felt by all.

The question that most World War II writers chose to keep in suspension was that of the nature of the war itself. Unlike most of the writers of the First World War, who viewed it, quite justifiably, as a catastrophic folly, the majority of novelists and poets in World War II regarded the battle against

Germany and Japan as, at least a necessary evil, if not a "good war." Many others suspended all larger questions in order to look with a dispassionate eye on military life itself, as in James Jones's (1921–77) *From Here to Eternity* (1951) and Norman Mailer's (1925–) *The Naked and the Dead* (1948) (see WAR IN THE PACIFIC).

One work that looks at the implications of the war while at the same time casting a satiric eye on army life is Evelyn Waugh's (1903–66) *Sword of Honor* trilogy: *Men at Arms* (1952), *Officers and Gentlemen* (1955), and *Unconditional Surrender* (1961). Guy Crouchback, the hero of these novels, is a 35-year-old conservative English-Catholic gentleman, who despite his relatively advanced age is eager to join the service as soon as he reads of the 1939 Hitler-Stalin pact: "The enemy at last was plain in view, huge and hateful, all disguise cast off." He obtains a commission with the Halberdiers, a regiment rooted in the glory days of the British Empire. After extensive training, which Guy undergoes enthusiastically, the regiment is assigned to West Africa, but the planned military engagement (against a Vichy French garrison) is called off, and Guy is sent back to England, charged with accidentally causing the death of a fellow officer. In the second volume, Guy joins a commando unit in training, while his ex-wife has an affair with one of his fellow officers. He is sent to CRETE, where he participates in the English evacuation of the island. The chaos of the evacuation and the behavior of his superior officers cause him to disobey orders to remain on the island. At the last moment, he leaps into a boat that carries him safely to Egypt. Recuperating there, he experiences fierce disillusion about his own behavior and that of his commanding officer. Added to this is the news of Hitler's invasion of the Soviet Union. Guy's sense of honor is now completely tarnished, as he recognizes that England's ally is the totalitarian Communist state. In the last volume, *Unconditional Surrender*, Guy is dispatched as a military liaison to Marshal Tito's Communist partisans in Yugoslavia, where Guy's worst fears about communists are confirmed. He makes an effort, partly successful, to aid a group of Jewish refugees, who are receiving no help from the partisans. In a telling conversation with a Jewish woman, one of the refugees, he speculates about the nature of the war. She observes that the Nazis were not the only ones who wanted war, that there was "a will to war, a death wish everywhere. Even good men thought their private honor would be satisfied by war." To which Guy replies, "God forgive me, I was one of them."

Readers familiar with Ford Madox Ford's *Parade's End* (1924–28) (see WORLD WAR I) will note the strong parallel between Ford's tetralogy and Waugh's trilogy, but although there is some indebtedness on Waugh's part, the military experiences that he records are those Waugh himself underwent in World War II. In relation to Ford's hero, Christopher Tietjens, Waugh's military career is an example of life imitating art. It also serves as confirmation of the theory that the first war created the issues of the second.

The most important novel of the Second World War is also the funniest and the saddest, the craziest and the sanest. Joseph Heller's (1923–2002) *Catch-22* (1961) is not the first novel to subject war to the merciless eye of the satirist. Jaroslav Hasek's (1883–1923) World War I masterpiece *The Good Soldier Schweik* (see EASTERN FRONT) can lay claim to that title. But Hasek's novel is entirely comic. It does not explore the dark side of comedy, that point on the emotional spectrum where it merges with tragedy. Its willingness to pursue the absurdity of the life it depicts to its logical, and very dark, conclusion is the distinctive feature of *Catch-22*.

The famous title, by now familiar to almost everyone, refers in the novel to the air force regulation stating that anyone who willingly continues to fly combat missions is insane and should be sent home, but there's a catch. Take the case of Lieutenant Orr: "Orr was crazy and could be grounded. All he had to do was ask; and, as soon as he did, he would no longer be crazy and have to fly more missions. Orr would be crazy to fly more missions and sane if he didn't, but if he was sane, he had to fly them. If he flew them he was crazy and didn't have to, but if he didn't want to, he was sane and had to." Or, as the novel's central figure, Yossarian, a veteran flyer of 44 missions, puts it, "That's some catch, that Catch-22." Yossarian's commander, Colonel Cathcart, keeps raising the number needed to be rotated home, thereby invoking another version of catch-22. Yossarian is becoming acutely conscious that the world he lives in is his enemy because it wants him dead: "You have a morbid aversion to dying," an army psychologist tells him, but Yossarian's sense is that morbidity lies in the casual acceptance of death that the war encourages. Early in the novel, the story has a lighter, satirical tone, depicting the military as a mirror of society, with each person scrambling for his place. The more serious theme of life and death emerges in the final section of the novel, climaxing in the unforgettable scene in which Yossarian confronts the eviscerated body of young Snowden, recalling the last line of Randall Jarrell's (1914–65) powerful poem "The Death of the Ball Turret Gunner": "When I died, they washed me out of the turret with a hose." Yossarian, reading "the message in Snowden's entrails," discovers Snowden's secret: "Man was matter, that was Snowden's secret. Drop him out a window and he'll fall, set fire to him and he'll burn. Bury him and he'll rot, like other kinds of garbage. The spirit gone, man is garbage. That was Snowden's secret. Ripeness was all." The last sentence is derived from Shakespeare's *King Lear* ("Ripeness is all") and is spoken by Edgar, the good son of Gloucester, who has earned his wisdom by assuming, like Yossarian, the role of a "poor naked wretch"; it is his insanity, like that of Yossarian, that puts him in touch with a deeper wisdom, the reverence for life.

FURTHER READING

John Keegan's *The Second World War* (1995) is an authoritative military history. Paul Fussell's *Wartime* (1989) takes an angry look at "the rationalizations and euphemisms people needed to deal with an unacceptable actuality from 1939 to 1945." John Aldridge's *After the Lost Generation* (1951) critically surveys World War II American fiction.

WORLD WAR II: AFTERMATH

The worldwide conflagration that ended in 1945 soon led to two other massive conflicts, the COLD WAR, which pitted the two remaining superpowers, the United States and the Soviet Union, against each other, and the battles against COLONIALISM, which Asian and African colonies raged in their desire for independence. But preceding these events was the wrenching spectacle of 20 million people roaming through Europe in the summer of 1945. Ten million of these were ethnic Germans expelled from Poland and Czechoslovakia. Added to these were the so-called displaced persons, the millions from all over Europe, once forced to do slave labor in German factories, now homeless, either because there was no home to go to, or because they feared to go home, as was the case with many Russians who knew they would either be killed or sent to the GULAG. Also among the displaced were many Jews who had survived the death camps and now sought a new home in Palestine. The year 1945 also saw the creation of the charter of the United Nations, the attempt to create an international peacekeeping organization. Organizers hoped to avoid the problems of the old League of Nations by giving greater power to an executive body, the Security Council. In the United States, the most significant domestic events were the enactment of the G.I. Bill of Rights, which opened American universities to middle-class and working-class veterans, providing a skilled and educated workforce for the postindustrial age looming on the horizon, and the growth of suburbia which offered veterans a low-cost down payment, low-mortgage version of the American dream.

The most surprising political development of 1945 was the defeat of Prime Minister Winston Churchill at the hands of a British Labour Party that ushered in an ambitious program of "welfare state" measures, notably the National Health Service; however, the new government was unable to restore Britain to economic health, as the privations of wartime persisted. The rest of Europe struggled to reconstruct a world from the psychological as well as physical rubble the war had created. In France, the rebuilding of the nation found its intellectual equivalent in the movement known as EXISTENTIALISM. Although existentialism had emerged in the 1930s, the war and the Nazi occupation gave the existentialist themes of freedom, choice, and death an immediate reality. Despite its frequently dark and somber representation, the philosophy represented a call to action for a morally engaged commitment to social justice. Human existence might be absurd, but the individual was still capable of meaningful action.

THE LITERATURE

These conditions and currents of thought informed the literature of the post-war world, sometimes indirectly but always powerfully. The physical and moral devastation experienced by Germans is captured in Heinrich Böll's (1917–85) *The Silent Angel* (1994), a novel that depicts the ruined, despairing world that was the legacy of the Third Reich. It is a story of suffering and horror, mediated only by the fact of survival. Hans Schnitzler, a returning soldier, arrives in his native city, which has been reduced to rubble by incessant bombing. The unnamed city is based upon Cologne, but its stark, desolate emptiness suggests a primitive world in which human existence itself is in peril. The rest of the novel explores the spiritual desperation of its characters while anticipating the greed and venality that will define the future.

David Lodge, (1935–   ), the British novelist best known for his satiric comedies of academic life (*Changing Places* [1975], *Small World* [1984]), has also written an affecting postwar novel, *Out of the Shelter* (1970; rev. ed. 1985), which offers a sympathetic, but not uncritical, view of English-American relations, using occupied Germany as its setting. Central to the historical background of the novel is the severe hardship of ordinary English life after the war. For a variety of reasons, England was very slow in making an economic recovery. A government policy of "austerity," extending into the early 1950s, included rationing of food and shortages of fuel and affordable clothing, even after France and defeated Germany had rebounded economically from the effects of the war. In 1951, 16-year-old Timothy Young, a survivor of the BLITZ and a docile participant in the lean years, receives an invitation to vacation with his sister, Kate, a secretary working for the American army occupying Heidelberg. On arrival, he plunges into a world of plentiful food, fun, and adventure that constitute a coming of age for the teenager. Caught up in the fun-loving, free-spending spirit of his sister's American friends, he begins to spread his wings, becoming more like a "Yank" while, at the same time, becoming more observant of his surroundings. He moves from seeing life in limited terms to seeing its possibilities and choices. His life had been *sheltered* in both senses of the term—enclosed and cramped—and, in the literal World War II sense, shaped by the experience of the blitz. At the age of five, he had been trapped with his mother in a bomb shelter after a direct hit that killed his playmate. What he has learned from that experience and what is reinforced in his encounter with the Americans is the recognition that "history is the verdict of the lucky on the unlucky," that the good life is a precarious one at best and at worst a giddiness that precedes a fall.

In the author's afterword, Lodge acknowledges that the details of his novel are modeled on his own experience as a teenager: "It seemed to me that by virtue of my encounter with the American expatriate community in Germany in 1951, I had been granted a privileged foretaste of the hedonistic, materialistic good life that the British and most of the developed or developing nations of the world would soon aspire to, and in some measure enjoy. . . . Is this a new freedom for man, or a new enslavement? I do not presume to give an answer, but the question is raised obliquely in Timothy Young's story." Reading his novel, one has the sense that the answer his head gives is freedom, while his heart senses enslavement.

The existentialist emphasis on free choice is confronted and challenged in William Styron's *Sophie's Choice* (1979), which explores the destructive afterlife of the HOLOCAUST. The narrator is Stingo, a young white southerner living in a Brooklyn boardinghouse with two lovers, Sophie, a refugee from Poland, and Nathan, a Jewish American subject to wide mood swings. Both Sophie and Nathan need "help"—she uses alcohol, he drugs—in order to deal with their separate hidden injuries. Stingo falls in love with Sophie, complicating the volatile relationship further. The wrenching climax of the novel occurs with the revelation alluded to in the book's title: During the war, Sophie, who is not Jewish, is shipped to a concentration camp, where she is forced to choose between her son and daughter; one child will be sent to the gas chamber, the other will survive. Haunted by that moment, by the choice that was not a choice, she has lied about her past, but, like Nathan, can find no peace. For Sophie, the horror has not ended with the war and can only end with her death.

In "The Displaced Person," Flannery O'Connor's (1925–64) remarkable short story, the plight of the uprooted people of Europe is seamlessly meshed with the issue of American racism. Mrs. McIntyre, a widow and small farm owner in Georgia, hires a European displaced family to work her farm. The father of the family proves to be an extraordinarily good worker, a "savior," as Mrs. McIntyre repeatedly says, until the immigrant tries to arrange a marriage between his relative and a black farmhand working for Mrs. McIntyre. She now sees her "savior" as a threat to the established order of things in the segregated South, as do the other workers on the farm. As a result, they silently collude in his "accidental" death. As in most O'Connor stories, the religious theme is clearly visible, but it is beautifully incorporated here into the story's texture and the painful realities of the postwar world.

FURTHER READING

A. S. Milward's *The Reconstruction of Western Europe, 1945–51* (1987) is an authoritative account of the postwar period. Tony Tanner's *City of Words: American Fiction 1950–1970* (1971) is an excellent guide to postwar American fiction.

Y

YOM KIPPUR WAR

See ARAB-ISRAELI CONFLICT.

YPRES, BATTLES OF (WORLD WAR I) (1914–1917)

Ypres, a town in northwestern Belgium, was the site of three major battles in WORLD WAR I. In October–November 1914, a German attack failed to capture the town but succeeded in securing the strategically important MESSINES ridge. In this first encounter, the Allies were able to occupy the "Ypres salient," a wedge extending into the German front line approximately five miles deep and six miles wide. In the second Ypres battle (April–May, 1915), German forces attacked the salient with a large number of troops, employing the use of poison gas for the first time in history. The gas used was chlorine, which has a corrosive effect on the lungs. The Allied troops fled in panic, except for the Canadian troops in one sector who fought valiantly and suffered terrible casualties. Fortunately for the Allies, the German commander failed to capitalize on the advantage the gas attack afforded. As a result the Germans did recover the area of the salient, but they were again unable to capture the town. The third battle of Ypres, or PASSCHENDAELE (July–November 1917), came on the heels of two British victories at Vimy and Messines and saw the Allies on the offensive.

At Ypres, as it had at other key battles on the WESTERN FRONT, the Canadian army displayed extraordinary courage and skill. At the second battle, the Canadians stood fast in the face of poison gas while other Allied troops fled in panic, and they were responsible for the final capture of that village at the disaster of Passchendaele. But the cost of their valor was high: 60,000 Canadians were killed in action during the war.

THE LITERATURE

The Canadian novelist Timothy Findley has recounted some of the Canadian army's history in his novel *The Wars* (1977). Findley focuses on the action on the Ypres front between the second and third Ypres battles. Robert Ross leaves his native Toronto home to enlist as an officer in Canadian forces headed for France. Assigned to an artillery unit at Ypres, Ross and his men face a gas attack without having been issued gas masks. Ross controls the panicky reaction of the men by forcing them at gunpoint to adopt the one technique that can save their lives: to tear off the tails of their shirts, to urinate on them, and to press the rags to their faces. His men survive, and when they make their way back to their own trenches, no one there is alive.

Instead of becoming inured to the carnage all around him, Ross's consciousness and sensitivity seem to expand. He becomes particularly concerned with the plight of the tortured, hysterical horses slaughtered in battle. When a group of trapped horses under heavy bombardment seem certain to be killed, he disobeys orders and frees them. When his sadistic commanding officer tries to stop him, he shoots the man and becomes an outcast. Tracked down by military police to a barn where he is sheltering horses, he is surrounded; when he refuses to surrender, the troops set the barn on fire. The horses are all killed, and Robert suffers severe burns to his face and body. He is so badly burned and blinded that the authorities forego the usual punishment. He returns to a hospital in England, where a woman who comes to love him cares for him. He dies in 1922 at the age of 26.

The title *The Wars* suggests that the author is not looking simply at World War I, but at war in general, at the destruction of innocence, reflected in the naïve Canadian soldiers and in the horses Robert tries in vain to save. But in order to be effective as fiction, the general must be grounded and shrouded in concrete particulars, which is precisely the case in this powerful recreation of the action on the western front.

FURTHER READING

James Stokesbury's *A Short History of World War I* (1981) provides a lively, accessible account of the Ypres battles.

Chronology of Entries

INDEX OF AUTHORS, TITLES, AND ENTRIES